PLANT NAMES
SIMPLIFIED

3rd Edition

PLANT NAMES SIMPLIFIED

3rd Edition

Their Pronunciation, Derivation and Meaning

 5m Publishing

First published by W. H. & L. Collingridge, 1931
Third revised edition published by 5m Publishing Ltd, 2019
Reprinted by 5m Books Ltd, 2021

Published by
5M Publishing Ltd,
Benchmark House,
8 Smithy Wood Drive,
Sheffield, S35 1QN, UK
Tel: +44 (0) 1234 81 81 80
www.5mpublishing.com

A Catalogue record for this book is available from the British Library

ISBN 9781910455067

The publishers would like to thank Peter Stewart for assisting in the
publication of this book

Frontispiece: Escholscholzia californica, by Victoria Begbie

Book layout by Servis Filmsetting Ltd, Stockport, Cheshire
Printed and bound by TJ Books Limited, Padstow, Cornwall

PREFACE TO THE SECOND EDITION

My endeavour in preparing this glossary has been to offer the reader a simple translation and pronunciation of the names of such plants, trees and shrubs as are commonly grown in the average garden. As they stand, such names are to most of us something more than an awkward obstacle barring way to any real intimacy with elements of botany. They are a direct hindrance to our progress as gardeners, and tend to complicate rather than to elucidate the difficulties of a vast and absorbing subject.

Centuries ago each plant was known by a long, descriptive sentence, which was unwieldy, to say the least. Then Caspar Bauhin (1560–1624) devised a plan of adopting two names only for each plant. But it was not until the great Swedish naturalist, Carl Linnaeus (1707–1778), undertook the task of methodically naming and classifying the whole living world 'from buffaloes to buttercups' that the dual system became permanently established. Linnaeus brought order out of chaos and indexed the vegetable world on a basis so sound and universally acceptable to the people of all nations that most of his names are in use today.

One of the two names given to each plant, the first, which may be likened to our surname, is the generic, or group, name. This can only occur once that is, as a group name – but while the second, the specific name or species is only given to one plant of the same genus – as is a first name in a family – it may occur in many different genera. Plants of garden origin, or those which are mere variations from the true species, usually have a third, such as *Campanula* (generic), *rotundifolia* (specific), 'Alba' (varietal). But since most of these varietal names occur as specific names they have not been generally included in the glossary. Names of plants which are hybrids, or which otherwise have a garden origin, have also been omitted. A very large subject has demanded as much brevity as possible, the writer realising that a dictionary of this kind might defeat its own object were it too bulky. Regarding such specific names as must constantly recur – *japonica, chinensis, wilsonii, vulgare, floribunda*, and the like – I have avoided the usual method of a single mention followed by cross references which is apt to waste the reader's time and patience. Instead of this, such words have been repeated throughout the work in all genera with which they are most closely associated.

Generic names, being the more important, are accorded the fuller explanation, and most of the more familiar groups are afforded more liberal treatment than those not so well known. Specific names are treated on similar lines. These are mainly adjectival or descriptive of the plant's colour, form or habit, but space only allows us to give to each of these a literal translation of the word with a brief indication as to what it alludes. Where a specific name is plainly derived from a name of a person (often merely commemorative) or place, its meaning is usually sufficiently obvious without explanation.

It is felt that with a translation of these words before him, the average amateur will be afforded not only an interesting glimpse into the past history of his plants, but that the names will lose much of that awkwardness with which they are so often invested. Further, the second, or specific name, alluding as it so often does to some marked character in the plant, will, in its translated form, often be helpful in aiding the identification of doubtful species. And, after all, these Greek and Latin names which are so disturbing to some people need not themselves be any more foreign and unintelligible than many other words now recognised as English and in daily use. It is entirely a matter of custom, and when we realise how freely we now use such beautiful botanical names as *Campanula*, *Veronica* and *Clematis* now that they have become familiar to us, one may with confidence express the belief that the time will come when the multitude of plant names which are not so well known will be spoken with the ease of the examples given. And it is to the furtherance of that desirable end that this glossary has been prepared. *Fuchsia*, *Geranium*, *Pelargonium*, *Dahlia*, *Aster*, *Primula*, *Calendula*, *Chrysanthemum*, *Pyrethrum* are a few additional botanical plant names that have become absorbed into everyday language.

Regarding pronunciation, this is given by phonetic spelling, each syllable being sounded as it is spelt. But in this matter the writer claims no infallibility. Just as in English (as departures in broadcasting have pointed out), where classical accuracy is sometimes superseded by custom, so is the pronunciation of these Latin and Greek names often decided by common usage. The correct pronunciation of *Anemone*, for example, is an-e-MO-NE, with the accent on each of the last two vowels. But we shall continue to say an-EM-on-e. *Hypericum* will always be hy-PER-ik-um, rather than hy-per-I-kum; and *Erica* will be ER-ik-a and not er-I-ka, as the learned would have such names said. The fact is no arbitrary rules of pronunciation can be laid down. Even such a great authority as the *Oxford English Dictionary* will give a choice of two pronunciations for the same word; and when we are given full licence by such exalted powers to pronounce chauffeur as 'shofer', fauteuil as 'fotill', cinema as 'sinnema', and Celtic as 'seltik', one may grieve for the traditions of the classics, but give courage its due and adopt in the pronunciation of our botanical names an equally liberal attitude.

Apropos the subject of pronunciation we may quote some lines on 'cyclamen' which appeared in the pages of an old-time gardening periodical:

> How shall we sound its mystic name
> Of Greek descent and Persian fame?
> Shall 'y' be long and 'a' be short,
> Or will the 'y' and 'a' retort?
> Shall 'y' be lightly rippled o'er,
> Or should we emphasise it more?
> Alas! The doctors disagree,
> For 'y's' a doubtful quantity.
> Some people use it now and then,
> As if 'twere written 'Sickly-men';
> But as it comes from *kuklos*, Greek,
> Why not 'kick-laymen', so to speak?
> The gardener, with his ready wit,
> Upon another mode has hit;
> He's terse and brief – long names dislikes,
> And so he renders it as 'Sykes'.

At the same time one must have a working principle as a basis in the pronunciation of scientific plant names, and the most important point, perhaps, is to get the correct vowel sound, or stress, in the right place, and this in each case is indicated by the syllable being printed in [uppercase]. With few exceptions the accented vowel (in [uppercase]) is long when alone or following a consonant (O as in 'mole', A as in 'pate', E as in 'been'), short when preceding a consonant or between two (O as in 'on', or 'pon', A as in 'an' or 'pan', E as in 'en' or 'pen'). The U is given the letter (ew) sound, as in 'due'. The G is hard (as in 'get'), but soft when the phonetic sound gives it the J sound (as in 'gem'), and C is hard (as in 'can'), when given the K sound, or soft (as in 'pace'), when it is given the sound of S.

Although usage is accepted as an influence in fixing the pronunciation of many words, the rules of the language to which a word belongs must always be the deciding factor in many cases. In the compilation of this glossary much guidance has been obtained from the *Oxford English Dictionary*, *Nuttall's Standard Dictionary*, *Nicholson's Dictionary of Gardening*, *Johnson's Gardener's Dictionary* (Fraser and Hemsley), Bentham and Hooker's botanical works, Dr. B. Daydon Jackson's *Glossary of Botanical Terms*, Dr. R.T. Harvey-Gibson's *Plant Names and their Derivatives*, and G.F. Zimmer's *Popular Dictionary of Botanical Terms*, among other works.

In offering this book to the public I may add in conclusion that while I claim no profound knowledge of the classics or of botany I do know something of the simple wants of my fellow amateur gardeners. It is with that conviction that I have made this effort to smooth down one of the roughest places in our common pursuit. To satisfy and to please everyone is far beyond my aspirations. But if in this work I have succeeded in reducing even by a little the menace presented us by that 'pile of heterogeneous names which stand as a barrier between our people and the fairest gates of knowledge' (*Botany*, by Professor Earle), I shall feel that I have done my bit in a good cause.

1931   A.T. JOHNSON

It has fallen to my lot to tread delicately in the footsteps of the author of the original edition of this work, and to graft, more or less successfully, my work upon his. To this end many more genera and species of plants appear than in the first edition, which was mainly limited to hardy plants, shrubs etc. The additions therefore comprise a large number of indoor temperate and tropical subjects, while also the opportunity has been taken to include the better known names of the new sectional genera into which the cacti, mesembryanthemums and houseleeks have been grouped in modern times.

It is therefore the hope of the publisher and joint author that PLANT NAMES SIMPLIFIED may appeal in a wider measure to the new generations of both amateur and professional gardeners and have as useful a life as the first edition enjoyed in the fifteen years of its existence.

1946   HENRY A. SMITH

INTRODUCTION

The updating of this book has been long overdue. Although it has undergone reprints there have been no major revisions to the text for over seventy years. Where plant names have changed overtime, and given the advances in science, I felt it prudent to carry out some renovation work. Notwithstanding *Plant Names Simplified* has remained a stock tome with amateurs and professionals alike. This is testament to its simplicity.

In revising this edition I have tried to remain faithful to Johnson's original tenet of furthering the ease with which botanical names are used. The revisions have been made in accordance with the *International Code of Botanical Nomenclature*. This edition uses as a starting point The Plant List, an online database which is a collaboration between the Royal Botanic Gardens Kew and Missouri Botanical Gardens. The database identifies the currently accepted name for any plant. Where there have been name changes I have cross referenced from the original entry to the new entry. Interestingly when the first edition was published in 1931 *Hebe* was not a recorded generic name rather they were classified as *Veronica*. Phil Garnock-Jones, emeritus professor, Victoria University, undertook nomenclature work into New Zealand *Veronica*. This casts doubt and *Hebe* transfers back into *Veronica*. The work utilises phylogenetic analyses and identifies that Northern Hemisphere *Veronica* and New Zealand *Hebe* share a common ancestor, now extinct. Therefore, I felt it pertinent, although not all taxonomists will agree, to record the original plant names as presented in the second edition.

This edition includes family names and where possible dates of birth and death for specific epithets that are commemorative. Geographical names are identified and where regions have changed the modern place name is recorded alongside that of antiquity. The convention for Botanical names has improved significantly since the first edition. The procedure for Botanical naming of plants is written in italics with the genus treated as a noun with a capital letter proceeding it, for example,

Campanula, the species is written in lowercase, *C. patula*. Where there are subspecies, varieties or forms these are written in lowercase italics, for example, *Campanula patula* subsp. *abietina*. Intergeneric and interspecific hybrid name changes have been included in this edition. For commemorative genus and species names I have referred to Stearn's *Dictionary of Plant Names for Gardeners*, 2nd edn (1992), the Royal Horticultural Society's *Dictionary of Gardening*, (1992) and the Harvard University Herbaria (online database of botanists) which have been invaluable in checking dates and details.

With respect to pronunciation I recall the advice given to me by my tutor at Writtle College. They would remind you to 'pronounce all the vowels' in the plant name. In addition, when presented with commemorative names such as wilsonii the first 'i' is 'e' as in bee, and the second 'i' is 'eye' as in time.

It has been a privilege to update this edition of *Plant Names Simplified*, with thanks to my parents, Bill and Maureen Stockdale, Roger Smith, who took me up on the offer, and 5M Publishing, especially Sarah Hulbert for her advice and guidance. *Plant Names Simplified* is a functional text book designed to be to on hand when needed. It is my hope that the reader feels more at ease in using Botanical names.

2019   A.P. Stockdale

Dedicated to my wife Victoria and daughters
Tashan-Rose, Amélie-Ferne and Freyja-Lily.

PLANT NAMES SIMPLIFIED

Abelia, a-BEEL-e-a; after Dr. Clarke Abel (1780–1826), physician, and author on China, who discovered *A. chinensis*, 1816–1817. Flowering shrubs. *Caprifoliaceae.*
chinensis, tshi-NEN-sis, of China.
floribunda, see *Vaselea floribunda.*
grandiflora, gran-dif-LO-ra, large flowered.
triflora, tri-FLOR-a, three flowered, i.e. flowers in three.
uniflora, uni-FLOR-a, one flowered, that is blooms solitary.

Abelmoschus, a-BEL-mos-kus; from Arabic, *Abu-l-misk*, father of musk, in allusion to the smell of the seeds of *A. moschatus*. Annual and perennial herbs. *Malvaceae.*
manihot, MAN-e-hot, palmate resembling the Manihot.

Abies, a-BE-es (commonly A-beez); an ancient Latin name, possibly from L. *abeo*, depart, that is, from the ground, referring to great height attained by some species. Conifers. *Pinaceae.*
alba, AL-ba, from the L. *alba*, white.
amabilis, am-A-bil-is, lovely.
balsamea, bal-SA-me-a, aromatic (Balm of Gilead fir).
brachyphylla, see *A. homolepis.*
bracteata, brak-te-A-ta, having bracts, or modified leaves, at bases of leaf stalks.
cephalonica, sef-a-LON-ik-a, of Cephalonia.
concolor, kon-KOL-or, one-coloured, that is, a uniform tint.
grandis, GRAN-dis, of great size.
homolepis, hom-o-LEP-is, having structurally similar scales.
magnifica, mag-NIF-ik-a, magnificent, beautiful.
nobilis, see *A. alba.*
pectinata, see *Picea abies.*

Abobra, a-BOB-ra; native Brazilian name. Scarlet fruited climber of the cucumber family. *Cucurbitaceae.*

tenuifolia, ten-u-e-FO-le-a, slender leaved.
viridiflora, see *A. tenuifolia.*

Abronia, A-BRO-ne-a; from Gr. *abros*, delicate, alluding to the leafy involucre enclosing unopened blossoms. Trailing plants. *Nyctaginaceae.*
latifolia, lat-if-O-le-a, broad-leaved.
umbellata, um-bel-LA-ta, having blossoms in umbels.

Abrus, A-brus; from Gr. *abros*, delicate with reference to the soft leaves. Warm house climber. *Leguminosae.*
precatorius, prek-a-TOR-e-us, entreating. The reference being to the black and red seeds of which rosaries are made.

Abutilon, a-BU-til-on; the Arabic name for a mallow-like plant. Greenhouse shrubs. *Malvaceae.*
darwinii, DAR-win-e-i, after Charles Darwin (1809–1882), english naturalist and botanist.
insigne, in-SIG-ne, handsome.
megapotamicum, meg-ap-o-TAM-ik-um, meaning big river – the Rio Grande.
pictum, pic-TUM, painted; brightly coloured.
sellowianum, see *Bakeridesia sellowiana.*
thompsonii, see *A. pictum.*
vexillarium, see *A. megapotamicum.*
vitifolium, see *Corynabutilon vitifolium.*

Acacia, a-KA-she-a; Gr. *akis*, needle, referring to the thorn. Tender trees and shrubs. *Leguminosae.*
armata, see *A. paradoxa.*
baileyana, ba-le-A-na, after Frederick Manson Bailey (1827–1915), colonial botanist of Queensland. The Golden Mimosa.
dealbata, de-al-BA-ta, whitened – the foliage. The mimosa of florists' shops.
drummondii, drum-MON-de-i, in honour of James Drummond (1784–1863), curator of Cork botanic gardens 1809–1829, who collected in Western Australia.

paradoxa, pa-ra-DOKS-a, paradoxical, contrary to exception.

riceana, rice-A-na, after Thomas Spring Rice, Chancellor of the Exchequer.

verticillata, ver-tis-il-LA-ta, whorl-leaved.

Acaena, ak-E-na (or ass-E-na); from Gr. *akanthos*, a thorn, referring to the spiny calyx. Creeping rock plants. *Rosaceae*.

buchananii, bu-kan-A-nei, after John Buchanan (1819–1898), Scottish botanist who collected in New Zealand.

microphylla, mi-krof-IL-la, small leaved.

novae-zelandiae, NOV-e-zeel-AND-e-e, of New Zealand.

Acalypha, a-KAL-y-fa; Gr. *akalepe*, Hippocrates name for nettle. Warm-house shrubby plants with variegated foliage. *Euphorbiaceae*.

australis, aws-TRA-lis, Southern.

godseffiana, see *A. wilkesiana*.

hispida, HIS-pid-a, bristly.

macrostachya, mak-ro-STAK-e-a, large flower spike.

musaica, see *A. wilkesiana*.

sanderi, see *A. hispida*.

wilkesiana, wilk-see-A-na, after Charles Wilkes (1798–1877), American naval officer, leader of the United States Exploring Expedition of 1838–1842 in the Pacific Ocean.

Acanthocereus, a-KAN-tho-SE-re-us; from Gr. *acanthos*, a thorn and *cereus*, a well known genus of cacti. Greenhouse cactus. *Cactaceae*.

pentagonus, see *A. tetragonus*.

tetragonus, te-tra-GO-nus, from Gr. *tessara* four and *gonus* angle.

Acantholimon, ak-an-THOL-e-mon; derivation obscure, but Gr. *akanthos*, a prickle, alludes to spiny foliage; *limon*, *Limonium*, a related genus. Rock plants. *Plumbaginaceae*.

glumaceum, glu-MA-se-um, with chaffy bracts.

venustum, ven-US-tum, pleasing, lovely.

Acanthus, Ak-AN-thus; Gr. *akanthos*, a prickle, some species being spiny. A conventional form of the leaf is used in architecture. Herbaceous plants. *Acanthaceae*.

mollis, MOL-lis, soft or tender, usually means velvety.

spinosus, spi-NO-sus, spines.

Acer, A-ser; Classical Latin name, possibly from L. *acer*, hard or sharp, the wood once been used for writing tablets. Also pronounced AK-er. Trees. *Sapindaceae*.

campestre, kam-PES-tre, growing in fields. The English Maple.

cappadocicum, kap-pa-DO-se-kum, Cappadocian.

dasycarpum, see *A. saccharinum*.

davidii, DA-vid-e-i, after Père Armand David (1826–1900), French missionary and plant collector in China who first discovered it. Re-discovered by Charles Maries.

ginnala, see *A. tataricum* subsp. *ginnala*.

glabrum, GLAB-rum, smooth, hairless.

griseum, GREE-see-um, grey.

insigne, see *A. velutinum*.

japonicum, jap-ON-ik-um, of Japan.

macrophyllum, mak-rof-IL-lum, large leaved.

palmatum, pal-MA-tum, leaves palmate, like a hand.

pennsylvanicum, pen-sil-VA-nik-um, of Pennsylvania.

platanoides, plat-an-OY-des, resembles *Platanus* (plane tree). The Norway maple.

pseudoplatanus, sued-o-plat-A-nus, false plane tree. The Sycamore.

rubrum, ROO-brum, red-flowered.

saccharinum, sak-kar-I-num, sugary. The Sugar Maple.

tataricum, tat-TAR-e-kum, of the Tatar Mountains, Russia.

tataricum subsp. *ginnala*, jin-NA-la, vernacular name.

velutinum, vel-u-TE-num, velvety – young wood and buds are downy.

Aceranthus, misapplied see below.

diphyllus, see *Epimedium diphyllum*.

Aceras, misapplied see below.

anthropophorum, see *Orchis anthropophora*.

Achillea, ak-il-E-a; after Achilles, the Greek hero, who first used the plant in medicine. Herbaceous and rock plant. *Compositae*.

ageratifolia, aj-er-a-tee-FO-le-a, with leaves like *Ageratum*.

ageratifolia subsp. *serbica*, SER-bik-a, of Serbia.

alpina, al-PINE-a (or al-PIN-a), of the Alps or alpine.

argentea, see *Tanacetum argenteum*.

coarctata, ko-ARC-ta-ta, pressed or crowded together.

compacta, see *A. coarctata*.

filipendulina, fil-e-pen-DO-le-na, resembling *Filipendula* (meadowsweet).

millefolium, mil-le-FO-le-um, thousand-leaved. The Yarrow or Milfoil of which there are cultivated forms.

mongolica, see *A. alpina*.

montana, mon-TA-na, of mountains.

ptarmica, TAR-mik-a, Greek *ptarmos*, sneezing, dried flowers once used for snuff. The Sneezewort.

rupestris, roo-PES-tris, growing on rocks.

santolina, san-to-LE-na, resembles *Santolina*.

serbica, see *A. ageratifolia* subsp. *serbica*.

tomentosa, to-men-TO-sa, downy foliage.

Achimenes, ak-e-MEE-neez; from Latin *cheimanos*, tender, as to cold. Greenhouse herbaceous perennials. Many florists' hybrids. *Gesneriaceae*.

carminata, kar-MIN-a-ta, carmine.

coccinea, see *A. erecta*.

erecta, e-REK-ta, erect; upright.

longiflora, long-if-LO-ra, long-flowered.

Acineta, ak-in-E-ta; from Latin *akineta*, immovable, the lip being jointless. Coolhouse orchid. *Orchidaceae*.

humboltii, see *A. superba*.

superba, su-PER-ba, superb.

Acmispon, ak-ME-spon; from Gr. *akme*, point; *spon*, derivation unknown however the genus was described by Rafinesque as the pod being hooked at the point. Herbaceous perennials. *Leguminosae*.

americanus, a-mer-ik-A-nus, of America.

Acokanthera, ak-O-kan-THE-ra; from Gr. *akoke*, a mucron or point; *anthera*, an anther, the anthers are mucronate. Greenhouse flowering shrubs. *Apocynaceae*.

oblongifolia, ob-long-if-O-le-a, oblong-leaved.

spectabilis, see *A. oblongifolia*.

Aconitum, ak-o-NI-tum; ancient classical name, probable origin, Gr. *akon*, a dart, arrows at one time being poisoned with the juices of the plant. Herbaceous plants. *Ranunculaceae*.

carmichaelii, kar-my-KAY-le-i, commemorating Dr. J. R. Carmichael (d. 1877), plant collector in China from 1863–1877.

carmichaelii var. *truppelianum*, trup-pel-e-A-num, after Oscar von Truppel (1854–1931), German Admiral and Governor of Kaio Chau (Jiaozhou Bay) from 1901 to 1911.

fischeri, fish-ER-i, after Fischer, a professor of botany.

forrestii, for-RES-te-i, after George Forrest (1873–1932), Scottish plant collector. Forrest collected in China between 1904 and 1932.

fortunei, see *A. carmichaelii* var. *truppelianum*.

japonicum, jap-ON-ik-um, Japanese.

lycoctonum, lik-OK-to-num, wolf's bane.

napellus, nap-EL-lus, turnip rooted. The Monkshood.

variegatum, var-e-eg-A-tum, variegated.

wilsonii, see *A. carmichaelii*.

Acorus, ak-OR-us; ancient name, possibly from Greek *a*, without; *kore*, pupil of the eye, alluding to the ancient use of the plant in medicine. Aquatics. *Acoraceae*.

calamus, KAL-a-mus; from *kalon*, Arabic for reed; *Calamus*, L. name for the Sweet-flag.

gramineus, gram-IN-e-us, grass leaved.

Acroclinium, misapplied see below.

roseum, see *Rhodanthe chlorocephala* subsp. *rosea*.

Acrostichum, ak-ROS-tik-um; from Gr. *akros*, top and *stichos*, a row, application unknown. Tropical ferns. *Pteridaceae*.

crinitum, see *Elaphoglossum crinitum*.

peltatum, see *Elaphoglossum obovatum*.

Actaea, ak-TE-a; from Gr. *aktaia*, elder, the leaves resembling those of that tree. Herbaceous plants. *Ranunculaceae*.

alba, see *A. rubra*.

dahurica, da-UR-ik-a, of Dahuri, Asia, a mountainous region to the east of Lake Baikal.

japonica, jap-ON-ik-a, of Japan.

racemosa, ras-em-O-sa, resembling a raceme.

rubra, ROO-bra, red-coloured.

simplex, SIM-pleks, simple – the spikes unbranched.

spicata, spe-KA-ta, spiked, alluding to the inflorescence.

Actinella, ak-tin-ELL-a; from Gr. *aktis*, a ray, flowers being rayed like small sunflowers; literally a little ray. Rock and border perennials. *Compositae.*

acaulis, see *Tetraneuris acaulis.*
grandiflora, see *Hymenoxys grandiflora.*

Actinidia, ak-tin-ID-e-a; from Gr. *aktis*, a ray, referring to star like flowers, or to rayed stigmas of female blooms. Climbing shrubs. *Actinidiaceae.*

arguta, ar-GU-ta, sharp-toothed or serrated.
chinensis, tshi-NEN-sis, of China.
henryi, HEN-re-i, after Dr. A. Henry (1857–1930), plant collector and dendrologist.
polygama, pol-e-GAM-a, with male, female and bisexual flowers on the same plant.
volubilis, see *A. polygama.*

Actinotus, ak-tin-O-tus; from L. *actinotus*, rayed, referring to the involucre. Tender perennial. *Apiaceae.*

helianthi, he-le-ANTH-i, sunflower like – the petal-like involcre. The Australian Flannel Flower.

Ada, A-da; a complimentary name after the queen of Caria in Asia Minor. Greenhouse orchid. *Orchidaceae.*

aurantiaca, see *Brassia aurantiaca.*
pygmaea, PIG-me-a, dwarf.

Adelocaryum, a-del-o-KAR-ee-um; from the Gr. *adelo*, unknown or secret; *karyo*, nut. Perennial. *Boraginaceae.*

coelestinum, se-les-TE-num, heavenly blue.

Adenophora, ad-en-OF-or-a; from Gr. *aden*, a gland, and *phoreo*, to bear; reference obscure. Herbaceous plants. *Campanulaceae.*

denticulata, see *A. tricuspidata.*
latifolia, see *A. pereskiifolia.*
liliiflora, lil-e-i-FO-le-a, lily leaved.
pereskiifolia, per-esk-e-i-O-le-a, resembling *Pereskia.*
polymorpha, see *A. liliiflora.*
stylosa, see *A. liliiflora.*
tricuspidata, try-kusp-e-DA-ta, three-pointed.
triphylla, trif-IL-la, three-leaved.
verticillata, see *A. triphylla.*

Adiantum, ad-e-AN-tum; from Gr. *a*, not; *diantos*, moistened (*adiantos*, dry), the fronds of the Maidenhair Fern being supposed to remain dry even after being plunged under water. Greenhouse and hardy ferns. *Pteridaceae.*

affine, af-FIN-e, related.
capillus-veneris, kap-IL-lus VEN-er-is, Venus' hair. The Maidenhair Fern.
caudatum, kaw-DA-tum, tailed.
concinnum, kon-SIN-num, neat.
concinnum var. *latum*, LA-tum, broad, that is, broader than the type. A native of Muna Island, Indonesia exhibited in 1867 by the nurseries of James Veitch.
cuneatum, see *A. raddianum.*
decorum, dek-OR-um, decorous – shapely or becoming.
farleyense, far-ley-EN-se, of Farley Hill, Barbados, where it originated.
formosum, see *A. capillus-veneris.*
fulvum, FUL-vum, tawny.
gracillimum, gra-SIL-lim-um, most graceful.
macrophyllum, mak-ROF-il-lum, large fronds – the size of the pinnae.
pedatum, ped-A-tum, like a bird's foot – the fronds.
princeps, PRIN-seps, princely.
raddianum, ray-dee-A-num, in honour of Giuseppe Raddi (1770–1829), Italian botanist who collected in Brazil and Egypt and gave special attention to cryptogams.
reniforme, ren-e-FOR-me, kidney-shaped – the fronds.
tenerum, TEN-er-um, tender.
tetraphyllum, tet-raf-IL-lum, four leaved, i.e. the pinnae.
trapeziforme, trap-e-zif-OR-me, rhomboid leaved – the pinnae.
williamsii, WILL-yams-e-i, after B.S. Williams, nurseryman, of Holloway.

Adlumia, ad-LU-me-a; named after Major John Adlum (1759–1836), grape breeder and American author. Biennial climber. *Papaveraceae.*

cirrhosa, see *A. fungosa.*
fungosa, fun-GO-sa, resembling fungus, the flower.

Adonis, ad-O-nis; after Adonis of the classics, one of Aphrodite's lovers, whose blood is supposed to have stained the petals of the

Pheasant-eye Adonis (*A. annua*). Annuals and perennials. *Ranunculaceae.*

aestivalis, es-tiv-ALE-is, of summertime referring to the flowering.

amurensis, am-oor-EN-sis, the region of the Amur river.

annua, ann-U-a, annual.

autumnalis, see *A. annua.*

pyrenaica, pir-en-A-ik-a, Pyrenean.

vernalis, ver-NA-lis, of spring – time of flowering.

Aechmea, EEK-me-a; from Gr. *aichme*, a point; referring to the rigid points on the sepals in the bud stage. Warm house herbaceous plants. *Bromeliaceae.*

coelestis, se-LES-tis, sky blue.

fasciata, fas-SEE-a-ta, banded.

fulgens, FUL-jenz, glowing red.

mariae-reginae, MAR-e-e re-JI-ne, after Queen Maria.

Aeonium, a-O-ne-um; an ancient name used by Dioscorides for a plant similar to *A. arboreum*. Greenhouse succulents. *Crassulaceae.*

arboreum, ar-bor-E-um, tree like.

arboreum var. *holochrysum*, hol-o-KRI-sum, entirely yellow – the flowers.

aureum, AW-re-um, golden.

caespitosum, see *Sempervivum caespitosum.*

canariense, ka-nar-e-EN-se, of the Canary Islands.

haworthii, ha-WORTH-e-i, after Adrian Hardy Haworth (1768–1833), author of literature on succulents.

holochrysum, see *A. arboreum* var. *holochrysum.*

spathulatum, spath-ul-A-tum, from L. *spatula*, a spoon – the shape of the leaves.

tabuliforme, tab-ul-e-FOR-me, table like, the rosettes have a flat top.

Aerides, a-er-I-deez; from L. *aer*, the air; some of the species obtain all their nurishment from the atmosphere through aerial roots. Tropical orchids. *Orchidaceae.*

crispum, KRISP-um, curly – the leaves waved.

odorata, od-o-RA-ta, sweet smelling.

Aeschynanthus, ees-kin-ANTH-us; from Gr. *aischuno*, to be ashamed; and *anthos*, a flower, referring to the modest flowers of some species. Warm house shrubby and pendent plants. *Gesneriaceae.*

fulgens, FUL-jenz, glowing red.

pulcher, PUL-ker, beautiful.

speciosus, spes-e-O-sus, handsome.

Aesculus, ES-ku-lus; ancient L. name of an oak or mast-bearing tree. Flowering trees. *Sapindaceae.*

californica, kal-if-OR-nik-a, of California.

× *carnea*, KAR-ne-a, flesh-coloured.

glabra, GLAB-ra, smooth; hairless.

hippocastanum, hip-po-KAS-ta-num, from Gr. *hippos*, a horse; and L. *castanea*, the chestnut tree of Virgil. The Horse Chestnut.

indica, IN-dik-a, of India.

macrostachya, see *A. parviflora.*

parviflora, par-vif-LOR-a, from L. *parvus*, small; *flor*, flower.

rubicunda, see *A. glabra.*

Aethionema, eth-e-O-ne-ma; origin obscure, said to be derived from Gr. *aitho*, to burn; *nema*, a filament, alluding to the burnt appearance of the stamens. More probable origin, the burning or acrid taste of some species. Rock plants. *Brassicaceae.*

armenum, ar-ME-num, of Armenia.

grandiflorum, gran-dif-LO-rum, large flowered.

iberideum, i-ber-ID-e-um, like an *Iberis* (candytuft).

pulchellum, see *A. grandiflorum.*

Agalinis, a-ga-LIN-is; irregular from Greek *aga*, wonder; Latin *linum*, flax. Remarkable flax. *Orobanchaceae.*

purpurea, pur-PUR-e-a, purple coloured.

Agapanthus, ag-a-PAN-thus; from the Greek *agape*, love; *anthos*, a flower. Greenhouse herbaceous plants. *Amaryllidaceae.*

africanus, af-rik-A-nus, African.

umbellatus, see *A. africanus.*

Agaricus, ag-AR-ik-us; probably from Agari, a district in Sarmatia, present day Iran. Fungi, including the edible mushroom. *Agaricaceae.*

campestris, kam-PES-tris, growing in fields or plains. The edible Field Mushroom.

Agathaea, ag-a-THE-a; from Gr. *agathos*, good; alluding to the beauty of the flower. Greenhouse sub-shrub. *Compositae.*

coelestis, see *Felicia amelloides.*

Agave, ag-AH-vee; from Gr. *agauos*, noble; referring to the stately form when in flower. Tender succulents. *Asparagaceae*.

  americana, a-mer-ik-A-na, of South America. The American Aloe (of gardens).

  atrovirens, a-tro-VER-enz, dark green.

  attenuata, at-ten-u-A-ta, attenuated or drawn out.

  horrida, HOR-rid-a, horrid, having strong spines.

  shawii, SHAW-e-i, after Henry Shaw (1800–1889), English born merchant and founder of the Missouri Botanical Garden (Shaw's Garden).

  univittata, u-ne-vit-TA-ta, one line, or stripe – on the leaves.

  utahensis, u-tah-EN-sis, of Utah.

Ageratina, a-jer-a-TEE-na; diminutive form of Ageratum. *Compositae*.

  aromatica, ar-o-MAT-ik-a, aromatic.

  ligustrina, lig-us-TRIN-a, resembling *Ligustrum* (privet).

Ageratum, aj-er-A-tum; from Gr. *a*, not, and *geras*, old; or Gr. *ageratus*, not growing old, presumably meaning that the flowers do not readily assume a withered appearance. Summer bedding. *Compositae*.

  altissima, al-TIS-sim-a, tallest.

  conyzoides, kon-iz-OY-dez, resembling *Conyza*.

  houstonianum, hows-to-ne-A-num, commemorating Dr. William Houston (1695–1733), Scottish surgeon and plant collector.

  mexicanum, see *A. houstonianum*.

Aglaonema, ag-la-on-E-ma; from Gr. for bright thread, possibly referring to the stamens. Tropical aroids. *Araceae*.

  costatum, kos-TA-tum, leaves strongly ribbed.

  pictum, PIK-tum, painted – the blotched leaves.

Agoseris, a-go-SER-is; possibly from L. *aigos*, goat; Gr. *seris*, lettuce, Goat chicory. Annual and perennial herbs. *Compositae*.

  glauca, GLAW-ka, sea-green, the foliage.

Agrostis, a-GROS-tis; from Gr. *agros*, a field, the Greek name for grass. Ornamental grasses. *Poaceae*.

  nebulosa, neb-ul-O-sa, nebulous or cloud like referring to the inflorescence. The Cloud Grass.

Aichryson, a-KRY-son; ancient name used by Dioscorides for a plant similar to *Aeonium*

arboreum. Greenhouse succulents. *Crassulaceae*.

  × *aizoides*, ay-ZOY-dees, resembling *Aizoon*.

  × *aizoides* var. *domesticum*, do-MES-tik-um, frequently used as a houseplant.

  dichotomum, see *A. laxum*.

  divaricatum, di-va-rik-A-tum, wide spreading branches.

  × *domesticum*, do-MES-tik-um, frequently used as a houseplant.

  laxum, LACK-sum, loose or open.

Ailanthus, a-LAN-thus; from *ailanto*, the native Chinese name for one of the species. Signifying tall enough to reach the skies. Deciduous tree. *Simaroubaceae*.

  altissima, al-TIS-sim-a, tallest. The Tree of Heaven.

Ajuga, a-JU-ga; a corruption of L. *abiga*, a plant used in medicine, or (more probably) from *a*, no, and *zugon*, a yoke, in reference to the calyx lobes being equal – not bilabiate. Creeping plants. *Lamiaceae*.

  genevensis, jen-e-VEN-sis, of Geneva.

  reptans, REP-tans, creeping. Several forms of this are cultivated.

Akebia, a-KE-be-a; an adaptation of the Japanese name *akebi* for these shrubby twining plants. *Lardizabalaceae*.

  lobata, see *A. trifoliata*.

  quinata, kwin-A-ta, five lobed – the leaves.

  trifoliata, tri-fo-li-A-ta, from the L. *tri*, three; *folium*, a leaf; because of the three lobed leaves.

Albuca, al-BU-ka; from L. *albicans* or *albus*, white – the prevailing colour. Greenhouse bulbous plants. *Asparagaceae*.

  bracteata, brak-te-A-ta, having bracts, or modified leaves.

  nelsonii, nel-SO-ne-i, after William Nelson (1852–1922), British nurseryman who first collected the species.

Alcea, al-SEE-a; from Gr. *alkaia*, a kind of mallow. Hollyhocks. Herbaceous perennial. *Malvaceae*.

  rosea, RO-ze-a, red or rosy. The Hollyhock.

  rosea subsp. *ficifolia*, fi-kif(or sif)-OL-e-a, *Ficus* or fig leaved.

Alchemilla, al-kem-IL-a; from the Arabic *alkemelych*, alluding to use of the plants in alchemy. Rock plants. *Rosaceae.*
 alpina, al-PINE-a, alpine.
 mollis, MOL-lis, with soft hairs. The Lady's Mantle.
 sericea, ser-IS-e-a, silky – the leaves.
 vulgaris, see *A. xanthochlora*.
 xanthochlora, zanth-o-KLOR-a, yellowish green.

Alisma, al-IZ-ma; water plantain, the Classical Greek name for this plant. Aquatic or bog plants. *Alismataceae.*
 natans, see *Luronium natans*.
 plantago-aquatica, plan-TA-go a-KWAT-ik-a, an old generic name referring to the *Plantago* (plantain) like leaves; L. *aquaticus*, growing in water. The Water Plantain.

Allamanda, al-la-MAN-da; in honour of Dr. Allamand (1735–1803), professor of natural history at Leiden. Warm-house shrubby climbers. *Apocynaceae.*
 cathartica, kath-AR-tik-a, purgative, cathartic.
 hendersonii, see *A. cathartica*.
 nobilis, NO-bil-is, large or noble.
 schottii, SHOT-te-i, after Heinrich Wilhelm Schott (1794–1865), Austrian Botanist who with Pohl was a participant on the Austrian Brazil Expedition from 1817–1821.

Allium, AL-le-um; the Latin term for garlic; now the name for all the onion family, or from the Celtic *all*, meaning pungent or burning. Bulbous perennials and culinary herbs. *Amaryllidaceae.*
 ampeloprasum, am-pe-LOW-pray-sum, from Gr. *ampelos*, vine; *prasum*, leek; a wild leek associated with vineyards.
 ascalonicum, as-kal-O-nik-um, of Askelon, Palestine. The shallot or eschalot.
 beesianum, bees-e-A-num, commemorating the nursery firm Bees.
 carinatum, ka-ri-NA-tum, keeled.
 carinatum subsp. *pulchellum*, pul-KEL-um, beautiful but small.
 carolinianum, ka-ro-li-ne-A-num, from Carolina, USA.
 cepa, KE-pa, headed, probably from Celtic *cep*, head. The onion.
 chrysanthum, kris-AN-thum, golden flowered.
 cristophii, kris-TOF-e-i, named after Christophe, origin unknown.

cyaneum, sy-A-ne-um, blue flowered.
descendens, see *A. sphaerocephalon*.
fistulosum, fis-tu-LO-sum, fistular or hollow leaved. Welsh onion.
flavidum, FLA-vid-um, pale yellow.
giganteum, ji-GAN-te-um, gigantic.
kansuense, see *A. sikkimense*.
moly, MO-le, old Greek name of a magic herb of uncertain identity.
narcissiflorum, nar-sis-e-FLOR-um, Narcissus flowered.
neapolitanum, ne-a-pol-e-TA-num, from Naples.
oreophilum, o-re-O-fa-lum, from Gr. *oreo*, mountain; *phila*, loving.
ostrowskyanum, see *A. oreophilum*.
paniculatum, pan-ik-u-LA-tum, panicled.
polyphyllum, see *A. carolinianum*.
porrum, see *A. ampeloprasum*.
pulchellum, see *A. carinatum* subsp. *pulchellum*.
purdomii, see *A. cyaneum*.
roseum, RO-ze-um, rosy.
sativum, SAT-iv-um, cultivated. The garlic.
schoenoprasum, sken-OP-ras-um, old Greek name for leek. The chives.
scorodoprasum, scor-od-OP-ras-um, combination of both Greek for onion and leek, signifying the plant is both onion and leek. The sand leek.
sikkimense, sik-kim-EN-se, from Sikkim.
sphaerocephalon, sfer-o-SEF-al-on, old generic name meaning round-headed – the flower head.
triquetrum, tri-KWET-rum, three cornered – the stalks.

Alnus, AL-nus; *alnus*, Latin name for alder. Trees. *Betulaceae.*
 cordata, kor-DA-ta, heart shaped, the leaves.
 glutinosa, glu-tin-O-sa, sticky referring to the foliage. Alder.
 incana, in-KA-na, grey or hoary-leaved.

Alocasia, al-o-KAS-e-a; from L. *a*, without; *colocasia*, similar to, without being a closely related plant *Colocasia*. Tropical ornamental leaved plant. *Araceae.*
 jenningsii, see *Colocasia affinis*.
 longiloba, lon-ge-LO-ba, with long lobes.
 macrorrhizos, mac-row-RY-zos, long rooted.
 metallica, see *A. macrorrhizos*.
 sanderiana, san-der-e-A-na, after Messrs. Sander of St. Albans, nurserymen.
 thibantiana, see *A. longiloba*.
 watsoniana, see *A. longiloba*.

Aloe, AL-o-e; old Arabic name, possibly from Arabic *alloch*, referring to species used medicinally. Greenhouse succulent plants. English name, Aloe; al-o. *Xanthorrhoeaceae*.
  abyssinica, ab-is-IN-ik-a, Abyssinian.
  arborescens, ar-bor-ES-cenz, tree like.
  humilis, HUM-il-is, dwarf, humble as to stature.
  mitriformis, see *A. perfoliata*.
  perfoliata, per-fo-le-A-ta, the leaf surrounding the stem.
  succotrina, suc-cot-RE-na, of Socotra.
  variegata, var-e-eg-A-ta, variegated. Partridge-breasted Aloe or Mackerel Plant.
  vera, VE-ra, the true or type species.

Alonsoa, al-on-SO-a; after Alonzo Zanoni, Secretary of State of Columbia. Half-hardy shrubby plants. *Scrophulariaceae*.
  incisifolia, see *A. meridionalis*.
  linearis, lin-e-AR-is, linear leaved, narrow, with nearly parallel sides.
  linifolia, see *A. linearis*.
  meridionalis, me-rid-e-o-NAL-iz, noonday, flowering at midday.
  warscewiczii, see *A. meridionalis*.

Aloysia, al-OY-se-a; named in honour of Maria Louisa (d. 1819), Queen of Spain. Half-hardy shrub. *Verbenaceae*.
  citriodora, sit-re-o-DOR-a, lemon scented. The Lemon Scented Verbena.

Alpinia, al-PIN-e-a; after P. Alpinus, an Italian botanist. Tropical herbaceous perennials. *Zingiberaceae*.
  nutans, nu-tanz, drooping or nodding.
  sanderiana, see *A. vittata*.
  vittata, vit-TA-ta, striped.

Alrawia, al-RA-we-a; in honour of Dr. Ali al-Rawi (fl. 1966), curator of the National Herbarium of Iraq. Bulbs. *Asparagaceae*.
  bellii, bel-LE-i, discovered by Major Frank Bell (fl. 1884), plant collector in Iran.

Alsine, al-SEEN-e; Gr. *alsos*, a grove, often a habitat of the chick weeds, according to some authorities; more probably derived from the Greek name given by Dioscorides to a *Cerastium*. Rock plants. *Caryophyllaceae*.
  laricifolia, see *Minuartia laricifolia*.

Alsophila, al-SOF-il-a; Gr. *alsos*, a grove; *phileo*, to love, shade loving tree-ferns. Greenhouse ferns. *Cyatheaceae*.
  australis, aws-TRA-lis, Southern.

Alstroemeria, al-stro-MEER-i-a; named in honour of Baron Claus Alstroemer (1736–1794), a Swedish botanist and friend of Linnaeus. Half-hardy herbaceous plants. Peruvian Lily. *Alstroemeriaceae*.
  aurantiaca, see *A. aurea*.
  aurea, AW-re-a, golden – the flower.
  chilensis, see *A. ligtu*.
  ligtu, LIG-too, the Chilean vernacular name for this plant.
  pelegrina, pel-e-GREE-na, spotted blooms.

Alternanthera, al-tern-AN-ther-a; alternate anthers, alluding to the anthers being alternately barren and fertile. Dwarf, tropical, coloured leaved plants, used for carpet bedding. *Amaranthaceae*.
  amabilis, am-A-bil-is, lovely.
  bettzickiana, bets-ik-i-A-na, named after August Bettzick (1814–1865), German gardener.
  ficoidea, fi-KOY-de-a, resembling *Ficus*.
  paronychioides, par-on-ik-OY-des, *Paronychia* like, several varieties.

Althaea, al-THE-a; Gr. *althaia*, a healing medium, referring to its use in medicine. Hardy herbaceous and biennials. *Malvaceae*.
  ficifolia, see *Alcea rosea* subsp. *ficifolia*.
  officinalis, of-fis-in-A-lis, of the shop (apothecary's), applied to plants always kept "in stock" by herbalists.
  rosea, see *Alcea rosea*.

Alyssoides, al-is-OY-dees; resembling *Alyssum*. Herbaceous perennial. *Brassicaceae*.
  utriculata, u-trik-ul-A-ta, from L. *utriculus*, a small bottle; bladder like, the seed pods.

Alyssum, AL-iss-um; from Gr. *a*, not; *lyssa*, madness, the plant once being considered a remedy for a bite by a mad dog, hence the popular name, Madwort. Rock plants. *Brassicaceae*.
  argenteum, ar-JEN-te-um, silvery.
  corymbosum, see *Aurinia corymbosa*.
  maritimum, see *Lobularia maritima*.
  montanum, mon-TA-num, of mountains.
  pyrenaicum, see *A. serpyllifolium*.

saxatile, see *Aurinia saxatilis*.
serpyllifolium, ser-pil-if-O-le-um, *Thymus serpyllum* (thyme) leaved.

Amaranthus, am-a-RANTH-us; from Gr. *a*, not; *maraino*, to fade, or *amarantos*, unfading, referring to the durability of the flowers of some species. Tender annuals. *Amaranthaceae*.
   caudatus, kaw-DA-tus, tailed, the shape of the inflorescence. The Love-lies- bleeding.
   cruentus, kru-EN-tus, dark blood-red.
   hypochondriacus, hy-pok-ON-dre-ak-us, of melancholy appearance; sombre-coloured flowers. The Prince's Feather.
   tricolor, TRIK-o-lor, three coloured.

Amaryllis, am-a-RIL-is; a classical name, after a beautiful shepherdess in the poetry of Theocritus and Virgil. Half-hardy bulb. *Amaryllidaceae*.
   belladonna, bel-la-DON-na, Ital. *bella*, pretty; *donna*, lady, an extract from the plant used to brighten the eyes. The Belladonna Lily.

Amasonia, am-as-O-ne-a; after Thomas Amason, an American traveller. Tropical coloured-foliage plants. *Lamiaceae*.
   calycina, kal-ik-EEN-a, with showy calyces.
   campestris, kam-PES-tris, growing in fields.
   punicea, see *A. campestris*.

Amberboa, am-BER-bo-a; from a Turkish name for *A. moschata*. Annual or biennial herbs. *Compositae*.
   amberboi, am-BER-bo-e, is the Turkish name given to some species of this kind.
   moschata, mos-KA-ta, musky.

Amelanchier, am-el-AN-ke-er; name adapted from Fr. *amelancier*, an old name in the Savoy region for *A. ovalis*, the Snowy Mespilus. Small flowering trees. *Rosaceae*.
   alnifolia, al-nif-O-le-a, alder-leaved.
   canadensis, kan-a-DEN-sis, of Canada.
   lamarckii, la-MARK-e-i, named after Jean Baptiste de Monet Lamarck (1744–1829), French naturalist and author.
   ovalis, o-VAR-lis, oval, broadly elliptic. The Snowy Mespilus, having edible fruits.
   vulgaris, see *A. ovalis*.

Amianthium, am-e-AN-thee-um; meaning 'unspotted' either because of the glandless

perianth or the pure white flowers. Bulbs. *Melanthiaceae*.
   muscitoxicum, mus-ke-TOKS-ik-um, old name referring to 'fly-poison'.

Ammobium, am-MO-be-um; from Gr. *ammos*, sand; *bio*, to live. Thriving in sandy places. Perennial. *Compositae*.
   alatum, al-A-tum, winged – the stems.

Ammogeton, misapplied see below.
   scorzonerifolius, see *Agoseris glauca*.

Amomyrtus, am-o-MER-tus; from the Gr. *amos*, fragrant; *myrtus*, the family name. Trees and shrubs. *Myrtaceae*.
   luma, LEU-ma, old name of Chilean origin.

Amorpha, am-OR-fa; from Gr. *a*, not; *morphe*, form, referring to the irregular shapes of the leaves. Shrubs. *Leguminosae*.
   canescens, kan-ES-ens, grey or hoary.
   fruticosa, frut-ik-O-sa, shrubby.
   nana, NA-na, dwarf.

Ampelopsis, am-pel-OP-sis; from Gr. *ampelos*, a vine; *opsis*, resemblance. Resembling a grapevine. *Vitaceae*.
   glandulosa, glan-du-LO-sa, glandular.
   glandulosa var. *heterophylla*, het-er-of-IL-la, variable leaf form.
   quinquefolia, see *Parthenocissus quinquefolia*.
   tricuspidata, see *Parthenocissus tricuspidata*.
   veithchii, see *Parthenocissus tricuspidata*.

Amsonia, am-SO-ne-a; after Charles Amson, a scientific American explorer. Herbaceous perennials. *Apocynaceae*.
   angustifolia, see *A. ciliata*.
   ciliata, sil-e-AH-ta, from L. *cilium*, eyelid, then eyelash, fringed with hairs.
   salicifolia, see *A. tabernaemontana* var. *salicifolia*.
   tabernaemontana, tab-er-ne-mon-TA-na, after Jacob Theodore (1525–1590), called Tabernaemontanus from his birthplace; German physician, herbalist and early botanist.
   tabernaemontana var. *salicifolia*, sal-is-if-O-le-a, *Salix* (willow) leaved.

Amygdalus, misapplied see below.
   communis, see *Prunus duleis*.

Anacamptis, a-na-KAMP-tis; from Gr. *anakampto*, bend back; in allusion to the spur of the flower. Pyramid Orchid. *Orchidaceae.*

laxiflora, laks-if-LOR-a, with loose flowers.

pyramidalis, pir-AM-id-al-is, pyramid or coned shaped, the flower spike.

Anacharis, misapplied see below.

alisinastrum, see *Elodea canadensis.*

Anagallis, an-a-GAL-is; from a Gr. word meaning delightful, or possibly from a fable ascribing to the Pimpernel the power to alleviate melancholy. Annuals, biennials and perennials. *Primulaceae.*

arvensis, ar-VEN-sis, growing in cultivated fields. The Scarlet Pimpernel.

indica, see *A. arvensis.*

linifolia, see *A. monellii.*

monelli, mo-NEL-e, after Monell.

tenella, ten-EL-la, somewhat delicate i.e. frail.

Ananas, an-A-nas (or an-AN-as); from *nanas*, the South American (Tupi) name for pineapple. Tropical fruiting plant. *Bromeliaceae.*

comosus, kom-O-sus, furnished with a tuft.

sativa, see *A. comosus.*

Anaphalioides, an-a-FA-lee-oy-dees; resembling *Anaphalis*. Herbaceous perennial. *Compositae.*

bellidioides, bel-lid-e-OY-dees, resembling *Bellis* (the daisy).

Anaphalis, an-a-FAR-lis; old Gr. name: De Candolle said the name was an ancient Gr. one for a similar plant. Herbaceous perennials. *Compositae.*

margaritacea, mar-gar-it-A-se-a, from L. *margarita*, a pearl. The Pearly Everlasting.

Anastatica, an-as-TAT-ik-a; from Gr. *anastasis*, resurrection. Called the Resurrection Plant because the dry dead plants open flat when immersed in water. Supposed to be the "rolling thing before the whirlwind" (Isaiah XVII, 13). Annual. *Brassicaceae.*

hierochuntica, hy-er-OK-unt-E-ka, of Jericho – the L. name of Jericho.

Anchusa, an-KU-za or an-SHOO-za; from Gr. *anchousa*, a cosmetic plant for staining the skin, formerly made from *A. tinctoria.* Herbaceous and biennial. *Boraginaceae.*

azurea, a-ZOR-e-a, sky-blue, azure.

capensis, ka-PEN-sis, of the Cape of Good Hope.

italica, see *A. azurea.*

myosotidiflora, see *Brunnera macrophylla.*

officinalis, of-fis-in-A-lis, of the shop referring to the Apothecary.

sempervirens, see *Pentaglottis sempervirens.*

Andromeda, an-DROM-ed-a; named after the Grecian Princess who was bound to a rock and rescued by the hero Perseus. Low evergreen flowering shrubs. Bog Rosemary. *Ericaceae.*

floribunda, see *Pieris floribunda.*

japonica, see *Pieris japonica.*

polifolia, pol-if-O-le-a, smooth or polished – the leaves.

Androsace, an-dro-SA-se (or an-DRO-sa-se); from Gr. *andros*, male; *sakos*, buckler, the anther being supposed to resemble an ancient buckler. Rock plants. *Primulaceae.*

alpina, al-PINE-a (or al-PIN-a), of the Alps or alpine.

amurensis, am-oor-EN-sis, the region of the Amur river.

chamaejasme, kam-e-JAS-me, literally dwarf jasmine.

ciliata, sil-e-A-ta, an eyelash, fringed with hair.

filiformis, fil-if-OR-mis, thread-like.

foliosa, fo-le-O-sa, leafy.

glacialis, see *A. alpina.*

helvetica, hel-VET-ik-a, of Helvetia (Switzerland).

lactea, lak-TE-a, milky (white).

lactiflora, see *A. amurensis.*

lanuginosa, lan-u-jin-O-sa, with long woolly hairs.

primuloides, prim-ul-OY-dees, resembling *Primula* (primrose).

pubescens, pew-BES-senz, clothed with soft hairs.

sarmentosa, sar-men-TO-sa, twiggy that is many runners.

sempervivoides, sem-per-viv-OY-dees, like a *Sempervivum.*

septentrionalis, sep-ten-tre-o-NA-lis, Northern; from L. *septen*, seven; *triones*, oxen i.e. the stars of the Great Bear constellation, close to the North Star, hence northern.

tibetica, tib-ET-ik-a, of Tibet.

villosa, vil-LO-sa, shaggy, hairy.

Anemia, an-EE-me-a; from Gr. *aneimon*, naked; refers to the naked panicles of fruit-

ification. Tropical (flowering) ferns. *Anemiaceae.*
  phyllitidis, fil-LIT-id-is, like *Phyllitis.*

Anemone, an-EM-o-ne; some authorities state it is from Gr. *anemos*, wind; *mone*, a habitation, some species enjoying windy places, hence Windflower, the English name. However Stearn suggests it is more likely of Semitic origin referring to the slaying of Naamam (Adonis), whose blood is supposed to have stained the blood-red *Anemone coronaria* or *Adonis*. Herbaceous and tuberous perennials. *Ranunculaceae.*
  alpina, al-PINE-a (or al-PIN-a), of the Alps or alpine.
  angulosa, an-gu-LO-sa, angular.
  apennina, ap-en-NI-na, of the Apennines.
  baldensis, ball-DEN-sis, of Mt. Baldo, Italy.
  blanda, BLAN-da, enchanting or pleasing.
  coronaria, kor-on-AR-e-a, crown or wreath-like.
  fulgens, see *A. hortensis.*
  halleri, HAL-er-i, after Albrecht von Haller (1708–1777), a Swiss botanist.
  hepatica, hep-AT-ik-a, liver like, i.e., the lobed leaves.
  hortensis, hor-TEN-sis, of gardens.
  japonica, see *Clematis florida.*
  narcissiflora, nar-sis-i-FLOR-ra, *Narcissus* flowered.
  nemorosa, nem-or-O-sa, of open glades. The Wood Anemone.
  patens, PA-tens, spreading open, or standing out.
  pulsatilla, pul-sa-TIL-la, to shake that is in the wind.
  ranunculoides, ra-nun-kul-OY-dees, like a *Ranunculus* (buttercup).
  rivularis, riv-u-LAR-is, of brooks or streams.
  rupicola, ru-PIK-o-la, a rock-dweller.
  sulphurea, see *A. alpina.*
  sylvestris, sil-VES-tris, pertaining to the woods.
  vernalis, ver-NA-lis, of the spring.

Anemonopsis, an-em-on-OP-sis; from *Anemone*, and Gr. *opsis*, a resemblance, referring to the flowers. Herbaceous plant. *Ranunculaceae.*
  macrophylla, mak-rof-IL-a, with large leaves.

Anethum, a-NE-thum; Gr. name for Dill. Culinary herbs. *Apiaceae.*
  graveolens, GRAV-e-ol-enz, strong smelling.

Angelica, an-JEL-ik-a; from L. *angelus*, an angel, or angelic, alluding to the valuable healing properties. Waterside perennials. *Apiaceae.*
  archangelica, ar-ch-an-JEL-ik-a, named after the Archangel Raphael, who, according to medieval legend, revealed its virtues.
  hirsuta, see *A. venenosa.*
  officinalis, see *A. archangelica.*
  venenosa, ve-ne-NO-sa, very poisonous.

Angelonia, an-gel-O-ne-a; from *angelon*, its South American name. Tropical herbaceous perennials. *Plantaginaceae.*
  grandiflora, gran-dif-LO-ra, large flowered.

Angophora, an-GO-for-a; from Gr. *aggeion*, a vessel; *phoreo*, to bear, in reference to the cup-like fruit. Trees and shrubs. *Myrtaceae.*
  floribunda, flor-e-BUN-da, abundant or free flowering.

Angraecum, an-GRA-kum; L. form of *Angrek*, the Malay name for all orchids of this habit. Tropical epiphytal orchids. *Orchidaceae.*
  eburneum, eb-UR-ne-um, like ivory.
  sesquipedale, ses-kwip-ed-A-le, a foot-and-a-half, the reference being to the long floral spur or nectary.

Anguloa, ang-ul-O-a; after Francisco de Angulo, a Spanish naturalist. South American orchids. *Orchidaceae.*
  clowesii, KLOWES-e-i, after Rev. John Clowes (1777–1846), orchid grower, of Broughton Hall, Manchester (now Clowes Park), he gifted his orchid collection to the Royal Botanic Gardens, Kew.

Anhalonium, misapplied see below.
  fissuratum, see *Ariocarpus fissuratus.*
  prismaticum, see *Ariocarpus retusus.*

Anomatheca, misapplied see below.
  cruenta, see *Freesia laxa.*

Anredera, an-REE-der-a; named by Antoine-Laurant de Jussieu after Anreder whom little more is known. Evergreen climbing plants. *Basellaceae.*
  baselloides, bas-el-OY-dees, resembles *Basella.*

Antennaria, an-ten-NA-re-a; from L. *antenna*, a sail-yard, the hairs attached to the seed of the plant resembling the antennae (feelers) of insects. Antennae is the same derivation. Rock and border plants. *Compositae*.

carpatica, kar-PAT-ik-a, Carpathian.

dioica, di-OY-ka, literally two houses, that is, male and female parts being on separate plants, dioecious.

plantaginifolia, plan-ta-jin-if-O-le-a, *Plantago* (Plantain) leaved.

Anthemis, AN-the-mis; Gr. name for chamomile. Annual, biennial and perennial herbs with strongly scented foliage. *Compositae*.

biebersteinii, see *A. marschalliana*.

cotula, KOT-u-la, cup-like, presumably the flower head.

macedonica, mas-e-DON-ik-a, of Macedonia.

marschalliana, mar-SHALL-e-a-na, in honour of Baron Friedrich August Marschall von Bieberstein, 19th century German explorer in southern Russia.

nobilis, see *Chamaemelum nobile*.

tinctoria, see *Cota tinctoria*.

Anthericum, an-THER-ik-um; from Gr. *anthos*, a flower; *kerkos*, a hedge, probably alluding to great height of some species. Bulbous plants. *Asparagaceae*.

liliago, lil-e-A-go, the silvery (St. Bernard's) Lily.

liliastrum, see *Paradisea liliastrum*.

ramosum, ram-O-sum, with many branches.

variegatum, see *Chlorophytum capense*.

yedoense, see *Comospermum yedoense*.

Antholyza, misapplied see below.

paniculata, see *Crocosmia paniculata*.

Anthriscus, an-THRIS-kus; the Gr. name of a similar plant described by Pliny. Culinary herb. *Apiaceae*.

cerefolium, ke-ref-O-le-um (or se-ref-o-le-um), waxy. The Chervil.

Anthurium, an-THU-re-um; from Gr. *anthos*, a flower; *oura*, a tail, alluding to the spadix. Tropical herbaceous plants, either fine foliage or floral. *Araceae*.

andraeanum, an-dre-AN-um, found growing in the Andes of Ecuador and Columbia and discovered in 1876 by Eduard André (1840–1911), French botanist.

crystallinum, kris-tal-LE-num, crystalline as to the veining.

scherzerianum, sher-zer-e-A-num, after Karl von Scherzer (1821–1903), Austrian explorer and author.

veitchii, VEECH-e-i, collected in Columbia by Gustav Wallis for James Veitch & Sons, Chelsea.

warocqueanum, war-ok-e-A-num, dedicated to Arthur Warocqué (1835–1880), Belgian industrialist and eminent horticulturist.

Anthyllis, an-THIL-is; from G. *anthos*, a flower, and *ioulos*, down, the calyx in many species being downy. Shrubs and perennials. *Leguminosae*.

barba-jovis, BAR-ba-JO-vis, Jupiter's or Jove's beard.

hermanniae, her-MAN-e-e, after Frau Hermann.

lagascana, lar-ga-SKA-na, named after Marianio La Gasca y Segura (1776–1839), Spanish botanist who spent many years in exile in England and Jersey.

sericea, see *A. lagascana*.

tetraphylla, see *Tripodion tetraphyllum*.

vulneraria, vul-ner-A-re-a, wound healing.

Antirrhinum, an-ter-RHI-num; from Gr. *anti*, resembling, and *rhis* (*rhinos*), a snout, alluding to the shape of the flower. Border and rock plants. *Plantaginaceae*.

majus, MA-jus, great. The Snapdragon.

Aotus, a-O-tus; from Gr. *a*, without; *ous*, an ear, certain calyx appendages are lacking that are present in an allied genus *Pultenaea*. Greenhouse evergreen shrubs. *Leguminosae*.

gracillima, gra-SIL-lim-a, most slender.

Aphelandra, af-el-AN-dra; from Gr. *apheles*, simple; *andros*, male, the anthers being one-celled. Tropical evergreen flowering shrubs. *Acanthaceae*.

aurantiaca, aw-ran-te-A-ka, golden orange.

aurantiaca var. *nitens*, NIT-enz, shining.

nitens, see *A. aurantiaca* var. *nitens*.

roezlei, see *A. aurantiaca*.

Aphyllanthes, af-il-AN-thes; from Gr. *a*, without; *phyllon*, a leaf, the flowers being borne at the tips of rush-like growth. Herbaceous perennials. *Asparagaceae.*
  monspeliensis, mon-spe-li-EN-sis, of Montpelier.

Apium, AP-i-um; from Celtic *apon*, water. Ditch plants and culinary vegetables. *Apiaceae.*
  graveolens, GRAV-e-ol-enz, strong smelling. The Celery.
  graveolens var. *rapaceum*, rap-A-se-um, turnip like. The turnip-rooted Celery or Celeriac.

Aponogeton, a-pon-o-GE-ton; from Celtic, *apon*, water; *geiton*, neighbour; or Gr. *apo*, away from; *ge*, the earth, i.e. living in water. Floating aquatic. *Aponogetonaceae.*
  distachyos, dis-TAK-e-os, from Gr. two spiked, the V-shaped flower spike.

Aporocactus, a-por-o-KAK-tus; from Gr. *aporos*, not open or impenetrable, and *cactus*. Possibly from the difficulty in classification. Cactus. *Cactaceae.*
  flagelliformis, see *Disocactus flagelliformis*.
  × *mallisonii*, see *Disocactus* × *mallisonii*.

Aptenia, misapplied see below.
  cordifolia, see *Mesembryanthemum cordifolium*.

Aquilegia, ak-wil-E-je-a; origin doubtful, possibly from L. *aquila*, an eagle, the flower spur resembling an eagle's claw; English name, Columbine, from L. *columba*, a dove, the form of the flowers suggesting a group of doves. Herbaceous perennials; many hybrid strains. *Ranunculaceae.*
  bertolonii, ber-tol-O-ne-i, after Antonio Bertoloni (1775–1869), Italian botanist, professor at Bologna.
  caerulea, se-RU-le-a, dark blue.
  canadensis, kan-a-DEN-sis, Canadian.
  flabellata, flab-el-LA-ta, fan-shaped.
  fragrans, FRA-granz, fragrant.
  glandulosa, glan-dul-O-sa, glandular.
  glauca, see *A. fragrans*.
  jucunda, see *A. glandulosa*.
  kitaibelii, kit-a-BEL-e-i, after Paul Kitaibel (1757–1817), professor of botany at Pest.
  nevadensis, nev-a-DEN-sis, of Nevada.
  reuteri, see *A. bertolonii*.

skinneri, SKIN-er-i, sent to Woburn Abbey by George Ure Skinner (1804–1867), British merchant in Guatemala.
  thalictrifolia, thal-ik-trif-O-le-a, leaves like a *Thalictrum*.
  viridiflora, vir-id-if-LO-ra, green flowered.
  vulgaris, vul-GAR-is, common. The Columbine.

Arabidopsis, AR-a-be-dop-sis; from *Arabis* and Gr. *opsis*, its appearance resembling this. Rock plants. *Brassicaceae.*
  lyrata, li-RA-ta, pinnately divided leaf with an enlarged terminal lobe.
  lyrata subsp. *petraea*, pet-RE-a, of rocks.
  thaliana, thar-li-AR-na, named in honour of Johannes Thal (1542–1583), German physician at Nordhausen.

Arabis, AR-ab-is; from Gr. *arabis*, Arabia, the home of several species. Rock plants. *Brassicaceae.*
  albida, see *A. caucasica*.
  aubrietioides, aw-bre-te-OY-dees, like an *Aubrietia*.
  bellidifolia, see *A. pumila*.
  caucasica, kaw-ka-SIK-a, of the Caucasus.
  lucida, LU-sid-a, shining that is the leaves.
  petraea, see *Arabidopsis lyrata* subsp. *petraea*.
  pumila, PU-mil-a, dwarf.

Aralia, ar-A-le-a; from the old French-Canadian vernacular name *aralie*. Herbaceous plants and shrubs. *Araliaceae.*
  cachemirica, Kash-MIR-ik-a, of Kashmir.
  chinensis, tshi-NEN-sis, Chinese.
  elata, e-LA-ta, tall.
  elata var. *mandshurica*, man-SHEM-ree-ka, of Manchuria.
  elegantissima, see *Schefflera elegantissima*.
  japonica, see *Fatsia japonica*.
  spinosa, spi-NO-sa, spiny.
  veitchi, see *Schefflera veitchi*.

Araucaria, a-raw-KAR-e-a; from Araucani the local tribe whose province it is native. Coniferous trees. *Araucariaceae.*
  araucana, a-raw-KAR-na, from the Province of Araneo, Chile, where it was first found. The Monkey Puzzle.
  columnaris, kol-LUM-nair-is, columnar. Cook Pine.
  excelsa, see *A. columnaris*.
  heterophylla, het-er-of-IL-la, Gr. *hetero*, diverse; *phylla*, leaves. Norfolk Island Pine.
  imbricata, see *A. araucana*.

Araujia, a-RAU-je-a; the Brazilian name for these vines. *Apocynaceae.*

graveolens, GRAV-e-ol-enz, strong smelling.

Arbutus, AR-bu-tus; L. name for *A. unedo*, the Strawberry Tree. Some authorities derive word from Celtic *arboise*, rough-fruited. Small trees. *Ericaceae.*

menziesii, men-ZE-se-i, after Archibald Menzies (1754–1842), the Scottish botanist.

unedo, u-NED-o or u-NE-do, meaning obscure. Pliny, the Roman naturalist, derives the word from *unus*, one; *edo*, to eat. That is to eat one only – pleasant but unwholesome. The Strawberry Tree.

Arctanthemum, ark-TAN-the-mum; from Gr. *arktikos*, northern; *anthemon*, a flower. Herbaceous perennials. *Compositae.*

arcticum, ARK-tik-um, Artic.

Arctostaphylos, ark-to-STAF-il-os; from Gr. *arktos*, a bear, and *staphyle*, a bunch of grapes, the berries of some species being eaten by bears, hence bear-berry. Shrubs. *Ericaceae.*

manzanita, man-zan-IT-a, a Spanish-Californian name for the genus generally.

uva-ursi, U-va-UR-see, bear's grape. The bear-berry.

Arctotis, ark-TO-tis; from Gr. *arktos*, a bear; *ous, otos*, an ear, probably in reference to the shaggy fruit. Annuals and perennials. *Compositae.*

acaulis, a-KAW-lis, stemless or with short stems.

aspera, AS-per-a, rough that is the leaves.

breviscapa, see *A. leporhiza.*

fastuosa, fas-tu-O-sa, stately.

grandis, see *A. stoechadifolia.*

leptorhiza, lep-to-RE-za, having fine (slender) roots.

scapigera, see *A. acaulis.*

stoechadifolia, sto-cha-DEE-fo-lia, meaning obscure, could be from Gr. *stoechas* in a row; or referring to the Greek name for mint as the leaves are aromatic.

Ardisia, ar-DIS-e-a; from Gr. *ardis*, a spearhead, alluding to the shape of the anthers. Greenhouse berry-bearing shrub. *Primulaceae.*

crenata, kren-A-ta, crenate or round-notched – the leaves.

Areca, ar-E-ka; from *areec*, the vernacular name of the Palm used by the inhabitants of Malabar. Tropical Palm. Areca Palm. *Arecaceae.*

lutescens, see *Hyophorbe indica.*

Arenaria, ar-en-AR-e-a; from L. *arena*, sand, that is inhabiting sandy places, hence sandwort. Rock plants. *Caryophyllaceae.*

balearica, bal-e-AR-ik-a, of the Balearic Islands.

gothica, GO-thik-a, of Gothland, North Germany.

laricifolia, see *Minuartia laricifolia.*

ledebouriana, see *Eremogone ledebouriana.*

montana, mon-TA-na, of mountains.

purpurascens, pur-pur-ES-ens, purple – the flowers.

tetraquetra, tet-ra-KWET-ra, four angled – the leaves in four.

verna, see *Minuartia verna.*

villarsii, see *Minuartia villarsii.*

Arequipa, ar e QUIP a; the name of the town in Peru where the species is found. Greenhouse cacti. *Cactaceae.*

leucotricha, loo-ko-TRIK-a, white-haired.

Argemone, ar-gem-O-ne; from Gr. *argemos*, a white spot (cataract) on the eye which the plant was supposed to cure; or from Gr. *argos*, slothful, i.e. from the narcotic effects of the poppy. Annuals and perennials. The Mexican poppy. *Papaveraceae.*

grandiflora, gran-dif-LO-ra, large flowered.

mexicana, meks-e-KAN-a, of Mexico.

platyceras, plate-e-SE-ras, having broad prickles.

Argyranthemum, ar-je-RAN-the-mum; from Gr. *argyros*, silver; *anthemon*, a flower. Perennials. *Compositae.*

frutescens, fru-TES-senz, shrubby. The Paris Daisy.

Argyrochosma, ar-gy-ro-KOS-ma; from Gr. *argyros*, silver; *chosma*, powder, referring to the white farina covering the leaf. Fern. *Pteridaceae.*

dealbata, de-al-BA-ta, whitewashed – the farina.

nivea, NIV-e-a, white – the farina.

nivea var. *tenera*, TEN-er-a, soft, delicate, slender.

Argyroderma, ar-gy-rod-ER-ma; from Gr. *argyros*, silver; *derma*, skin, referring to the silvery deposit on the skin. Greenhouse succulent. *Aizoaceae.*

　testiculare, tes-tik-u-LAR-e, tubercle like.

Ariocarpus, AR-e-o-KAR-pus; compound of *aria* (Whitebeam – *Sorbus aria*) and Gr. *carpos*, fruit, the fruits suggesting those of the Whitebeam. Greenhouse cacti. *Cactaceae.*

　fissuratus, fis-sur-A-tum, cleft.
　prismaticus, see *A. retusus.*
　retusus, ret-U-sus, with a rounded, slightly notched tip.

Arisaema, ar-is-E-ma; from Gr. *aris*, arum; *haima*, blood, name referring to the red-blotched leaves of some species. Tuberous-rooted perennials. *Araceae.*

　ringens, RIN-gens, gaping – the open spathe.
　speciosum, spes-e-O-sum, showy.
　triphyllum, trif-IL-lum, three-leaves, i.e. the leaf divisions.

Arisarum, ar-is-AR-um; possibly from Gr. *arista*, a bristle, or awn; *arum*, to which the genus is allied, the spathe, or sheath of the flower, having a spike. Herbaceous perennials. *Araceae.*

　proboscideum, pro-bos-SID-e-um, having a proboscis or tail-like appendage; literally like a snout.
　vulgare, vul-GAR-e, common.

Aristolochia, ar-is-to-LO-ke-a; from Gr. *aris*, best (most useful); *locheia*, childbirth, alluding to the ancient use in maternity – the Birthwort. Tropical and hardy climbing plants and shrubs. *Aristolochiaceae.*

　clematitis, klem-at-I-tis, resembling *Clematis.*
　elegans, see *A. littoralis.*
　gigas, see *A. grandiflora.*
　grandiflora, gran-dif-LO-ra, large flowered.
　littoralis, lit-tor-A-lis, of the seashore.

Aristotelia, ar-is-to-TE-le-a; believed to be named in honour of the philosopher Aristotle. Shrubs. *Elaeocarpaceae.*

　chilensis, chil-EN-sis, of Chile.
　macqui, see *A. chilensis.*

Armeria, ar-MEER-e-a; old Latin name. English name, Thrift or Sea Pink. Rock and border plants. *Plumbaginaceae.*

alliacea, al-le-A-see-a, *Allium* (onion) like in appearance.
arenaria, ar-en-AR-e-a; from L. *arena*, sand, that is inhabiting sandy places. Jersey Thrift.
caespitosa, kees-pit-O-sa (or ses-pit-O-sa), closely tufted (literally turf-like).
cephalotes, see *A. alliacea.*
fasciculata, see *A. pungens.*
juncea, see *A. alliacea.*
latifolia, see *A. pseudoarmeria.*
maritima, mar-IT-im-a, of the sea. Sea Pink or Thrift.
plantaginea, see *A. arenaria.*
pseudoarmeria, sued-o-ar-MEER-e-a, false sea thrift.
pungens, PUN-jenz, sharp pointed.
splendens, SPLEN-denz, splendid.

Armoracia, ar-mo-RA-se-a; the Latin name for a related plant. Horse-Radish. *Brassicaceae.*

　rusticana, russ-te-KA-na, pertaining to the country.

Arnebia, ar-NE-be-a; from Arabic, *arneb*, name for one of the species. Rock or border plants. *Boraginaceae.*

　benthamii, ben-THAM-e-i, named in honour of George Bentham (1800–1884) botanist and author.
　echioides, see *Nonea echioides.*

Arnica, AR-nik-a; origin uncertain, possibly from Gr. *arnakis*, a lamb's skin (or Gr. *arnion*, a lamb), the leaves a soft texture. Herbaceous plants. *Compositae.*

　amplexicaulis, see *A. lanceolata* subsp. *prima.*
　lanceolata, lan-se-o-LA-ta, the leaves spear-shaped.
　lanceolata subsp. *prima*, PRY-ma; from L. *primus*, foremost; most distinguished.
　montana, mon-TA-na, of mountains.
　sachalinensis, sak-al-in-EN-sis, of Sakhalin Island.

Aronia, a-ROW-ne-a; from Gr. *aria*, Whitebeam; in allusion to the resemblance of the Chokeberry fruits. *Rosaceae.*

　arbutifolia, ar-bew-tif-OL-e-a, resembling *Arbutus* leaves. Red Chokeberry.
　melanocarpa, mel-an-ok-AR-pa, black-fruited. The Black Chokeberry.
　× *prunifolia*, proo-nif-O-le-a, plum-leaved. Purple Chokeberry.

Artemisia, ar-tem-EES-e-a; called after Artemis (Diana), one of the divinities of Ancient Greece. Perennials. *Compositae.*

abrotanum, ab-ROT-a-num, Ancient Latin name for Southernwood.

absinthium, ab-SIN-the-um, Latin and Pre-Linnean name for Wormwood.

alpina, al-PINE-a (or al-PIN-a), of the Alps or alpine.

arborescens, ar-bor-ES-senz, tree-like.

cana, KA-na, hoary.

dracunculus, drak-UN-ku-lus, Latin word meaning a small dragon. The Tarragon.

frigida, FRIJ-id-a, growing in cold regions.

gnaphalioides, naf-a-le-OY-dees, resembling *Gnaphalium* (Cudweed).

gracilis, see *A. scoparia.*

lactiflora, lak-tif-LO-ra, flowers are milk-white.

lanata, see *A. pedemontana.*

laxa, see *A. umbelliformis.*

ludoviciana, lu-do-VIS-e-a-na (or lu-do-vik-e-A-na), of Louisiana (U.S.A.).

pedemontana, ped-e-mon-TA-na, from Piedmont.

pontica, PON-tik-a, Pontus, the shores of the Black Sea.

scoparia, sko-PAR-e-a, having twiggy braches like *Cytissus scoparius.*

stellariana, stel-lar-e-A-na, starry.

tanacetifolia, tan-a-set-if-O-le-a, leaves like *Tanacetum* (Tansy).

umbelliformis, um-bel-IF-or-miss, furnished in umbels.

Arthropodium, arth-ro-pod-e-um; from Gr. *arthron*, a joint; *pous*, a foot. The floral foot stalks are jointed. Greenhouse herbaceous plants. *Asparagaceae.*

cirrhatum, kir-ha-tum, having curls.

milleflorum, mil-li-FLOR-um, many flowered; literally a thousand flowers.

paniculatum, see *A. milleflorum.*

Arum, a-RUM; ancient name, possibly from Arabic, *ar*, fire, in reference to the burning taste of the plant. Herbaceous perennials. *Araceae.*

creticum, KRET-ik-um, of the Island of Crete.

dracunculus, see *Dracunculus vulgaris.*

italicum, it-AL-ik-um, Italian.

maculatum, mak-ul-A-tum, spotted that is the leaves.

palaestinum, pal-es-TIN-um, of Palestine.

Aruncus, a-RUN-kus; named used by Pliny for these herbs. Perennial herbs. *Rosaceae.*

dioicus, di-OY-kus, literally two houses, that is, male and female parts being on separate plants, dioecious.

Arundinaria, ar-un-din-A-re-a; from L. *arundo*, a reed. Bamboos. *Poaceae.*

anceps, see *Yushania anceps.*

appalachiana, ap-pa-la-chee-A-na, of the Appalachian mountains.

auricoma, see *Pleioblastus viridistriatus.*

fortunei, see *Pleioblastus fortunei.*

gigantea, ji-GAN-te-a, unusually tall or big.

metake, see *Pseudosasa japonica.*

palmata, see *Sasa palmata.*

pumila, see *Pleioblastus argenteostriatus.*

veitchii, see *Sasa veitchii.*

Arundo, ar-UN-do; from L. *arundo*, a reed. Reeds. *Poaceae.*

donax, DO-naks, name for the Greek Reed of Provence.

phragmites, see *Phragmites australis.*

Asarum, as-AR-um; from ancient name, meaning not clear. Herbaceous plants. *Aristolochiaceae.*

caudatum, kaw-DA-tum, tailed.

europaeum, u-ro-PE-um, of Europe.

virginicum, vir-JIN-ik-um, of Virginia.

Asclepias, as-KLE-pe-as; in honour of Asklepios, Greek god of medicine, who in Latin was called Aesculapius. Some of the species were used in medicine. Asklepios carried a snake intwined rod which is still used today as the sign of healing. Milkweed. Herbaceous and sub-shrubby. *Apocynaceae.*

curassavica, ku-ras-SAV-ik-a, of Curaçao, Dutch Antilles, Carribean Sea.

incarnata, in-kar-NA-ta, flesh-coloured.

obtusifolia, ob-tu-sif-O-le-a, blunt-leaved.

tuberosa, tu-ber-O-sa, bearing tubers.

Ascocentrum, as-ko-SEN-trum; from Gr. *askos*, bladder; *kentron*, spur. Orchid. *Orchidaceae.*

ampullaceum, am-pul-LA-se-um, bottle shaped.

Asparagus, as-PAR-ag-us; ancient Greek name, said to be derived from Gr. *a*, intensive; *sparasso*, to tear, alluding to the prickles of some species. Herbaceous and climbing plants. *Asparagaceae.*

aethiopicus, e-thee-O-pik-us, Africa (especially South Africa); name derived from Aethiops, an African and son of Vulcan, the Greek God of metalworking and fire.

asparagoides, as-par-ag-OY-dees, resembling *Asparagus.*

officinalis, of-fis-in-A-lis, of the shop (apothecary's), applied to plants always kept "in stock" by herbalists.

plumosus, see *A. setaceus.*

setaceus, se-TAY-see-us, from L. *seta,* a bristle.

sprengeri, see *A. aethiopicus.*

Asperula, as-PER-u-la; from L. *asper,* rough, alluding to the leaves. Rock plants. *Rubiaceae.*

arcadiensis, ar-ka-de-EN-sis, Arcadian.

azurea, see *A. orientalis.*

cynanchica, si-NAN-chik-a, Greek name for quinsy. The Squinancy-wort.

gussonei, GUS-on-e-i, named for Giovanni Gussone (1787–1866), a professor of botany who studied the flora of Sicily.

hexaphylla, heks-af-IL-la, having six leaves or leaflets.

hirta, HER-ta, rough or shaggy.

odorata, see *Galium odoratum.*

orientalis, or-e-en-TA-lis, Eastern.

suberosa, su-ber-O-sa, corky, that is, the stems.

Asphodeline, as-fod-el-E-ne; allied to *Asphodelus.* Herbaceous plants. *Xanthorrhoeaceae.*

liburnica, li-BER-nik-a, of Liburnia, Eastern Adriatic.

lutea, LU-te-a, yellow.

tenuior, ten-U-e-or, more slender.

Asphodelus, as-FOD-el-us; Greek name for the true asphodel, *Asphodelus ramosus,* and allied species. Herbaceous perennials. *Xanthorrhoeaceae.*

fistulosus, fis-tu-LO-sus, pipe-like, hollow.

ramosus, ra-MO-sus, with many branches. The Asphodel.

Aspidistra, as-pe-DIS-tra; from Gr. *aspidion,* a small round shield, referring to the mushroom shaped stigma. The cast-iron plant. House plant. *Asparagaceae.*

elatior, e-LA-te-or, taller.

lurida, LU-ri-da, sallow-coloured – the flowers.

Aspidium, as-PID-e-um; from Gr. *aspidion,* a shield, alluding to the spore-covering or indusium. Greenhouse and hardy ferns. *Tectariaceae.*

acrostichoides, a-kros-tik-OY-dees, like *Acrostichum.*

aculeatum, see *Polystichum tetragonum.*

aculeatum var. *angulare,* a-ku-le-A-tum, prickly; ang-ul-A-re, angular. The Soft Shield Fern.

angulare, see *A. aculeatum* var. *angulare.*

capense, ka-PEN-se, of the Cape.

falcatum, see *Cyrtomium falcatum.*

lonchitus, see *Polystichum lonchitis.*

munitum, see *Polystichum munitum.*

vestitum, see *Polystichum chilense.*

Asplenium, as-PLE-ne-um; from Gr. *a,* not; *splene,* spleen, the Black Spleenwort (*A. adiantum-nigrum*) once being regarded as a cure for diseases of the spleen. Greenhouse and hardy ferns. *Aspleniaceae.*

adiantum-nigrum, a-de-AN-tum-NI-grum, the Maiden hair, NI-grum, black, the stems, the Black Maidenhair Spleenwort.

bulbiferum, bul-BIF-er-um, bulbil-bearing.

ceterach, see *Ceterach officinarum.*

filix-femina, see *Athyrium filix-femina.*

fontanum, see *Asplenium yunnanense.*

× *germanicum,* jer-MAN-e-kum, of Germany.

lucidum, LU-sid-um, shining.

marinum, see *Asplenium sulcatum.*

monanthemum, mon-ANTH-em-um, one flowered, that is, one sorus per pinna.

nidus, NY-dus, Latin for nest. Bird's-nest Fern.

ruta-muraria, ROO-ta-mu-RA-re-a, rue of the wall. The Wall-rue Fern.

scolopendrium, skol-o-PEN-dre-um; from Gr. *scolopendra,* a centipede, the ripe sori are very suggestive of centipedes. Hart's Tongue Fern.

sulcatum, sul-KA-tum, furrowed.

thelypteroides, thel-ip-ter-OY-dees, like a *Thelypteris.*

trichomanes, trik-OM-an-ez, a thin hair or bristle. The Maidenhair Spleenwort.

viride, VIR-id-e, green.

viviparum, vi-VIP-ar-um, plant-bearing – plantlets on the fronds.

yunnanense, yun-nan-EN-se, from Yunnan, west China.

Aster, AS-ter; from Gr. *aster,* a star, which the flower is supposed to resemble. Herbaceous perennials. Michaelmas Daisy. Many hybrid forms. *Compositae.*

 acris, AK-ris, acrid, pungent.

 albescens, al-BES-senz, whitish.

 alpinus, al-PINE-us, alpine.

 amellus, a-MEL-lus, name given by Virgil to a blue aster-like plant by the River Mella.

 cordifolius, see *Symphyotrichum cordifolium.*

 delavayi, see *A. diplostephioides.*

 diffusus, dif-FU-sus, spread out.

 diplostephioides, DIP-lo-stef-e-OY-dees, resembling *Diplostephium.*

 dumosus, du-MO-sus, bushy.

 ericoides, see *Symphyotrichum ericoides.*

 farreri, FAR-rer-i, in honour of Reginald John Farrer (1880–1920), plant hunter and botanist.

 laevis, LE-vis, smooth, polished.

 linosyris, lin-OS-er-is, resembling *Linum* (flax). The Goldilocks.

 novae-angliae, see *Symphyotrichum novae-angliae.*

 novi-belgii, see *Symphyotrichum novi-belgii.*

 puniceus, see *Symphyotrichum puniceum.*

 subcaerulens, sub-see-RU-lenz, somewhat or slightly blue.

 vimineus, vim-IN-e-us, with long pliant growths, like an Osier.

 yunnanensis, yun-nan-EN-sis, from Yunnan, west China.

Astilbe, as-TIL-be; from Gr. *a,* without; *stilbe,* brightness; in allusion to the dullness of the leaves of the type species. Herbaceous plants. *Saxifragaceae.*

 × *arendsii,* ar-ENDS-e-i, named after German nurseryman Georg Arends (1863–1952).

 chinensis, see *A. rubra.*

 davidii, see *A. rubra.*

 japonica, jap-ON-ik-a, of Japan.

 rivularis, riv-u-LAR-is, of streams.

 rubra, ROO-bra, red-coloured.

 simplicifolia, sim-plis-e-FO-le-a, having simple (not compound) leaves.

 thunbergii, thun-BER-ge-i, after Carl Peter Thunberg (1743–1828), Swedish botanist, a student of Linnaeus.

Astilboides, as-TIL-boy-dees; resembling *Astilbe.* Perennial herbs. *Saxifragaceae.*

 tabularis, tab-ul-AR-is, table-like, the leaves.

Astragalus, as-TRAG-a-lus; from Gr. *astragalos,* one of the bones of the human ankle-bone, alluding to the shape of the seed. Another explanation is suggested by supposed likeness of the root to the ankle-bone. The Milkvetch. Herbaceous plants and shrubs. *Leguminosae.*

 alopecuroides, al-o-pek-u-ROY-dez, resembles *A. alopecurus* (fox-tail like).

 monspessulanus, mon-spes-sul-A-nus, of Montpellier.

 onobrychis, on-o-BRI-kis, literally an ass's fodder. The Sainfoin.

 tragacantha, trag-a-KAN-tha, goat's-thorn (from Gr. *tragos,* goat; *akantha,* thorn).

Astrantia, as-TRAN-te-a; derivation obscure, a medieval plant-name possibly corrupted from Magistrantia and so derived from L. *magister,* master, or from *aster,* star, referring to the star-like flower umbels. Herbaceous plants. *Apiaceae.*

 biebersteinii, bi-ber-STI-ne-i, in honour of Baron Friedrich August Marschall von Bieberstein, 19th century German explorer in southern Russia.

 carniolica, kar-ne-OL-ik-a, of Carniola a historical region of present day Slovenia.

 major, MA-jor, greater.

 minor, MI-nor, smaller.

Astrolepis, as-tro-LEP-is; from Gr. *aster,* a star; *lepis,* a scale, referring to the shape of the indusium covering the spore cases. Ferns. *Pteridaceae.*

 sinuata, sin-u-A-ta, wavy.

Astrophytum, as-tro-FY-tum; from Gr. *aster,* a star; *phytos,* a plant, the plants are star-shaped. Greenhouse cacti. *Cactaceae.*

 myriostigma, my-re-os-TIG-ma, many-dotted.

Athyrium, a-thee-REE-um; from the Gr. *a,* without; *thurium,* shield, referring to the enclosed sori. Ferns. *Athyriaceae.*

 alpestre, AL-pes-tre, of mountains.

 angustum, see *A. filix-femina.*

 asplenioides, as-ple-nee-OY-dees, *Asplenium* like.

 distentifolium, see *A. alpestre.*

 filix-femina, FE-liks-FEM-in-a, female fern. The Lady Fern – in allusion to its elegance.

 flexile, FLEKS-il-e, pliant, limber.

 medium, MEE-dee-um, intermediate, middle.

 yokoscense, yo-ko-SEN-see, of Yokohama, Japan.

Atragene, misapplied see below.
  alpina, see *Clematis alpina*.

Atriplex, A-trip-leks; the Greek name for
orach, a species of this genus of herbs and
shrubs which can be used like spinach. The
genus also includes salt-bush. *Amaranth-aceae*.
  halimus, HAL-im-us, from Gr. *halimon*, sea
    orach.
  hortensis, hor-TEN-sis, of gardens. The Orach.

Atropa, AT-ro-pa; from Gr. *atropos*, one of
the three Fates of Grecian mythology from
whom there was no escape. This genus of
herbs, whilst very poisonous, has important
uses in medicine. *Solanaceae*.
  belladonna, bel-la-DON-na, from Italian
    meaning beautiful lady. The name arises
    from the fact that the juice was used to dilate
    the pupil to make the eye appear larger and
    brighter.

Aubrieta, aw-BRE-she-a; from Claude
Aubriet (1668–1743), a French botanical
artist. Rock-cress. *Brassicaceae*.
  deltoidea, del-TOY-de-a, three-angled, like the
    Greek letter *Delta* and *oides*, resembles; said
    to allude to the triangular petals.

Aucuba, aw-KU-ba; the Japanese name.
Evergreen shrubs. *Garryaceae*.
  japonica, jap-ON-ik-a, of Japan.

Audouinia, aw-do-IN-e-a; after Jean Victor
Audouin (1797–1841), a French naturalist,
founder of the Annales des Sciences Natur-
elles, along with Brongniart who named the
genus. Evergreen shrubs. *Bruniaceae*.
  capitata, kap-it-A-ta, growing in a dense head.

Aureolaria, awe-re-o-LAR-e-a; golden-like.
Herbs. *Orobanchaceae*.
  virginica, ver-JIN-ik-a, of Virginia, U.S.A, the
    state being named after Queen Elizabeth I,
    England's 'Virgin Queen'.

Aurinia, AW-rin-e-a; from L. *aureus*, golden,
in allusion to the flowers of *A. saxatilis*. Biennial and perennial herbs. *Brassicaceae*.
  corymbosa, kor-im-BO-sa, flowers in corymbs.
  saxatilis, saks-A-til-is, haunting rocks.

Avena, a-VE-na; from L. *avena*, a grass.
Poaceae.
  sativa, SAT-iv-a, cultivated. Common Oats.
  sterilis, ster-IL-is, barren. Wild oats.

Azalea, az-A-le-a; Gr. *azaleos*, dry or
parched, probably from *A. pontica*, inhabiting dry places. Evergreen shrubs. *Ericaceae*.
  alabamensis, al-la-ba-MEN-sis, from the state of
    Alabama, U.S.A.
  indica, see *Rhododendron indicum*.
  kurume, see *Rhododendron amoenum*.
  mollis, see *Rhododendron molle*.

Azara, az-AR-a; named after J.N. Azara, a
Spanish patron of botany. Shrubs. *Salicaceae*.
  dentata, den-TA-ta, toothed, the leaves.
  gilliesii, see *A. petiolaris*.
  microphylla, mi-kro-FIL-la, small-leaved.
  petiolaris, pet-e-o-LAR-is, furnished with a leaf-
    stalk or a particularly long one.

Azolla, a-ZOL-la; from Gr. *azo*, dry; *ollymi*,
to destroy – the plant being killed by dryness.
Floating aquatics. *Salviniaceae*.
  caroliniana, kar-o-LIN-e-an-a, from Carolina.

Babiana, bab-e-A-na; from Dutch *babianer*,
a baboon, which is said to devour the bulbs,
hence Baboon-root. Tender bulbous plants.
Iridaceae.
  disticha, see *B. fragrans*.
  fragrans, FRA-granz, fragrant.
  plicata, see *B. fragrans*.
  stricta, STRIK-ta, upright.

Baccharis, BAK-a-ris; from Gr. *Bacchus*,
the God of wine, a spicy extract from some
species having been used for mixing with
wine. Shrubs. *Compositae*.
  halimifolia, hal-im-if-O-le-a, leaves like *Atriplex
    halimus*. The Groundsel Tree.

Bakeridesia, baker-id-ES-e-a; after Edmund
Gilbert Baker (1864–1949), British plant
collector and botanist. Shrubs and small
trees. *Malvaceae*.
  sellowiana, sel-lo-VE-a-na, after Friedrich Sellow
    (1789–1831), German traveller and natural-
    ist, who made extensive collections in Brazil
    and Uruguay.

Balantium, bal-AN-tee-um, from Gr. *balantion*, a purse or depository in reference to the indusium. Tree fern. *Dicksoniaceae.*
   antarcticum, an-TARK-tik-um, southern.

Bambusa, bam-BU-sa; from the Malay vernacular. Bamboo. *Poaceae.*
   palmata, see *Sasa palmata.*
   vulgaris, vul-GAR-is, common.

Banksia, BANGK-se-a; after Sir Joseph Banks (1743–1820), President of the Royal Society. Banks collected the first specimens of this genus whilst aboard Cook's Endeavour. Greenhouse shrubs. *Proteaceae.*
   dryandroides, dry-an-DROY-dees, resembling *Dryandra.*
   quercifolia, kwer-ke-FOL-e-a, leaves resembling *Quercus* (oak).

Baptisia, bap-TIS-e-a; from Gr. *bapto*, to dye, some species yielding dyer's tinctures. Hardy herbaceous plants. *Leguminosae.*
   australis, aws-TRA-lis, southern.
   tinctoria, tink-TOR-e-a, of dyers, *tingo*, to dye.

Barbarea, bar-bar-E-a; called after St. Barbara, to whom the Winter Cress was dedicated. Herbaceous salad plant. Winter or American Cress. *Brassicaceae.*
   praecox, see *B. verna.*
   verna, VER-na, spring, spring-flowering.
   vulgaris, vul-GAR-is, common.

Bartlettina, bart-LET-te-na; after Harley Harris Bartlett (1886–1960), American botanist, director of the Botanical Gardens at the University of Michigan (1919–1955). Shrubs and small trees. *Compositae.*
   sordida, SAW-did-a, dirty.

Bartonia, bar-TO-ne-a; after Benjamin Smith Barton (1766–1815), professor of natural history and botany, University of Pennsylvania. Advisor to the Lewis and Clark Expedition. Half-hardy annual. *Gentianaceae.*
   aurea, see *Mentzelia aurea.*

Bassia, BASS-e-a; in honour of Ferdinando Bassi (1710–1774), Italian botanist. Annual occasionally perennial herbs. *Amaranthaceae.*
   scoparia, sko-PAR-e-a, broom like.

Bauhinia, baw-IN-i-a; commemorates the Swiss botanists, Johann (Jean) Bauhin (1541–1613) and Caspar (Gaspard) Bauhin (1560–1624). The two lobes of the leaf signify the two brothers. Warm-house evergreen flowering shrubs. *Leguminosae.*
   aculeata, ak-u-le-A-ta, prickly.
   aculeata subsp. *grandiflora*, gran-dif-LOR-a, large-flowered.
   grandiflora, see *B. aculeata* subsp. *grandiflora.*
   natalensis, na-tal-EN-sis, from Natal.
   purpurea, pur-PUR-e-a, purple coloured.

Beaucarnea, bow-KAR-ne-a; commemorates Jean-Baptiste Beaucarne, a nineteenth century Belgian plant collector. Ornamental foliage plants. *Asparagaceae.*
   glauca, see *B. stricta.*
   recurvata, rek-ur-VA-ta, curved backwards – the leaves.
   stricta, STRIK-ta, upright.

Begonia, be-GO-ne-a; named by Charles Plumier for Michel Begon (1638–1710), French official, patron and plant collector. Tender bedding and indoor perennials; flowering and ornamental foliage. *Begoniaceae.*
   albococcinea, AL-bow-kok-SIN-e-a, white and scarlet.
   boliviensis, bol-iv-e-EN-sis, Bolivian.
   capensis, ka-PEN-sis, of the Cape of Good Hope.
   coccinea, kok-SIN-e-a, scarlet.
   cucullata, kuk-ul-A-ta, hooded – the upper petals bent over.
   evansiana, see *B. grandis.*
   froebelii, fre-BEL-e-i, after Karl Otto Froebel (1844–1906), German botanist.
   fuchsioides, few-she-OY-dees, resembling *Fuchsia.*
   glabra, GLA-bra, smooth – without hairs.
   gracilis, GRAS-il-is, graceful.
   grandis, GRAN-dis, of great size.
   haageana, see *B. scharffii.*
   hydrocotylifolia, hy-dro-KOT-il-if-O-le-a, leaves resemble *Hydrocotyl* (Pennywort).
   incarnata, in-kar-NA-ta, flesh-coloured.
   lloydii, LOY-dee-I, a seedling strain first raised by Frank Lloyd of Coombe House, Croydon, Surrey.
   maculata, mak-ul-A-ta, blotched – the leaves.
   manicata, man-ik-A-ta, collared (sleeved) with fleshy, scale-like bristles on the leaf-stalk.
   metallica, see *B. incarnata.*
   octopetala, ok-to-PET-a-la, eight-petalled.

olbia, olb-E-a, rich.

rex, reks, a King, presumably the handsome foliage.

scandens, see *B. glabra.*

scharffii, SKARF-e-i, after Scharff, German plant collector in South America for Haage and Schmidt, nurseryman of Erfurt, Germany.

semperflorens, see *B. cucullata.*

socotrana, sok-O-tra-na, of the Island of Socotra, Indian Ocean.

tuberosa, see *B. capensis.*

× *weltoniensis*, wel-ton-e-EN-sis, introduced by Col. Trevor Clarke of Welton Place, Daventry.

× *worthiana*, wurth-e-A-na, after Worth.

Bellevalia, bel-ee-VAL-e-a; in honour of Pierre Richer de Belleval (1564–1632), professor of anatomy and botany at Montpellier. Bulbous plants. *Asparagaceae.*

ciliata, sil-e-A-ta, an eyelash, fringed with hair.

romana, ro-MA-na, Roman.

Bellidastrum, bel-lid-AS-trum; from L. *bellis*, a Daisy; *astrum*, a star. Rock plant. *Compositae.*

michelii, MI-kel-e-i, named for Pietro Antonio Micheli (1679–1737), Florentine botanist.

Bellis, BEL-lis; from L. *bellus*, pretty; Anglo Saxon *daeges eage*, day's-eye, the Daisy. Herbaceous and rock plants. *Compositae.*

perennis, per-EN-nis, perennial.

rotundifolia, ro-tun-dif-O-le-a, round-leaved.

sylvestris, sil-VES-tris, of woods.

Bellium, BEL-le-um; derivation as above, the flowers being Daisy like. Rock plants. *Compositae.*

bellidioides, bel-lid-e-OY-dees, resembles *Bellis* (daisy-like).

minutum, min-U-tum, small, minute.

Beloperone, bel-o-PER-o-ne; from Gr. *belos*, an arrow; *perone*, a clasp or buckle. The arrow-shaped connective, the part of the stamen connecting the anther cells. Tender flowering plants. *Acanthaceae.*

violacea, see *Justicia carthaginensis.*

Benthamia, ben-THA-me-a; after George Bentham (1800–1884), the English botanist. Shrubs. *Boraginaceae.*

fragifera, see *Cornus capitata.*

Berberidopsis, ber-ber-e-DOP-sis; from *Berberis*, and Gr. *opsis*, a resemblance, being like a *Berberis*. Coral plant. Twining shrub. *Berberidopsidaceae.*

corallina, kor-a-LINE-a, coral – the flowers.

Berberis, BER-ber-is; from the Arabic name *berberys*. Shrubs. *Berberidaceae.*

aggregata, ag-gre-GA-ta, heaped together – the clustered fruits.

aquifolium, ak-we-FO-le-um, sharp, or holly-leaved.

aristata, ar-is-TA-ta, bristled.

buxifolia, see *B. microphylla.*

darwinii, DAR-win-e-i, after Charles Darwin (1809–1882), geologist, zoologist and botanist, who discovered it in 1835 whilst collecting plants on the voyage of the 'Beagle'.

dictyophylla, dik-ti-OF-il-la, with net-veined leaves.

empetrifolia, em-pet-rif-O-le-a, with leaves resembling *Empetrum.*

gagnepainii, GAG-ne-pain-e-i, after Francois Gagnepain (1866–1952), French botanist.

hookeri, HOO-ke-ri, after Sir William Jackson Hooker (1785–1865), professor of botany, first Director of the Royal Botanic Gardens, Kew.

ilicifolia, il-lis-if-O-le-a, *Ilex* (holly) leaved.

japonica, jap-ON-ik-a, Japanese.

lycium, LIS-e-um, resembling the genus *Lycium.*

microphylla, mi-krof-IL-la, small leaved.

nepalensis, nep-al-EN-sis, of Nepal.

nervosa, ner-VO-sa, large-nerved.

nevinii, ne-VEN-e-i, after Reuben Denton Nevius (1827–1913), American missionary and plant collector who corresponded with Asa Gray.

polyantha, pol-e-AN-tha, many-flowered.

pruinosa, pru-in-O-sa, covered in a waxy bloom, frosted, the glaucous fruits.

repens, RE-pens, creeping.

sanguinea, san-GWIN-e-a, blood-red – the calyx.

sargentiana, sar-jen-te-A-na, after Charles Sprague Sargent (1841–1927), professor of arboriculture at Harvard University and the first Director of the Arnold Arboretum.

sinensis, sin-EN-sis, of China.

× *stenophylla*, sten-o-FIL-la, narrow-leaved.

thunbergii, thun-BERJ-e-i, after Carl Peter Thunberg (1743–1828), Swedish botanist, a student of Linnaeus.

verruculosa, ver-ru-ku-LO-sa, warty – the bark.

virescens, vir-ES-sens, greenish – the flowers.

vulgaris, vul-GAR-is, common. The Barberry.

wilsoniae, wil-so-NE-e, named for Mrs Helen Wilson (d.1930), Mrs Wilson's Barberry.

Berchemia, ber-SHE-me-a; after Jacob-Pierre von Berchem (1763–1832), Dutch botanist, who studied the flora of Switzerland. Climbing shrubs. *Rhamnaceae*.

flavescens, fla-VES-sens, yellowish.

scandens, SKAN-denz, climbing.

volubilis, see *B. scandens*.

Bergenia, ber-ghee-NE-a; after Karl von Bergen (1704–1759), professor at Frankfurt (Oder). Herbaceous perennials. *Saxifragaceae*.

ciliata, sil-e-A-ta, an eyelash, fringed with hair.

cordifolia, see *B. crassifolia*.

crassifolia, kras-sif-OL-e-a, thick-leaved.

purpurascens, pur-pur-AS-senz, purple – the flowers.

stracheyi, STRAK-e-i, after Sir Richard Strachey (1817–1908), British army officer and Indian administrator, who collected with J.E. Winterbottom in Tibet.

Bergerocactus, ber-ger-o-KAK-tus; after Alwin Berger (1871–1931), German botanist and horticulturist, curator of Hanbury Garden at La Mortola, Italy. Greenhouse cacti. *Cactaceae*.

emoryi, e-MOR-e-i, after Major William Hemsley Emory (1811–1887), United States Army officer and surveyor. Emory corresponded will George Engelmann.

Bertolonia, ber-tol-O-ne-a; after Antonio Bertoloni (1775–1869), Italian botanist, professor at Bologna. Dwarf tropical plants with ornamental foliage. *Melastomataceae*.

guttata, see *Gravesia guttata*.

houtteana, hoot-A-na, named after Louis Benoit Van Houtte (1810–1876), Belgian horticulturist, nurseryman and plant collector.

maculata, mak-ul-A-ta, spotted.

marmorata, mar-mor-A-ta, like marble.

Bessera, BES-ser-a; after Dr. Wilibald Swibert Joseph Gottlieb von Besser (1784–1842), Austrian born botanist. Bulbous plants. *Asparagaceae*.

elegans, EL-e-ganz, elegant.

Beta, BE-ta; from L. *beta*, Beetroot; or Celtic, *bett*, red. Biennials. Ornamental and culinary. *Amaranthaceae*.

chilensis, chil-EN-sis, of Chile. The Chilean Beet.

cicla, see *B. vulgaris*.

c. variegata, see *B. chilensis*.

vulgaris, vul-GAR-is, common. The Beetroot.

Betonica, bet-ON-ik-a; from Celtic *bentonic*; *ben*, head; *ton*, good, referring to herbalists use of the common kind. Herbaceous perennials. *Lamiaceae*.

grandiflora, see *Stachys macrantha*.

Betula, BET-u-la; the Latin name for Birch; Anglo-Saxon, *birce*. Trees and shrubs. *Betulaceae*.

alba, see *B. pubescens*.

humilis, HUM-il-is, lowly – on the ground.

nana, NA-na, dwarf.

nigra, NY-gra, black, the bark markings.

papyrifera, pa-pir-IF-er-a, papery – the bark.

pendula, PEN-du-la, pendulous or weeping.

populifolia, pop-u-lif-O-le-a, leaves resemble *Populus* (poplar).

pubescens, pew-BES-senz, downy.

verrucosa, see *B. pendula*.

Bidens, BI-dens; from L. *bis*, twice; *dens*, teeth, the seed having two tooth-like projections. Half-hardy perennial. *Compositae*.

aristosa, ar-is-TO-sa, bearded – the seed.

dahlioides, see *Cosmos diversifolius* var. *dahlioides*.

ferulifolia, fer-u-le-FO-le-a, leaves resembling *Ferula* (Fennel).

laevis, LE-vis, smooth.

Bifrenaria, bi-fren-A-re-a; from L. *bis*, twice; *frenum*, a bridle, in reference to the two caudicles connecting the pollen masses to their glands. Epiphytic orchids. *Orchidaceae*.

harrisoniae, har-ris-O-ne-e, after Elizabeth Harrison (1792–1834), Orchid collector at Aigburth, Liverpool.

Bignonia, big-NO-ne-a; after Abbe Bignon, librarian to Louis XIV of France. Climber. *Bignoniaceae*.

capreolata, kap-re-o-LA-ta, furnished with tendrils.

tweedieana, see *Dolichandra unguis-cati*.

venusta, see *Pyrostegia venusta*.

Billardiera, bil-lard-e-AIR-a; named after Jacques Julien Houtou de Labillardière (1755–1834), French botanist. Evergreen vine. *Pittosporaceae*.
  heterophylla, het-er-of-IL-la, Gr. *hetero*, diverse; *phylla*, leaves.
  longiflora, long-if-LO-ra, long-flowered.

Billbergia, bil-BER-je-a; after Gustaf Johan Billberg (1772–1844), Swedish botanist. Tropical flowering plants. *Bromeliaceae*.
  chlorosticta, klo-row-STIK-ta, from Gr. *chloros*, green; *stiktos*, spotted.
  liboniana, see *Quesnelia liboniana*.
  marmorata, see *Quesnelia marmorata*.
  nutans, NU-tanz, nodding.
  saundersii, see *B. chlorosticta*.
  vittata, vit-TA-ta, striped.
  zebrina, ze-BRY-na, zebra-striped.

Blechnum, BLEK-num; from Gr. *blechnon*, a fern, the ancient name for a fern. Hardy and Greenhouse ferns. *Blechnaceae*.
  boreale, bor-e-A-le, northern.
  brasiliense, braz-il-e-EN-se, Brazilian.
  occidentale, ok-se-den-TA-le, western.
  penna-marina, PEN-na-ma-RE-na, from L. *penna*, feather or wing; *marina*, of or belonging to the sea. Alpine Water Fern.
  spicant, SPE-kant, spiked – the appearance of the fertile fronds.

Bletia, BLET-e-a; after Don Luis Blet, Spanish apothecary and botanist, who established a botanic garden in Algeciras towards the end of the eighteenth century. Orchids. *Orchidaceae*.
  hyacinthina, see *Bletilla striata*.

Bletilla, BLET-il-la; resembles *Bletia* which see. Terrestrial orchids. *Orchidaceae*.
  striata, stri-A-ta, striped.

Blitum, BLY-tum; from Celtic *blith*, insipid, referring to the fruits. Hardy annual. *Amaranthaceae*.
  capitatum, see *Chenopodium capitatum*.

Blumenbachia, blu-men-BAK-e-a; after John Frederick Blumenbach MD (1752–1840), professor of medicine at Gottingen. Tender plants covered in stinging hairs. *Loasaceae*.

insignis, in-SIG-nis, striking.
lateritia, see *Caiophora lateritia*.

Bocconia, bok-KO-ne-a; after Paolo Boccone (1633–1703), Italian monk and botanist. Herbaceous plants. *Papaveraceae*.
  cordata, see *Macleaya cordata*.
  microcarpa, mi-kro-KAR-pa, bearing small fruits.

Bolanthus, bol-AN-thus; from Gr. *bolos*, hump; *anthos*, a flower; a rounded mass of flowers. Dwarf perennial herbs. *Caryophyllaceae*.
  frankenioides, frank-en-e-OY-dees, resembling *Frankenia*.

Boltonia, bol-TO-ne-a; after James Bolton (c1758–1799), British botanist. Herbaceous perennials. *Compositae*.
  asteroides, as-ter-OY-dees, resembling *Aster*.

Bomarea, bo-MA-re-a; after Jacques-Christophe Valmont de Bomare (1731–1807), French naturalist. Greenhouse flowering twiners. *Alstroemeriaceae*.
  carderi, kar-DER-i, after Carder who collected for William Bull in Columbia.
  conferta, see *B. patocoensis*.
  multiflora, mul-tif-LO-ra, many flowered.
  oligantha, see *B. multiflora*.
  patacoensis, pat-ak-o-EN-sis, of Patococha, Ecuador.

Borago, bor-A-go; derivation uncertain, may be from medieval L. *borra*, rough hair; or *burra*, a shaggy garment; in reference to the rough foliage. Linnaeus states the name to be a corruption of *corago* (L. *cor*, the heart; *ago*, to act) from its use in medicine as a heart sedative. Hardy annual and biennial herbs. *Boraginaceae*.
  laxiflora, see *B. pygmaea*.
  officinalis, of-fis-in-A-lis, of the shop (apothecary's), applied to plants always kept "in stock" by herbalists.
  pygmaea, PIG-me-a, dwarf.

Boronia, bor-ON-ne-a; after Francesco Borone (1769–1794), Italian botanist engaged by Sir James Smith. He fell to his death from a hotel window in Athens, whilst accompanying John Sibthorp in collecting for the Flora Graecae. Shrubs. *Rutaceae*.

drummondii, see *B. pulchella*.
elatior, e-LA-te-or, taller.
heterophylla, het-er-of-IL-la, Gr. *hetero*, diverse; *phylla*, leaves.
megastigma, meg-as-TIG-ma, having a large stigma.
pulchella, pul-KEL-la, pretty.
serrulata, ser-rul-A-ta, leaves finely toothed.

Bougainvillea, boo-gain-VIL-le-a; after Louis Antoine de Bougainville (1729–1811), French navigator who circumnavigated the globe. Tender climbers. *Nyctaginaceae*.
glabra, GLA-bra, smooth – without hairs.
speciosa, see *B. spectabilis*.
spectabilis, spek-TAB-il-is, notable.

Boussingaultia, misapplied see below.
baselloides, see *Anredera baselloides*.

Bouvardia, boo-VARD-e-a; after Dr. Charles Bouvard (1572–1658), keeper of the Jardin du Roi, Paris. Perennial herbs and shrubs. *Rubiaceae*.
humboldtii, see *B. longiflora*.
longiflora, long-if-LO-ra, long-flowered.
jasminiflora, jas-min-if-LO-ra, jasmine-flowered.

Brachyglottis, brak-e-GLOT-iss; from Gr. *brachys*, short; *glotta*, a tongue; referring to the ray florets. Shrubs. *Compositae*.
greyi, GRAY-i, after Sir George Grey (1812–1898), Governor of New Zealand.
laxifolia, laks-e-FO-le-a, loosely spread leaves.

Brachyscome, brak-es-KO-me; from Gr. *brachys*, short; *comus*, hair. Annual. *Compositae*.
iberidifolia, i-ber-id-if-O-le-a, leaves resembling *Iberis*.

Brasenia, bra-SEE-ne-a; commemorating Christoph Brasen (1738–1774), Danish surgeon and plant collector, who collected in Greenland and Labrador. Aquatic herb. *Cabombaceae*.
schreberi, shre-BER-i, named after Johann Christian Daniel von Schreber (1739–1810), German naturalist, who named the genus.

Brasiliorchis, braz-il-e-OR-kis; a new genus of orchid native to Brazil. Orchids. *Orchidaceae*.
picta, PIK-ta, painted.

Brassavola, bras-sa-VO-la; after Antonio Musa Brassavola (1500–1555), Italian botanist. Orchids. *Orchidaceae*.
digbyana, see *Rhyncholaelia digbyana*.

Brassia, BRAS-se-a; after William Brass (d. 1783), English botanist, who collected for Sir Joseph Banks in West Africa. Orchids. *Orchidaceae*.
aurantiaca, aw-ran-te-A-ka, orange coloured.
brachiata, see *B. verrucosa*.
maculata, mak-ul-A-ta, spotted.
verrucosa, ver-ru-KO-sa, warty.

Brassica, BRAS-sik-a; from L. *brassica*, used by Pliny; Celtic *bresic*, the name for cabbage. Culinary vegetables. *Brassicaceae*.
cretica, KRE-tik-a, of Crete. Broccoli and Cauliflower.
juncea, JUNK-e-a, rush-like. The Mustard.
napus, NAP-us, diminutive to turnip. The Swede.
oleracea, ol-er-A-se-a, of the vegetable garden. The Brussels Sprouts, Cabbage, Kale, and Savoys.
o. acephala, see *B. oleracea*.
o. botrytis, see *B. cretica*.
o. bullata, see *B. oleracea*.
o. capitata, see *B. oleracea*.
o. cauliflora, see *B. oleracea*.
o. caulorapa, see *B. oleracea*.
o. major, see *B. oleracea*.
rapa, RA-pa, the Turnip.

Bravoa, misapplied see below.
geminiflora, see *Polianthes geminiflora*.

Breynia, BRAY-ne-a; in memory of the botanist Jacob Breyne (1637–1697), and his son Johann Philipp Breyne (1680–1764), a physician, both from Danzig. Tender shrubs and small trees. *Phyllanthaceae*.
disticha, DIS-tik-a, leaves in two rows.

Briza, BRI-za; from Gr. *brizo*, to nod, from the movement of the spikelets. The Ancient Greek name for a grass, probably rye. Grasses. Quaking Grass. *Poaceae*.
maxima, MAKS-im-a, greatest.
media, ME-de-a, midway, medium.
minor, MY-nor, smallest.

Brodiaea, bro-DE-e-a; named after James Brodie (1744–1824), Scottish botanist. Bulbous plants. *Asparagaceae*.

bridgesii, see *Triteleia bridgesii.*
capitata, see *Dichelostemma capitatum.*
congesta, see *Dichelostemma congestum.*
coronaria, kor-on-AR-e-a, crowned.
grandiflora, see *B. coronaria.*
hendersonii, see *Triteleia hendersonii.*
howellii, see *Triteleia grandiflora.*
ixioides, see *Leucocoryne ixioides.*
laxa, see *Triteleia laxa.*
uniflora, see *Tristagma uniflorum.*

Bromelia, bro-ME-le-a; named by Plumier after Olof Bromel (1629–1705), Swedish botanist. Herbaceous plants. *Bromeliaceae.*
urbaniana, ur-bar-NE-a-na, belonging to towns.

Bromus, BRO-mus; from Gr. *bromos*, oats. A borrowed word referring initially to wild oats *Avena sativa.* Ornamental Grasses. *Poaceae.*
briziformis, bri-ze-FOR-mis, formed like *Briza* or Quaking Grass.

Browallia, brow-AL-le-a; named after Johan Browall (1707–1755), Bishop of Abo, Sweden. Greenhouse annuals. *Solanaceae.*
americana, a-mer-ik-A-na, of America.
elata, see *B. americana.*
speciosa, spes-e-O-sa, showy.

Brugmansia, brug-man-SEE-a; named in honour of Sebald Justinus Brugmans (1763–1819), professor of natural history at the University of Leiden. Tender perennial shrubs. *Solanaceae.*
sanguinea, san-GWIN-e-a, blood red.
sauveolens, swa-VE-o-lenz, sweet smelling.

Brunfelsia, brun-FELZ-e-a; after Otto Brunfels (1489–1534), Carthusian monk and German botanist. Warm-house evergreen flowering shrubs. *Solanaceae.*
calycina, see *B. pauciflora.*
pauciflora, paw-se-FLOR-a, with few flowers.

Brunnera, brun-NE-ra; named for Samuel Brunner (1790–1844), Swiss botanist. Perennial herbs. *Boraginaceae.*
macrophylla, mak-rof-IL-a, with large leaves.

Bryanthus, bry-AN-thus; from Gr. *bryon*, moss; *anthos*, flower, found growing among mosses. Low shrubs. *Ericaceae.*

empetriformis, em-pet-rif-OR-mis, resembling *Empetrum.*

Bryophyllum, bry-of-IL-um; from Gr. *bryo*, to sprout; *phyllon*, a leaf, alluding to the leaves bearing plantlets round their edges. Greenhouse succulents. *Crassulaceae.*
calycinum, see *B. pinnatum.*
pinnatum, pin-NA-tum, with pinnate leaves.

Buddleja, BUD-le-a; called after Rev. Adam Buddle (1660–1715), English botanist and vicar at Farmbridge, Essex. Mostly deciduous shrubs. *Scrophulariaceae.*
alternifolia, al-ter-ne-FO-le-a, alternate leaved.
colvilei, COL-vil-LE-i, named after Sir James William Colvile (1801–1880), Scottish lawyer and judge.
davidii, DA-vid-e-i, after Pere Armand David (1826–1900), French missionary and plant collector in China who sent specimens back to Adrien René Franchet in 1869.
fallowiana, fal-low-e-A-na, named in honour of Sergeant George Fallow (1890–1915), a probationer gardener at the Royal Botanic Gardens Edinburgh and student of Prof. Isaac Bailey Balfour prior to enlisting. The specimen was collected by George Forrest in 1906 and again in 1910 before being named in 1917.
globosa, glo-BO-sa, globular, the flower clusters.
nanhoensis, see *B. davidii.*
nivea, NIV-e-a, snowy – the leaves and shoots are white.
variabilis, see *B. davidii.*

Buglossoides, bu-gloss-OY-dees; resembling bugloss. Annual and perennial herbs. *Boraginaceae.*
purpurocaerulea, pur-PEW-ro-se-RU-le-a, purple and blue flowers.

Bulbocodium, misapplied see below.
vernum, see *Colchicum bulbocodium.*

Buphthalmum, bup (or buf)-THAL-mum; from Gr. *bous*, ox; *ophthalmos*, an eye, the large rayed flower supposed to resemble the eye of an ox. Hardy herbaceous. *Compositae.*
salicifolium, sal-is-if-O-le-um, leaves resembling *Salix* (willow).
speciosum, see *Telekia speciosa.*

Bupleurum, bu-PLU-rum; from Gr. *boupleuros*, ox-rib, name for another umbelliferous plant. Hardy shrubs. *Apiaceae*.
  fruticosum, frut-ik-O-sum, shrubby.

Burchellia, bur-CHEL-le-a; after William Burchell (1781–1863), an English traveller and collector in Brazil and South Africa. Warm-house evergreen shrub. *Rubiaceae*.
  bubalina, bub-A-le-na, from L. *bubalina*, buff-coloured, possibly in reference to the yellowish hairs found on some forms.
  capensis, see *B. bubalina*.

Butomus, BU-to-mus; from Gr. *bous*, an ox; *temno*, to cut, the sharp-edged leaves being said to injure the mouths of cattle. Aquatic plant. *Butomaceae*.
  umbellatus, um-bel-LA-tus, umbelled – the flowers.

Buxus, BUKS-us; ancient L. name for Box tree. Shrubs and trees. *Buxaceae*.
  microphylla, mi-krof-IL-la, small leaved.
  sempervirens, sem-per-VEER-enz, from L. *semper*, ever; *virens*, green. Always green.
  suffruticosa, see *B. sempervirens*.

Cabomba, cab-OM-ba; latinised form of the native Guiana name. Greenhouse submerged aquatic. *Cabombaceae*.
  caroliniana, car-ol-in-i-A-na, native of Carolina State. Considered an invasive species in the U.K.

Cacalia, ka-KA-le-a; ancient Gr. name, possibly from Gr. *kakos*, pernicious; *lian*, very much, supposed to be harmful to the soil. *Compositae*.
  coccinea, see *Emilia coccinea*.

Cactus, KAK-tus; from Gr. *kaktos*, a name used by Theophrastus for an unknown prickly plant. Now applied to a group of cacti of which the Melon cactus is the type and was the first cactus brought to Europe (1581). This plant was called *Cactus melocactus*, since changed to *Melocactus intortus*. *Cactaceae*.
  stella-aurata, STEL-la-aw-RA-ta, golden star.

Caesalpinia, seez-al-PIN-e-a; after Andrea Cesalpino (1519–1603), Italian botanist, director of the Botanical Garden of Pisa.

Instrumental in laying the foundation for Linnaeus' binomial system. Tropical and subtropical woody plants. *Leguminosae*.
  decapetala, dek-a-PET-al-a, ten-petalled.
  gilliesii, gil-LEEZ-e-i, after John Gillies (1792–1834), Scottish collector in South America.
  japonica, see *C. decapetala*.
  pulcherrima, pul-KER-rim-a, most beautiful.
  sepiaria, see *C. decapetala*.

Caiophora, ka-o-FOR-a; from Gr. *kaios*, a burn; *phoreo*, to bear; in reference to bristly, stinging hairs. Annual or short-lived herbaceous climbing perennials. *Loasaceae*.
  lateritia, lat-er-IT-e-a, brick-red; the colour of the flowers.

Caladium, kal-A-de-um; origin uncertain, said to be from Malay *kaladi*, the native name of the tuberous root. Tropical tuberous-rooted foliage plants. *Araceae*.
  argyrites, see *C. humboldtii*.
  bicolor, BIK-ol-or, two-coloured.
  humboldtii, hum-BOLT-e-i, after Alexander von Humboldt (1769–1859), Prussian naturalist and explorer.

Calamintha, misapplied see below.
  alpina, see *Clinopodium alpinum*.
  grandiflora, see *Clinopodium grandiflorum*.

Calamistrum, kal-a-MIS-trum; L. *calamister*, curling-iron; from Gr. *kalamus*, a reed, in allusion to the hollow stem. Aquatic ferns. *Marsileaceae*.
  globuliferum, glob-ul-IF-er-um, resembling a globe, the spore cases. The Pillwort.

Calandrinia, kal-an-DRIN-e-a; after Jean Louis Calandrini (1703–1758), Swiss scientist. Rock garden annuals and perennials. *Portulacaceae*.
  grandiflora, see *Cistanthe grandiflora*.
  umbellata, see *Montiopsis umbellata*.

Calanthe, kal-AN-thee; from Gr. *kalos*, beautiful; *anthos*, a flower. Deciduous terrestrial orchids. *Orchidaceae*.
  × *veitchii*, VEECH-e-i, hybrid produced by Mr Dominy, Veitch & Sons, of Exeter.
  vestita, ves-TEE-ta, clothed.

Calathea, kal-ATH-e-a; from Gr. *kalathos*, a basket, referring to a native use of the tough fibrous leaves. Tropical ornamental leaved plants. *Marantaceae.*

bella, BEL-la, pretty.

bellula, BEL-lu-la, little, pretty – neat, diminutive.

concinna, kon-SIN-na, neat, pretty.

illustris, il-LUS-tris, brilliant.

lancifolia, lan-sif-O-le-a, leaves lance shaped.

massangeana, see *Maranta leuconeura.*

makoyana, ma-koy-A-na, after Jacob Makoy Lambert (1790–1873), Belgian plant collector in Brazil.

ornata, or-NA-ta, adorned.

regalis, re-GA-lis, Royal, stately.

roseopicta, RO-ze-o-PIC-ta, rosy painted.

sanderiana, san-der-e-A-na, first described by Henry Frederick Conrad Sander (1847–1920), nurseryman.

variegata, var-e-eg-A-ta, variegated.

veitchiana, veech-e-A-na, collected by Richard Pearce and named by James Veitch Junior to commemorate his late father James Veitch (1792–1863).

warszewiczii, var-skew-IK-ze-i, after Joseph Warszewicz, who collected in Central and South America between 1844–1850 and 1851–1853.

zebrina, ze-BRY-na, zebra-striped.

Calceolaria, kal-se-o-LAIR-e-a; from L. *calceolus*, a slipper or little shoe, alluding to the shape of the flower. Half-hardy rock, herbaceous perennials and shrubs. *Calceolariaceae.*

biflora, bif-LO-ra, two-flowered, that is, in pairs.

× *burbidgei*, bur-BIJ-e-i, after Frederick William Burbidge (1847–1905), curator of the botanical gardens, Trinity College, Dublin at Glasnevin.

corymbosa, kor-im-BO-sa, corymbose, flowers in corymbs.

integrifolia, in-teg-rif-O-le-a, leaves entire, not broken at the edges.

rugosa, see *C. integrifolia.*

violacea, vi-o-LA-se-a, violet-coloured.

Calendula, kal-EN-du-la; from L. *calandae*, the first day of the month, probably alluding to the flowering of the plant throughout the year. Hardy annual. *Compositae.*

officinalis, of-fis-in-A-lis, of the shop (apothecary's), applied to plants always kept "in stock" by herbalists.

Calla, KAL-la; ancient name probably from Gr. *kallos*, beauty. Aquatic and marginal herb. *Araceae.*

palustris, pal-US-tris, found in marshy places.

Callianthemum, kal-le-an-THEE-mum; from Gr. *kallos*, beauty; *anthemon*, a flower. Perennial herbs. *Ranunculaceae.*

anemonoides, an-em-on-OY-dees, resembling *Anemone.*

angustifolium, an-gus-tif-O-le-um, having narrow leaves.

Callicarpa, kal-le-KAR-pa; from Gr. *kalli*, beautiful; *karpos*, fruit. Trees and shrubs. *Lamiaceae.*

bodineiri, bod-e-NE-er-i, commemorating Emile Marie Bodinieri (1842–1901), French missionary in Guizhou Province, China, and plant collector.

giraldii, jer-al-DE-i, after Giuseppe Giraldi (1848–1901), Italian missionary, plant collector in China.

Callirhoe, kal-lir-HO-e; after Callirhoe, the name of a divinity of the ancient Greeks. Hardy herbaceous. *Malvaceae.*

involucrata, in-vol-u-KRA-ta, from L. *involucrum*, roll in, envelop, the leaf edges rolled together.

Callisia, kal-LIS-e-a; from Gr. *kalos*, beauty. Herbaceous perennials. *Commelinaceae.*

rosea, RO-ze-a, rose-coloured.

Callistemon, kal-le-STEM-on; from Gr. *kallistos*, most beautiful; *stemon*, a stamen; the beauty of the flowers residing in the coloured stamens. Greenhouse flowering shrubs. The Bottlebrush. *Myrtaceae.*

linearis, lin-e-AR-is, linear leaved, narrow, with nearly parallel sides.

speciosus, spes-e-O-sus, handsome.

Callistephus, kal-lis-TEF-us; from Gr. *kallostos*, most beautiful; *stephos*, a crown, referring to the flower. The China Aster. Annual. *Compositae.*

chinensis, tshi-NEN-sis, of China.

hortensis, see *C. chinensis.*

Callitriche, kal-LIT-rik-e; from Gr. *kalos*, beautiful; *thrix*, hair – resembling beautiful hair. Submerged aquatics. *Plantaginaceae.*

autumnalis, see *C. hermaphroditica*.

hermaphroditica, her-ma-fro-DIT-ik-a, stamens and pistol in the same flower.

palustris, pal-US-tris, found in marshy places.

verna, see *C. palustris*.

Calluna, kal-LU-na; from Gr. *kalluno*, to cleanse, alluding to the use of this heather as a broom. Ericaceous Shrub. *Ericaceae*.

vulgaris, vul-GAR-is, common.

Calocedrus, kal-o-SED-rus; from Gr. *kalos*, beautiful; *cedrus*, cedar (which see). Trees. *Cupressaceae*.

decurrens, de-KUR-rens, running-down – the lower parts of the leaves clasping the branches. The Incense Cedar.

Calocephalus, KAL-o-SEF-a-lus; from Gr. *kalos*, beautiful; *kephale*, a head, alluding to the white cord-like stems forming a "beautiful head". Bedding foliage plant. *Compositae*.

brownii, see *Leucophyta brownii*.

Calochortus, kal-o-KOR-tus; from Gr. *kalos*, beautiful; *chortus*, grass, referring to the leaves. Half-hardy bulbs. The Mariposa Lily. *Liliaceae*.

albus, AL-bus, from the L. *alba*, white.

coeruleus, se-RU-le-us, blue.

lilacinus, see *C. uniflorus*.

lyallii, LI-al-e-i, after David Lyall (1817–1895), physician, botanist and collector.

nuttallii, NUT-al-le-i, after Thomas Nuttall (1786–1859), English botanist and plant collector. A curator of Harvard Botanic Garden from 1822 to 1834 Nuttall is remembered as a father of American botany.

pulchellus, pul-KEL-lus, small and beautiful.

uniflorus, uni-FLOR-us, one flowered, that is blooms solitary.

venustus, ven-US-tus, charming.

Calomeria, kal-o-MER-e-a; dedicated to Napoleon Bonaparte from Gr. *kalos*, Fr. *bon*, good; Gr. *meris*, Fr. *partie*, a part. Annual and perennial herbs. *Compositae*.

amaranthoides, am-a-RANTH-oy-dees, resembling *Amaranth*.

Calopogon, kal-o-PO-gon; from Gr. *kalos*, beautiful; *pogon*, a beard, referring to the fringed floral lip. Terrestrial Orchid. *Orchidaceae*.

tuberosus, tu-ber-O-sus, bearing tubers.

Caltha, KAL-tha; from Gr. *kalathos*, a goblet, alluding to the form of the flower. Bog perennials. *Ranunculaceae*.

leptosepala, lep-to-SEP-a-la, having thin sepals.

palustris, pal-US-tris, found in marshy places.

polypetala, see *C. palustris*.

radicans, see *C. palustris*.

Calycanthus, kal-e-KANTH-us; from Gr. *kalyx*, calyx; *anthos*, a flower, in reference to the coloured sepals and petals being alike. Shrubs. *Calycanthaceae*.

floridus, FLOR-id-us, from L. *floridus*, flowering abundantly.

floridus var. *glaucus*, GLAW-kus, sea-green, the foliage.

occidentalis, oks-se-DEN-ta-lis, western – North America.

Calypso, kal-IP-so; called after the Ancient Greek goddess of that name. Terrestrial Orchid. *Orchidaceae*.

borealis, see *C. bulbosa*.

bulbosa, bul-BO-sa, bulbous.

Calystegia, kal-is-TE-je-a; from Gr. *kalyx*, calyx; *stege*, a covering, the calyx of some of the Bindweeds being enclosed in two bracts. Twining plants. *Convolvulaceae*.

hederacea, hed-er-A-se-a, resembling *Hedera* (ivy).

pubescens, pew-BES-senz, downy.

pubescens flore pleno, see *C. hederacea*.

sepium, SE-pe-um, of hedges.

silvatica, sil-VAT-ik-a, of the woods.

soldanella, sol-dan-EL-la, leaves like a *Soldanella*.

Camassia, kam-AS-se-a; from *Quamash*, the Native American name for *C. quamash*. Hardy bulbs. *Asparagaceae*.

cusickii, ku-SIK-ke-i, after William Conklin Cusick (1842–1922), self-taught botanist.

esculenta, see *C. quamash*.

leichtlinii, lecht-LE-ne-i, commemorates Maximilian Leichtlin (1831–1910), German horticulturalist, who specialised in growing bulbs.

quamash, KWA-mash, Native American name. The Quamash.

Camellia, ka-ME-le-a; after George Josef Kamel (Camellus) (1661–1706), a Jesuit of

Moravia, who travelled in Asia and the East. Evergreen flowering shrubs. *Theaceae*.

japonica, jap-ON-ik-a, of Japan.

sasanqua, sas-ANG-kwa, native Japanese name.

sinensis, si-NEN-sis, Chinese. The leaves and buds of which are used to produce tea.

sinensis var. *assamica*, ass-SAM-i-ka, of the region of Assam, India. Assam Tea.

thea, see *C. sinensis*.

theifera, see *C. sinensis* var. *assamica*.

Campanula, kam-PAN-u-la; from L. *campanula*, little bell – the bellflower. Annuals, biennials and herbaceous perennials. *Campanulaceae*.

abietina, see *C. patula* subsp. *abietina*.

arvatica, ar-VAT-ik-a, from Arvas in the Cantabrian Mountains.

barbata, bar-BA-ta, bearded – the flowers being hairy.

carpatica, kar-PAT-ik-a, Carpathian.

excisa, eks-SI-sa, cut, that is, the cleft at the base of the bloom segments.

fragilis, FRAJ-il-is, fragile.

garganica, gar-GAN-ik-a, from Gargano, Italy.

glomerata, glom-er-A-ta, clustered – the flowers.

grandis, GRAN-dis, of great size.

hofmannii, hof-MAN-ne-i, named by Pantocsek after Hofmann a dear friend.

isophylla, i-so-FI-la, leaves equal.

lactiflora, lak-tif-LO-ra, flowers milk-white.

latiloba, see *C. grandis*.

medium, MEE-dee-um, from the Italian vernacular name *erbe media*. Canterbury Bells.

muralis, see *C. portenschlagiana*.

patula, PAT-u-la, spreading open – the bells or flowers.

patula subsp. *abietina*, ab-e-TE-na, of coniferous woods.

pendula, PEN-du-la, pendulous or weeping.

persicifolia, per-sis-if-O-le-a, resembling *Prunus persica* (peach) leaves.

portenschlagiana, por-ten-shlag-e-A-na, commemorates Franz von Portenschlag-Ledermermeyer (1772–1822), Austrian botanist.

pulla, PUL-la, dark-coloured.

punctata, punk-TA-ta, dotted or speckled.

pusilla, pu-SIL-la, dwarf.

pyramidalis, pir-AM-id-al-is, pyramid or coned shaped, the flower spike. The Chimney Bellflower.

raddeana, rad-de-A-na, commemorates Gustav Ferdinand Richard Radde (1831–1903),

German naturalist, who collected plants in the Caucasus.

rapunculus, ra-PUN-ku-lus, little turnip. The Rampion.

rotundifolia, ro-tun-dif-O-le-a, round-leaved. The Harebell.

sarmatica, sar-MAT-ik-a, Sarmatian (Poland).

sibirica, si-BIR-ik-a, of Siberia.

trachelium, trak-E-le-um, from Gr. *trachelos*, a neck; old generic name for Throatwort.

Campsis, KAMP-sis; from Gr. *kampsis*, bending, referring to the curved stamens. Climber. *Bignoniaceae*.

grandiflora, gran-dif-LO-ra, large-flowered.

radicans, RAD-e-kanz, trailing and rooting.

Canna, KAN-na; from L. *cana*, cane or reed. Tropical herbaceous perennials used for summer bedding. *Cannaceae*.

indica, IN-di-ka, of India.

Cannabis, KAN-na-bis; from Gr. *kannabis*, hemp. An annual grown for its seeds and fibres. *Cannabaceae*.

sativa, SAT-iv-a, cultivated. The Common Hemp.

Capsicum, KAP-sik-um; from Gr. *kapto*, to bite, referring to the pungency of the fruits. Warm-house annual. *Solanaceae*.

annuum, AN-nu-um, of annual duration.

Caragana, kar-a-GAN-a; from the Mongolian name, *Caragan*. Shrubs or small trees. *Leguminosae*.

arborescens, ar-bor-ES-cenz, tree like.

frutescens, see *C. frutex*.

frutex, FRUT-ex, from L. *frutex*, a shrub; shrubby or bushy.

pygmaea, PIG-me-a, dwarf.

spinosa, spi-NO-sa, spiny.

Carbeni, misapplied see below.

benedicta, see *Centaurea benedicta*.

Cardamine, kar-dam-I-ne; from Gr. *cardamon*, cress. A derivative from Gr. *kardia*, heart; *damao*, to subdue, a plant of the cress family once used as a heart sedative in medicine. Hardy herbaceous. *Brassicaceae*.

bulbifera, bul-BIF-er-a, bearing bulblets.

enneaphyllos, en-ne-af-IL-los, from Gr. nine-leaved – leaflets.

pentaphyllos, pen-ta-FIL-los, five-leaved or leaflets divided into five.

pratensis, pra-TEN-sis, of meadows. A double form of this species being cultivated.

trifolia, trif-O-le-a, three-leaved.

Cardiomanes, kar-de-o-MAN-ez; from Gr. *kardio*, heart; *manos*, soft, the fronds vague resemblance to a heart and soft sheen. Fern. *Hymenophyllaceae*.

reniforme, ren-e-FOR-me, kidney-shaped – the fronds.

Carex, KAR-eks; the L. name for some kind of sedge, now applied to the genus. Grass-like herbs. *Cyperaceae*.

acutiformis, ak-u-te-FOR-mis, pointed shape the leaf.

japonica, jap-ON-ik-a, of Japan.

paludosa, see *C. acutiformis*.

pendula, PEN-du-la, pendulous or weeping.

riparia, re-PAIR-e-a, frequenting river banks.

Carnegiea, kar-NEE-gee-a; after Andrew Carnegie (1835–1919), Scottish American industrialist and philanthropist, whose Institute financed collectors of cacti in America. Greenhouse cacti. *Cactaceae*.

gigantea, ji-GAN-te-a, unusually tall or big. The Giant Cactus of the Sonoran Desert, Arizona and areas of California. Synonymous image of the American Southwest.

Carpanthea, kar-PAN-the-a; from the Gr. *karpos*, a fruit; *anthos*, a flower, probably in allusion to the open fruits that look like a star-shaped flower. Greenhouse succulent. *Aizoaceae*.

pomeridiana, po-mer-ID-e-A-na, post meridian, that is, flowers opening after midday.

Carpenteria, kar-pen-TEER-e-a; named in honour of William Marbury Carpenter (1811–1848), physician and naturalist, professor of botany and geology then dean, Medical College of Louisiana (Tulane University). Shrub. *Hydrangeaceae*.

californica, kal-if-OR-nik-a, of California.

Carpinus, kar-PINE-us; ancient L. name for Hornbeam. Deciduous trees. *Betulaceae*.

betulus, BET-u-lus; *Betula* the generic name for Birch, which it resembles. The Hornbeam.

caroliniana, car-ol-in-i-A-na, native of Carolina State.

cordata, kor-DA-ta, heart shaped, the leaves.

Carpobrotus, kar-po-BRO-tus; from Gr. *karpos*, a fruit; *brotos*, edible, the fruits edible. Greenhouse succulents. *Aizoaceae*.

acinaciformis, a-sin-AS-if-OR-mis, shaped like a scimitar, that is, the leaf curved and thick on the outer edge and thin on the inner.

edulis, ed-U-lis, edible, the fruit.

Carum, KA-rum; Latinised form of the Gr. word *karon*, from Caria, in Asia Minor where it was widely grown. The Caraway. Biennials and perennials. *Apiaceae*.

carvi, KAR-vi, from Caria, in Asia Minor where it was widely grown. The Caraway.

petroselinum, see *Petroselinum crispum*.

Caryopteris, kar-e-OP-ter-is; from Gr. *karnon*, a nut; *pteron*, a wing, the fruits being winged. Shrub. *Lamiaceae*.

× *clandonensis*, klan-don-EN-sis of Clandon Park, Surrey, U.K.

incana, in-KA-na, hoary.

mastacanthus, see *C. incana*.

Cassandra, misapplied see below.

calyculata, see *Chamaedaphne calyculata*.

Cassia, KAS-se-a; from Gr. *kasian*, Greek name of the subject. Greenhouse shrubby plants. *Leguminosae*.

corymbosa, see *Senna corymbosa*.

marylandica, see *Senna marilandica*.

Cassinia, kas-SIN-e-a; named after Count Alexandre Henri Gabriel de Cassini (1781–1832), French botanist and naturalist. Shrub. *Compositae*.

fulvida, see *Ozothamnus leptophyllus*.

Cassiope, kas-se-O-pe; named after a Queen of Ethiopia, the mother of Andromeda, in Greek mythology. Shrub. *Ericaceae*.

fastigiata, fas-tij-e-A-ta, pointed and erect.

tetragona, te-tra-GO-na, from Gr. *tessara* four; *gonus* angle, the leaves in fours.

Castanea, kas-TA-ne-a; from Gr. *kastanon*, a chestnut, said to be after Kastana, a district in Thessaly, Greece. L. *castanea*, a Chestnut tree. Trees. *Fagaceae*.

sativa, SAT-iv-a, cultivated, that is, for crops. The edible Chestnut.

Castilleja, kas-STIL-e-a; after Domingo Castillejo (d. 1786), Spanish botanist, surgeon, and professor. Annuals and herbaceous perennials. *Orobanchaceae*.
exserta, eks-SER-ta, protruding.

Catabrosa, cat-a-BRO-sa; from Gr. *katabrosis*, a gnawing; in allusion to the irregular margins of the glumes, as if gnawed. Grasses. *Poaceae*.
aquatica, a-KWAT-ik-a, growing in water.

Catalpa, kat-AL-pa; a North American vernacular name for *C. bignonioides*. Flowering trees. *Bignoniaceae*.
bignonioides, big-no-ne-OY-dees, resembling *Bignonia*. The Indian Bean tree.

Catananche, kat-an-ANG-ke; from Gr. *katananke*, a strong incentive, alluding to the ancient custom among Greeks, who used it in love potions. Hardy herbaceous. *Compositae*.
caerulea, se-RU-le-a, sky-blue. The Blue Cupidone.

Catharanthus, kath-ar-AN-thus; from Gr. *katharos*, pure; *anthos*, a flower. Annuals and herbaceous perennials. *Apocynaceae*.
roseus, ro-ZE-us, rose-coloured.

Cathcartia, kath-KAR-te-a; called after John Fergusson Cathcart (1802–1851), botanist and Judge in the Indian Civil Service. Hardy herbaceous. *Papaveraceae*.
villosa, see *Meconopsis villosa*.

Cattleya, KAT-le-a; after William Cattley (d.1832), of Barnet, a keen cultivator of tropical plants. Cattley successfully propagated plant material which flowered in 1818. The resultant type species *Cattleya labiata* was described by Dr John Lindley. Tropical orchids. *Orchidaceae*.
aclandiae, ak-LAND-ee-e, after Lady Lydia Elizabeth Acland (1786–1856), who first grew the orchid.
bowringiana, see *Guarianthe bowringiana*.
cinnabarina, kin- (or sin-) nab-ar-EE-na, cinnabar; from Gr. *kinnabari*, a Persian dye.

coccinea, kok-SIN-e-a, scarlet.
crispa, KRIS-pa, curled.
× *elegans*, EL-e-ganz, elegant.
gigas, see *C. warscewiczii*.
harrisoniana, har-ris-on-e-A-na, after Elizabeth Harrison (1792–1834), Orchid collector at Aigburth, Liverpool.
intermedia, in-ter-MED-e-a, between.
labiata, lab-e-A-ta, from L. *labium*, meaning lip, the flamboyant trumpet-shaped lip created a sensation when first seen.
mendelii, men-DEL-e-i, after Samuel Mendel (1811–1884), merchant and Orchid collector from Manchester.
mossiae, MOSS-ee-e, after Hannah Moss (fl.1838), botanical artist and orchid collector, from Otterspool, Liverpool. National flower of Venezuela.
pumila, PU-mil-a, dwarf or diminutive.
purpurata, pur-pur-A-ta, purple.
trianae, tree-A-ne, after José Jerónimo Triana Silva (1828–1890), Colombian botanist.
warscewiczii, war-skew-IK-ze-i, after Joseph Warszewicz, who was interested in orchids and collected in Central and South America between 1844 and 1850.

Ceanothus, se-an-O-thus; ancient Gr. name, supposed to have been applied to an unknown plant by Theophrastus, the Greek philosopher. Shrubs. *Rhamnaceae*.
americanus, am-er-ik-A-nus, American.
arboreus, ar-BOR-e-us, tree-like. Tending to be woody.
azureus, see *C. caeruleus*.
caeruleus, se-RU-le-us, sky-blue.
cuneatus, ku-ne-A-tus, wedge-shaped, the leaves.
cuneatus subsp. *rigidus*, RIG-id-us, rigid, stiff.
dentatus, den-TA-tus, toothed, the leaf margin.
floribundus, see *C. dentatus*.
griseus, GRE-se-us, grey.
integerrimus, in-teg-ER-rim-us, entire, the leaves having unbroken margins.
papillosus, pap-il-O-sus, pimpled, that is, the leaves nippled with glands.
rigidus, see *C. cuneatus* subsp. *rigidus*.
thyrsiflorus, ther-sif-LO-rus, flowers in thyrses, that is, the middle blooms having longer stalks than those above and below.
× *veitchianus*, veech-e-A-nus, introduced from California by William Lobb for James Veitch & Sons.

Cedronella, sed-ron-EL-la; from Gr. *kedros*, the Cedar of Pliny, the Roman naturalist, alluding to the fragrance – Balm of Gilead. Aromatic herbs. *Lamiaceae.*
  canariensis, ka-nar-e-EN-sis, of the Canary Islands.
  triphylla, see *C. canariensis.*

Cedrus, SE-drus; from Gr. *kedros*, cedar; some suggest the name is derived from Kedron, a river in Judea. Trees. *Pinaceae.*
  atlantica, at-LAN-tik-a, of the Atlas Mountains.
  deodara, de-o-DAR-a, from Deodar, an Indian State.
  libani, LIB-an-i, of Mount Lebanon. The Cedar of Lebanon.

Celastrus, se-LAS-trus; from Gr. *kelastros*, an evergreen tree. Shrubs, usually climbers. *Celastraceae.*
  articulatus, see *C. orbiculatus.*
  flagellaris, flaj-el-LAR-is, whip-like.
  orbiculatus, or-bik-ul-A-tus, shaped like a disc, the leaves.
  scandens, SKAN-denz, climbing.

Celosia, se-LO-se-a; probably from Gr. *keleos*, burning, in reference to the burned appearance of the flowers of some species. Greenhouse annuals. *Amaranthaceae.*
  argentea, ar-JEN-te-a, silvery, the foliage.
  cristata, see *C. argentea.*
  plumosa, see *C. argentea.*

Celsia, misapplied see below.
  arcturus, see *Verbascum arcturus.*
  cretica, see *Verbascum creticum.*

Centaurea, sen- (or ken-) TAW-re-a; from Gr. *kentauros*, centaur. Annuals and perennials. *Compositae.*
  babylonica, bab-e-LON-ik-a, Babylonian.
  benedicta, ben-e-DIK-ta, blessed. The Blessed Thistle.
  cineraria, sin-er-AIR-e-a, from L. *cinereus*, ash-coloured, referring to the grey down on the undersides of the leaves,.
  cyanus, see *Cyanus segetum.*
  dealbata, see *C. cineraria.*
  gymnocarpa, see *C. cineraria.*
  macrocephala, mak-ro-SEF-a-la, large headed.
  montana, mon-TA-na, of mountains.
  moschata, see *Amberboa moschata.*
  ruthenica, ru-THEN-ik-a, Russian.

  scabiosa, skay-be-O-sa, from L. *scabies*, itch.
  suaveolens, see *Amberboa amberboi.*

Centaurium, sen-TOR-e-um; from Gr. *kentauros*, centaur; in reference to Chiron, whom it is stated first used herbs in the medicinal art of surgery. Annual, biennial and perennial plants. *Gentianaceae.*
  erythraea, er-re-THREE-a, from Gr. *erythros*, red.
  maritimum, mar-IT-im-um, maritime, coastal; in reference to the sea.

Centradenia, sen- (or ken-) tra-DE-ne-a; from Gr. *kentron*, a spur; *aden*, a gland, spur-like glands on the anthers. Perennial herbs and subshrubs. *Melastomataceae.*
  floribunda, flor-e-BUN-da, abundant or free flowering.

Centranthus, sen- (or ken-) TRAN-thus; from Gr. *kentron*, a spur; *anthos*, a flower, the flower having a spur-like base. Hardy herbaceous perennial. Red Valerian. *Caprifoliaceae.*
  macrosiphon, mak-ro-SY-fon, long tubed – the flowers have a long spur.
  ruber, RU-ber, red.

Centropogon, sen- (ken-) tro-PO-gon; from Gr. *kentron*, a spur; *pogon*, a beard; the fringed or bearded stigma. Greenhouse perennial. *Campanulaceae.*
  × *lucyanus*, loo-se-A-nus, hybrid created by M. Desponds in honour of M. Lucy, then president of the Horticultural Society of Marseille.

Cephalaria, sef- (or kef-) al-AR-e-a; from Gr. *kephale*, a head – flowers collected into heads. Hardy herbaceous perennials. *Caprifoliaceae.*
  gigantea, ji-GAN-te-a, unusually tall or big.
  tatarica, see *C. gigantea.*

Cephalocereus, sef- (or kef-) al-o-SER-e-us; from Gr. *kephale*, a head; *cereus*, a cactus, alluding to the woolly headed flowering zone. Cactus. *Cactaceae.*
  senilis, sen-E-lis, old – the appearance given by the long white hairs. The Old Man Cactus.

Cephalophyllum, sef- (or kef-) al-o-FI-lum; from Gr. *kephale*, a head; *phyllon*, a leaf, alluding to the compact head of leaves. Succulents. *Aizoaceae.*

tricolorum, trik-ol-OR-um, three-coloured.

Cephalotaxus, sef- (or kef-) al-o-TAKS-us; from Gr. *kephale*, a head; *taxus*, yew, resembling yew with a inflorescence head. Evergreen shrubs and small trees. *Taxaceae.*

harringtonii, har-ring-TO-ne-i, after Major-General Charles Stanhope, 4th Earl of Harrington (1780–1851), said to be one of the first to grow the plant in Europe.

Cephalotus, sef- (or kef-) al-O-tus; from Gr. *kephalotes*, small head, referring to the glandular head of stamens. Greenhouse herbaceous plants. *Cephalotaceae.*

follicularis, fol-lik-ul-A-ris, like a follicle – the leaves.

Cerastium, ser-AS-te-um; from Gr. *keras*, a horn, the seed capsules of some species appearing like horns as they emerge from the calyx. Rock and border plants. *Caryophyllaceae.*

biebersteinii, bi-ber-STI-ne-i, after Friedrich August Marschall von Bieberstein (1768–1826), botanist and plant collector in Russia.

tomentosum, to-men-TO-sum, felted – the leaves.

Cerasus, misapplied see below.

avium, see *Prunus avium.*
japonica, see *Prunus japonica.*
laurocerasus, see *Prunus laurocerasus.*
lusitanica, see *Prunus lusitanica.*

Ceratophyllum, ser-at-o-FIL-lum; from Gr. *keras*, a horn; *phyllon*, a leaf, the divisions of the leaves suggesting horns. Submerged aquatics. Hornwort. *Ceratophyllaceae.*

demersum, de-MER-sum, down under – the water.

submersum, sub-MER-sum, submerged.

Ceratostigma, ser-at-o-STIG-ma; from Gr. *keras*, a horn and *stigma*; alluding to the horn-like branches of the stigma. Shrubs. *Plumbaginaceae.*

plumbaginoides, plum-bay-gee-NOY-dees, resembling *Plumbago.*

willmottianum, wil-mot-te-A-num, commemorating Miss Ellen Ann Wilmott (1858–

1934), English horticulturist, who developed the gardens at Warley Place, Essex.

Cercis, SIR-sis; from Gr. *kerkis*, a weaver's shuttle; a name given by Theophrastus from the resemblance in the shape of the flattened fruits. Trees and shrubs. *Leguminosae.*

canadensis, kan-a-DEN-sis, of Canada.

siliquastrum, sil-e-KWAS-trum, from siliqua, a botanic name for pods having a partition between the seeds. The Judas Tree.

Cereus, SE-re-us; from L. *cereus*, wax taper, referring to the candle-like shape of some of the species. Cacti. *Cactaceae.*

flagelliformis, see *Disocactus flagelliformis.*
grandiflorus, see *Selenicereus grandiflorus.*
hystrix, HIS-trix, like a porcupine.
macdonaldiae, see *Selenicereus macdonaldiae.*
nycticalus, see *Selenicereus grandiflorus.*
speciosissimus, see *Heliocereus speciosus.*
spegazzinii, speg-az-ZIN-e-i, after Carlo Luigi Spegazzini (1858–1926), Italian born Argentinian botanist.

Cerinthe, ser- (or ker-) IN-thee; from Gr. *keros*, wax; *anthos*, a flower, once believed that the flowers were frequented by bees. Half-hardy annual. The Honeyworts. *Boraginaceae.*

major, MA-jor, greater.

Ceropegia, ker-o-PE-je-a; from Gr. *keros*, wax; *pege*, a fountain, referring to the form and waxy appearance of the flowers. Greenhouse trailing plants. *Apocynaceae.*

elegans, EL-e-ganz, elegant.

sandersonii, san-der-SO-ne-i, discovered in 1867 by John Sanderson (1829–1881), Scottish plant collector, who emigrated to the Natal in 1850.

woodii, WOOD-e-i, named after John Medley Wood (1827–1915), South African botanist, curator of the Durban Botanic Gardens. Wood discovered it in 1881 growing on Groenberg in Natal.

Cestrum, KES-trum (or SES-trum); Greek name however applied to another subject. Greenhouse flowering shrubby plants. *Solanaceae.*

aurantiacum, aw-RAN-te-a-kum, orange-coloured.

elegans, EL-e-ganz, elegant.

fasciculatum, fas-sik-ul-A-tum, bundled, that is, the flowers.

newellii, see *C. fasciculatum*.

Ceterach, SET-er-ak; origin obscure; said to be an ancient Persian name for Fern. The Scale Fern. *Aspleniaceae*.

officinarum, of-fis-in-AR-um, of the shop, herbal.

Chaenomeles, sha-no-MA-leez; from Gr. *chaino*, to split ground; *melon*, apple. *Rosaceae*.

japonica, jap-ON-ik-a, of Japan.

sinensis, si-NEN-sis, Chinese.

speciosa, spes-e-O-sa, showy.

× *superba*, su-PER-ba, superb.

Chamaecyparis, kam (sham)-e-SIP-a-ris, from Gr. *chamai*, on the ground; *kuparissos*, cypress. Coniferous trees. *Cupressaceae*.

lawsoniana, law-so-ne-A-na, after Charles Lawson (1794–1873), an Edinburgh nurseryman, who introduced this species from North America in 1854.

obtusa, ob-TU-sa, blunt.

pisifera, pis-IF-e-ra, pea-bearing, the cones being round like peas.

Chamaecytisus, kam-e-SY-tis-us; from Gr. *chamai*, on the ground; *cytisus*, *Cytisus* – a low growing broom. Small trees and shrubs. *Leguminosae*.

albus, AL-bus, white.

Chamaedaphne, kam (sham)-e-DAF-ne; from Gr. *chamai*, on the ground; *Daphne*, laurel – a dwarf plant resembling laurel. Herbaceous perennial. *Ericaceae*.

calyculata, kal-ik-u-LA-ta, small-calyxed.

Chamaelirium, kam-e-LIR-e-um; from Gr. *chamai*, on the ground; *leirion*, Lily – a dwarf lily-like plant. Herbaceous perennial. *Melanthiaceae*.

carolinianum, see *C. luteum*.

luteum, LU-te-um, yellow.

Chamaemelum, kam-E-mel-um; from Gr. *chamai*, on the ground; *melon*, apple. Annual and herbaceous perennial plants. *Compositae*.

nobile, no-bil-e, noble referring to the large flowers for a small plant. The Chamomile.

Chamaepeuce, misapplied see below.

casabonae, see *Ptilostemon casabonae*.

diacantha, see *Cirsium diacanthum*.

Chamaerops, kam-E-rops; from Gr. *chamai*, on the ground or dwarf; *rhops*, a twig, suggesting the form in contrast to the tall palms. Greenhouse palms. *Arecaceae*.

excelsa, see *Rhapis excelsa*.

fortunei, see *Trachycarpus fortunei*.

humilis, HUM-il-is, low or dwarf.

Chara, KAR-a; possibly from Gr. *karis*, grace or beauty. Submerged Algae. *Characeae*.

aspera, AS-per-a, rough to the touch.

fragifera, frag-IF-er-a, the red fruiting bodies resembling *Fragaria* (strawberry).

vulgaris, vul-GAR-is, common.

Charieis, misapplied see below.

heterophylla, see *Felicia heterophylla*.

Cheilanthes, ky-LANTH-eez; from Gr. *cheilos*, a lip; *anthos*, a flower, referring to the indusium. Greenhouse ferns. *Pteridaceae*.

elegans, see *C. myriophylla*.

hirta, HER-ta, hairy.

myriophylla, mir-e-OF-il-a, many leaved. The Lace Fern.

Cheiranthus, misapplied see below.

× *allionii*, see *Erysimum* × *marshallii*.

× *cheiri*, see *Erysimum* × *cheiri*.

Cheiridopsis, ky-rid-OP-sis; from Gr. *cheiris*, a sleeve; *opsis*, like, refers to the withered sheath surrounding the new foliage. Greenhouse succulents. *Aizoaceae*.

candidissima, see *C. denticulata*.

caroli-schmidtii, kar-O-le-smid-e-i, after Carl Schmidt (1848–1919), German nurseryman, owner of Haage & Schmidt, Erfurt.

denticulata, den-tik-u-LA-ta, toothed, the leaves.

Chelidonium, kel-id-O-ne-um; from Gr. *chelidon*, a swallow, the plant (Greater Celandine) being supposed to flower and fade with the arrival and departure of the swallow. Hardy herbaceous. *Papaveraceae*.

majus, MA-jus, great. There is a double form.

Chelone, ke-LO-ne; Gr. *kelone*, a tortoise, the helmet of the flower suggesting the shape of that reptile. Herbaceous plants. *Plantaginaceae.*

barbata, see *Penstemon barbatus.*
glabra, GLAB-ra, smooth – the leaves.
obliqua, ob-LEE-kwa, with unequal sides.

Chenopodium, ken-o-POD-e-um; from Gr. *chen*, a goose; *podion*, a little foot; from the shape of the leaves. Hardy culinary and ornamental plants. *Amaranthaceae.*

bonus-henricus, BO-nus-hen-REE-kus, literally good Henry. Good King Henry or Lincolnshire Spinach.
capitatum, kap-it-A-tum, in heads – the fruits. Strawberry Spinach or Strawberry Blite.

Chimaphila, kim-AF-il-a; from Gr. *cheima*, winter; *phileo*, to love, the plants are green in winter. Dwarf shrubs. *Ericaceae.*

maculata, mak-ul-A-ta, spotted. The Spotted Wintergreen.
umbellata, um-bel-LA-ta, flowers in an umbel.

Chimonanthus, kim-on-AN-thus; from Gr. *cheima*, winter; *anthos*, a flower, alluding to the flowering of *Chimonanthus praecox* (Winter Sweet) in the early year. Shrub. *Calycanthaceae.*

fragrans, see *C. praecox.*
praecox, PRA-koks, early flowering.

Chionodoxa, misapplied see below.
luciliae, see *Scilla luciliae.*
sardensis, see *Scilla sardensis.*

Chionoscilla, misapplied see *Scilla × allenii.*

Chlidanthus, kly-DAN-thus; from Gr. *chlideios*, delicate; *anthos*, a flower. Half-hardy bulbous plants. *Amaryllidaceae.*

fragrans, FRA-granz, fragrant.

Chlorophytum, klo-rof-it-um; from Gr. *chloros*, green; *phyton*, a plant. Greenhouse herbaceous plant with variegated leaves. *Asparagaceae.*

capense, ka-pen-se, of the Cape of Good Hope, South Africa.
elatum, see *C. capense.*

Choisya, CHOY-se-a; in honour of Jacques Denys Choisy (1799–1859), Swiss clergyman and botanist. Shrub. *Rutaceae.*

× *dewitteana*, de-wit-TE-a-na, dedicated to Dominique de Witt, nurseryman of Try, Ceroux, Belgium.
ternata, ter-NA-ta, with three leaflets. The Mexican Orange.

Chorizema, kor-is-E-ma; Legume discovered by Labillardière in 1792 in Australia. A contraction from Gr. *choris*, separate; *nema*, thread, the filaments of their stamina being separate from each other. Greenhouse flowering shrubs. *Leguminosae.*

cordatum, kor-DA-tum, heart shaped.
ilicifolium, il-is-if-O-le-um, *Ilex* (holly) leaved.

Christella, kris-TEL-la; in honour of Konrad Hermann Heinrich Christ (1833–1933), Swiss botanist, who specialised in ferns. Tropical and subtropical ferns. *Thelypteridaceae.*

dentata, den-TA-ta, toothed, the leaves.

Chrysalidocarpus, misapplied see below.
lutescens, see *Dypsis lutescens.*

Chrysanthemum, kris-AN-the-mum; from Gr. *chrysos*, gold; *anthemum*, a flower, the flowers being golden, or with yellow disks. Annuals and perennials. *Compositae.*

arcticum, see *Arctanthemum arcticum.*
carinatum, see *Ismelia carinata.*
coronarium, see *Glebionis coronaria.*
frutescens, see *Argyranthemum frutescens.*
indicum, IN-dik-um, Indian. The Greenhouse Chrysanthemum.
leucanthemum, see *Leucanthemum vulgare.*
maximum, MAKS-e-mum, largest. The Shasta Daisy.
× *morifolium*, mor-e-FO-le-um, leaves resembling *Morus* (mulberry). The greenhouse and border chrysanthemums.
segetum, seg-E-tum, of cornfields. The Corn Marigold.
× *sinense*, see *C.* × *morifolium.*
uliginosum, see *Leucanthemella serotina.*

Chrysogonum, kris-OG-o-num; from Gr. *chrysos*, gold; *gonu*, a joint, the golden flowers appearing at the joints of the stem. Hardy herbaceous. *Compositae.*

virginianum, vir-jin-e-A-num, of Virginia, U.S.A.

Chrysosplenium, kris-os-PLE-ne-um; from Gr. *chrysos*, gold; *splen*, spleen, the colour of the flowers and medicinal use for the spleen. Dwarf hardy plants. *Saxifragaceae*.
  alternifolium, al-ter-ne-FO-le-um, leaves alternate.
  oppositifolium, op-pos-it-e-FO-le-um, leaves opposite.

Chysis, KY-sis; from Gr. *chysis*, melting; fused appearance of pollen masses. Warmhouse orchids. *Orchidaceae*.
  aurea, AW-re-a, golden.
  bractescens, brak-TES-enz, with bracts.

Cichorium, sik-OR-e-um; an old Arabic name for Chicory. Gr. *kichore*. Salad and root vegetable. *Compositae*.
  endivia, en-DEE-ve-a. The Endive.
  intybus, IN-tib-us, from L. *intubus*, wild chicory, the old name for Chicory. The Chicory.

Cimicifuga, sim-is-if-U-ga; from L. *cimex*, a bug; *fugio*, to run away, the plant once being used to ward off fleas. Hence the English common name Bugbane. *Ranunculaceae*.
  dahurica, see *Actaea dahurica*.
  japonica, see *Actaea japonica*.
  racemosa, see *Actaea racemosa*.
  simplex, see *Actaea simplex*.

Cineraria, sin-er-AIR-e-a; from L. *cinereus*, ash-coloured, referring to the grey down on the undersides of the leaves. Herbaceous plants and subshrubs. *Compositae*.
  cruenta, see *Pericallis cruenta*.
  maritima, see *Jacobaea maritima*.

Cionura, ki-on-UR-a; from Gr. *kion*, column or pier; *oura*, a tail, the upright habit. Deciduous shrub exuding an irritating latex. *Apocynaceae*.
  erecta, e-REK-ta, erect; upright.

Cirsium, SIR-se-um; comes from the Gr. *kirsos*, varicose veins, it was believed the herb was good at soothing the pain from varicose veins. Herbaceous perennials. *Compositae*.
  diacanthum, di-ak-AN-thum, having two spines. The Fishbone Thistle.

Cissus, SIS-sus; from Gr. *kissos*, ivy, in reference to the climbing habit of these plants. Greenhouse climbers. *Vitaceae*.
  antarctica, an-TARK-tik-a, southern.
  discolor, see *C. javana*.
  javana, ja-VAR-na, of Java.
  striata, stri-A-ta, fluted or grooved – presumably the angled stems.

Cistanthe, sis-TAN-the; the name alludes to the appearance of the flowers, which resemble those of *Cistus*. Succulent flowering plants. *Portulacaceae*.
  grandiflora, gran-dif-LO-ra, large-flowered.

Cistus, SIS-tus; ancient Gr. *kistos*, name of the plant. The Rock Rose. Flowering Shrubs and rock plants. *Cistaceae*.
  albidus, AL-bid-us, nearly white – the leaves.
  × *corbariensis*, kor-bar-e-EN-sis, Corbiere, South France.
  creticus, KRE-tik-us, of Crete.
  crispus, KRIS-pus, curly – the leaves waved.
  × *cyprius*, SIP-re-us, of Cyprus.
  × *florentinus*, flor-en-TE-nus, of Florence, Italy.
  ladaniferus, see *C. creticus*.
  laurifolius, law-rif-O-le-us, *Laurus* (Laurel) leaved.
  monspeliensis, mon-spe-le-EN-sis, of Montpellier.
  populifolius, pop-u-lif-O-le-us, *Populus* (Poplar) leaved.
  salviifolius, sal-ve-i-FO-le-us, *Salvia* (Sage) leaved.
  villosus, see *C. creticus*.

Citrullus, sit-RUL-lus; Citrus or Citron-like. The Water Melon. *Cucurbitaceae*.
  lanatus, la-NA-tus, soft-leaved.

Citrus, SIT-rus; classical name first applied to another tree. Greenhouse flowering and fruiting evergreen shrubs. *Rutaceae*.
  × *aurantium*, aw-RAN-te-um, orange. The Orange.
  limon, LI-mon, lemon. The Lemon.
  medica, ME-dik-a, median or between. The Citron.
  trifoliata, trif-o-le-A-ta, three-leaved.

Cladium, KLAD-e-um; from Gr. *kladion*, a small branch. The flowering stems have twiggy branches. Bog perennial. *Cyperaceae*.
  mariscus, mar-IS-kus, after the genus *Mariscus*.

Cladrastis, klad-RAS-tis; from Gr. *klados*, a branch; *thraustos*, fragile, in allusion to the brittle twigs. Flowering shrubs. *Leguminosae.*

kentukea, ken-TUK-e-a, from Kentucky, U.S.A.
tinctoria, see *C. kentukea*.

Clarkia, KLAR-ke-a; after Capt. William Clark (1770–1838), companion of Capt. Meriwether Lewis, explorer of the Rocky Mountain region in 1806. Hardy annuals. *Onagraceae.*

amoena, am-E-na, pleasing.
amoena subsp. *lindleyi*, LIND-le-i, after John Lindley (1799–1865), British botanist, appointed first chair of botany at University College London.
amoena subsp. *whitneyi*, WHIT-ne-i, after Josiah Whitney (1819–1896), professor of geology Harvard University, head of the California State Geological Survey, in whose pursuit it was discovered.
breweri, BROO-er-i, after William Henry Brewer (1828–1910), American botanist, pioneer explorer in California.
concinna, kon-SIN-na, neat, pretty.
elegans, see *C. unguiculata.*
pulchella, pul-KEL-la, pretty.
unguiculata, un-gwik-ul-A-ta, narrow-clawed, the lower end of the petal.

Claytonia, klay-TO-ne-a; after John Clayton (1686–1773), pioneer American plant collector. Succulent perennial herbs. *Montiaceae.*

perfoliata, per-fo-le-A-ta, the leaf-stem pierced.
sibirica, si-BIR-ik-a, of Siberia.

Clematis, KLEM-a-tis; from Gr. *klema*, a vine branch, alluding to the vine-like habit of the climbing species. Climbers and woody-based perennials. *Ranunculaceae.*

alpina, al-PINE-a (or al-PIN-a), of the Alps or alpine.
armandii, ar-MAN-de-i, after Armand David (1826–1900), French missionary in China.
coccinea, see *C. texensis.*
davidiana, see *C. heracleifolia.*
flammula, FLAM-u-la, a little flame.
florida, FLOR-id-a, from L. *floridus*, flowering abundantly.
graveolens, GRAV-e-ol-enz, strong smelling.

heracleifolia, her-ak-le-FO-le-a; with leaves resembling *Heracleum.*
lanuginosa, lan-u-jin-O-sa, downy.
montana, mon-TA-na, of mountains.
orientalis, or-e-en-TA-lis, eastern – Eastern Asia (China).
paniculata, pan-ik-ul-A-ta, flowers in a panicle or branching inflorescence.
recta, REK-ta, upright.
tangutica, tan-GU-te-ka, Tangusian, Siberia.
terniflora, ter-ne-FLOR-a, flowers in clusters of three. Sweet Autumn Clematis.
texensis, TEX-en-sis, of Texas, U.S.A.
vitalba, vit-AL-ba, the white vine. The Wild Clematis, Virgin's Bower or Traveller's Joy.
viticella, vit-e-SEL-la, vine-bower.

Cleome, kle-O-me; derivation uncertain. Tropical plants. *Cleomaceae.*

gigantea, see *C. viridiflora.*
viridiflora, vir-id-e-FLOR-a, with green flowers.

Clerodendrum, kler-o-DEN-drum; from Gr. *kleros*, chance; *dendron*, a tree, in allusion to the various medicinal qualities of the genus, Greenhouse and hardy shrubs and climbers. *Lamiaceae.*

balfourii, see *C. thomsoniae.*
bungei, BUN-je-e, after Alexander Andrejewitsch von Bunge (1803–1890), a Russian botanist.
chinense, tshi-NEN-se, of China.
fallax, see *C. speciosissimum.*
fargesii, see *C. trichotomum* var. *fargesii.*
foetidum, see *C. bungei.*
fragrans, see *C. chinense.*
speciosissimum, spes-e-o-SIS-se-mum, most showy.
thomsoniae, tom-SO-ne-e, discovered by Rev. W.C. Thomson in Old Calabar (Akwa Akpa – now Calabar, Nigeria), who wished it to be named after his late wife.
trichotomum, try-KO-to-mum, branches or stems dividing into three.
trichotomum var. *fargesii*, FAR-ge-se-i, after Père Paul Guillaume Farges (1844–1912), missionary and plant collector in China.

Clethra, KLE-thra; from Gr. *klethra*, name for an Alder, which some species resemble. Shrubs and trees. *Clethraceae.*

acuminata, a-ku-min-A-ta, long-pointed, the leaves.
alnifolia, al-nif-O-le-a, *Alnus* (Alder) leaved.

Clianthus, kli-AN-thus; from Gr. *kleios*, glory; *anthos*, a flower. Climbing shrubs. *Leguminosae*.
  puniceus, pu-NIK-e-us, reddish-purple. New Zealand Glory Pea.

Clinopodium, klin-o-PO-de-um; from Gr. *kline*, bed; *podion* diminutive of *pous*, a foot, the flowers being in whorls one above another in the shape of an old fashioned bed's foot. Perennial herbs. *Lamiaceae*.
  alpinum, al-PINE-um (or al-PIN-um), of the Alps or alpine.
  grandiflorum, gran-dif-LO-rum, large flowered.
  thymifolium, ty-mif-OL-e-um, *Thymus* (Thyme) leaved.

Clintonia, klin-TO-ne-a; after DeWitt Clinton (1769–1828), Governor of New York and botanist. Woodland herbs. *Liliaceae*.
  uniflora, uni-FLOR-a, one flowered, that is blooms solitary.

Clivia, KLY-ve-a; named after Charlotte Percy, Duchess of Northumberland (1787–1866), member of the Clive family. Herbaceous perennials. *Amaryllidaceae*.
  miniata, min-e-A-ta, vermilion coloured.
  nobilis, NO-bil-is, large or noble.

Cnicus, NY-kus; L. name of safflower, early name applied to thistles. Annual herb. *Compositae*.
  casabonae, see *Ptilostemon casabonae*.
  diacantha, see *Ptilostemon diacantha*.
  pungens, PUN-jenz, piercing – the leaves are sharp pointed.

Cobaea, ko-BE-a; after Bernabé Cobo (1580–1657), Spanish Jesuit priest and naturalist in Mexico, whence most species come. Half-hardy climbing plants. *Polemoniaceae*.
  scandens, SKAN-denz, climbing.

Coccothrinax, kok-o-THRIN-aks, from Gr. *kokkos*, a berry; *thrinax*, a trident. Warmhouse palms. *Arecaceae*.
  argentea, ar-JEN-te-a, silvery, the foliage.

Cochlearia, kok-le-AR-e-a; from L. *cochlea*, spoon; refers to concave leaves of Scurvy Grass (*C. officinalis*). Annual and perennial herbs. *Brassicaceae*.
  acaulis, a-KAW-lis, stalkless, the plants.
  armoracia, see *Armoracia rusticana*.
  officinalis, of-fis-in-A-lis, of the shop (herbal).

Cocos, ko-kos; from Portuguese *coco* a mask, in allusion to the face like appearance of the nut. *Arecaceae*.
  nucifera, nu-SIF-er-a, nut-bearing.
  weddelliana, see *Lytocaryum weddellianum*.

Codariocalyx, ko-da-re-O-ka-liks; from Gr. *koidarion*, sheepskin; *kalyx*, calyx. Shrubs. *Leguminosae*.
  motorius, mo-tor-E-us, from L. *motus*, to move, capable of rapid movement.

Codiaeum, ko-de-EE-um; from the Ternate native name *kodiho*. Tropical variegated shrubs. *Euphorbiaceae*.
  angustifolium, see *C. variegatum*.
  chelsonii, see *C. variegatum*.
  interruptum, see *C. variegatum*.
  variegatum, var-e-eg-A-tum, leaves variegated.
  warrenii, see *C. variegatum*.

Codonopsis, ko-don-OP-sis; from Gr. *kodon*, a bell; *opsis*, resemblance, the flowers being bell-shaped. Tender perennials. *Campanulaceae*.
  clematidea, klem-at-ID-e-a, resembling *Clematis*.
  ovata, o-VA-ta, egg-shaped; the leaves.

Coelogyne, se-LOG-e-ne; from Gr. *koilos*, hollow; *gyne*, woman, in allusion to the pistil. Cool-house orchids. *Orchidaceae*.
  cristata, kris-TA-ta, crested lipped.
  dayana, see *C. pulverula*.
  massangeana, see *C. tomentosa*.
  pulverula, pul-ver-U-la, powdered.
  speciosa, spes-e-O-sa, showy.
  tomentosa, to-men-TO-sa, downy foliage.

Coffea, KOF-fe-a; from *quahouch*, the Arabic name for the liquor of coffee. Tropical shrub. *Rubiaceae*.
  arabica, ar-AB-ik-a, from Arabia. The Coffee Tree.

Coix, KO-iks; name given by Theophrastus for a reed-leaved plant. Annual ornamental grass. *Poaceae*.

lacryma-jobi, LAK-rim-a-JO-be, literally Job's tears.

Colchicum, KOL-chi-kum; named after Colchis, a region on the coast of the Black Sea, where the plant abounds. Hardy bulbs. *Colchicaceae*.
  autumnale, aw-tum-NA-le, autumnal flowering.
  bulbocodium, bul-bo-KO-de-um, from L. *bulbus*, a globular root (bulb); *kodion*, wool, with which the bulbs are covered.
  × *byzantinum*, bi-zan-TE-num, from Byzantium, a hybrid first described by Clusius in 1601.
  giganteum, see *C. speciosum*.
  speciosum, spes-e-O-sum, showy.

Coleus, misapplied see below.
  blumei, see *Plectranthus scutellarioides*.
  fredericii, see *Plectranthus welwitschii*.
  thyrsoideus, see *Plectranthus thyrsoideus*.
  verschaffeltii, see *Plectranthus scutellarioides*.

Colletia, kol-LE-te-a; called after Philibert Collet (1643–1718), French botanist. Shrubs. *Rhamnaceae*.
  armata, see *C. hystrix*.
  cruciata, see *C. paradoxa*.
  hystrix, HIS-trix, like a porcupine.
  paradoxa, pa-ra-DOKS-a, paradoxical, contrary to exception.

Collinsia, kol-LIN-se-a; called after Zaccheus Collins (1764–1831), a naturalist, of Philadelphia. Hardy annuals. *Plantaginaceae*.
  bicolor, see *C. verna*.
  heterophylla, het-er-of-IL-la, Gr. *hetero*, diverse; *phylla*, leaves.
  verna, VER-na, spring, spring-flowering.

Collomia, kol-LO-me-a; from Gr. *kolla*, glue, referring to the mucilage around the seeds. Hardy annuals. *Polemoniaceae*.
  biflora, bif-LO-ra, two-flowered, that is, in pairs.
  coccinea, see *C. biflora*.

Colocasia, kol-o-KAS-e-a; from Gr. *kolokasia*, name for the root of an Egyptian plant. Tropical tuberous rooted foliage plants. *Araceae*.
  affinis, af-FIN-nis, related or similar to.
  antiquorum, an-te-KOR-um, ancient.
  esculenta, es-kul-EN-ta, esculent or edible.

Columnea, kol-UM-ne-a; in honour of Fabius Columna (1567–1640), Italian writer on plants. Shrubs. *Gesneriaceae*.
  gloriosa, see *C. microcalyx*.
  magnifica, mag-NIF-ik-a, magnificent.
  microcalyx, mi-kro-KA-liks, from Gr. *mikros*, small; *kalyx*, calyx.

Coluria, ko-LUR-e-a; from Gr. *kolos*, clipped; *oura*, tail. Herbaceous perennials. *Rosaceae*.
  longifolia, long-if-OL-e-a, long leaves.

Colutea, ko-LU-te-a; from the Gr. *koloutea*, name used by Theophrastus. Shrubs. *Leguminosae*.
  arborescens, ar-bor-ES-cenz, tree like.
  cruenta, see *C. orientalis*.
  media, ME-de-a, midway, medium.
  orientalis, or-e-en-TA-lis, eastern – Eastern Asia (China).

Commelina, kom-me-LE-na; named after Jan Commelin (1629–1692) and Caspar Commelin (1667–1731), Dutch botanists. Annuals and perennials. *Commelinaceae*.
  coelestis, se-LES-tis, sky blue.
  tuberosa, tu-ber-O-sa, tuberous rooted.

Comospermum, ko-mo-SPUR-mum; from Gr. *koma*, tuft of hairs; *sperma*, a seed. A genus of one species of flowering plant. *Asparagaceae*.
  yedoense, yed-o-EN-se, of Yeddon, Japan.

Conicosia, kon-e-KO-se-a; from Gr. *konikos*, conical, the conical top of the fruit. Greenhouse succulent. *Aizoaceae*.
  pugioniformis, pu-je-e-o-nif-OR-mis, dagger shaped.

Coniogramme, ko-ne-o-GRAM-me; from Gr. *konis*, dusty; *gramme*, line, in allusion to the sori being continuous along the veins. Ferns. *Pteridaceae*.
  japonica, jap-ON-ik-a, of Japan.

Conophytum, kon-OF-i-tum; from Gr. *konos*, a cone; *phyton*, a plant, in allusion to the form of many species – an inverted cone. Greenhouse succulents. The Pebble Plants. *Aizoaceae*.
  aggregatum, see *C. piluliforme*.

globosum, glo-BO-sum, spherical.

longum, LONG-um, long – the leaves, for the genus.

minutum, min-U-tum, small, minute.

mundum, see *C. obcordellum*.

obcordellum, ob-kor-DEL-lum, obversely heart-shaped. The narrow end being at the base.

piluliforme, pil-ul-e-FOR-me; from L. *pilula*, a pill; *forma*, shape, forming mats or domes.

Consolida, kon-soh-LID-a; from L. *consolido*, to make firm, medieval name applied to another plant (a wound-healing herb) and transferred to this genus. Annuals. The Larkspur. *Ranunculaceae.*

ajacis, aj-A-kis, this name has been stated to be found on some marks at the base of the united petals which were compared to the Greek letters AIAI.

regalis, re-GA-lis, Royal, stately.

sulphurea, sul-FU-re-a, sulphur yellow, the flowers.

Convallaria, kon-val-LAIR-e-a; from L. *convallium*, a valley, the natural habitat of the Lily of the Valley. Hardy herbaceous. *Asparagaceae.*

majalis, maj-A-lis, May – the time of flowering.

Convolvulus, kon-VOL-vu-lus; from L. *convolvo*, to entwine, alluding to the twining habit of some species. Shrubby, herbaceous and rock plants. *Convolvulaceae.*

althaeoides, al-the-OY-dees, resembling *Althaea* (Hollyhock) – the flowers.

cantabrica, kan-TAB-rik-a, Cantabria, Spain.

cneorum, ne-OR-um, from Gr. *kneoron*, the shrub resembling olive.

lineatus, lin-e-A-tus, with lines.

mauritanicus, see *C. sabatius*.

nitidus, NIT-id-us, shining.

sabatius, sa-BA-te-us, native to Vado Ligure, in antiquity Vada Sabatia, north-west Italy.

soldanella, see *Calystegia soldanella*.

tenuissimus, ten-u-IS-sim-us, most slender.

tricolor, TRIK-o-lor, three coloured.

Coprosma, kop-ROZ-ma; from Gr. *kopros*, dung; *osme*, a smell; alluding to the unpleasant odour. Greenhouse shrub. *Rubiaceae.*

baueri, bo-EE-re, collected by Ferdinand Bauer (1760–1826), in 1803–1805.

Cordyline, kor-dil-Y-ne; from Gr. *kordyle*, a club, in reference to the thickened roots. Greenhouse palm-like plants. *Asparagaceae.*

australis, aws-TRA-lis, southern.

fruticosa, frut-ik-O-sa, shrubby.

indivisa, in-de-VY-sa, not divided.

lineata, see *C. indivisa*.

Coreopsis, kor-e-OP-sis; from Gr. *koris*, a bug or tick; *opsis*, resemblance, from the appearance of the seed, hence the common name of Tickseed. Annuals and perennials. *Compositae.*

aristosa, see *Bidens aristosa*.

atkinsoniana, see *C. tinctoria*.

auriculata, aw-rik-ul-A-ta, ear-shaped – the leaves.

coronata, see *C. nuecensis.*

douglasii, dug-LAS-e-i, after David Douglas (1799–1834), Scottish plant collector.

drummondii, drum-MON-de-i, in honour of Thomas Drummond (1780–1835), who collected across North America.

grandiflora, gran-dif-LO-ra, large-flowered.

lanceolata, lan-se-o-LA-ta, the leaves lance-shaped.

maritima, mar-IT-im-a, of the sea.

nuecensis, new-SEN-sis, native to the Nueces river area in SE Texas.

rosea, RO-ze-a, rose-coloured.

stillmanii, STIL-man-e-i, after Jacob David Babcock Stillman (1819–1888), physician and botanist.

tinctoria, tink-TOR-e-a, reference to dyeing – the variously coloured flowers.

verticillata, ver-tis-il-LA-ta, whorled – the leaves.

Coriaria, kor-e-AIR-e-a; from L. *corium*, hide, from the use made of some kinds in tanning leather. The Tanner's tree. Shrubs. *Coriariaceae.*

terminalis, ter-min-A-lis, flowers terminal.

Cornus, KOR-nus; the Latin name for Cornelian Cherry (*C. mas*). Trees and shrubs. *Cornaceae.*

alba, AL-ba, from the L. alba, white.

canadensis, kan-a-DEN-sis, of Canada.

candidissima, see *C. florida.*

capitata, kap-it-A-ta, growing in a dense head.

florida, FLOR-id-a, from L. *floridus*, flowering abundantly.

glabrata, gla-BRA-ta, glabrous.

kousa, KOO-sa, a Japanese name.

mas, mas, male (*mascula* of Linnaeus).

nuttallii, NUT-al-le-i, after Thomas Nuttall (1786–1859), English botanist and plant collector. Nuttall found this specimen near Fort Vancouver.

sanguinea, san-GWIN-e-a, blood red.

sericea, ser-IS-e-a, silky – the leaves.

stolonifera, see *C. sericea*.

Corokia, kor-O-ke-a; adapted from *korokia-taranga*, the Maori name. Shrubs. *Argophyllaceae*.

buddlieoides, bud-le-e-OY-dez, resembling *Buddleja*.

cotoneaster, ko-to-ne-AS-ter, resembling *Cotoneaster*.

macrocarpa, mak-ro-KAR-pa, large fruits.

× *virgata*, vir-GA-ta, with willowy twigs.

Coronilla, kor-o-NIL-la; meaning a little crown, from L. *corona*, a crown or garland, in reference to the disposition of the umbels. Rock plants and shrubs. *Leguminosae*.

cappadocica, see *Securigera orientalis*.

emeroides, see *Hippocrepis emerus* subsp. *emeroides*.

emerus, see *Hippocrepis emerus*.

glauca, see *C. valentina* subsp. *glauca*.

minima, MIN-e-ma, from L. *minimus*, smallest.

valentina, val-en-TE-na, from Valencia, Spain.

valentina subsp. *glauca*, GLAW-ka, sea-green, the foliage.

varia, see *Securigera varia*.

Correa, kor-RE-a; after Jose Francesco Correa de Serra (1750–1823), a Portuguese botanist. Greenhouse evergreen flowering shrubs. *Rutaceae*.

cardinalis, see *C. reflexa* var. *cardinalis*.

reflexa, re-FLEKS-a, leaves bent back, recurved.

reflexa var. *cardinalis*, kar-din-A-lis, scarlet, cardinal red.

speciosa, see *C. reflexa*.

ventricosa, see *C. reflexa*.

Cortaderia, kaw-ta-deer-E-a; from the vernacular Argentine name *cortadera* meaning cutting. Ornamental grasses. *Poaceae*.

selloana, sel-lo-A-na, after Friedrich Sellow (1789–1831), German traveller and naturalist, who made extensive collections in Brazil and Uruguay.

Cortusa, misapplied see below.

matthioli, see *Primula matthioli*.

Corydalis, kor-ID-a-lis; from Gr. *korydalis*, the crested lark (derivation *korys*, a helmet), alluding to the shape of the petals. Herbaceous and rock plants. *Papaveraceae*.

bulbosa, see *C. solida*.

cava, KA-va, hollow, or cave-like – the bulbous root.

cheilanthifolia, ky-lanth-e-FO-le-a, with foliage resembling *Cheilanthus*.

lutea, see *Pseudofumaria lutea*.

solida, SOL-id-a, solid – the fleshy root.

thalictrifolia, thal-ik-trif-O-le-a, leaves resembling *Thalictrum*.

Corylopsis, kor-il-OP-sis; from Gr. *korylos*, hazel; *opsis*, like, the leaves resembling *Corylus*. Shrubs and small trees. *Hamamelidaceae*.

pauciflora, paw-se-FLOR-a, with few flowers.

spicata, spe-KA-ta, spiked – the inflorescence.

Corylus, KOR-il-us; the Gr. name, possibly from Gr. *korys*, hood or helmet; the calyx covering the nut. Shrubs. *Betulaceae*.

avellana, av-el-LA-na, after Avella Vecchia near Naples, Italy, where the Hazel was grown for its nuts. The Hazel and Cobnut.

colurna, ko-LUR-na, classical name.

maxima, MAKS-im-a, greatest. The Filbert.

Corymbia, ko-RIM-be-a; from Gr. *korymbos*, cluster, the genus distinguished as forming corymb inflorescences. Trees. *Myrtaceae*.

citriodora, sit-re-o-DOR-a, lemon scented.

Corynabutilon, kor-IN-a-BU-til-on; from Gr. *koryne*, a club; and *Abutilon*. Shrubs. *Malvaceae*.

vitifolium, vi-tif-O-le-um, the leaves resembling *Vitis* (grape vine).

Coryphantha, kor-if-ANTH-a; from Gr. *koryphe*, summit; *anthos*, a flower, the flowers appearing at the top of the plant. Cacti. *Cactaceae*.

chlorantha, see *Escobaria dasyacantha*.

clava, KLA-va, club shaped.

echinus, ek-IN-us, from Gr. *echinos*, hedgehog.

elephantidens, el-ef-AN-tid-enz, elephant's tooth.

macromeris, mak-rom-E-ris, large-flowered.

ottonis, ot-TO-nis, after Christoph Friedrich Otto (1783–1856), German botanist, curator of the Berlin Botanic Garden.

pectinata, see *C. echinus*.
pycnacantha, pik-nak-AN-tha, densely spined.
sulcolanata, see *C. elephantidens*.

Cosmea, KOS-me-a; from Gr. *kosmos*, beautiful. Annual and perennial herbs. *Compositae*.
bipinnata, bi-pin-A-ta, the leaves double pinnate.
diversifolia, di-ver-see-FO-le-a, diversely leaved.

Cosmos, KOS-mos; from Gr. *kosmos*, beautiful; in reference to the flowers. Half-hardy annuals. *Compositae*.
bipinnatus, bi-pin-A-tus, the leaves double pinnate.
diversifolius, di-ver-see-FO-le-us, diversely leaved.
diversifolius var. *dahlioides*, day-le-OY-deez, resembling *Dahlia*.
sulphureus, sul-FUR-e-us, sulphur coloured – the flowers.

Cota, KO-ta; possibly from classical generic name used as a specific epithet for *Anthemis cota*. Herbs. *Compositae*.
tinctoria, tink-TOR-e-a, of dyers, tingo, to dye. Dyer's Chamomile.

Cotinus, KOT-in-us; old generic name for this plant, signifying wild olive. The Smoke Bush. Trees and shrubs. *Anacardiaceae*.
coggygria, kog-GY-gre-a, incorrect interpretation of the Gr. word *kokkugia*, name for the smoke tree.
obovatus, ob-ov-A-tus, egg-shaped, the broadest part near the tip.

Cotoneaster, ko-to-ne-AS-ter; from L. *cotoneum*, quince; *aster*, a likeness, leaves been quince like in some species. Shrubs. *Rosaceae*.
adpressus, ad-PRES-sus, close, pressed down growth; or fruits closely pressed against the branch.
applanatus, ap-lan-A-tus, the branches plane-like, or flat.
bullatus, bul-LA-tus, wrinkled – the upper surface of the leaves.
buxifolius, buks-e-FO-le-us, resembling *Buxus* (Box) leaves.
congestus, kon-JES-tus, crowded – the habit.
dammeri, DAM-mer-i, after Carl Lebrecht Udo Dammer (1860–1920), German botanist.
divaricatus, di-var-e-KA-tus, spread-out, forking – the branches.
franchetii, fran-SHET-e-i, after Adrien René Franchet (1834–1900), French botanist at

the Muséum national d'histoire naturelle in Paris.
frigidus, FRIJ-id-us, growing in cold regions.
harrovianus, har-ro-VE-a-nus, after George Harrow (1858–1940), manager of Veitch's Coombe Wood nursery.
henryanus, hen-re-A-nus, after Dr. Augustine Henry (1857–1930), plant collector and dendrologist.
horizontalis, hor-e-zon-TA-lis, horizontal – the habit of growth.
humifuus, see *C. dammeri*.
lucidus, LU-sid-us, shining that is the leaves.
microphyllus, mi-krof-IL-lus, small leaved.
multiflorus, mul-tif-LO-rus, many flowered.
pannosus, pan-NO-sis, tattered – the foliage.
rotundifolius, ro-tun-dif-O-le-us, round-leaved.
salicifolius, sal-is-if-O-le-us, *Salix* (Willow) leaved.
simonsii, SI-mons-e-i, after Charles J. Simons (fl. 1820–1854), apothecary and plant collector in Assam and Khasia.

Cotula, KOT-u-la; from Gr. *kotyle*, a cup, the bases of the leaves. Dwarf creeping plants. *Compositae*.
barbata, bar-BA-ta, having hooked hairs.
squalida, SKWOL-id-a, squalid or lowly – flower-heads dingy.

Cotyledon, kot-e-LE-don; from Gr. *kotyle*, meaning cup-shaped, from the round, concave leaves of Navalwort. Mainly Greenhouse succulent perennials. *Crassulaceae*.
agavoides, see *Echeveria agavoides*.
atropurpurea, see *Echeveria atropurpurea*.
fulgens, see *Echeveria fulgens*.
gibbiflora, see *Echeveria gibbiflora*.
gibbiflora var. *metallica*, see *Echeveria gibbiflora*.
retusa, see *Echeveria fulgens*.
secunda, see *Echeveria secunda*.
simplicifolia, sim-plis-e-FO-le-a, having simple (not compound) leaves.
umbilicata, see *Umbilicus rupestris*.

Crambe, KRAM-bee; from Gr. *krambe*, cabbage. Hardy herbaceous plants. *Brassicaceae*.
cordifolia, kor-dif-OL-e-a, heart shaped.
maritima, mar-IT-im-a, of the sea. The Sea Kale.
orientalis, or-e-en-TA-lis, eastern – Eastern Asia (China).

Crassula, CRAS-sul-a; diminutive form from L. *crassus*, thick, referring to the thick or fleshy leaves. Greenhouse succulents. *Crassulaceae*.
  arborescens, ar-bor-ES-senz, tree-like.
  coccinea, kok-SIN-e-a, scarlet.
  cotyledon, see *C. arborescens*.
  dichotoma, dye-ko-TOME-a, repeatedly dividing into two branches.
  falcata, see *C. perfoliata* var. *falcata*.
  lactea, LAK-te-a, milk white.
  obtusa, ob-TU-sa, blunt.
  perfoliata, per-fol-e-A-ta, perfoliate leaved – the leaves pierced by the stem.
  perfoliata var. *falcata*, fal-KA-ta, sickle-shaped – the leaves.

Crataegus, kra-TE-gus; Gr. *krataigos*, a flowering thorn, believed to be derived from *kratos*, strength, alluding to the hardness of the wood. Shrubs and trees. *Rosaceae*.
  calpodendron, kal-po-DEN-dron, from Gr. *kalpis*, urn; *dendron*, tree, the flowers being upright and urn-shaped.
  coccinea, kok-SIN-e-a, scarlet.
  cordata, kor-DA-ta, heart shaped, the leaves.
  crus-galli, kroos-GAL-le, literally a cock's leg. The Cockspur Thorn.
  laevigata, leve-GA-ta, smooth.
  macracantha, mak-kra-KAN-tha, with large spines.
  mollis, MOL-lis, soft, with soft hairs.
  monogyna, mon-o-JIN-a, having a single pistil.
  orientalis, or-e-en-TA-lis, eastern – Eastern Asia (China).
  oxyacantha, see *C. laevigata*.
  phaenopyrum, fe-no-PY-rum, from Gr. *phaeno*, visible; *pyrus*, pear, alluding to its likeness. Washington Thorn.
  punctata, punk-TA-ta, the fruits are speckled.
  tomentosa, see *C. calpodendron*.

Crepis, KRE-pis; from Gr. *krepis*, a sandal, reference not clear. Hardy annuals. *Compositae*.
  barbata, see *Tolpis barbata*.
  rubra, ROO-bra, red.

Crinodendron, kry-no-DEN-dron; from Gr. *krinon*, lily; *dendron*, tree, in reference to the flowers. Large shrubs or small trees. *Elaeocarpaceae*.

  hookerianum, hook-er-e-A-num, after Sir William Jackson Hooker (1785–1865), professor of botany, director of the Royal Botanic Gardens, Kew.
  patagua, pa-TAG-u-a, Mapuche name for this plant.

Crinum, KRY-num; from Gr. *krinon*, a lily. Greenhouse and hardy bulbous plants. *Amaryllidaceae*.
  bulbispermum, bul-be-SPER-mum, from Gr. *bolbos*, a bulb; *sperma*, a seed.
  capense, see *C. bulbispermum*.
  moorei, MOOR-e-e, after Dr. David Moore (1808–1879), Scottish botanist, director of National Botanic Gardens, Glasnevin from 1838–1879.
  × *powellii*, POW-el-e-i, raised by Mr. Powell of Old Hall, Southborough, Tonbridge Wells.

Crocosmia, kro-KOS-me-a; from Gr. *krokos*, saffron; *osme*, odour. The dried flowers emit a strong saffron smell when placed in water. Perennial monocot. *Iridaceae*.
  × *crocosmiiflora*, kro-kos-me-i-FLOR-a, flowers like *Crocosmia*.
  paniculata, pan-ik-ul-A-ta, flowers in a panicle or branching inflorescence.
  pottsii, POTTS-e-i, named in honour of Mr George Honington Potts of Lasswade, Edinburgh.

Crocus, KRO-kus; from Gr. *krokos*, saffron, possibly from *kroke*, a thread, the filaments of the styles being the source of the dye. Bulbous perennials. *Iridaceae*.
  angustifolius, an-gus-tif-O-le-us, having narrow leaves.
  aureus, see *C. flavus*.
  biflorus, bi-FLOR-us, two-flowered. The Scotch Crocus.
  chrysanthus, kris-ANTH-us, golden-flowered.
  flavus, FLA-vus, pure yellow – the flowers.
  minimus, MIN-e-mus, smallest.
  nudiflorus, nu-de-FLOR-us, naked-flowered – no foliage present.
  ochroleucus, ok-ro-LEW-kus, yellowish white flower.
  sativus, SAT-iv-us, cultivated. The Saffron Crocus.
  sieberi, SI-ber-e, possibly named after Franz Wilhelm Sieber (1789–1844), plant collector.
  susianus, see *C. angustifolius*.

vernus, VER-nus, spring flowering. The Dutch or spring crocuses are derived from this species.

versicolor, ver-SIK-o-lor, changing or varied colour.

Crossandra, kros-SAN-dra; from Gr. *krossos*, a fringe; *aner*, a man – fringed anthers. Evergreen shrubs and subshrubs. *Acanthaceae*.

infundibuliformis, in-fun-de-bul-E-for-mis, funnel-shaped.

Crucianella, kru-se-an-EL-la; diminutive form of L. *crux*, cross, the Crosswort. Herbaceous and rock plants. *Rubiaceae*.

maritima, mar-IT-im-a, of sea coasts.

stylosa, see *Phuopsis stylosa*.

Cryophytum, misapplied see below.

crystallinum, see *Mesembryanthemum crystallinum*.

Cryptocoryne, krip-to-KOR-in-e; from Gr. *kryptos*, hidden; *koryne*, a club – the club-like spadix is enclosed in the spathe. Tropical submerged aquatics. *Araceae*.

ciliata, sil-e-A-ta, an eyelash, fringed with fine hairs – the spath.

cordata, kor-DA-ta, heart shaped, the leaves.

Cryptogramma, krip-to-GRAM-ma; from Gr. *kryptos*, hidden; *gramme*, a line, the region of fruiting (spores) being concealed. Hardy ferns. *Pteridaceae*.

crispa, KRIS-pa, curled. The Parsley Fern.

Cryptomeria, krip-to-MEER-e-a; from Gr. *krytos*, hidden; *meris*, part, alluding to the hidden floral parts. Coniferous trees. *Cupressaceae*.

japonica, jap-ON-ik-a, of Japan.

Cucumis, KU-ku-mis; from L. *cucumis*, cucumber. Greenhouse climbing plants. *Cucurbitaceae*.

citrullus, see *Citrullus lanatus*.

melo, MEE-lo, melon. The Melon.

sativus, SAT-iv-us, cultivated. The Cucumber.

Cucurbita, ku-KER-bit-a; from L. *curbita*, a gourd. Greenhouse and tender climbing plants. Gourds and pumpkins. *Cucurbitaceae*.

pepo, PEEP-o, the pre-Linnaean name. The Vegetable Marrow.

pepo subsp. *ovifera*, o-VIF-er-a, egg-like, the fruit.

Cuitlauzina, ku-it-LAW-zee-na; named after Cuitlahuatzin, governor of Iztapalapa, Mexico. Orchids. *Orchidaceae*.

pendula, PEN-du-la, pendulous or weeping.

Cuphea, KU-fe-a; from Gr. *kyphos*, curved, the form of the seed pods. Greenhouse and bedding plants. *Lythraceae*.

ignea, IG-ne-a, fiery – the colour of flowers. The Cigar Plant.

llavea, la-VE-a; after Pablo de La Llave (1773–1833), Mexican priest, politician and naturalist.

miniata, see *C. llavea*.

platycentra, see *C. ignea*.

Cupressus, ku-PRES-sus; classical name, said to be from Gr. *kuo*, to produce; *parissos*, equal, alluding to the symmetrical form of *C. sempervirens;* possibly from an ancient L. word signifying a box, the wood once used for coffins. Coniferous trees – the Cypresses. *Cupressaceae*.

arizonica, ar-i-ZON-ik-a, from Arizona, U.S.A.

funebris, fu-NE-bris, pertaining to funerals.

lawsoniana, see *Chamaecyparis lawsoniana*.

lusitanica, loo-sit-A-nik-a, of Lusitania (Portugal).

macrocarpa, mak-ro-KAR-pa, large fruits.

nootkatensis, noot-ka-TEN-sis, of Nootka, North America.

obtusa, see *Chamaecyparis obtusa*.

pisifera, see *Chamaecyparis pisifera*.

sempervirens, sem-per-VEER-enz, from L. *semper*, ever; *virens*, green. Always green.

Cyananthus, sy-an-AN-thus; from Gr. *kyanos*, dark blue; *anthos*, a flower. Rock plants. *Campanulaceae*.

incanus, in-KA-nus, hoary or grey, the leaves.

Cyanus, sy-AN-us; from Gr. *kyanos*, dark blue, the name for the Cornflower. Annuals. *Compositae*.

segetum, seg-E-tum, of cornfields. The Cornflower.

Cyathea, sy-a-THE-a; from Gr. *kyatheion*, a little cup, the shape of the sori. Greenhouse tree Fern. *Cyatheaceae*.

dealbata, de-al-BA-ta, whitewashed, the colour of the under surface of the frond.

Cycas, SY-kas; from Gr. *kykas*, the name of a palm tree. *Cycadaceae*.
revoluta, rev-ol-U-ta, revolute or rolled back, the leaves.

Cyclamen, SIK-la-men; name a contraction of Gr. *kyklaminos*, from *kyklos*, a circle, alluding to the coiled stem of the seed vessel. Herbaceous plants. *Primulaceae*.
cilicicum, si-LIS-ik-um, from Cilicia, an ancient region of Asia Minor.
coum, COO-um, of Kos, a Greek Island.
coum subsp. *caucasicum*, kaw-KAS-ik-um, Caucasian.
europaeum, see *C. purpurascens*.
hederifolium, hed-er-e-FO-le-um, the leaves resembling *Hedera* (ivy).
ibericum, see *C. coum* subsp. *caucasicum*.
latifolium, see *C. persicum*.
neapolitanum, see *C. hederifolium*.
persicum, PER-sik-um, of Persia.
purpurascens, pur-pur-AS-senz, purple – the flowers.
repandum, re-PAN-dum, scalloped, the leaf margins.

Cydonia, sy-DO-ne-a; classical name for the common quince, derived from the town of Cydon, Crete. Trees. *Rosaceae*.
japonica, see *Chaenomeles japonica*.
maulei, see *Chaenomeles japonica*.
oblonga, ob-LON-ga, oblong the leaves.
vulgaris, see *C. oblonga*.

Cymbalaria, sim-bal-AR-e-a; from Gr. *kymbalon*, a cymbal; the shape of the leaves in some species. The Ivy-leaved Toadflax. Herbaceous perennials. *Plantaginaceae*.
aequitriloba, e-kwit-ril-O-ba, three equal lobes, the leaves.
muralis, mu-RA-lis, from L. *muralis*, of walls; found on walls.

Cymbidium, sim-BID-e-um; from Gr. *kymbe*, a boat, referring to the hollow in the lip. Cool-house orchids. *Orchidaceae*.
eburneum, eb-UR-ne-um, like ivory.
lowianum, low-e-A-num, after Messrs. Low & Co. Clapham nurseries.

tracyanum, tra-se-A-num, after Henry Amos Tracy (1850–1910), Orchid and bulb specialist of Twickenham.

Cynara, sin-AR-a; from Gr. *kyon*, a dog, with reference to spines on involucre suggesting dog's teeth. Perennial herbs. *Compositae*.
cardunculus, kar-DUN-ku-lus, resembles a thistle. The Cardoon or Spanish Artichoke.
scolymus, SKOL-im-us, after or like *Scolymus*. The Giant Artichoke.

Cynoglossum, sin-o-GLOS-sum; from Gr. *kyon*, dog; *glossa*, a tongue. The Hound's-tongue. Annuals, biennials and perennials. *Boraginaceae*.
amabile, am-A-bil-e, lovely.
coelestinum, see *Adelocaryum coelestinum*.
wallichii, wol-LICH-e-i, after Nathaniel Wallich (1786–1854), Danish surgeon and botanist, who worked for the East India Company and became superintendent of the Calcutta Botanic Garden.

Cyperus, SY-per-us; from old Gr. name *kypeiros*, for a sedge. Waterside perennials. *Cyperaceae*.
alternifolius, al-ter-ne-FO-le-us, alternate leaved.
longus, LONG-us, long, tall.
papyrus, pa-PY-rus, paper. The Egyptian Papyrus.

Cyphomandra, misapplied see below.
betacea, see *Solanum betaceum*.

Cypripedium, sip-re-PE-de-um; from Gr. *kypris*, one of the names of Venus, and *podion*, a little foot or slipper, literally Venus' Slipper, now referred to as Lady's Slipper Orchid. Greenhouse and hardy terrestrial orchids. *Orchidaceae*.
bellatulum, see *Paphiopedilum bellatulum*.
calceolus, kal-se-O-lus, a little slipper.
insigne, see *Paphiopedilum insigne*.
macranthos, mak-RANTH-os, large-flowered.
reginae, re-JI-ne, of the queen – Queen Victoria.
spectabile, see *C. reginae*.
spicerianum, see *Paphiopedilum spicerianum*.
superbiens, see *Paphiopedilum superbiens*.
venustum, see *Paphiopedilum venustum*.
villosum, see *Paphiopedilum villosum*.

Cyrtanthus, ser-TAN-thus; from Gr. *kyrtos*, arched; *anthos*, a flower; the flowers bend

down from the main stalk. Greenhouse
bulbs. *Amaryllidaceae.*

angustifolius, an-gus-tif-O-le-us, having narrow
leaves.

elatus, e-LA-tuss, tall.

lutescens, see *C. ochroleucus*.

mackenii, mak-KEN-e-i, discovered at Port Natal,
by Mr Mark J. McKen.

macowanii, mak-KOW-an-e-i, named for Mr
MacOwan, who sent specimens to England
from Africa.

ochroleucus, ok-ro-LEW-kus, yellow-white or
cream-coloured.

Cyrtochilum, ker- (or ser-) to-KIL-um; from
Gr. *kyrtos*, curved; *cheilos*, lip. Orchids.
Orchidaceae.

flexuosum, fleks-u-O-sum, zig-zag – the flower
stem.

macranthum, mak-RANTH-um, large-flowered.

Cyrtomium, kyr-TO-me-um; from Gr.
kyrtos, arched; in allusion to its growth
habit. Ferns. *Dryopteridaceae.*

falcatum, fal-KA-tum, hooked – curved pinnae.
The False Holly Fern.

Cystopteris, sist-OP-ter-is; from Gr. *kystis*, a
bladder; *pteris*, a fern. Bladder Fern. Hardy
ferns. *Cystopteridaceae.*

bulbifera, bul-BIF-er-a, referring to the little
green balls or buds under fronds.

fragilis, FRAJ-il-is, fragile – finely leaved.

montana, mon-TA-na, of mountains.

Cytisophyllum, sy-tis-o-FIL-lum; derived
from the genus and section. One species a
shrub. *Leguminosae.*

sessilifolium, ses-sil-if-O-le-um, sessile leaved, that
is, stalkless.

Cytisus, SY-tis-us; from Gr. *kytisos*, trefoil,
pertaining to the leaves of many species.
Shrubs. *Leguminosae.*

albus, AL-bus, white.

ardoinii, ar-DO-in-e-i after Honoré Jean Baptiste
Ardoino (1819–1874) French botanist, who
discovered it.

× *dallimorei*, dal-le-MORE-i, after William Dal-
limore (1871–1959), English botanist.

decumbens, de-KUM-benz, prostrate.

emeriflorus, em-er-e-FLOR-us, possibly meaning
cultivated flower.

fragrans, see *C. supranubius.*

hirsutus, hir-SU-tus, hairy.

× *kewensis*, kew-EN-sis, of Kew Gardens.

leucanthus, see *Chamaecytisus albus.*

purgans, PUR-gans, purging – its use in medicine.

purpureus, pur-PUR-re-us, purple.

scoparius, sko-PAR-e-us, from L. *scopae*, a broom,
a broom made of twigs. The Common
Broom.

sessilifolius, see *Cytisophyllum sessilifolium.*

supranubius, sue-pra-NEW-be-us, above the
clouds, growing at altitude.

Daboecia, da-bo-E-se-a; from its Irish
name, St. Dabeoc's Heath. Dwarf shrub.
Ericaceae.

cantabrica, kan-TAB-rik-a, Cantabria, Spain.

polifolia, see *D. cantabrica.*

Dactylis, DAK-til-is; from Gr. *daktylos*, a
finger, from the shape of the panicle. The
Cocksfoot Grass. Ornamental grass. *Poaceae.*

glomerata, glom-er-A-ta, clustered.

Dactylorhiza, dak-til-o-RHY-za; from Gr.
daktylos, finger; *rhiza*, a root, referring to the
shape of the tubers. Orchids. *Orchidaceae.*

foliosa, fo-le-O-sa, profusely leaved, notably the
flower stalks.

maculata, mak-ul-A-ta, spotted.

sambucina, sam-BU-kin-a, *Sambucus* (scent
resembling elder).

Dahlia, DAH-le-a; named after Andreas
Dahl (1751–1789), a Swedish botanist and
pupil of Linnaeus. Originally (and still in
America) pronounced DAH-le-a and not
DAY-le-a as commonly heard. The dahlias
usually grown in gardens are from hybrids
from species rarely seen. Half-hardy tuberous herbaceous perennials. *Compositae.*

coccinea, kok-SIN-e-a, scarlet.

imperialis, im-peer-e-A-lis, powerful.

juarezii, ju-a-REZ-e-i, after President Benito
Jaurez (1806–1872) of Mexico, introduced
to the Netherlands from Mexico although
possibly itself an early Mexican cultivar.

merckii, MERK-e-i, after Heinrich Johann Merck
(1770–1853), Merchant banker and Senator
of Hamburg.

variabilis, var-e-AB-il-is, variable coloured.

zimapani, see *Cosmos diversifolius.*

Dalea, DAY-le-a; after Dr. Samuel Dale (1659–1739), English botanist, from Braintree, Essex. Hardy annual and Greenhouse sub-shrub. *Leguminosae.*

  alopecuroides, see *D. leporina.*

  mutabilis, see *D. obovatifolia.*

  leporina, lep-o-RE-na, hare-like from L. *lepus*, hare. Hare's Foot Prairie Clover.

  obavatifolia, o-bow-VAR-te-fo-le-a, inverted ovate, that is egg shaped with the broadest end uppermost.

Danae, DAN-ee; in Greek mythology the name of the daughter of King Acrisius of Argos. Shrub. *Asparagaceae.*

  racemosa, ras-em-O-sa, resembling a raceme.

Daphne, DAF-ne; Gr. name of *Laurus nobilis*, some say named after the river god's daughter in Grecian mythology, who, on being pursued by Apollo, prayed for aid, and was transformed into a Laurel tree. Shrubs. *Thymelaeaceae.*

  blagayana, blag-ay-A-na, discovered in Sveti Lavrent region of Slovenia by a local farmer in 1837. A flowering branch was presented to Count Rihard Blagnay who forwarded the specimen to his friend, the botanist, Henrik Freyer.

  cneorum, ne-OR-um, old Greek name.

  collina, see *D. sericea.*

  indica, IN-dik-a, of India.

  laureola, LAW-re-o-la, a little laurel. The Spurge Laurel.

  mezereum, me-ZE-re-um, probably from Persian, *mazaryum*, the Spurge Olive; some authorities believe the word to signify death, the berries being poisonous. The Mezerion.

  odora, od-O-ra, sweetly scented.

  petraea, pet-RE-a, growing on rocks.

  pontica, PON-tik-a, Pontic, the shores of the Black Sea.

  rupestris, see *D. petraea.*

  sericea, ser-IS-e-a, silky – the leaves.

Darlingtonia, dar-ling-TO-ne-a; after Dr. William Darlington (1782–1863), of Philadelphia, physician and botanist. Hardy herbaceous foliage plant. Insectivorous. *Sarraceniaceae.*

  californica, kal-if-OR-nik-a, of California.

Darmera, DAR-mer-a; in honour of Karl Darmer (1843–1918), founder and first president of the Allgemeinen Deutschen Gartner-Verein. Perennial herb. *Saxifragaceae.*

  peltata, pel-TA-ta, shaped like a shield, the leaves.

Dasylirion, das-e-LIR-e-on; from Gr. *dasys*, thick; *leirion*, lily; referring to the crowded leaves and flowers. Greenhouse evergreen foliage plants. *Asparagaceae.*

  glaucophyllum, glaw-ko-FIL-um, glaucous-coloured – the leaves.

Datura, day-TU-ra; vernacular East Indian name. Half-hardy annuals and greenhouse perennials and shrubs. *Solanaceae.*

  ceratocaula, ser-at-o-KAW-la, horn-stalked.

  cornucopia, see *D. metel.*

  fastuosa, see *D. metel.*

  inermis, see *D. stramonium.*

  innoxia, in-nox-E-a, from L. *innoxia*, harmless, not having prickles.

  metel, ME-tel, from Arabic *matil*, referring to the apothecaries nut, of metel, origin uncertain.

  meteloides, see *D. innoxia.*

  sanguinea, see *Brugmansia sanguinea.*

  sauveolens, see *Brugmansia suaveolens.*

  stramonium, stra-MO-ne-um, old botanic name for the Thorn Apple of medicine. The Thorn Apple.

Daucus, DAW-kus; from the ancient Gr. name *daukos*. Annual and biennial. *Apiaceae.*

  carota, ka-RO-ta, red-rooted. The Carrot.

Davallia, da-VAL-le-a; after Edmund Davall (1763–1798), Swiss botanist. Tropical and temperate ferns. *Davalliaceae.*

  bullata, bul-LA-ta, blistered.

  canariensis, ka-nar-e-EN-sis, of the Canary Islands.

  decora, dek-OR-a, from L. *decorus*, graceful, neat or becoming.

  denticulata, den-tik-u-LA-ta, toothed, the leaves.

  elegans, see *D. denticulata.*

  fijiensis, fee-jee-EN-sis, of the Fiji Islands.

  hirta, HER-ta, hairy.

  mariesii, mar-EES-e-i, after Charles Maries (1851–1902), plant collector and botanist, who worked for the firm of James Veitch & Sons collecting in Japan and China.

mooreana, moor-e-AN-a, after Thomas Moore (1821–1887), botanist and gardener, author of The Ferns of Great Britain and Ireland.

tyermanni, ty-er-MAN-e, after Mr. Tyerman, curator of Waverley Botanic Garden and Park, Liverpool.

Davidia, da-VID-e-a; after Abbe Jean Pierre Armand David (1826–1900), French missionary and plant collector in China. Tree. *Cornaceae.*

involucrata, in-vol-u-KRA-ta, from L. *involucrum*, roll in, envelop, referring to the bracts covering the inflorescence.

Decumaria, dek-u-MA-re-a; from L. *decimus*, ten, the number of the calyx and seed-pods often being in tens. Twining plants. *Hydrangeaceae.*

barbara, BAR-bar-a, foreign.

Deinanthe, de-in-AN-the; from Gr. *deinos*, wonderful; *anthos*, flower. Herbaceous perennial. *Hydrangeaceae.*

caerulea, se-RU-le-a, sky-blue.

Delonix, de-LON-ix; from Gr. *delos*, conspicuous; *onux*, a claw, alluding to the long clawed petals. Trees. *Leguminosae.*

regia, RE-je-a, royal, princely.

Delosperma, de-lo-SPER-ma; from Gr. *delos*, manifest; *sperma*, seed. The seeds being clear or obvious, exposed to the eye. Perennials. *Aizoaceae.*

cooperi, KOO-per-e, after Thomas Cooper (1815–1913), English plant collector, who collected in South Africa between 1859 to 1862.

echinatum, ek-in-A-tum, the spines resembling a hedgehog.

Delphinium, del-FIN-e-um; from Gr. *delphin*, a dolphin, from the fancied resemblance of the flower-spur to a dolphin's head. Annuals, biennials and herbaceous perennials. *Ranunculaceae.*

ajacis, see *Consolida ajacis.*

californicum, kal-if-OR-nik-um, native habitat California.

cardinale, kar-din-A-le, scarlet.

consolida, see *Consolida regalis.*

elatum, e-LA-tum, tall.

formosum, for-MO-sum, beautiful.

grandiflorum, gran-dif-LO-rum, large flowered.

nudicaule, nu-di-KAW-le, naked-stemmed.

sulphureum, see *Consolida sulphurea.*

tatsienense, tat-SE-en-EN-se, from Tasienlu (Kangding), western China.

triste, TRIS-te, sad, the dull blue of the flowers.

zalil, ZAL-il, after *Zalil*, the vernacular Afghanistan name.

Dendrobium, den-DRO-be-um; from Gr. *dendron*, a tree; *bios*, life, in allusion to the wild plants being found on trees. Tropical orchids, many species epiphytes on trees. *Orchidaceae.*

bigibbum, big-IB-bum, two-humped.

chrysanthum, kris-ANTH-um, golden flowered.

chrysotoxum, kris-ot-OX-um, golden arched.

dalhousianum, see *D. pulchellum.*

densiflorum, den-sif-LOR-um, dense flowered.

fimbriatum, fim-bre-A-tum, fringed.

infundibulum, in-fun-DIB-u-lum, shaped like a funnel.

nobile, NO-bil-e, notable, renowned.

polyanthum, pol-e-ANTH-um, many flowered.

primulinum, see *D. polyanthum.*

pulchellum, pul-KEL-um, beautiful.

speciosum, spes-e-O-sum, showy.

wardianum, ward-e-A-num, after Nathaniel Bagshaw Ward (1791–1868), English doctor and inventor of the Wardian case.

Dendrochilum, den-dro-KI-lum; from Gr. *dendron*, a tree; *cheilos*, a lip, referring to lipped flowers and growing on trees. Tropical orchids. *Orchidaceae.*

cobbianum, kob-i-A-num, after William Cobb (died 1922), businessman and orchid collector.

filiforme, fil-if-OR-me, thread-like.

glumaceum, glu-MA-see-um, flower spike resembling grass.

Dendromecon, den-DROM-e-kon; from Gr. *dendron*, a tree; *mecon*, a poppy. Shrubby perennial. *Papaveraceae.*

rigida, RIG-id-a, rigid, the Bush Poppy.

Dentaria, den-TAR-e-a; from L. *dens*, a tooth, in reference to the tooth-like scales on the roots. Herbaceous perennials. *Brassicaceae.*

bulbifera, see *Cardamine bulbifera.*

digitata, see *Cardamine pentaphyllos.*

enneaphylla, see *Cardamine enneaphyllos.*

Desfontainia, des-fon-TA-ne-a; after Rene Louiche Desfontaines (1750–1833), French botanist, professor of botany at the Jardin des Plantes, Paris. Evergreen shrub. *Columelliaceae.*
  spinosa, spi-NO-sa, spiny.

Desmodium, des-MO-de-um; from Gr. *desmon*, chain, referring to the jointed pod. Tender shrubs. *Leguminosae.*
  canadense, kan-a-DEN-se, of Canada.
  elegans, EL-e-ganz, elegant.
  gyrans, see *Codariocalyx motorius.*
  tiliifolium, see *D. elegans.*

Deutzia, DOYTS-e-a; named in commemoration of Johan van der Deutz (1743–1788), Dutch patron of Carl Thunberg. Shrubs. *Hydrangeaceae.*
  corymbosa, kor-im-BO-sa, corymbose, flowers in broad corymb.
  crenata, kre-NA-ta, cut in round scallops; leaves crenate.
  discolor, DIS-ko-lor, various colours – the flowers.
  gracilis, GRAS-il-is, slender.
  scabra, SKA-bra, rough, the bark.
  setchuenensis, setsh-u-en-EN-sis, of Sichuan province, China.
  sieboldiana, se-bold-e-AN-a, after Philipp Franz Balthazar von Siebold ((1796–1866), botanist, traveler in Japan and author.
  vilmorinae, see *D. discolor.*

Dianthus, di-AN-thus; from Gr. *dios*, God or divine in respect of Zeus; *anthos*, a flower. A plant name used by Theophrastus. The Divine flower. Annuals, biennials and perennials. The Carnation and Pink family. *Caryophyllaceae.*
  allwoodii, hybrid crosses produced from *D. caryophyllus* × *D. plumarius*. Allwoodii group.
  alpinus, al-PINE-us, alpine.
  anatolicus, an-at-OL-ik-us, of Anatolia, Turkey.
  atrorubens, see *D. carthusianorum* subsp. *atrorubens.*
  barbatus, bar-BA-tus, bearded. The Sweet William.
  caesius, SE-se-us, light blue. The Cheddar Pink.
  callizonus, kal-e-ZO-nus, beautifully zoned or banded.
  carthusianorum, kar-THU-se-an-OR-um, of the Carthusian Monastery of Grand Chartreuse, France.

carthusianorum subsp. *atrorubens*, at-ro-RU-bens, dark red.
  caryophyllus, kar-e-o-FIL-lus, from Gr. *karya*, walnut; *phyllon*, a leaf, in reference to the clove-like fragrance. An old name used for an unrelated shrub producing the cloves of commerce. The Clove Pink.
  chinensis, tshi-NEN-sis, of China.
  cruentus, kru-EN-tus, dark blood-red.
  deltoides, del-TOY-dees, triangular, shape of the Greek letter delta on the petals. The Maiden Pink.
  glacialis, glas-e-A-lis, from Alpine glacier regions.
  graniticus, gran-IT-ik-us, of granite rocks.
  gratianopolitanus, gra-te-an-o-pol-e-TA-nus, for Grenoble, Dauphine, France.
  microlepis, mi-kro-LE-pis, having small scales.
  neglectus, see *D. seguieri* subsp. *gautieri.*
  plumarius, plu-MAR-e-us, from L. *plumeus*, feathery. The flowers being frilled or feathered. The Pink.
  seguieri, say-gu-e-AYR-re, after Jean-Francois Seguier (1703–1784), French astronomer and botanist.
  seguieri subsp. *gautieri*, gaw-te-AYR-i, after Maria Clement Gaston Gautier (1841–1911) French botanist and collector.
  sinensis, see *D. chinensis.*
  squarrosus, skwar-RO-sus, rough or scurfy.
  superbus, su-PER-bus, superb. The Fringed Pink.

Diascia, di-AS-ke-a; from Gr. *di*, two; *askos*, a pouch, referring to the two-spurred corolla. Low slender herbs. *Scrophulariaceae.*
  barberae, BAR-ber-e, collected in South Africa by Col. James Henry Bowker and sent in 1870 to Kew by his sister Mary Elizabeth Barber (1818–1899).

Dicentra, di-SEN-tra; from Gr. *di*, two; *kentron*, a spur, alluding to the two Spurs of the petals. Hardy herbaceous. *Papaveraceae.*
  chrysantha, see *Ehrendorferia chrysantha.*
  cucullaria, ku-kul-LAR-e-a, hooded.
  eximia, eks-IM-e-a, excellent, choice.
  formosa, for-MO-sa, handsome.
  spectabile, see *Lamprocapnos spectabilis.*

Dichelostemma, dy-kel-O-stem-a; from Gr. *dichelos*, with two prongs; *stemma*, wreath or garland. Corms. *Asparagaceae.*
  capitatum, kap-it-A-tum, flowers clustered in a head.
  congestum, kon-JES-tum, crowded, the flowers.

Dichorisandra, dik-or-e-ZAN-dra; from Gr. *dis*, two; *choris*, apart; *aner*, man; referring to the way two stamens stand apart. Perennial herbs. *Commelinaceae.*
 mosaica, mo-SA-ik-a, mosaic variegation.
 reginae, re-JI-ne, queen – Queen Victoria.
 thyrsiflora, thir-sif-LOR-a, thyrse flowered.

Dicksonia, dik-SO-ne-a; after James Dickson (1738–1822), British botanist. Tree ferns. *Dicksoniaceae.*
 antarctica, see *Balantium antarcticum.*
 squarrosa, skwar-RO-sa, rough or shaggy.

Dictamnus, dik-TAM-nus; Classical Greek name for a perennial herb, *diktamnon*, dittany, the plant possibly being named after the Dikti mountain range, Crete where it occurs. Hardy herbaceous. *Rutaceae.*
 albus, AL-bus, white.
 fraxinella, see *D. albus.*

Didiscus, did-IS-kus; from Gr. *di*, two; *diskos*, a flat disk; the form of the flower head. Half-hardy annual. *Apiaceae.*
 caeruleus, ser-U-le-us, sky-blue.

Dieffenbachia, deef-fen-BAK-e-a; named by Schott after Herr Joseph Dieffenbach (1790–1863), plant collector and later gardener at the Royal Palace Gardens Schonbrunn, Vienna. Evergreen perennial herbs. *Araceae.*
 × *bausei*, BAWS-e-i, after C.F. Bause (c. 1839–1895), German born nurseryman, South Norwood, Middlesex.
 × *memoria-corsii*, me-MOR-e-a-KOR-se-i, hybrid cross dedicated to the memory of Marquis Corsi Salviati, by his son.
 shuttleworthiana, shutl-WORTH-e-an-a, after Edward Shuttleworth (1829–1909), plant collector and nurseryman. Shuttleworth collected in South America around 1873 for William Bull.

Dierama, di-er-A-ma; from Gr. *dierama*, a funnel, alluding to the shape of the flowers. Bulbous perennial. *Iridaceae.*
 pulcherrimum, pul-KER-rim-um, most beautiful.

Diervilla, di-er-VIL-la; after M. Dierville, a French surgeon who travelled in Canada. Flowering shrubs. *Caprifoliaceae.*

 floribunda, see *Weigela floribunda.*
 florida, FLO-rid-a, from L. *floridus*, flowery.
 rosea, RO-ze-a, rose-coloured.

Dietes, dy-E-teez; from Gr. *di*, two; *etes*, affinities. Rhizomatous plants. *Iridaceae.*
 bicolor, BIK-ol-or, two-coloured.
 robinsoniana, rob-in-SO-ne-A-na, named by Mueller commemorating Sir Hercules Robinson, Governor of New South Wales.

Digitalis, dij-it-A-lis; Latinized version of the German name (Fingerhut) from L. *digitus*, a finger, the flower resembling the finger of a glove. Biennials and herbaceous perennials. *Plantaginaceae.*
 ferruginea, fer-ru-JIN-e-a, rusty – the flowers being brownish.
 lutea, LU-te-a, yellow.
 purpurea, pur-PUR-e-a, purple coloured.

Dimorphanthus, misapplied see below.
 mandschuricus, see *Aralia elata* var. *mandshurica.*

Dimorphotheca, DI-mor-FOTH-eek-a; from Gr. *di*, two; *morphe*, shape; *theka*, a case or capsule, in reference to the two kinds of achenes formed. The achenes of the disc and ray florets differ. Annuals and perennials. *Compositae.*
 aurantiaca, see *D. sinuata.*
 pluvialis, plu-ve-A-lis, rainy, presumably alluding to the natural season of flowering.
 sinuata, sin-u-A-ta, wavy margin or scalloped-leaved.

Dionaea, di-o-NE-a; from Gr. Dione, the mother of Aphrodite. Greenhouse herbaceous insectivorous plant. *Droseraceae.*
 muscipula, mus-KIP-u-la, fly-catching. The Venus Flytrap.

Dioscorea, di-o-SKOR-e-a; after Dioscorides, a Greek physician. Hardy tuberous-rooted climber. *Dioscoreaceae.*
 elephantipes, el-ef-AN-tip-ez, elephant's foot. In allusion to the shape of the rootstock.
 polystachya, pol-e-STAK-e-a, many spiked. Chinese yam.

Diosma, di-OZ-ma; from Gr. *dios*, divine; *osme*, odour, referring to the perfume. Greenhouse shrub with fragrant leaves. *Rutaceae.*

capitata, see *Audouinia capitata*.
ericoides, see *D. hirsuta*.
hirsuta, hir-SU-ta, hairy.

Diospyros, di-o-SPY-ros; from Gr. *dios*, divine; *puros*, wheat or food; food of the gods. Persimmon or Date Palm. *Ebenaceae*.
   kaki, KA-ke, native Japanese name. The Persimmon of Japan.
   lotus, LO-tus, after the Lotus, which if eaten causes forgetfulness. The Persimmon of Southern Europe. The Date-plum.
   virginiana, vir-jin-e-A-na, of Virginia. The Virginian Date Plum.

Dipelta, di-PEL-ta; from Gr. *di*, two; *pelta*, and shield, referring to the pair of opposite bracts. Shrubs. *Caprifoliaceae*.
   floribunda, flor-e-BUN-da, abundant or free flowering.
   ventricosa, see *D. yunnanensis*.
   yunnanensis, yun-nan-EN-sis, of Yunnan, west China.

Diplacus, DIP-la-kus; from Gr. *dis*, two; *plakos*, placenta, seed capsule with two placentas. Greenhouse flowering shrub. *Phrymaceae*.
   glutinosus, glu-tin-O-sus, sticky.
   puniceus, pu-NIK-e-us, reddish-purple.

Dipladenia, dip-la-DE-ne-a; from Gr. *diploos*, double; *aden*, gland, two gland-like developments on the ovary. Tropical evergreen flowering climbers. *Apocynaceae*.
   × *amabilis*, am-A-bil-is, lovely.
   boliviensis, see *Mandevilla boliviensis*.
   brearleyana, see *Odontadenia macrantha*.

Diplopappus, dip-lo-PAP-pus; from Gr. *diploos*, double; *pappos*, a plume, in allusion to the feathery awns which crown the seed. Annual and perennial herbs. *Compositae*.
   chrysophyllus, kris-of-IL-lus, golden leaves.

Dipsacus, DIP-sa-kus; from Gr. *dipsa*, thirst, referring to the cavity formed by the uniting of the leaves round the stem, which collects and holds water. Biennial or short-lived perennial. *Caprifoliaceae*.
   acaulis, a-KAW-lis, stemless.
   fullonum, ful-LO-num, relating to fullers. The technique of raising the nap in woollen cloth. The Fullers' Teasel.

inermis, in-ER-mis, unarmed.
sylvestris, see *D. fullonum*.

Disa, DY-sa; the net-veined dorsal sepal of the flowers; alluding to the mythical Queen Disa who came to the King of Sveas clad in a fishing-net. Greenhouse terrestrial orchids. *Orchidaceae*.
   grandiflora, see *D. uniflora*.
   uniflora, uni-FLOR-a, one flowered, that is blooms solitary.

Disocactus, dis-o-KAK-tus; from Gr. *dis*, two or twice and *cactus*. Two-shaped cactus. Greenhouse cacti. *Cactaceae*.
   ackermannii, ak-er-MAN-ne-i, named after Georg Ackermann (fl. 1824), who collected it in Mexico.
   biformis, bif-OR-mis, two forms – simulating both *Epiphyllum* and *Phyllocactus*.
   flagelliformis, flaj-el-lif-OR-mis, flagellant or whip-like. The Rats-tail Cactus.
   × *mallisonii*, mal-le-SON-e-i, after Mr Mallinson, gardener to Sir Samuel Scott, who raised this hybrid.
   phyllanthoides, fil-lanth-OY-dees, resembling *Phyllanthus*.

Dodecatheon, do-dek-ATH-e-on; ancient name signifying 'Flower of the Twelve Gods'; from *dodeka*, twelve; *theos*, god. Herbaceous perennials. *Primulaceae*.
   clevelandii, KLEEVE-land-e-i, after Daniel Cleveland (1838–1929), natural historian and San Diego lawyer.
   hendersonii, hen-der-SO-ne-i, after Louis Forniquet Henderson (1853–1942), American Botanist and the first professor of botany at the University of Idaho.
   jeffreyi, JEF-re-e, after John Jeffrey (1826–1854), Scotish botanist and plant collector in North America.
   meadia, ME-de-a, after Richard Mead (1673–1754), English physician, Meadia was first suggested for the name of the genus, but not accepted by Linnaeus.

Dolichandra, DOL-e-kan-dra; from Gr. *dolikos*, long; *andros*, male; alluding to the long anthers. Climbing shrub. *Bignoniaceae*.

unguis-cati, un-gwis-KAT-e, cat's claw. The Cat's Claw vine.

Dolichos, DOL-ik-os; from Gr. *dolikos*, long; old Gr. name of a bean transferred to these closely related climbers. *Leguminosae.*
  lablab, see *Lablab purpureus.*

Dolichothele, dol-ik-o-THE-le; from Gr. *dolikos*, long; *thele*, a nipple, the elongated tubercles. Greenhouse cacti. *Cactaceae.*
  longimamma, long-im-AM-ma, long tubercled.

Doodia, DOOD-e-a; after Samuel Doody (1656–1706), a London apothecary and botanist, keeper of Chelsea Physic Garden. Evergreen ferns. *Blechnaceae.*
  aspera, AS-per-a, rough to the touch.
  caudata, kaw-DA-ta, tailed – the fronds.

Doronicum, dor-ON-ik-um; from the Arabic name *doronigi* or *doronakh*. Herbaceous perennials. *Compositae.*
  austriacum, AWS-tre-ak-um, of Austria.
  caucasicum, see *D. orientale.*
  orientale, or-e-en-TA-le, Eastern.
  plantagineum, plan-ta-JI-ne-um, leaves resembling *Plantago* (Plantain).

Doryopteris, dor-re-OP-teh-ris; from Gr. *dory*, a spear; *pteris*, a fern. Ferns. *Pteridaceae.*
  pedata, ped-A-ta, footed – the bird's claw-like fronds.
  pedata var. *palmata*, pal-MA-ta, palmate, like a hand – the fronds.

Douglasia, misapplied see *Vitaliana.*

Downingia, down-ING-e-a; after Andrew Jackson Downing (1815–1852), horticulturist and landscape gardener. Annuals. *Campanulaceae.*
  elegans, EL-e-ganz, elegant.
  pulchella, pul-KEL-la, pretty.

Draba, DRA-ba; old Gr. name for a cress. Annual or perennial herb. *Brassicaceae.*
  aizoides, ay-ZOY-dees, resembling *Aizoon.*
  aizoon, see *D. lasiocarpa.*
  bruniifolia, bru-ne-e-FO-le-a, *Brunia* leaved.
  dedeana, DED-e-an-a, after James Dede author of the English Botanist's Pocket Companion (1809).
  lasiocarpa, las-e-o-KAR-pa, hairy fruits.

pyrenaica, see *Petrocallis pyrenaica.*
× *suendermannii*, SOON-der-MAN-e-i, named for Franz Sundermann, nurseryman and hybridiser who established the Botanic Alpine Garden, Lindau, Bavaria in 1886.

Dracaena, drak-E-na; from Gr. *drakaina*, a female dragon, the juice when thickened supposed to resemble dragon's blood. Perennial herbs, shrubs and trees. *Asparagaceae.*
  amabilis, see *Cordyline fruticosa.*
  draco, DRAK-o, dragon.
  fragrans, FRA-granz, fragrant.
  godseffiana, see *D. surculosa.*
  goldieana, gold-e-A-na, after Rev. Hugh Goldie who collected it for Edinburgh Botanic Garden in 1870.
  surculosa, sir-KOO-lo-sa, producing suckers.
  terminalis, see *Cordyline fruticosa.*

Dracocephalum, drak-o-SEF-a-lum; from Gr. *drakon*, dragon; *kephale*, head, in allusion to the gaping mouth of the flower. Annuals and perennials. Dragon's Head. *Lamiaceae.*
  forrestii, for-RES-te-i, after George Forrest (1873–1932), Scottish plant collector. Forrest collected in China between 1904 and 1932.
  moldavica, mol-DA-ve-ka, Moldovian.
  nutans, nu-tanz, drooping or nodding.
  ruyschiana, rews-ki-AN-a, after Frederick Ruysch (1638–1731), Dutch botanist.
  virginianum, see *Physostegia virginiana.*

Dracula, dra-KU-la; diminutive form of Gr. *draco*, little dragon. Orchids. *Orchidaceae.*
  bella, BEL-la, beautiful or pretty.
  chimaera, KI-mer-a, weird, fanciful – the flowers.

Dracunculus, drak-UN-ku-lus, Latin name for another plant. The Dragon Arum. Herbaceous perennials. *Araceae.*
  vulgaris, vul-GAR-is, common.

Drimys, DRIM-is; from Gr. *drimus*, acrid, referring to the pungent taste of the bark and foliage. Evergreen trees and shrubs. *Winteraceae.*
  winteri, WIN-ter-i, after John Winter, the aromatic bark (Winter's Bark) being used as a preventative for scurvy. Winter captained the Elizabeth, one of Drakes ships.

Drosera, DROS-e-ra; from Gr. *droseros*, dewy, referring to the gland tipped hairs on the leaves. Bog plants. Insectivorous. *Droseraceae*.
  anglica, ANG-lik-a, of England.
  binata, bi-NA-ta, from L. *bina*, pairs; the type species having a 'T' leaf form splitting into pairs.
  capensis, ka-PEN-sis, of the Cape of Good Hope.
  dichotoma, see *D. binata*.
  longifolia, see *D. anglica*.
  rotundifolia, ro-tun-dif-O-le-a, round-leaved. The Sundew.

Dryas, DRI-as; from Gr. *dryas*, a Dryad or wood nymph; some authorities derive from Gr. *drys*, an oak, leaves of the *D. octopetala* resemble those of oak. Rock Plants. *Rosaceae*.
  drummondii, drum-MON-de-i, after Thomas Drummond (1780–1835), plant collector in Canada and the United States of America for Veitch Nurseries.
  octopetala, ok-to-PET-a-la, eight-petalled.

Dryopteris, dri-OP-ter-is; from Gr. *drys*, oak; *pteris*, a fern. The plants characteristically being found in oak woods. Ferns. *Dryopteridaceae*.
  cristata, kris-TA-ta, crested. In this case the word refers to the fringed margins of the fronds.
  erythrosora, er-ith-RO-sor-a, from Gr. *erythros*, red; *soros*, stack, pile or heap, having red spore cases.
  filix-mas, FIL-iks-mas, male fern, it being of tall and robust growth. The Male Fern.

Dypsis, DIP-sis; origin obscure named by Domini Francisci Noronha in 1787. Evergreen palms. *Arecaceae*.
  lutescens, lu-TES-senz, becoming yellow.

Ecballium, ek-bal-LE-um; from Gr. *ekballein*, to cast out, the seeds violently ejected. Herbaceous perennial. *Cucurbitaceae*.
  elaterium, el-at-E-re-um, impelling, the seeds expelled from ripe fruits. The Squirting Cucumber.

Eccremocarpus, ek-krem-o-KAR-pus; from Gr. *ekkremes*, pendant; *karpos*, fruit, the seed vessels being a slender pendulous pod. Half-hardy, sub-shrubby climber. *Bignoniaceae*.
  scaber, SKA-ber, rough – to the touch.

Echeveria, esh-e-VE-re-a; after Atanasio Echeverria y Godoy (fl. 1771–1803), Mexican botanical artist. Tender succulents. *Crassulaceae*.
  agavoides, ag-a-VOY-dees, resembling *Agave*.
  atropurpurea, atro-pur-PUR-e-a, deep purple.
  fulgens, FUL-jenz, shining or glowing.
  gibbiflora, gib-bif-LO-ra, humped flowers.
  metallica, see *E. gibbiflora*.
  retusa, see *E. fulgens*.
  secunda, sek-UN-da, one-sided flower spike.

Echinacea, ek-in-A-se-a; from Gr. *echinos*, hedgehog, referring to the prickly involucre. Hardy herbaceous perennials. *Compositae*.
  purpurea, pur-PUR-e-a, purple coloured.

Echinocactus, EK-in-o-KAK-tus; from Gr. *echinos*, a hedgehog; *cactus*, referring to the spiny plants. Greenhouse cacti. *Cactaceae*.
  grusonii, GRUS-o-ne-i, after Herman Gruson (1821–1895), German industrialist and avid cacti collector.
  horizonthalonius, hor-E-zon-thal-ON-e-us, with horizontal areoles.
  ingens, see *E. platyacanthus*.
  platyacanthus, plat-e-a-KAN-thus, with broad spines.
  polycephalus, pol-e-KEF-a-lus, alternatively pol-e-SEF-a-lus, many headed.

Echinocereus, EK-e-no-SE-re-us; from Gr. *echinos*, hedgehog; *cereus*, an allusion to the prickly plants. Greenhouse cacti. *Cactaceae*.
  chloranthus, klo-RANTH-us, green – the flowers.
  dasyacanthus, day-ze-a-KAN-thus, thick spines or spines close together.
  fendleri, FEND-ler-i, after August Fendler (1813–1883), German plant collector in North and Central America.
  pectinatus, pek-tin-A-tus, like a comb, the spines.
  poselgeri, pos-EL-ger-e, after Heinrich Poselger (1818–1883), plant collector South West United States (1850–1856).
  pulchellus, pul-KEL-lus, small and beautiful.
  viridiflorus, vir-id-e-FLOR-us, with green flowers.

Echinofossulocactus, EK-in-o-FOS-sul-o-KAK-tus; from Gr. *echinos*, a hedgehog; L. *fossula*, a groove; and *cactus*, the plants being prickly and grooved. Cacti. *Cactaceae*.
  coptonogonus, kop-ton-OG-on-us, notched or wavy – the ribs.

crispatus, kris-PA-tus, curled.

obvallatus, ob-val-LA-tus, fortified as with a rampart.

Echinops, EK-e-nops; from Gr. *echinos*, a hedgehog; *opsis*, like, in reference to the spines which surround the flower. Herbaceous perennials and biennials. *Compositae.*

banaticus, ban-NAT-ik-us, from Banat, a historical region in Central Europe.

ritro, RE-tro, South European vernacular name possibly meaning small.

sphaerocephalus, sfer-o-SEF-a-lus, round-headed – the flower head.

Echinopsis, ek-in-OP-sis; from Gr. *echinos*, a hedgehog; *opsis*, like; the plants are balls of spines. Greenhouse cacti. *Cactaceae.*

eyriesii, ey-REE-se-i, named for Alexander Eyries of Le Havre, cactus collector, who first introduced it from South America.

ferox, FE-roks, from L. *ferox*, fierce, very prickly.

macrogona, mak-ro-GO-na, large angled.

maximiliana, MAX-e-mil-e-A-na, after Prince Maximilian of Wied-Neuwied (1782–1867), German explorer, ethnologist and naturalist.

maximiliana subsp. *caespitosa*, ses-pit-O-sa, growing in tufts.

oxygona, ox-e-GO-na, with sharp angles.

pentlandii, PENT-land-e-i, after Joseph Barclay Pentland (1797–1873), Irish geographer, natural scientist and traveller. Whilst in Bolivia Pentland discovered and sent samples of this cacti to the Royal Botanic Gardens, Kew.

spachiana, spash-e-A-na, of Spachia, Mexico.

Echium, EK-e-um; from Gr. *echis*, a viper, an old belief in the plant (Viper's Bugloss) as a remedy for adder's bite or from Gr. *echion*, classical name used by Dioscorides. Annuals, biennials and perennials. *Boraginaceae.*

albicans, AL-bi-kans, whitish.

creticum, KRET-ik-um, Cretan.

plantagineum, plan-ta-JI-ne-um, leaves resembling *Plantago* (Plantain).

vulgare, vul-GAR-e, common.

Edraianthus, ed-ray-e-ANTH-us; from Gr. *edraios*, sessile; *anthos*, a flower. Rock plants. *Campanulaceae.*

dalmaticus, dal-MAT-ik-us, of Dalmatia.

graminifolius, gram-in-if-OL-e-us, grass-leaved.

pumilio, pew-MIL-e-o, rather dwarf.

serpyllifolius, ser-pil-if-O-le-us, leaves resemble *Thymus serpyllum* (thyme).

Edwardsia, misapplied see below.

grandiflora, see *Sophora tetraptera.*

Ehrendorferia, e-ren-DOR-fe-re-a; named in honour of Friedrich Ehrendorfer (1927 –), Austrian botanist, on his seventieth birthday. Biennial and perennial plant. *Papaveraceae.*

chrysantha, kris-ANTH-a, golden-flowered.

Eichhornia, ish-HOR-ne-a; after Johann Albrecht Friedrich Eichhorn (1779–1856), Prussian politician. Aquatic herbs. *Pontederiaceae.*

azurea, a-ZOR-e-a, Sky-blue, azure.

crassipes, KRAS-sip-eez, with a thick stem.

speciosa, see *E. crassipes.*

Elaeagnus, el-e-AG-nus; said to be from Gr. *elaia*, olive; *agnos*, the Greek name for *Vitex agnus-castus*. Stearn attributes it to Theophrastus and probably *heleagnos*, for a *Salix*, from Gr. *helodes*, marshy; *agnos*, lamb, or *hagnos*, pure, as in white. The masses of pure white fruits. Shrubs. *Elaeagnaceae.*

angustifolia, an-gus-tif-O-le-a, having narrow leaves. The Oleaster.

argentea, see *E. angustifolia.*

glabra, GLAB-ra, smooth – the leaves.

macrophylla, mak-rof-IL-a, with large leaves.

multiflora, mul-tif-LO-ra, many flowered.

pungens, PUN-jenz, piercing – the twigs are sharp pointed.

rhamnoides, ram-NOY-dees, like *Rhamnus* (buckthorn). The Sea Buckthorn.

Elaphoglossum, e-la-foe-GLOS-sum; from Gr. *elaphos*, a stag; *glossa*, a tongue, alluding to the shape of the fronds. Ferns. *Dryopteridaceae.*

crinitum, KRYN-it-um, hairy.

obovatum, ob-o-VAY-tum, inverted ovate, that is, egg-shaped with the broadest end uppermost.

Elatine, e-LAT-e-ne; ancient Gr. name used by Dioscorides. Submerged aquatics. *Elatinaceae.*

hexandra, hex-AN-dra, with six stamens.

macropoda, mak-ro-PO-da, from Gr. *macro*, large; *poda*, foot – stout stalked.

Elisena, misapplied see below.
  longipetala, see *Ismene longipetala*.

Elodea, el-O-de-a; from Gr. *helodes*, a marsh, the native habitat. Submerged aquatics. *Hydrocharitaceae*.
  canadensis, kan-a-DEN-sis, of Canada. Invasive pond weed.
  densa crispa, see *Lagarosiphon major.*

Embothrium, em-BOTH-re-um; from Gr. *en*, in; *bothrion*, a pit, referring to the structure of the anthers. Shrubs. *Proteaceae*.
  coccineum, kok-SIN-e-um, scarlet flowers.

Emilia, em-IL-e-a; derivation unknown probably commemorative. Half-hardy annual. *Compositae*.
  coccinea, kok-SIN-e-a, scarlet flowers.
  sagitta, see *Emilia coccinea*.

Empetrum, em-PE-trum; from Gr. *en*, in; *petros*, a rock, the plant haunting rocky places. Shrub. *Ericaceae*.
  nigrum, NI-grum, black – the berries.

Encelia, en-SE-le-a; named in honour of Christopher Encel, author on oak galls, 1577. Shrubs. *Compositae*.
  californica, kal-if-OR-nik-a, of California. The Californian Bush Sunflower.

Enkianthus, en-ki-AN-thus; from Gr. *enkyos*, pregnant; *anthos*, flower, in reference to the round, bell-shaped blossoms that give the allusion of a flower within a flower. Shrubs. *Ericaceae*.
  campanulatus, kam-pan-u-LAH-tus, bell-shaped.
  cernuus, SER-nu-us, drooping – the flowers.
  japonicus, jap-ON-ik-us, of Japan.

Ensete, en-SE-te; probably the Abyssinian vernacular name. Monocarpic perennial. *Musaceae*.
  ventricosum, ven-trik-O-sum, having a swelling on one side.

Eomecon, e-om-E-kon; from Gr. *eos*, dawn; *mecon*, a poppy, the Japanese 'Poppy of the Dawn'. Hardy perennial. *Papaveraceae*.
  chionantha, ki-on-AN-tha, snowy – the white flowers.

Epacris, e-PAK-ris; from Gr. *epi*, upon; *akros*, a summit; habitat on high ground. Greenhouse flowering shrubs. *Ericaceae*.
  hyacinthiflora, hy-a-SINTH-if-LO-ra, resembling hyacinth flowers.
  impressa, im-PRES-sa, flower tube with two depressions.
  longiflora, long-if-LO-ra, long-flowered.

Epidendrum, ep-e-DEN-drum; from Gr. *epi*, upon; *dendron*, a tree; growing upon trees. Epiphytic orchids. *Orchidaceae*.
  fragrans, see *Prosthechea fragrans*.
  radicans, RAD-e-kanz, producing roots.
  vittellinum, see *Prosthechea vitellina*.
  wallisii, wal-LIS-e-i, introduced in 1874 from New Grenada by Gustav Wallis (1830–1878), German born plant collector, employed by James Veitch and Sons, Chelsea.

Epigaea, ep-e-GAY-a; from Gr. *epi*, upon; *gaia*, earth, in allusion to its creeping habit. Creeping shrub. *Ericaceae*.
  repens, RE-penz, creeping.

Epilobium, ep-e-LO-be-um; from Gr. *epi*, upon; *lobos*, pod, the flowers appearing to be growing on the pod-like ovary. The Willow Herbs. Perennial herbs. *Onagraceae*.
  angustifolium, an-gus-tif-O-le-um, having narrow leaves. The Rose Bay Willow herb.
  dodonaei, dod-on-A-e, after Rembert Dodoens (1517–1585), Flemish Royal physician and herbalist, professor of medicine at Leiden.
  fleischeri, FLI-sher-i, after Johann Gottlieb Fleischer (1797–1838), German botanist and ornithologist.
  glabellum, glab-EL-um, small and smooth – the leaves.
  hirsutum, hir-SU-tum, hairy. Codlins and Cream.
  nummularifolium, num-mul-AR-e-FO-le-um, rounded leaves resembling money.
  obcordatum, ob-kor-DA-tum, obversely heart-shaped. The narrow end being at the base.
  rosmarinifolium, see *E. dodonaei*.

Epimedium, ep-im-E-di-um; Gr. name of obscure meaning for another plant. Herbaceous and rock plants. The Barrenworts. *Berberidaceae*.
  alpinum, al-PINE-um, alpine.
  diphyllum, dif-IL-lum, two-leaved.
  grandiflorum, gran-dif-LO-rum, large flowered.

macranthum, see *E. grandiflorum*.

pinnatum, pin-NA-tum, with pinnate leaves.

Epipactis, ep-ip-AK-tis; a name given by the Ancient Greeks and adopted for this genus. Orchids. *Orchidaceae*.

helleborine, hel-le-BOR-in-e, resembling *Helleborus* (hellebore).

latifolia, see *E. helleborine*.

palustris, pal-US-tris, found in marshy places.

Epiphyllum, ep-e-FIL-lum; from Gr. *epi*, upon; *phyllon*, a leaf; flowers borne on leaf-like branches. Greenhouse cacti. *Cactaceae*.

crenatum, kre-NA-tum, scallop-edged.

gaertneri, see *Hatiora gaertneri*.

oxypetalum, ox-e-PET-a-lum; blended from Gr. *oxys*, sharp; L. *petalum*, a petal – the petals being sharp pointed.

russellianum, see *Schlumbergera russelliana*.

truncatum, see *Schlumbergera truncata*.

Epithelantha, ep-e-thel-AN-tha; from Gr. *epi*, upon; *thele*, a nipple; *anthos*, a flower. The flowers are borne on tubercles. Cacti. *Cactaceae*.

micromeris, mi-kro-MER-is, small in all its parts.

Equisetum, ek-we-SE-tum; from L. *equus*, horse; *seta*, a bristle, the barren growths resembling horses' tails. Herbaceous perennial. The Horsetails. *Equisetaceae*.

sylvaticum, sil-VAT-ik-um, inhabiting woods.

Eragrostis, er-a-GROS-tis; from Gr. *eros*, love; *agrostis*, grass; in allusion to its beauty. Ornamental annual grass. *Poaceae*.

elegans, see *E. japonica*.

japonica, jap-ON-ik-a, of Japan.

Eranthemum, e-RAN-the-mum; from Gr. *eros*, love; *anthemon*, flower; referring to the beauty of the flowers. Tropical sub-shrubby flowering plants. *Acanthaceae*.

albiflorum, see *Pseuderanthemum albiflorum*.

andersonii, see *Pseuderanthemum andersonii*.

cooperi, see *Pseuderanthemum cooperi*.

Eranthis, e-RAN-this; from Gr. *er*, spring; *anthos*, a flower; referring to the early flowering. Tuberous perennials. *Ranunculaceae*.

cilicica, si-LIS-ik-a, from Cilicia, an ancient region of Asia Minor.

hyemalis, hi-em-A-lis, pertaining to winter. The Winter Aconite.

Ercilla, er-SIL-la; in honour of Don Alonso de Ercilla y Zuniga (1533–1594), Spanish poet. Hardy evergreen creeper. *Phytolaccaceae*.

spicata, spe-KA-ta, spiked – the inflorescence.

volubilis, see *E. spicata*.

Eremogone, er-e-MO-go-ne; from Gr. *eremos*, a desert; *gonu*, a joint or angle. Herbaceous perennials. Sandwort. *Caryophyllaceae*.

ledebouriana, led-e-boo-re-A-na, after Carl Friedrich von Ledebour (1785–1851), professor of science at the University of Tartu, Estonia.

Eremurus, er-e-MU-rus; from Gr. *eremos*, desert; *oura*, a tail; alluding to the single flower-spike. Herbaceous perennials. Desert Candle or the Foxtail Lily. *Xanthorrhoeaceae*.

aitchisonii, aitch-e-SO-ne-i, after Dr James Aitchison (1836–1898), British physician and botanist, who collected in India and Afghanistan.

bungei, see *E. stenophyllus*.

elwesii, see *E. aitchisonii*.

himalaicus, him-al-A-ik-us, Himalayan.

robustus, ro-BUS-tus, strong or robust.

stenophyllus, sten-o-FIL-lus, narrow-leaved.

Erepsia, e-REP-se-a; from Gr. *erepo*, to cover with a roof, in allusion to the hidden stamens. Succulent. *Aizoaceae*.

inclaudens, in-KLAW-denz, the flowers remaining expanded, not closing.

Erica, ER-ik-a (more correctly e-RI-ka); from Gr. *ereike*, Heath or heather. Shrubs. *Ericaceae*.

arborea, ar-BOR-e-a, tree-like.

australis, aws-TRA-lis, southern.

carnea, see *E. herbacea*.

× *cavendishiana*, KAV-en-dish-e-A-na, after William Cavendish (1790–1858), 6th Duke of Devonshire.

ciliaris, sile-AR-is, fringed with fine hairs – the leaves.

cinerea, sin-er-E-a, grey or ashen, the underparts of the leaves.

× *darleyensis*, dar-le-EN-sis, originated at the Darley Dale nursery.

gracilis, GRAS-il-is, slender.

herbacea, her-BA-se-a, herbaceous.

hyemalis, hi-em-A-lis, pertaining to winter.

lusitanica, loo-sit-A-nik-a, of Lusitania (Portugal).

mediterranea, see *E. herbacea*.

melanthera, mel-AN-ther-a, black anthers.

stricta, see *E. terminalis*.

terminalis, ter-min-A-lis, flowers terminal.

tetralix, te-TRA-liks, four leaves arranged crosswise.

vagans, VA-gans, wandering, widespread.

ventricosa, ven-trik-O-sa, swollen or bellied.

Erigeron, er-IJ-er-on; from Gr. *eri*, early (or ear, spring); *geron*, old (an old man), alluding to the hairy seed pappus; or, more probably, to the hoary appearance of the leaves of some species in spring. Herbaceous perennials. *Compositae.*

coulteri, KOL-ter-e, after Thomas Coulter (1793–1843), Irish botanist who collected in California and Mexico.

karvinskianus, kar-vin-sky-A-nus, after Wilhelm Friedrich Karwinsky von Karmin (1780–1855), German plant collector who introduced the species from Mexico.

mucronatus, see *E. karvinskianus*.

multiradiatus, mul-te-RA-de-a-tus, many-rayed.

philadelphicus, fil-a-DEL-fik-us, of Philadelphia, USA.

speciosus, spes-e-O-sus, handsome.

strigosus, strig-O-sus, bristly.

Erinacea, er-in-A-se-a; from L. *erinaceus*, a hedgehog, the branches being spiny. Evergreen shrub. *Leguminosae.*

anthyllis, an-THIL-is, from Gr. *anthos*, a flower; *ioulos*, down; the calyx being covered in a silky hair.

pungens, see *E. anthyllis*.

Erinus, er-I-nus; Greek name *erinos*, used by Dioscorides for a kind of basil and transferred to this genus. Perennial herbs. *Plantaginaceae.*

alpinus, al-PINE-us, alpine.

Eriobotrya, er-e-o-BOT-re-a; from Gr. *erion*, wool; *botrys*, a bunch of grapes; referring to the downy flower clusters. Frost tender evergreen shrubs and trees. *Rosaceae.*

japonica, jap-ON-ik-a, of Japan.

Eriocaulon, er-e-o-KAW-lon; from Gr. *erion*, wool; *kaulon*, a stem; alluding to the woolly stems of some species. Submerged aquatics. *Eriocaulaceae.*

aquaticum, a-KWAT-ik-um, aquatic.

septangulare, see *E. aquaticum*.

Eriogonum, er-e-o-GO-num; from Gr. *erion*, wool; *gonu*, a joint; the joints of the stems being downy. Hardy perennials. *Polygonaceae.*

compositum, kom-POS-it-um, compound – the flowers in a composite head.

fasciculatum, fas-sik-ul-A-tum, bundled, that is, the flowers.

umbellatum, um-bel-LA-tum, flowers in umbels.

Eriophorum, er-e-o-FOR-um; from Gr. *erion*, wool; *phoreo*, to bear, in allusion to the hairy fruits. Perennial grass-like herbs. Cottongrass. *Cyperaceae.*

angustifolium, an-gus-tif-O-le-um, having narrow leaves.

polystachion, see *E. angustifolium*.

vaginatum, va-jin-A-tum, sheathed.

Eriostemon, er-e-os-TE-mon; from Gr. *erion*, wool; *stemon*, a stamen; the downy stamens. Greenhouse shrubs. *Rutaceae.*

buxifolius, bux-if-O-le-us, resembling *Buxus* (Box) leaves.

× *pulchellus*, pul-KEL-lus, small and beautiful.

Erodium, er-O-deum; from Gr. *erodios*, a heron, in reference to the resemblance of the style and ovaries to the head and beak of that bird. Herbaceous and rock plants. The Heron's Bill or Storksbill. *Geraniaceae.*

amanum, am-A-num, from Mt. Amano, Syria.

chamaedryoides, see *E. reichardii*.

chrysanthum, kris-ANTH-um, golden flowered.

corsicum, KOR-sik-um, of Corsica.

glandulosum, glan-dul-O-sum, glandular.

guttatum, gut-TA-tum, spotted – the flowers.

macradenum, see *E. glandulosum*.

manescavi, man-es-KA-ve-i, after its finder M. Manescau, Mayor of Pau, France.

olympicum, ol-IM-pe-kum, Olympian, that is Mount Olympus.

pelargonifolium, see *E. trifolium*.

reichardii, ri-KAR-de-i, after Johann Jacob Reichard (1743–1782), German botanist and editor of several works of Linnaeus.

trichomanefolium, trik-o-ma-ne-FO-le-um, leaves resembling *Trichomanes*, a genus of ferns.

trifolium, trif-OL-e-um, from L. *tres*, three; *folium*, a leaf.

Eryngium, e-RING-e-um (or er-IN-je-um); from Gr. *eryngion*, a name for some sort of thistle with spiny-toothed leaves described by Theophrastus. Herbaceous perennials. The Eryngoes. *Apiaceae.*

alpinum, al-PINE-um, alpine.

amethystinum, am-e-this-TE-num, violet-blue.

bourgatii, boor-GA-te-i, after a French medical practitioner Bourgat who collected plants in the Pyrenees with Gouan in 1766–1767.

maritimum, mar-IT-im-um, belonging to the sea coasts. The Sea Holly.

planum, PLA-num, flat, with flat leaves.

Erysimum, er-IS-im-um; from Gr. *eryo*, to draw up; some of the species being supposed to raise blisters. Biennial and perennial, rock and border plants. *Brassicaceae.*

arkansanus, see *E. capitatum.*

capitatum, kap-it-A-tum, flowers clustered in a head.

× *cheiri*, KY-re, meaning obscure although some suggest it is from Arabic *keiri*, a name for a sweet smelling red flower, others from Gr. *cheir*, a hand; the flowers being suitable for hand bouquets.

linifolium, li-nif-O-le-um, resembling *Linum* (flax) leaves.

× *marshallii*, mar-SHAL-le-i, raised by John Marshall of Limburn.

ochroleucum, ok-ro-LEW-kum, yellow-white or cream-coloured.

perofskianum, per-of-SKE-a-num, possibly after Count Vasily Perovsky (1794–1857), military general and governor of Orenburg.

Erythraea, misapplied see below.

centaurium, see *Centaurium erythraea.*

massonii, see *Centaurium maritimum.*

Erythrina, er-ith-RE-na; from Gr. *erythros*, red, referring to colour of flowers. Half-hardy flowering shrub. The Coral tree. *Leguminosae.*

crista-galli, KRIS-ta-GAL-li, a cock's comb.

Erythronium, er-ith-RO-ne-um; from Gr. *erythros*, red; that being the colour of the flowers of the European species. Bulbous plants. *Liliaceae.*

americanum, a-mer-e-KAY-num, of the Americas.

californicum, kal-if-OR-nik-um, native habitat California.

citrinum, sit-RI-num, citron-yellow, the flowers.

dens-canis, dens-KA-nis, a dog's tooth. The Dog's-tooth violet.

hartwegii, see *E. multiscapideum.*

howellii, HOW-el-e-i, after Thomas Howell (1842–1912), plant collector in Oregon.

multiscapideum, mul-te-ska-pe-DE-um, with many scapes, leafless flower stems.

revolutum, rev-ol-U-tum, revolute or rolled back, the leaves.

Escallonia, es-kal-LO-ne-a; in commemoration of Señor Escallon, a Spanish traveller in the eighteenth century. Mostly evergreen shrubs and trees. *Escalloniaceae.*

bifida, bi-FID-a, cleft in two.

× *edinensis*, see *E.* × *rigida.*

× *exoniensis*, ex-o-ne-EN-sis, of Exeter.

floribunda, see *E. paniculata* var. *floribunda.*

illinita, il-LIN-it-a, varnished or glossy, the leaves.

macrantha, mak-RANTH-a, large-flowered.

montevidensis, see *E. bifida.*

paniculata, pan-ik-ul-A-ta, with flowers arranged in panicles.

paniculata var. *floribunda*, flor-e-BUN-da, abundant or free flowering.

pterocladon, see *E. rosea.*

pulverulenta, pul-ver-ul-EN-ta, powdered.

punctata, see *E. rubra.*

× *rigida*, rij-ID-a, rigid; stiff.

rosea, RO-ze-a, rose-coloured.

rubra, ROO-bra, red, the flowers.

Eschscholzia, esh-SHOL-se-a; after Dr. J. F. Eschscholtz, naturalist and physician, attached to a Russian exploring expedition to N.W. America. Usually treated as annuals. *Papaveraceae.*

californica, kal-if-OR-nik-a, of California. The Californian Poppy.

Escobaria, es-ko-BAR-e-a; after the brothers Romulo Escobar Zerman (1872–1946) and Numa Pompilio Escobar Zerman (1874–1949), Mexican agriculturists. Cacti. *Cactaceae.*

dasyacantha, day-ze-a-KANTH-a, thick spines or spines close together.

tuberculosa, TU-ber-ku-LO-sa, tubercled.

vivipara, vi-VIP-ar-a, from L. *vivus*, alive; *parere*, bring forth, producing young stem plants.

Eucalyptus, u-kal-IP-tus; from Gr. *eu*, good or well; *kalyptos*, covered, in allusion to the calyx and petals forming a lid (operculum) which is shed when the flower opens. Trees and shrubs. *Myrtaceae.*
  citriodora, see *Corymbia citriodora.*
  coccifera, kok-SIF-er-a, from L. *coccus*, grain; *fera*, bearing; in reference to the coccoid insects that infest some plants.
  globulus, GLOB-ul-us, globular.
  gunnii, GUN-e-i; after Ronald Gunn (1808–1881), Tasmanian magistrate, landowner and botanist.

Eucharidium, misapplied see below.
  breweri, see *Clarkia breweri.*
  concinnum, see *Clarkia concinna.*
  grandiflorum, see *Clarkia concinna.*

Eucharis, U-kar-is; from Gr. *eucharis*, charming, referring to the pleasing fragrance of the flowers. Tropical evergreen bulbous plants. *Amaryllidaceae.*
  amazonica, am-a-ZON-ik-a, Amazonian.
  candida, KAN-did-a, white.
  × *grandiflora*, gran-dif-LO-ra, large flowers.

Eucnide, u-NID-e; from Gr. *eu*, good; *knide*, stinging nettle, in allusion to the nettle-like hairs. Annual and biennial herbs. *Loasaceae.*
  bartonioides, bar-ton-e-OY-dez, resembling *Bartonia.*

Eucomis, U-kom-is; from Gr. *eukomus*, beautiful hair, referring to the leafy tuft surmounting the flower spike. Perennial bulbs. *Asparagaceae.*
  comosa, ko-MO-sa, hairy.
  punctata, see *E. comosa.*

Eucryphia, u-KRIF-e-a; from Gr. *eu*, good; *kryphia*, a covering; in reference to the cap-like cover formed by the calyx. Flowering shrubs. *Cunoniaceae.*
  cordifolia, kor-dif-OL-e-a, heart shaped.
  pinnatifolia, see *E. cordifolia.*

Eulalia, u-LAL-e-a; named by Kunth in honour of Madame Eulaliae Delile (1800–1840), French botanical artist, who 'created elegant pencil drawings'. Hardy ornamental grasses. *Poaceae.*
  gracillima, see *Microstegium glabratum.*

  japonica, see *Miscanthus sinensis.*
  japonica var. *zebrina*, see *Miscanthus sinensis.*

Euonymus, u-ON-e-mus; from Gr. *eu*, good; *onoma*, a name; of good repute. Trees and shrubs. *Celastraceae.*
  alatus, al-A-tus, winged – the branches.
  atropurpureus, AT-ro-pur-PUR-e-us, dark purple.
  europaeus, u-ro-PE-us, European.
  fortunei, for-TOO-ne-i, after Robert Fortune (1812–1880), Scottish plant collector in China.
  japonicus, jap-ON-ik-us, of Japan.
  latifolius, lat-if-O-le-us, broad-leaves.
  radicans, see *E. fortunei.*
  sachalinensis, sak-al-in-EN-sis, of Sakhalin Island.

Eupatorium, u-pat-OR-e-um; commemorating Mithridates the Great (Eupator Dionysius) (135–63 BC), King of Pontus, who discovered in one species an antidote for poison. Hardy herbaceous plants and shrubs. *Compositae.*
  ageratoides, see *Ageratum altissima.*
  aromaticum, see *Ageratina aromatica.*
  cannabinum, kan-nab-EE-num, resembling *Cannabis* (hemp).
  ianthinum, see *Bartlettina sordida.*
  purpureum, pur-PUR-e-um, purple.
  riparium, re-PAIR-e-um, of river banks.
  weinmannianum, see *Ageratina ligustrina.*

Euphorbia, u-FOR-be-a; after Euphorbus, physician to Juba, King of Mauritania, who used the latex for medicinal purposes. Annuals, perennials and succulents. *Euphorbiaceae.*
  capitata, see *E. hirta.*
  characias, kar-ra-KEY-as, from Gr. *charakias*, fit for a stake, in reference to the upright or erect habit.
  characias subsp. *wulfenii*, wul-FEN-e-i, after Francis Xavier von Wulfen, professor of natural philosophy at Klagenfurt.
  cyparissias, si-par-IS-se-as, resembling a cypress – the foliage. The Cypress Spurge.
  epithymoides, ep-ith-e-MOY-dees, resembling *Epithymum.*
  fulgens, FUL-jenz, shining or glowing.
  heterophylla, het-er-of-IL-la, Gr. *hetero*, diverse; *phylla*, leaves.
  hirta, HER-ta, hairy.
  jacquiniiflora, see *E. fulgens.*
  lathyris, LATH-e-ris, old name for Caper Spurge.

marginata, mar-jin-A-ta, margined with another colour – white.

milii, MIL-e-i, named for Pierre Bernard Milius (1773–1829), explorer and governor of Reunion Island, who introduced it to France in 1821.

milii var. *splendens*, SPLEN-denz, splendid.

myrsinites, mir-sin-I-tees, from Ancient Greek name signifying myrtle, reference obscure.

obesa, o-BE-sa, obese, or tub-like.

pilosa, pil-O-sa, soft long hairs.

polychroma, see *E. epithymoides*.

pulcherrima, pul-KER-rim-a, most beautiful. Poinsettia.

splendens, see *E. milii* var. *splendens*.

wulfenii, see *E. characias* subsp. *wulfenii*.

Exacum, EKS-ak-um; of Pliny and Dioscorides derivation unknown. Possibly from L. *ex*, out; *actum*, to drive, in reference to the purgative properties of some species. Conservatory plants. *Gentianaceae*.

affine, af-FIN-ne, related or similar to.

trinervium, tri-ner-VEE-um, with three prominent veins (nerves).

zeylanicum, see *E. trinervium*.

Exochorda, eks-o-KOR-da; from Gr. *exo*, outside; *chorde*, a cord or thong, in reference to the structure of the ovary. Shrubs. *Rosaceae*.

albertii, see *E. racemosa*.

giraldii, see *E. racemosa* subsp. *giraldii*.

grandiflora, see *E. racemosa*.

× *macrantha*, mak-RANTH-a, large-flowered.

racemosa, ras-em-O-sa, resembling a raceme.

racemosa subsp. *giraldii*, jir-AL-de-i, introduced by Pere Giuseppe Giraldi (d. 1901), plant collector in China.

Fabiana, fab-E-a-na; in commemoration of Archbishop Francisco Fabian y Fuero (1719–1801), of Valencia, Spain, a promoter of botanical study. Half-hardy shrub. *Solanaceae*.

imbricata, im-bre-KA-ta, overlapping leaves.

Fagus, FA-gus; the Latin name for a Beech tree, some authorities deriving the word from Gr. *phago*, to eat, the seeds being edible. Trees. *Fagaceae*.

sylvatica, sil-VAT-ik-a, inhabiting woods – the Beech Tree.

Fallopia, fal-O-pe-a; commemorating Gabriele Fallopio (1523–1562), Italian anatomist, professor of Anatomy, Surgery and Botany at the University of Padua. Herbaceous perennials and climbers. *Polygonaceae*.

baldschuanica, bawld-shu-AN-ik-a, of Bal'juan, Tajikistan.

japonica, see *Reynoutria japonica*.

Farfugium, far-FEW-ge-um; name ascribed by Pliny. Evergreen herbaceous perennial. *Compositae*.

japonicum, jap-ON-ik-um, of Japan.

× *Fatshedera*, FATS-head-e-ra; an intergeneric hybrid (*Fatsia japonica* 'Moseri' × *Hedera hibernica*). Evergreen shrub. *Araliaceae*.

lizei, LY-zee-i, named for Lize Freres who created the hybrid in France in 1910.

Fatsia, FAT-se-a; from the Japanese name, *Fatsi*, for *Fatsia japonica*. Shrubs. *Araliaceae*.

japonica, jap-ON-ik-a, of Japan.

papyrifera, see *Tetrapanax papyrifer.*

Faucaria, fau-KAR-e-a; from L. *faux*, a gullet or throat, the pairs of leaves resemble the open mouth of a carnivore. Greenhouse succulents. *Aizoaceae*.

bosscheana, BOS-she-a-na, named after Leon Van den Bossche (1841–1911), of Tirlemont, Belgium, in whose garden the first plants were grown from seed in Europe.

felina, fe-LE-na, cat-like.

lupina, see *F. felina*.

tigrina, tig-RE-na, tiger-striped.

Felicia, fe-LIS-e-a; named after Herr Felix, a German official at Regensburg, who died in 1846. Annuals and perennials. *Compositae*.

abyssinica, ab-is-SIN-ik-a, Abyssinian, native to Ethiopia (Abyssinia).

amelloides, a-mel-LOY-deez, resembling *Amellus*.

fragilis, see *F. tenella*.

heterophylla, het-er-of-IL-la, Gr. *hetero*, diverse; *phylla*, leaves.

tenella, ten-EL-la, tender; delicate.

Fendlera, fend-LE-ra; after August Fendler (1813–1883), German plant collector in North and Central America. Shrubs. *Hydrangeaceae*.

rupicola, roo-PIK-o-la, rock inhabiting.

Ferocactus, fer-o-KAK-tus; from L. *ferox*, fierce, and *cactus*, refers to the very spiny plants. Greenhouse cacti. *Cactaceae*.
  cylindraceus, sil-in-DRAK-e-us, long and round, cylindrical.
  cylindraceus subsp. *lecontei*, lec-ON-te-i, named after Dr. John Lawrence LeConte (1825–1883), American entomologist and explorer who first noticed it.
  echidne, ek-ID-ne, viper's fang-like – the spines.
  latispinus, see *F. recurvus*.
  lecontei, see *F. cylindraceus* subsp. *lecontei*.
  recurvus, re-KER-vus, curved backwards.
  uncinatus, un-sin-A-tus, hooked – the spines.
  viridescens, vir-id-ES-senz, greenish flowered.
  wislizeni, wis-liz-EE-ne, after Friedrich Adolph Wislizenus (1810–1889), German-born American explorer and botanist who found it at El Paso.

Ferula, FER-u-la; name given to the Giant Fennel by Pliny, the Roman naturalist. Herb and perennials. *Apiaceae*.
  communis, kom-MU-nis, common, that is, in groups or communities.
  foetida, FET-id-a, bad-smelling.
  tingitana, ting-e-TA-na, of Tangiers.

Fessia, FESS-e-a; dedicated to Dr. Bernhard Heindl (1947-), philosopher and writer, on the basis of a moniker. Bulbous plants. *Asparagaceae*.
  puschkinioides, pus-kin-e-OY-dees, resembling Puschkinia.

Festuca, fes-TU-ka; from L. *festuca*, a stem or blade. Grasses. *Poaceae*.
  glauca, GLAW-ka, sea-green, the foliage.
  ovina, o-VE-na, pertaining to sheep (fodder plant), hence Sheep's Fescue.

Ficus, FI-kus; the Latin name for the Fig tree and one common to most European languages. Believed to be derived from the Hebrew name, *fag*. Trees, shrubs and vines. *Moraceae*.
  aspera, AS-per-a, rough.
  benjamina, ben-ja-ME-na, from Indian *benjan*, the name for this plant.
  carica, KAR-ik-a, of Caria, Asia Minor (ancient geography). The Fig.
  elastica, el-AS-tik-a, elastic. The Indian Rubber Tree.

  parcellii, see *F. aspera*.
  pumila, PU-mil-a, dwarf or diminutive.
  repens, RE-penz, creeping.
  stipulata, see *F. pumila*.

Filipendula, fil-e-PEN-du-la; from L. *filum*, a thread; *pendulus*, drooping, in allusion to the root tubers of some species. Herbaceous perennials. *Rosaceae*.
  camschatica, kams-KAT-ik-a, of Kamchatka Peninsula, Russia.
  × *purpurea*, pur-PUR-e-a, purple coloured.
  rubra, ROO-bra, red.
  ulmaria, ul-MAIR-e-a, old generic name for common Meadowsweet, meaning elm-leaved.
  vulgaris, vul-GAR-is, common.

Fittonia, fit-TO-ne-a; commemorative of Elizabeth and Sarah Mary Fitton, botanical authors. Tropical trailing foliage plants. *Acanthaceae*.
  albivenis, al-be-VEN-is, white-veined.
  argyroneura, see *F. albivenis*.
  gigantea, ji-GAN-te-a, of large size.
  pearcei, PEERS-e-i, after Pearce. Unresolved name.

Foeniculum, fee-NIK-u-lum; from L. *faenum*, hay, because of its odour. Perennial herb. *Apiaceae*.
  vulgare, vul-GAR-e, common. Fennel.

Fontinalis, FON-tin-a-lis; from L. *fons*, spring or fountain – alluding to habitat. Submerged aquatic moss. *Fontinalaceae*.
  antipyretica, an-te-py-re-TIK-a, anti-fire, the plant being used to plug spaces round chimneys in wood houses as a precaution against fire.

Forsythia, for-SI-the-a; after William Forsyth, superintendent of the Royal Gardens, Kensington (1737–1805). Shrubs. *Oleaceae*.
  densiflora, see *F. velutina*.
  × *intermedia*, in-ter-ME-de-a, intermediate that is between its two parents.
  spectabilis, see *F.* × *intermedia*.
  suspensa, sus-PEN-sa, hanging down, the flowers.
  velutina, vel-u-TE-na, velvety – young wood and buds are downy.
  viridissima, vir-id-IS-sim-a, greenest.

Fothergilla, foth-er-GILL-a; commemorating Dr. John Fothergill (1712–1780), Quaker and physician of Stratford, Essex. Noted for his collection of American plants. Shrubs. *Hamamelidaceae.*
gardenii, gar-DE-ne-i, of Dr. Garden (USA), who discovered it.
major, MA-jor, bigger; larger.
monticola, see *F. major.*

Fragaria, fraj-AR-e-a (or fra-GAR-e-a); from L. *fraga*, strawberry; presumably from *fragrans*, sweet-smelling, alluding to the fruit. Rock plants and fruit. *Rosaceae.*
elatior, see *F. virginiana.*
indica, IN-dik-a, of India.
monophylla, mon-of-IL-la, single leaved.
vesca, VES-ka, small or feeble. The Wild Strawberry.
virginiana, vir-jin-e-A-na, of Virginia.

Franciscea, fran-SIS-se-a; after Francis, Emperor of Austria and patron of botany. Tropical flowering shrub. *Solanaceae.*
calycina, see *Brunfelsia pauciflora.*

Francoa, fran-KO-a; after Fransisco Franco, 16th-century physician of Valencia, Spain. Greenhouse herbaceous. *Melianthaceae.*
appendiculata, ap-pen-dik-ul-A-ta, elongated or lengthened, the flowering stalks; literally appendaged.
ramosa, ra-MO-sa, branched.

Frangula, FRANG-ul-a; old name for the Alder Buckthorn. Shrubs and trees. *Rhamnaceae.*
alnus, AL-nus, resembling *Alnus* (alder).
purshiana, pursh-e-AN-a, after Federick Traugott Pursh (1774–1820), German explorer.

Frankenia, fran-KE-ne-a; after Johan Frankenius (1590–1661), professor of anatomy and botany at Uppsala, Sweden. Rock plants. *Frankeniaceae.*
laevis, LE-vis, smooth.
pulverulenta, pul-ver-ul-EN-ta, powdery.

Fraxinus, FRAKS-in-us; Latin name for an Ash tree, probably from Gr. *phrasso*, to fence, the wood being useful for fence-making. Trees. *Oleaceae.*
angustifolia, an-gus-tif-O-le-a, narrow-leaved.

excelsior, ek-SEL-se-or, taller. The Ash.
latifolia, lat-if-O-le-a, broad-leaved.
mandshurica, mands-HOO-rik-a, of Manchuria.
mariesii, see *F. sieboldiana.*
oregona, see *F. latifolia.*
ornus, OR-nus, old Latin name for Ash tree. The Flowering Ash.
sieboldiana, se-bold-e-A-na, after Philipp Franz van Siebold (1796–1866), German doctor, who travelled in Japan from 1823 to 1830 and again 1859 to 1863, introduced many Japanese plants into European gardens.

Freesia, FREE-se-a; after Dr. Freidrich Heinrich Theodor Freese (d. 1876), of Kiel, a friend of Ecklon who named the genus. Very fragrant cut flowers. *Iridaceae.*
alba, AL-ba, from the L. *alba*, white.
laxa, LACK-sa, loose or open.
leichtlinii, lecht-LE-ne-i, for Max Leichtlin (1831–1910) of Baden-Baden, who introduced many plants into cultivation, notably from the Near East.
refracta, re-FRAK-ta, bent back.

Fremontodendron, free-mon-toe-DEN-dron; named after Major-General John Charles Fremont (1813–1890), who between 1842 and 1848 made four hazardous explorations into the far west of the United States. Shrubs. *Malvaceae.*
californicum, kal-if-OR-nik-um, of California.
mexicanum, meks-e-KAN-um, of Mexico.

Fritillaria, frit-il-LAR-e-a; from L. *fritillus*, a dice-box, the markings on the flower resembling those on a chequer or chess-board, which is often associated with games of dice. Bulbous plants. *Liliaceae.*
armena, see *F. pinardii.*
aurea, aw-RE-a, golden.
bithynica, bith-e-NIK-a, from Bithynia, in ancient geography a region of North-west Asia Minor, now in Turkey.
citrina, see *F. bithynica.*
imperialis, im-peer-e-A-lis, imperial, majestic. The Crown Imperial.
meleagris, me-le-A-gris, Gr. name for Guinea-fowl, literally speckled – the flowers chequered.
pinardii, pin-ARD-e-i, after Christian Pinard (collected 1843 to 1846), who discovered it in Turkey.

Fuchsia, FEW-sche-a; after Leonhart Fuchs (1501–1566), a German physician and botanist, professor at Tubingen. Noted for his herbal published in 1542 and 1543 with beautiful woodcuts. Shrubs. *Onagraceae.*

corymbiflora, kor-im-bif-LO-ra, cluster flowered.

fulgens, FUL-jens, glowing.

gracilis, see *F. magellanica.*

macrostemma, see *F. magellanica.*

magellanica, maj-el-AN-ik-a, of the area of the Straits of Magellan.

procumbens, pro-KUM-benz, prostrate.

riccartonii, see *F. magellanica.*

splendens, SPLEN-denz, splendid.

triphylla, trif-IL-a, three-leaved – the leaves in threes around the stem.

Fumaria, few-MAR-e-a; from L. *fumus,* smoke, some species having a smoky odour. Annual climber. *Papaveraceae.*

capreolata, kap-re-o-LA-ta, provided with tendrils.

Funkia, misapplied see below.

fortunei, see *Hosta sieboldiana.*

grandiflora, see *Hosta plantaginea.*

lancifolia, see *Hosta lancifolia.*

sieboldiana, see *Hosta sieboldiana.*

subcordata, see *Hosta plantaginea.*

tardiflora, see *Hosta longipes.*

undulata, see *Hosta undulata.*

Gagea, GA-je-a; commemorating Sir Thomas Gage (1781–1820), a botanist. Hardy bulbs. *Liliaceae.*

lutea, LU-te-a, yellow.

Gaillardia, gal-LAR-de-a; after M. Gaillard de Charentonneau, a French patron of botany. Hardy perennials; most garden kinds are hybrids. *Compositae.*

amblyodon, am-BLY-od-on, blunt toothed.

aristata, ar-is-TA-ta, awned – the seeds.

picta, PIK-ta, painted.

pulchella, pul-KEL-la, pretty (diminutive).

Galanthus, gal-AN-thus; from Gr. *gala,* milk; *anthos,* a flower, alluding to its whiteness – the Snowdrop. Bulbous. *Amaryllidaceae.*

byzantinus, see *G. plicatus* subsp. *byzantinus.*

elwesii, el-WE-ze-i, after Henry John Elwes (1846–1922), botanist and author.

nivalis, niv-A-lis, snowy. The Common Snowdrop.

plicatus, plik-A-tus, pleated.

plicatus subsp. byzantinus, bi-zan-TE-nus, Byzantine.

Galax, GA-laks; from Gr. *gala,* milk, possibly in reference to the milk-white flowers. Woodland or peat plant. *Diapensiaceae.*

aphylla, af-IL-la, no leaves, that is, on the flower stalks.

Galega, ga-LE-ga; from Gr. *gala,* milk; *ago,* to lead, the plant once being esteemed as a fodder crop for cows and goats in milk, hence Goat's Rue. Hardy perennials. *Leguminosae.*

officinalis, of-fis-in-A-lis, of the shop (herbal).

Galium, GA-le-um; from Gr. *gala,* milk, the leaves of *G. verum* once having been used for the curdling of milk. Rock plants. *Rubiaceae.*

aparine, ap-AR-in-nee, the Greek name for cleavers.

odoratum, od-o-RA-tum, sweet-smelling. The Sweet Woodruff.

olympicum, ol-IM-pik-um, Mt. Olympus.

Galtonia, gawl-TO-ne-a; commemorating Francis Galton, anthropologist. Hardy bulb. *Asparagaceae.*

candicans, see *Ornithogalum candicans.*

viridiflora, ver-id-ee-FLOR-a, with green flowers.

Gamolepis, misapplied see below.

tagetes, see *Steirodiscus tagetes.*

Gardenia, gar-DE-ne-a; commemorating Dr. Alexander Garden (1730–1791), who corresponded with Linnaeus. Garden was born in Scotland and emigrated to Charleston, South Carolina where he was a physician and botanist. Tender shrubs. *Rubiaceae.*

florida, see *G. jasminoides.*

jasminoides, jaz-min-OY-dees, resembling *Jasminum* (Jasmine).

Garrya, GAR-re-a; named by Douglas in honour of Mr Garry, of the Hudson Bay Company who gave the former much assistance in his plant-collecting expeditions

(1820–1830) in the Pacific North West. Shrubs. *Garryaceae*.

elliptica, el-LIP-tik-a, ellipse-shaped, the leaves.

Gasteria, gas-TE-re-a; from Gr. *gaster*, belly, alluding to the swollen base of the flowers. Greenhouse succulents. *Xanthorrhoeaceae*.

brevifolia, brev-IF-ol-e-a, short-leaved.
carinata, kar-ee-NAH-tuh, having a keel.
carinata var. *verrucosa*, ver-ru-KO-sa, warted.
disticha, DIS-tik-a, leaves in two rows.
lingua, lin-GWA, tongue-like, the leaves.
verrucosa, see *G. carinata* var. *verrucosa*.

Gastrorchis, gast-ROAR-kis; from Gr. *gaster*, belly; *orchis*, orchid; in allusion to the swollen lip base. Orchids. *Orchidaceae*.

tuberculosa, tu-ber-kul-O-sa, tubercles.

Gaultheria, gawl-THE-re-a; commemorating Dr. Gaulthier, a botanist and physician, of Quebec, in the eighteenth century. Shrubs. *Ericaceae*.

nummularioides, num-mul-AR-e-oy-dees, like *Nummalaria* (moneywort), the leaves and growths.
mucronata, muk-ron-A-ta, from L. *mucro*, sharp point, leaves terminating in a point.
procumbens, pro-KUM-benz, prostrate, flat on the ground.
pyrolifolia, pir-ol-e-FO-le-a, leaves like *Pyrola* (wintergreen).
shallon, SHAL-lon, old Native American name.
trichophylla, trik-of-IL-la, hairy-leaved.

Gaura, GAW-ra; from Gr. *gauros*, superb. Hardy perennial. *Onagraceae*.

lindheimeri, lind-HI-mer-i, for Ferdinand Jacob Lindheimer (1801–1879), German American botanist.

Gaylussacia, gay-loo-SAK-e-a; named after a French chemist, Joseph Louis Gay-Lussac (1778–1850). Peat shrubs. *Ericaceae*.

baccata, bak-KA-ta, berry-like, having fruits with a pulpy texture. Black Huckleberry.
dumosa, du-MO-sa, bushy.
frondosa, fron-DO-sa, leafy.
resinosa, see *G. baccata*.

Gazania, gaz-A-ne-a; from L. *gaza*, treasure, or riches, in allusion to the large and gaudy flowers, or commemorating Theodore of Gaza (1398–1478) who translated into Latin the botanical works of Theophrastus. Half-hardy perennials and annuals. The Treasure Flower. *Compositae*.

linearis, lin-e-AR-is, linear leaved, narrow, with nearly parallel sides.
longiscapa, see *G. linearis*.
rigens, RI-gens, rigid.
splendens, see *G. rigens*.

Gelasine, je-LAS-e-ne; from Gr. *gelasinos*, a smiling dimple, referring to the flowers. Bulbs. *Iridaceae*.

azurea, see *G. elongata*.
elongata, e-long-GAH-tuh, lengthened or elongated.

Genista, jen-IS-ta; ancient Latin name from which the Plantagenet kings and queens of England took their name (*planta genista*). Flowering shrubs. *Leguminosae*.

aetnensis, et-NEN-sis, of Mount Etna.
cinerea, sin-er-E-a, greyish – the foliage.
dalmatica, see *G. sylvestris* subsp. *dalmatica*.
glabrescens, see *Cytisus emeriflorus*.
hispanica, his-PAN-ik-a, Spanish Broom.
pilosa, pil-O-sa, downy, covered in long soft hairs.
radiata, rad-e-A-ta, rayed – the form of the branches.
sagittalis, sag-it-TA-liss, like an arrow – the winged twigs.
sylvestris, sil-VES-tris, pertaining to the woods.
sylvestris subsp. *dalmatica*, dal-MAT-ik-a, of Dalmatia, on the Adriatic side of the Balkan Peninsula.
tinctoria, tink-TOR-e-a, of dyers, *tingo*, to dye. Dyer's Greenweed.
virgata, see *G. tinctoria*.

Gentiana, JEN-she-AN-a; (or JEN-te-AN-a); called after Gentius, King of Illyria, who first used the plant in medicine. Rock and border perennials. *Gentianaceae*.

acaulis, a-KAW-lis, stemless.
algida, al-GEE-da, cold, originating in high mountains.
algida var. *purdomii*, PUR-dom-e-i, in honour of William Purdom (1880–1921), British plant collector.
andrewsii, AN-drew-see-i, in honour of the English botanical artist Henry C. Andrews (fl. 1799–1830), illustrator of The Botanist's Repository (1797–1815).
bavarica, bav-AR-ik-a, of Bavaria.

farreri, see *G. lawrencei.*

freyniana, see *G. septemfida.*

kurroo, KER-roo, native name of habitat.

lawrencei, law-RENS-e-i, named after R. W. Lawrence, a nineteenth century amateur botanist who collected in Tasmania.

ornata, or-NA-ta, ornate.

pnuemonanthe, new-mon-AN-the, literally lung-flower, the plant once being used as a remedy for lung disease.

purdomii, see *G. algida* var. *purdomii.*

septemfida, sep-TEM-fid-a, seven-cleft, referring to the flowers.

sino-ornata, SI-no-or-NA-ta, Chinese ornate gentian.

verna, VER-na, spring, spring-flowering.

Geonoma, je-o-NO-ma; from Gr. *geonomos*, skilled in agriculture. These feather palms send out buds from the apex of the stems. These in turn forming new plants. Tender palms. *Arecaceae.*

cuneata, ku-ne-A-ta, wedge-shaped, the leaves, usually with the narrow end down.

gracilis, see *G. cuneata.*

Geranium, jer-A-nee-um; from Gr. *geranos*, a crane, the fruit of the plant resembling the head and beak of that bird, hence Cranesbill. Border perennials and rock plants. *Geraniaceae.*

albanum, al-BA-num, of Albania.

armenum, see *G. psilostemon.*

endressii, en-DRES-see-i, after Philip Anton Christoph Endress (1806–1831), German plant collector who died of malaria after a plant collecting trip to the Pyrenees.

grandiflorum, see *G. sanguineum.*

ibericum, i-BER-ik-um, of Iberia, that is Spain and Portugal.

macrorrhizum, mak-ror-RHIZ-um, large rooted.

nepalense, nep-al-EN-see, of Nepal.

nodosum, no-DO-sum, full of nodes, thick jointed.

phaeum, FE-um, brownish or dusky.

pratense, pra-TEN-see, of the meadows.

psilostemon, si-lo-STEM-on, with glabrous stamens.

pylzowianum, pil-zo-e-AN-um, after Mikhail Alexandrovich Pyltsov, Russian army officer, who accompanied Przewalski in China 1870–1873.

robertianum, ro-ber-te-AN-um, after Robert, a French abbot. The Herb Robert.

sanguineum, san-GWIN-e-um, blood red.

striatum, see *G. versicolor.*

traversii, tra-VER-see-i, after William Locke Travers (1819–1903), solicitor, parliamentarian and botanist.

versicolor, ver-SIK-o-lor, various colours.

wallichianum, wol-litsch-e-A-num, of Dr. Nathaniel Wallich (1786–1854), a director of the Botanical Gardens, Calcutta.

Gerardia, jer-ARD-e-a; named after John Gerard (1545–1612), barber-surgeon, garden superintendent to Lord Burghley, Minister to Queen Elizabeth I. He is famous for his Herball, first published in 1597. Parasitic plants. *Orobanchaceae.*

purpurea, see *Agalinis purpurea.*

quercifolia, see *Aureolaria virginica.*

Gerbera, JER-ber-a; after Traugott Gerber, a German naturalist who died in 1743. Tender perennials. *Compositae.*

aurantiaca, aw-ran-te-A-ka, golden-orange.

jamesonii, jame-SO-ne-i, commemorating Robert Jameson (1832–1908), Scottish born botanist who settled in South Africa. The Barberton Daisy.

Gesneria, GES-ner-e-a; after Conrad Gessner (1516–1565) of Zurich. Tropical flowering and foliage tuberous plants. *Gesneriaceae.*

calycina, ka-lee-SIN-a, calyx like.

cardinalis, see *Sinningia cardinalis.*

× *exoniensis*, eks-on-e-EN-sis, of Exeter, Devon, England.

× *naegelioides*, naeg-el-e-OY-dez, resembling *Naegelia.*

refulgens, misapplied, possibly a cultivar of *Smithiantha.*

Geum, JE-um; name used by Pliny, possibly from the Gr. *geuo*, to give an agreeable flavour (to taste), the roots of some species being aromatic. Herbaceous perennials. *Rosaceae.*

× *borisii*, see *G. coccineum.*

chiloense, chil-o-EN-se, of the Island of Chiloe.

coccineum, kok-SIN-e-um, scarlet.

× *heldreichii*, see *G. coccineum.*

montanum, mon-TA-num, of mountains.

rivale, re-VA-le, pertaining to brooks.

Gibbaeum, gib-BE-um; from L. *gibba*, a hump, referring to the humped appearance of the larger of the two leaves forming the new growth. Greenhouse succulents. *Aizoaceae.*
  album, AL-bum, white – the flowers.
  dispar, DIS-par, unequal – the leaves.
  gibbosum, gib-BO-sum, humped or swollen.
  heathii, HEETH-e-i, after Dr Francis Harold Rodier Heath (fl. 1910–1937), English grower of succulent plants.
  pubescens, pew-BES-senz, downy.

Gilia, GIL-e-a; dedicated to Fillipo Luigi Gilii (1756–1821), astronomer in Rome, author with Caspar Xuarez of Observazioni fitologiche (1789–1792). Mainly half-hardy annuals. *Polemoniaceae.*
  achilleifolia, a-kil-le-if-OL-e-a, leaves resembling *Achillea.*
  capitata, kap-it-A-ta, growing in a dense head.
  coronopifolia, kor-on-op-e-FO-le-a, leaves resembling *Coronopus.*
  tricolor, TRIK-ol-or, three coloured.

Gillenia, gil-LE-ne-a; named after Arnold Gille, German physician who wrote on horticulture in the seventeenth century and had a garden at Cassel. Rhizomatous perennial herbs. *Rosaceae.*
  trifoliata, see *Spiraea trifoliata.*

Ginkgo, GINK-go; from Chinese *yin*, silver; *kuo*, apricot, via Japanese pronunciation, *ginko*. Introduced into Europe from Japan. Tree. *Ginkgoaceae.*
  biloba, bi-LO-ba, two-lobed, the foliage.

Gladiolus, glad-e-O-lus; from L. *gladiolus*, a small sword, the shape of the leaf. Bulbous plants, mainly hybrids in common cultivation. *Iridaceae.*
  blandus, see *G. carneus.*
  × *brenchleyensis*, brench-ley-EN-sis, of Brenchley.
  byzantinus, see *G. communis.*
  cardinalis, kar-din-A-lis, scarlet, cardinal red.
  carneus, kar-NE-us, flesh-coloured, deep pink.
  colvillei, COL-vil-le-i, named after nurseryman James Colville of Chelsea, London.
  communis, kom-MU-nis, common, that is, in groups or communities.
  dalenii, da-LEN-e-i, after Cornelius Dalen, Director of Rotterdam Botanic Gardens who introduced the species into gardens.
  × *gandavensis*, gan-dav-EN-sis, relating to Ghent, Belgium.
  primulinus, see *G. dalenii.*
  psittacinus, see *G. dalenii.*
  tristis, TRIS-tis, dull, sad.

Glandora, GLAN-dor-a; in reference to the hairy corolla. Dwarf shrub. *Boraginaceae.*
  prostrata, pros-TRA-ta, prostrate, lying flat.

Glandularia, glan-do-LAIR-e-a; having small glands. Annual and perennial herbs. *Verbenaceae.*
  laciniata, las-in-e-A-ta, slashed or torn into narrow divisions.
  peruviana, pe-ru-ve-A-na, of Peru.
  tenera, TEN-er-a, soft, delicate, slender.

Glaucium, GLAW-ke-um (or GLAW-ce-um); from Gr. *glaukos*, blue-grey, the colour of the foliage. Hardy biennials. *Papaveraceae.*
  corniculatum, kor-nik-ul-A-tum, horned. The Horned Poppy.
  flavum, FLA-vum, yellow – the flowers.

Glebionis, gleb-e-O-nis; from L. *gleba*, soil; *ionis*, characteristic of, reference obscure. Herbaceous perennials. *Compositae.*
  coronaria, kor-on-AIR-e-a, crown or wreath-like.

Glechoma, glee-KO-ma; from Gr. *glechon*, a kind of mint. Perennial herbs. *Lamiaceae.*
  hederacea, hed-er-A-se-a, resembling *Hedera* (ivy).

Gleditsia, gled-ITS-see-a; named after Johann Gottlieb Gleditsch (1714–1786), director of the Botanical Garden, Berlin and friend of Linnaeus. Trees. Honey Locust. *Leguminosae.*
  caspia, KAS-pe-a, Caspian.
  triacanthos, tri-a-KAN-thos, three-spined.

Gleichenia, gle-KEE-ne-a; after Baron Gleichen (1717–1783), German botanist. Greenhouse ferns. *Gleicheniaceae.*
  circinnata, ser-sin-NA-ta, coiled.
  dicarpa, From Gr. *di*, two; *carpa*, fruits.
  rupestris, roo-PES-tris, rock loving.

Globularia, glob-u-LAR-e-a; from L. *globulus*, a small globe, in reference to the rounded flower heads. Sub-shrubs and perennials. Globe Daisy. *Plantaginaceae.*

bellidifolia, see *G. meridionalis.*
cordifolia, kor-dif-OL-e-a, heart shaped.
incanescens, in-ka-NES-sens, becoming hoary.
meridionalis, me-rid-e-o-NA-lis, of noonday;
blooming at midday.
trichosantha, trik-o-SAN-tha, hairy flowered, the
appearance of the blossoms.

Gloriosa, glo-re-O-sa; from L. *gloriosus*,
glorious, referring to the gorgeous flowers.
Tropical climbing tuberous rooted plants.
Glory-Lily. *Colchicaceae.*
superba, su-PER-ba, superb.

Glottiphyllum, glot-tif-IL-lum; from Gr.
glotta, tongue; *phylla*, leaf, referring to the
thick fleshy leaves. Greenhouse succulents.
Aizoaceae.
apiculatum, see *G. cruciatum.*
cruciatum, kroo-see-A-tum, in the form of a cross.
linguiforme, lin-gwe-FOR-me, tongue shaped.
longum, LONG-um, long, the leaves.

Gloxinia, gloks-IN-e-a, named after Benjamin Peter Gloxin (flourished 1785), a
botanical writer of Colmar. Tuberous perennials. *Gesneriaceae.*
perennis, per-EN-nis, perennial.
speciosa, see *Sinningia speciosa.*

Glyceria, glik-ER-e-a; (or gly-ce-re-a); from
Gr. *glykys*, sweet; with reference to the sweet
tasting of some seeds of the genus. Aquatic
grass. *Poaceae.*
aquatica, see *Catabrosa aquatica.*
canadensis, kan-a-DEN-sis, of Canada.

Glycyrrhiza, glik-er-RHE-za (or gly-ser-
RHY-za); from Gr. *glykys*, sweet; *rhiza*, a
root, referring to the sweet juice of the roots
from which liquorice is made. Perennial
herbs. *Leguminosae.*
glabra, GLAB-ra, smooth, destitute of hairs.

Gnaphalium, naf-A-le-um; from Gr. *gnaphal-
ion*, woolly, in allusion to the very woolly
foliage. Hardy herbaceous plants. *Compositae.*
supinum, sue-PINE-um, prostrate; low growing.

Gnidia, NID-e-a; Latin referring to the
Doric city and region of *Gnidus* (Gr. *Knidos*)
in Caria, Asia Minor (Turkey). Greenhouse
flowering shrubs. *Thymelaeaceae.*

denudata, de-nu-DA-ta, uncovered or not hairy.
pinifolia, py-nif-OL-e-a, *Pinus* (Pine) leaved.

Godetia, go-DE-she-a; after Charles H.
Godet, Swiss botanist and entomologist.
The genus is now included under Clarkia.
grandiflora, see *Clarkia amoena* subsp. *lindleyi.*
whitneyi, see *Clarkia amoena* subsp. *whitneyi.*

Goldfussia, gold-FUS-se-a; after Dr. Gold-
fuss (1782–1848), natural history professor in Bonn university. The genus is now
included under Strobilanthes.
anisophylla, see *Strobilanthes persicifolia.*
isophylla, see *Strobilanthes persicifolia.*

Gomesa, go-MESS-a; after Bernadino
Antonio Gomes (1768–1823), Portuguese
physician and botanist. Orchids. *Orchidaceae.*
concolor, KON-kol-or, one-coloured.
forbesii, FORBES-e-i, after John Forbes (1799–
1823), plant collector for the Horticultural
Society of London. Collected in Brazil and
Africa.
varicosa, var-ik-O-sa, dilated veins.

Gomphrena, gom-FREE-na; from an ancient
name for amaranth. Tender annuals. *Amaranthaceae.*
globosa, glob-O-sa, globular. The Globe Amaranth.

Goniolimon, gon-e-o-LI-mon; from Gr.
gonia, an angle; *limon*, after *Limonium*, a
related genus. The branches are angled. Perennial herbs. *Plumbaginaceae.*
eximium, eks-IM-e-um, excellent.
tataricum, tat-TAR-e-kum, of the Tatar Mountains, Russia.

Goniophlebium, gon-e-of-LEB-e-um; from
Gr. *gonia*, an angle; *phlebion*, a vein, alluding
to the angled veins. Epiphytic ferns. *Polypodiaceae.*
appendiculatum, ap-pen-dik-ul-A-tum, drooping
like an appendage.
subauriculatum, see *Schellolepis subauriculata.*

Gordonia, gor-DO-ne-a; named after James
Gordon (1708–1780), nurseryman of Mile
End, London. Trees. *Theaceae.*
lasianthus, las-e-AN-thus, hairy flowered.
pubescens, pew-BES-senz, downy.

Gossypium, gos-SIP-e-um; from L. *gossypion*, cotton plant. Annual and perennial herbs, subshrubs, shrubs and trees. *Malvaceae.*
barbadense, bar-bad-EN-see, from Barbados.
herbaceum, her-BA-se-um, herbaceous.

Grammanthes, misapplied see below.
gentianoides, see *Crassula dichotoma.*

Gravesia, GRAVE-see-a; possibly after George Graves (1784–1839), author of the 'Naturalist's Pocket-book or Tourist's Companion'. Annual and perennial herbs. *Melastomataceae.*
guttata, gut-TA-ta, speckled or spotted.

Greenovia, misapplied see below.
aurea, see *Aeonium aureum.*

Grevillea, gre-VIL-le-a; named after Charles F. Greville (1749–1809), a founder of the Horticultural Society of London (RHS), once vice-president of the Royal Society and patron of botany. Evergreen Trees and Shrubs. *Proteaceae.*
juniperina, ju-NIP-er-e-na, resembling *Juniperus* (juniper).
juniperina subsp. *sulphurea*, sul-FU-re-a, sulphur yellow, the flowers.
robusta, ro-BUS-ta, strong or robust.
rosmarinifolia, ros-mar-e-nif-OL-e-a, *Rosmarinus* (Rosemary) leaved.
sulphurea, see *G. juniperina* subsp. *sulphurea.*

Griffinia, grif-FIN-e-a; after William Griffin (d. 1827), a distinguished cultivator of bulbs. Tropical bulbs. *Amaryllidaceae.*
hyacinthina, hy-a-SINTH-in-a, dark purplish-blue; resembling *Hyacinthus* (hyacinth).

Griselinia, gris-el-IN-e-a; after Francesco Griselini (1717–1783), a Venetian botanist. Shrub. *Cornaceae.*
littoralis, lit-tor-A-lis, of the sea-shore.

Grusonia, grus-ON-e-a; after Hermann Gruson of Magdebourg, a cactus specialist. Greenhouse cacti. *Cactaceae.*
bradtiana, brad-tee-A-na, after George Bradt, editor of The Southern Florist and Gardener.
cereiformis, see *G. bradtiana.*

Guarianthe, gwa-re-AN-thee; from the Costa Rican native name for orchid. *Orchidaceae.*

bowringiana, bo-ring-e-A-na, introduced by Veitch and named after Mr J.C. Bowring of Forest Farm, Windsor, an ardent amateur orchid collector.
skinneri, SKIN-ner-i, after George Ure Skinner (1804–1867), botanist, plant collector in Guatemala and Honduras. The national flower of Costa Rica.

Guaiacum, gwa-e-AK-um; the native name for the tropical evergreen tree lignum vitae. Shrubs and trees. *Zygophyllaceae.*
officinale, of-FIS-in-A-lee, found in shops. Lignum vitae, the wood of life so named because of its high repute in medicine.

Gunnera, GUN-ner-a; named after Johan Ernst Gunnerus (1718–1773), Norwegian bishop and botanist. Author of Flora Norvegica (1766–1772). Herbaceous perennials. *Gunneraceae.*
chilensis, see *G. tinctoria.*
magellanica, maj-el-AN-ik-a, of the area of the Straits of Magellan.
manicata, man-ik-A-ta, literally sleeved, usually applied to pubescent material which may be stripped off in shreds.
scabra, see *G. tinctoria.*
tinctoria, tink-TOR-e-a, of dyers, *tingo*, to dye.

Guzmania, guz-MAN-e-a; named in honour of Anastasio Guzman (d. 1807), Spanish naturalist. Perennial herbs. *Bromeliaceae.*
lingulata, ling-ul-A-ta, tongue-shaped.

Gymnocalycium, gim-no-kal-IK-e-um; from Gr. *gymnos*, naked; *kalyx*, a bud, the flower buds having no covering. Cacti. *Cactaceae.*
denudatum, de-nu-DA-tum, denuded of covering.
gibbosum, gib-BO-sum, swollen on one side, humped.
leeanum, see *G. gibbosum.*
monvillei, mon-VIL-e-i, after Hippolyte Boissel (1794–1863), Baron de Monville, whose plant collection was sold by auction in 1846.
multiflorum, see *G. monvillei.*

Gymnocarpium, gyim-no-KAR-pe-um; from Gr. *gymnos*, naked; *karpus*, fruit. The sori being naked. Ferns. *Cystopteridaceae.*
dryopteris, dri-OP-ter-is; from Gr. *drys*, oak; *pteris*, a fern. The Oak Fern.

Gymnocladus, gim-no-KLA-dus; from Gr. *gymnos*, naked; *klados*, a branch. The branches are bare for many months in winter and the buds are barely visible. Trees. *Leguminosae.*

  canadensis, see *G. dioica.*

  dioica, di-OY-ka, literally two houses, that is, male and female parts being on separate plants, dioecious. The Kentucky Coffee Tree. The seeds of which were used as a coffee substitute by the American Pioneers.

Gymnogramma, gim-no-GRAM-ma; from Gr. *gymnos*, naked; *gramma*, lines, from the conspicuous naked sori being in lines. Ferns. *Pteridaceae.*

  argyrophylum, ar-ger-of-IL-la, silver-leaved.

  calomelanos, see *Pityrogramma calomelanos.*

  chrysophylla, kris-of-IL-lum, with golden leaves.

  dealbata, see *Pityrogramma dealbata.*

  japonica, see *Coniogramme japonica.*

  peruviana, see *Pityrogramma calomelanos* var. *peruviana.*

  tartarea, see *Pityrogramma ebenea.*

  wetenhalliana, wet-ten-hal-le-A-na, after Wetenhall.

Gynerium, gyn-EER-e-um; from Gr. *gyne*, woman; *erion*, wool, the hairy spikelets of the female plants. Grasses. *Poaceae.*

  argenteum, see *Cortaderia selloana.*

  sagittatum, sag-it-TA-tum, like an arrow. Uva grass.

Gypsophila, gip-SOF-il-la; from Gr. *gypsos*, chalk; *phileo*, to love, in reference to some species preference for chalky soils. Annual or perennials herbs of varying habit. *Caryophyllaceae.*

  cerastoides, se-rast-OY-dees, like *Cerastium.*

  elegans, EL-e-ganz, elegant.

  frankenioides, see *Bolanthus frankenioides.*

  paniculata, pan-ik-ul-A-ta, with flowers arranged in panicles.

  repens, RE-penz, creeping.

Habenaria, hab-en-AR-e-a; from L. *habena*, a strap, referring to the strap-shaped spur. Terrestrial orchids. *Orchidaceae.*

  bifolia, see *Platanthera bifolia.*

  blephariglottis, see *Platanthera blephariglottis.*

  fimbriata, see *Platanthera grandiflora.*

Haberlea, HAB-er-le-a; named after Karl Konstantin Haberle (1764–1832), teacher of botany, University of Pest, Hungary. Monotypic genus of rock plants. *Gesneriaceae.*

  ferdinand-coburgi, see *H. rhodopensis.*

  rhodopensis, ro-do-PEN-sis, from the Rhodope mountains, Bulgaria.

Habranthus, hab-RAN-thus; from Gr. *habros*, graceful; *anthos*, a flower, of graceful appearance. Half-hardy bulbs. *Amaryllidaceae.*

  pratensis, see *Rhodophiala pratensis.*

Habrothamnus, hab-roth-AM-nus; from Gr. *habros*, graceful; *thamnos*, a shrub, referring to the showy flowers. Greenhouse shrubs. *Solanaceae.*

  elegans, see *Cestrum elegans.*

  newelli, new-EL-le, bred by and named after a Mr Newell, Downham Market, Norfolk.

Hacquetia, hak-KWET-e-a; named after Belsazar de la Motte Hacquet (c.1740–1815), Slovenian physician of French descent. Perennial herb. *Apiaceae.*

  epipactis, ep-e-PAK-tis, an old generic name. The Greek word given to plants thought to curdle milk.

Haemanthus, ha-MAN-thus; from Gr. *haima*, blood; *anthos*, flower, alluding to the red colour of the flowers. Greenhouse bulbous plants. *Amaryllidaceae.*

  albiflos, AL-be-flos, white-flowered.

  coccineus, kok-SIN-e-us, scarlet.

  katharinae, see *Scadoxus multiflorus* subsp. *katharinae.*

  multiflorus, see *Scadoxus multiflorus.*

  natalensis, see *Scadoxus puniceus.*

Hakonechloa, hak-o-ne-KLO-a; from the Japanese region of Hakone; Gr. *chloi*, grass. *Poaceae.*

  macra, MAK-ra, large.

Halesia, hale-E-ze-a; commemorating Dr. Stephen Hales (1677–1761), curate of Teddington, botanical author. Shrubs. *Styracaceae.*

  carolina, ka-ro-LI-na, from Carolina, USA.

diptera, DIP-ter-a, from Gr. literally two-winged – the seed pods.

tetraptera, tet-RAP-ter-a, from Gr. literally four-winged – the seed pods.

tetraptera var. *monticola*, mon-TIK-o-la, growing on hills.

Halimium, hal-e-ME-um; from Gr. *halimos*, sea-coast. Shrubs and sub-shrubs. *Cistaceae*.
halimifolium, hal-im-if-OL-e-um, leaves resembling *Halimus*.
lasianthum, las-e-AN-thum, hairy flowered.
lasianthum subsp. *formosum*, for-MO-sum, beautiful.
ocymoides, os-e-MOY-dees, resembling *Ocimum*.

Halimodendron, hal-e-mod-EN-dron; from Gr. *halimos*, sea-coast; *dendron*, tree – a seaside shrub. *Leguminosae*.
argenteum, see *H. halodendron*.
halodendron, ha-lo-DEN-dron, literally Salt Tree.

Hamamelis, ham-a-MEL-is; from Gr. *hama*, together; *mela*, fruit, flowers and fruit being borne at the same time. Shrubs. *Hamamelidaceae*.
arborea, ar-BOR-e-a, tree-like.
japonica, jap-ON-ik-a, of Japan.
mollis, MOL-lis, downy.
virginiana, vir-jin-e-A-na, of Virginia, U.S.A.

Hamatocactus, ham-A-to-KAK-tus; from L. *hamatus*, hooked and *cactus*, refers to the hooked central spine. Greenhouse cactus. *Cactaceae*.
hamatocanthus, ham-A-to-KAN-thus; from L. *hamatus*, hooked; *anthos*, a flower.
setispinus, see *Thelocactus setispinus*.

Hardenbergia, har-den-BER-je-a; after Frances Countess Hardenburg, sister of Baron Hugel, a plant collector and whose plants his sister cared for while on his travels. Greenhouse twining plants. *Leguminosae*.
comptoniana, kom-ton-e-A-na, introduced by Lady Margaret Compton (1793–1830), wife of Spencer Compton second Marquess of Northampton.
monophylla, see *H. violacea*.
violacea, vi-o-LA-se-a, violet-coloured.

Harpalium, misapplied see below.
rigidum, see *Helianthus pauciflorus*.

Hatiora, hat-e-OR-a; an anagram of the genus *Hariota* which was renamed. In honour of Thomas Hariot (1560–1621), cartographer. Cactus. *Cactaceae*.
gaertneri, GEERT-ner-i, after Karl Friedrich von Gaertner (1772–1850), German botanist. Easter cactus.
salicornioides, sal-ik-or-me-OY-dees, resembling *Salicornia* (glasswort).

Haworthia, ha-WORTH-e-i; after Adrian Hardy Haworth (1768–1833), English botanist and writer on succulents. Greenhouse succulents. *Xanthorrhoeaceae*.
atrovirens, see *H. herbacea*.
herbacea, her-BA-se-a, herbaceous.
margaritifera, see *H. pumila*.
pumila, PU-mil-a, dwarf or diminutive.
reinwardtii, rin-WARD-e-i, after Caspar Georg Carl Reinwardt (1773–1854), Dutch botanist.

Hebe, not an accepted name when this book was first printed. It is being argued *Hebe* share a common ancestor with *Veronica* which see.

Hebenstretia, he-ben-STRY-te-a; after Professor John Ernest Hebenstreit (1703–1757), of Leipzig. Half-hardy annual. *Scrophulariaceae*.
comosa, ko-MO-sa, hairy.

Hedera, HED-er-a; the ancient Latin name for Ivy. Climbers. *Araliaceae*.
arborea, see *H. helix*.
canariensis, ka-nar-e-EN-sis, of the Canary Islands.
colchica, KOL-chik-a, from Colchis.
digitata, see *H. helix*.
helix, HE-liks, spiral, or twisted. The Common Ivy.
regneriana, see *H. colchica*.

Hedychium, he-DIK-e-um; from Gr. *hedys*, sweet; *chion*, snow, alluding to the snow-white fragrant flowers (of some species). Tropical herbaceous plants. *Zingiberaceae*.
coronarium, kor-on-AIR-e-um, crown or wreath-like.
gardnerianum, gard-ner-e-A-num, commemorates Col. Edward Gardner, East India Company.
maximum, see *H. coronarium*.

Hedysarum, hed-e-SAR-um; possibly from Gr. *hedys*, sweet, in reference to these fragrant plants. Herbaceous perennials subshrubs and shrubs. *Leguminosae.*
  coronarium, kor-on-AIR-e-um, crown or wreathlike – the flowers.
  multijugum, mul-te-JU-gum, many paired leaves.

Helenium, hel-E-ne-um; Gr. name for another plant honouring Helen of Troy. Herbaceous perennials. *Compositae.*
  autumnale, aw-tum-NA-le, autumnal.
  bigelovii, big-e-LOV-e-i, after Jacob Bigelow (1787–1879), physician and botanist, professor of materia medica at Harvard Medical School.
  bolanderi, bo-LAND-er-e, after Henry Nicholas Bolander (1831–1897), German-American botanist and educator.
  flexuosum, fleks-u-O-sum, zig-zag – the flower stem.
  grandicephalum, see *H. autumnale.*
  striatum, Hybrid see *H. flexuosum.*

Helianthemum, he-le-AN-the-mum; from Gr. *helios*, the sun; *anthemon*, a flower, the Sun Rose. Mainly dwarf shrubs. Also pronounced he-le-ANTH-em-um. *Cistaceae.*
  formosum, see *Halimium lasianthum* subsp. *formosum.*
  halimifolium, see *Halimium halimifolium.*
  nummularium, num-mul-AR-e-um, from L. *nummus*, a coin, the shape of the leaf.
  ocymoides, see *Halimium ocymoides.*
  vineale, vin-e-A-le, inhabiting vineyards.
  vulgare, see *H. nummularium.*

Helianthus, he-le-AN-thus; from Gr. *helios*, the sun; *anthos*, a flower, the Sunflower. Annuals and perennials. *Compositae.*
  annuus, AN-u-us, annual.
  argophyllus, ar-GO-fil-lus, silvery foliage – leaves clothed in white down.
  atrorubens, at-ro-RU-bens, dark red.
  debilis, DE-bil-is, weak, frail.
  debilis subsp. *cucumerifolius*, ku-ku-mer-e-FO-le-us, resembling *Cucumis* (cucumber) foliage.
  decapetalus, dek-a-PET-al-us, ten-petalled.
  giganteus, ji-GAN-te-us, gigantic.
  multiflorus, mul-tif-LO-rus, many flowered.
  pauciflorus, paw-sif-LO-rus, few-flowered.
  rigidus, see *H. pauciflorus.*

sparsifolius, see *H. atrorubens.*
tomentosus, to-men-TO-sus, felted, the leaf underparts.

Helichrysum, he-le-KRI-sum; from Gr. *helios*, the sun; *chrysos*, gold, alluding to the flowers of some species. Border plants and shrubs. *Compositae.*
  bellidioides, see *Anaphalioides bellidioides.*
  bracteatum, brak-te-A-tum, the flowers having many bracts.
  rosmarinifolium, ros-mar-e-nif-OL-e-um, *Rosmarinus* (Rosemary) leaved.
  triplinerve, trip-le-NER-ve, three-nerved – the leaves.

Heliconia, he-le-KO-ne-a; from Gr. *Helicon*, a mountain in Greece. Tropical herbaceous foliage plants. *Heliconiaceae.*
  aureo-striata, see *H. wagneriana.*
  illustris, see *H. indica.*
  indica, IN-di-ka, of India.
  rubricaulis, see *H. indica.*
  wagneriana, wag-ner-e-A-na, after Moritz Friedrich Wagner (1813–1887), German botanist.

Heliocereus, he-le-o-se-RE-us; from Gr. *helios*, the sun; *cereus*, cactus, flowers expand in sunlight. Greenhouse cacti. *Cactaceae.*
  speciosus, spes-e-O-sus, handsome.

Heliohebe, he-le-o-HEE-bee; from Gr. *helios*, the sun; *hebe*, Greek goddess of youth, cupbearer to the gods. Sun Hebe. Shrubs or subshrubs. *Plantaginaceae.*
  hulkeana, hul-ke-A-na, probably of native origin.

Heliophila, he-le-O-fil-a; from Gr. *helios*, the sun; *phileo*, to love. Half-hardy annuals. *Brassicaceae.*
  africana, af-re-KA-na, of Africa.
  arabioides, see *H. africana.*
  linearis, lin-e-AR-is, linear leaved, narrow, with nearly parallel sides.
  linearis var. *linearifolia*, lin-e-ar-if-OL-e-a, narrow leaved.
  pilosa, pil-O-sa, soft long hairs.

Heliopsis, he-le-OP-sis; from Gr. *helios*, the sun; *opsis*, a resemblance, the appearance of the flowers. Hardy perennials. *Compositae.*
  helianthoides, he-le-anth-OY-dees, resembling *Helianthus.*

helianthoides var. *scabra*, SKA-bra, rough.
laevis, see *Bidens laevis*.
scabra, see *H. helianthoides* subsp. *scabra*.

Heliotropium, he-le-o-TRO-pe-um; from Gr. *helios*, the sun; *trope*, to turn, the flowers were believed to turn to the sun. Greenhouse sub-shrubs. *Boraginaceae*.
arborescens, ar-bor-ES-cenz, tree like.
nicotianifolium, nik-o-te-A-ne-FO-le-um, resembling *Nicotiana* (Tobacco) leaves.
peruvianum, see *H. arborescens*.

Helipterum, hel-IP-ter-um; from Gr. *helios*, the sun; *pteron*, a wing, in reference to the plumed seed pappus. Hardy annuals. *Compositae*.
manglesii, mang-LES-e-i, after James Mangles (1786–1867), British naval officer, naturalist and horticulturist.
roseum, see *Rhodanthe chlorocephala* subsp. *rosea*.

Helleborus, hel-LE-bor-us; classical name of one of the species. Herbaceous perennials. *Ranunculaceae*.
caucasicus, kaw-KAS-ik-us, Caucasian.
colchicus, KOL-chik-us, from Colchis.
foetidus, FET-id-us, bad-smelling.
guttatus, see *H. caucasicus*.
lividus, LIV-id-us, leaves bluish grey or lead-coloured.
niger, NI-jer, black – the root. Christmas Hellebore or Christmas Rose.
viridis, VIR-id-is, green – the flowers.

Helonias, hel-O-ne-as; from Gr. *helos*, a marsh, *H. bullata* being a bog plant. *Melanthiaceae*.
bullata, bul-LA-ta, puckered – like a primrose leaf.

Heloniopsis, hel-o-ne-OP-sis; from Gr. *Helonias (q.v.)* and Gr. *opsis*, a resemblance. Herbaceous plants. *Melanthiaceae*.
orientalis, or-e-en-TA-lis, eastern – Eastern Asia (China).
orientalis var. *breviscapa*, brev-is-KA-pa, short-scaped (stalked).

Helxine, misapplied see below.
soleirolii, see *Soleirolia soleirolii*.

Hemerocallis, hem-er-o-KAL-lis; from Gr. *hemera*, a day; *kallos*, beauty. Herbaceous perennials. *Xanthorrhoeaceae*.
aurantiaca, see *H. fulva* var. *aurantiaca*.
dumortieri, do-mor-TE-ayr-e, in honour of Barthélemy Charles Joseph Dumortier (1797–1878), Belgian botanist and member of parliament.
flava, see *H. lilioasphodelus*.
fulva, FUL-va, tawny.
fulva var. *aurantiaca*, aw-ran-te-A-ka, golden orange.
graminea, see *H. minor*.
lilioasphodelus, le-le-o-as-FO-del-us; name given by Clusius.
middendorffii, mid-den-DORF-e-i, after Alexander von Theodorowitsch Middendorff (1815–1894), zoologist and botanist who was active in Siberia.
minor, MY-nor, dwarf.

Hemionitis, he-me-on-I-tis; from Gr. *hemionos*, a mule, the plants being thought sterile. Warm-house ferns. *Pteridaceae*.
arifolia, ar-if-OL-e-a, leaves resembling *Arum*.
cordata, see *H. arifolia*.
palmata, pal-MA-ta, palmate, like a hand – the leaves.

Hepatica, he-PAT-ik-a; from Gr. *hepar*, liver, which the lobed leaves are supposed to resemble. Perennials. *Ranunculaceae*.
angulosa, see *Anemone angulosa*.
triloba, see *Anemone hepatica*.

Heracleum, her-AK-le-um; named after Hercules, who is said to have discovered the plant's medicinal virtues; or after *heracles*, a plant consecrated to Hercules. Biennials and perennials. *Apiaceae*.
giganteum, ji-GAN-te-um, gigantic.
mantegazzianum, man-te-gats-e-A-num, dedicated to Paolo Mantegazza (1831–1910), a champion of Darwinian theory in Italy.
sphondylium, sfon-DIL-le-um, name given by Caspar Bauhin. Possibly referring to the similarity of the segmented stem to vertebrae.
sphondylium subsp. *sibiricum*, si-BIR-ik-um, Siberian.

Hereroa, her-e-RO-a; after Herer in Namibia, the native habitat. Succulent plants. *Aizoaceae*.

dolabriformis, dol-A-brif-OR-mis, axe or hatchet shaped leaves.

granulata, gran-u-LA-ta, granulated or rough.

Herniaria, her-ne-AR-e-a; from L. *hernia*, rupture, for which the plant was a supposed remedy. Creeping or carpeting rock plant. *Caryophyllaceae.*

glabra, GLAB-ra, smooth.

Herpestis, her-PES-tis; from Gr. *herpestes*, creeping – the habit of the plant. Aquatic. *Plantaginaceae.*

amplexicaulis, am-pleks-e-KAW-lis, leaves clasping the stem.

Hertia, her-TE-a; in honour of Joannes Casimirus Hertius (1679–1748), German physician and author. Herbaceous perennial. *Compositae.*

cheirifolia, ky-rif-O-le-a, leaves resembling see *Erysimum* × *cheiri* (the wallflower).

Hesperantha, hes-per-AN-tha; from Gr. *hespera*, evening; *anthos*, a flower. Corms. *Iridaceae.*

coccinea, kok-SIN-e-a, scarlet.

Hesperis, HES-per-is; from Gr. *hespera*, evening, the Sweet Rockets being more fragrant at this time of day. Biennial and herbaceous plants. *Brassicaceae.*

matronalis, mat-ro-NA-lis, pertaining to a matron or dame. Old English name, Dame's Violet.

Hesperoyucca, hes-per-o-YUK-ka; from Gr. *hesperos*, western and *yucca* (q.v.). Perennials. *Asparagaceae.*

whipplei, WHIP-ple-i, after Amiel Weeks Whipple (1817–1863), American military engineer and surveyor.

Heteromeles, he-ter-OM-el-eez; from Gr. *heteros*, variable; *melon*, an apple, alluding to the variable character of the fruits. Shrubs. *Rosaceae.*

arbutifolia, ar-bew-tif-OL-e-a, resembling *Arbutus* leaves.

Heuchera, HEW-ke-ra (or HOY-ker-a); named after Johann Heinrich von Heucher (1677–1747), German professor of medi-

cine and botany, correspondent of Linnaeus. Rock and border perennials. *Saxifragaceae.*

americana, a-mer-ik-A-na, of America.

× *brizoides*, briz-OY-dees, resembling *Briza*, Brizoides group.

hispida, HIS-pid-a, bristly.

micrantha, mi-KRAN-tha, small-flowered.

sanguinea, san-GWIN-e-a, blood red.

Hexacentris, unresolved see below.

mysorensis, see *Thunbergia mysorensis.*

Hibbertia, hib-BER-te-a; after George Hibbert (1757–1837), a patron of botany. Greenhouse climbers. *Dilleniaceae.*

dentata, den-TA-ta, toothed, the leaves.

volubilis, vol-U-bil-is, twining.

Hibiscus, hi-BIS-kus; name of very ancient origin used by Virgil for a mallow-like plant. Shrubs, perennials and annuals. *Malvaceae.*

africanus, see *H. trionum.*

manihot, see *Abelmoschus manihot.*

syriacus, syr-e-AK-us, Syrian, misleading name, since this shrub has been cultivated in Korea prior to the sixteenth century.

trionum, tre-O-num, three-coloured. The Flower of an Hour Hibiscus or Bladder Ketmia.

Hidalgoa, hid-AL-go-a; after Miguel Hidalgo (1753–1811), early Mexican leader. Half-hardy climber. *Compositae.*

wercklei, WERK-le-i, after Carlo Werckle (1860–1924), Costa Rican plant collector.

Hieracium, hi-er-AK-e-um; an ancient name from Gr. *hierax*, a hawk. Pliny, the Roman naturalist, believed hawks ate the plant to strengthen their eyesight. Also pronounced hi-er-A-se-um. The Hawkweed. Perennial herbs. *Compositae.*

aurantiacum, see *Pilosella aurantiaca.*

pannosum, pan-NO-sum, roughly hairy, like wool cloth.

pannosum subsp. *bornmuelleri*, born-MOOL-ler-i, after Joseph Friedrich Nicolaus Bornmüller (1862–1948), German botanist, who collaborated with Josef Freyn.

villosum, vil-LO-sum, covered with long, loose hairs.

Hierochloe, hi-er-o-KLO-e; from Gr. *hieros*, sacred; *chloe*, grass, alluding to the grass

being strewn on church floors, hence the English name of Holy Grass. *Poaceae.*
odorata, od-or-A-ta, sweet-scented.

Himantoglossum, he-man-toe-GLOS-um; from Gr. *himas*, strap; *glossa*, a tongue, alluding to the unusually long strap-like labellum. Greenhouse orchids. *Orchidaceae.*
hircinum, her-SE-num, from L. *hircus*, he-goat, pertaining to the smell.

Hippeastrum, hip-pe-AS-trum; from Gr. *hippeus*, a knight; *astron*, a star, from the fancied resemblance of the species to a horses head and associated with Knight's star. Greenhouse bulbs. *Amaryllidaceae.*
equestre, see *H. puniceum.*
pratense, see *Rhodophiala pratensis.*
puniceum, pu-NIS-e-um, reddish-purple.
reticulatum, re-tik-ul-A-tum, the colours forming a network.

Hippocrepis, hip-po-KRE-pis; from Gr. *hippo*, horse; *krepis*, a shoe, in reference to the shape of the seed pod, which resembles a horseshoe. Rock plants. *Leguminosae.*
comosa, ko-MO-sa, hairy, in tufts.
emerus, EM-er-us, old generic name, meaning cultivated.
emerus subsp. emeroides, em-er-OY-dees, resembling *emerus.*

Hippolytia, hip-po-LI-te-a; commemorates Ippolit Mikhailovich Krascheninnikov (1884–1947), Russian botanist. Herbaceous perennials. *Compositae.*
herderi, HERD-er-i, after Ferdinand Gottfried Theobald Herder (1828–1896), German botanist, in Russia.

Hippophae, hip-PO-fa-e; Gr. name for a spring plant. Shrub. *Elaeagnaceae.*
rhamnoides, see *Elaeagnus rhamnoides.*
salicifolia, sal-is-if-O-le-a, *Salix* (Willow) leaved.

Hippuris, hip-PUR-is; from Gr. *hippos*, a horse; *oura*, a tail – the stems, crowded with hair-like leaves, resemble a horse's tail. Submerged aquatics. *Plantaginaceae.*
vulgaris, vul-GAR-is, common.

Hoffmannia, hof-MAN-e-a; named after Georg Frank Hoffmann (1760–1826),

professor of botany at Göttingen. Herbs or woody plants with very showy foliage. *Rubiaceae.*
discolor, DIS-ko-lor, various colours.
regalis, re-GA-lis, royal.

Holboellia, hol-BEL-le-a; after Frederik Ludvig Holboell (1765–1829), of Copenhagen Botanic Garden. Greenhouse climber. *Berberidaceae.*
latifolia, lat-if-O-le-a, broad-leaved.

Holcoglossum, hol-ko-GLOS-sum; from Gr. *holkos*, furrow; *glossa*, a tongue. Orchid. *Orchidaceae.*
kimballianum, kim-bal-le-A-num, named in honour of the American orchid collector W.S. Kimball.

Holcus, HOL-kus; from Gr. *holkus*, the name of a grass. Hardy variegated grass. *Poaceae.*
lanatus, la-NA-tus, soft-leaved.

Holodiscus, ho-lo-DIS-kus; from Gr. *holos*, entire; *diskos*, a disk, in allusion to the flower disk. Shrubs. *Rosaceae.*
dumosus, dew-MO-sus, bushy or shrubby.

Homeria, ho-ME-re-a; said to be from Gr. *homereo*, alluding to the meeting or joining of the filaments. Greenhouse bulbous plants. *Iridaceae.*
collina, see *Moraea collina.*
tricolor, TRIK-o-lor, three coloured.

Hoodia, HOOD-e-a; Sweet commemorated the plant to Mr. Hood, a cultivator of succulent plants. Greenhouse succulents. *Apocynaceae.*
bainii, BANE-e-i, after Thomas Bain (1830–1893), South African plant collector.
gordonii, GOR-do-ne-i, after Robert Jacob Gordon (1743–1795), Dutch explorer collecting in South Africa.

Hordeum, HOR-de-um; Latin name for barley. Ornamental grasses. *Poaceae.*
jubatum, joo-BA-tum, crested or maned.

Hornungia, hor-NUN-ge-a; after Ernst Gottfried Hornung (1795–1862), German pharmacist. Annuals. *Brassicaceae.*
alpina, al-PINE-a (or al-PIN-a), of the Alps or alpine.

Hosackia, hos-AK-e-a; commemorating Dr. David Hosack (1769–1835), American botanist. Rock and border plants. *Leguminosae*.
  oblongifolia, ob-long-if-O-le-a, oblong-leaved.
  purshiana, see *Acmispon americanus*.

Hosta, HOS-ta; after Nicholaus Thomas Host (1761–1834), botanist and physician to the Emperor of Austria. Hardy foliage and flowering plants. *Asparagaceae*.
  lancifolia, lan-sif-O-le-a, leaves lance shaped.
  longipes, LON-gi-pez, long-footed.
  plantaginea, plan-ta-JIN-e-a, leaves resembling *Plantago* (plantain).
  sieboldiana, se-bold-e-A-na, after Philipp Franz Balthasar von Siebold (1796–1866), German physician, botanist, and traveller.
  undulata, un-du-LA-ta, waved – the leaves.

Hottonia, hot-TO-ne-a; after Peter Hotton (1648–1709), Dutch professor of botany at Leiden. Aquatics. *Primulaceae*.
  palustris, pal-US-tris, found in marshy places.

Houstonia, hows-TO-ne-a; commemorating William Houston (1695–1733), Scottish surgeon and plant collector. Rock plants. *Rubiaceae*.
  serpyllifolia, ser-pil-if-O-le-a, leaves like wild thyme, *Thymus serpyllum*.

Houttuynia, howt-too-IN-e-a; after Maarten Houttuyn (1720–1794), Dutch naturalist and physician. Marsh plants. *Saururaceae*.
  cordata, kor-DA-ta, heart shaped, the leaves.

Hovea, HO-ve-a; after Anton Pantaleon Hove (c.1762–1830), a Polish botanist. Greenhouse flowering shrub. *Leguminosae*.
  elliptica, el-LIP-tik-a, ellipse-shaped, the leaves.

Howea, HOW-e-a; after Lord Howe's Island, where these plants are found. Greenhouse and room palms. *Arecaceae*.
  belmoreana, bel-mor-e-A-na, after Somerset Richard Lowry-Corry, fourth Earl of Belmore (1835–1913), governor of New South Wales.
  forsteriana, fors-ter-e-A-na, after Johann Reinhold Forster (1729–1798) and Georg Forster (1754–1794), collectors on Cook's second voyage which included Norfolk Island.

Hoya, HOY-a; after Thomas Hoy (c.1750–1822), head gardener at Syon House, seat of the Duke of Northumberland. The Wax Flower. Evergreen perennial. *Apocynaceae*.
  bella, see *H. lanceolata* subsp. *bella*.
  carnosa, kar-NO-sa, fleshy or flesh coloured – the flowers.
  lanceolata, lan-se-o-LA-ta, the leaves spear-shaped.
  lanceolata subsp. *bella*, BEL-la, pretty.
  paxtonii, see *H. lanceolata* subsp. *bella*.

Humea, misapplied see below.
  elegans, see *Calomeria amaranthoides*.

Humulus, HU-mu-lus; origin uncertain, possibly from Latinised form of old German *humela*, hops, from L. *humus*, soil, that is lowly or trailing if not supported. Climbing or twining plants. *Cannabaceae*.
  japonicus var. *variegatus*, see *H. scandens*.
  lupulus, LOO-pul-us, the old herbalists' shop name for the Hop, meaning a wolf; also applied to hook-like teeth with which the stems are armed and by which it climbs or clings to a support.
  scandens, SKAN-denz, climbing.
  yunnanensis, yun-nan-EN-sis, of Yunnan, China.

Hunnemannia, hun-ne-MAN-ne-a; after John Hunneman (c. 1760–1839), London book-seller and introducer of plants. Half-hardy perennial. *Papaveraceae*.
  fumariifolia, fu-mar-e-i-FO-le-a, leaves resembling *Fumaria* (fumitory).

Hutchinsia, hut-CHIN-se-a; after Ellen Hutchins (1785–1815), Irish botanist, a specialist in non-flowering plants. Rock plants. *Brassicaceae*.
  alpina, see *Hornungia alpina*.

Hyacinthoides, hy-a-sinth-OY-dees; resembling *Hyacinthus* (hyacinth). Bulbs. *Asparagaceae*.
  hispanica, his-PAN-ik-a, of Spain. The Spanish Bluebell.
  italica, it-AL-ik-a, of Italy.
  lingulata, ling-ul-A-ta, tongue-leaved.
  non-scripta, non-SKRIP-ta, without markings.

Hyacinthus, hi-a-SIN-thus; named after Hyakinthos, the beautiful Spartan (Greek Mythology), who was accidentally killed by Apollo. The legend stating that a plant sprang up from where his blood was shed. Florists' hyacinths are forms of *H. orientalis*. Bulbous perennials. *Asparagaceae.*

　amethystinus, see *Hyacinthoides hispanica.*
　azureus, see *Bellevalia ciliata.*
　orientalis, or-e-en-TA-lis, eastern – Eastern Asia (China).
　romanus, see *Bellevalia romana.*

Hydrangea, hy-DRAN-je-a; from Gr. *hydor*, water; *aggeion*, a vessel, or vase, in reference to the shape of the seed capsule. Shrubs. *Hydrangeaceae.*

　arborescens, ar-bor-ES-cenz, tree like.
　aspera, AS-per-a, rough to the touch.
　heteromalla, het-er-o-MAL-la, woolly-leaved.
　hortensis, see *H. macrophylla.*
　macrophylla, mak-rof-IL-a, with large leaves.
　paniculata, pan-ik-ul-A-ta, flowers in a panicle or branching inflorescence.
　petiolaris, pet-e-o-LAR-is, with a long leaf-stalk.
　vestita, see *H. heteromalla.*

Hydrocharis, hi-DROK-ar-is; from Gr. *hydor*, water; *charis*, graceful, in allusion to the beauty of the floating flowers. Aquatics. *Hydrocharitaceae.*

　morsus-ranae, MOR-sus-RA-ne; from L. *morsus*, a bite; *rana*, a frog. The Frog-bit.

Hydrocotyle, hi-dro-KOT-il-e; from Gr. *hydor*, water; *kotyle*, a cup, in reference to the cup-like hollow at the centre of the leaf. Bog plants. *Araliaceae.*

　vulgaris, vul-GAR-is, common.

Hydropeltis, synonym please see below.

　purpurea, see *Brasenia schreberi.*

Hylocereus, hi-lo-SE-re-us; from Gr. *hyle*, a wood, and *cereus;* the habitat – epiphytic on trees. Greenhouse climbing cacti. *Cactaceae.*

　triangularis, see *H. trigonus.*
　trigonus, tri-GO-nus, three angled – the stem.

Hymenanthera, unresolved see below.

　crassifolia, see *Melicytus crassifolius.*

Hymenocallis, hi-men-o-KAL-is; from Gr. *hymen*, a membrane; *kalos*, beautiful, a reference to the membranous cup forming the flower centre. Bulbous plants. *Amaryllidaceae.*

　calathina, see *Ismene narcissiflora.*
　caribaea, ka-RIB-e-a, Caribbean.
　× *macrostephana*, mak-ros-TEF-an-a, large crowned.
　ovata, o-VA-ta, egg-shaped – the leaves.
　speciosa, spes-e-O-sa, showy.

Hymenophyllum, hi-men-of-IL-lum; from Gr. *hymen*, a membrane; *phyllon*, a leaf, alluding to the delicate membranous fronds. Greenhouse filmy ferns. *Hymenophyllaceae.*

　demissum, dem-IS-sum, hanging down.
　flabellatum, flab-el-LA-tum, fan-shaped.
　pulcherrimum, pul-KER-rim-um, most beautiful.
　tunbrigense, tun-brij-EN-se, of Tunbridge Wells. Tunbridge Wells Filmy Fern.

Hymenoxys, hi-men-OX-is; from Gr. *hymen*, a membrane; *oxys*, sharp. Herbaceous perennials and sub-shrubs. *Compositae.*

　grandiflora, gran-dif-LO-ra, large flowered.

Hyophorbe, hi-o-FOR-be; from Gr. *hys*, pig; *phorbe*, food. The fruits eaten by pigs. Palms. *Arecaceae.*

　indica, IN-di-ka, of India.

Hypericum, hi-PER-ik-um (in Classical Greek, hi-per-E-kum); Gr. name of obscure meaning; some authorities derive word from Gr. *hyper*, above; *eikon*, image, flowers being placed above images to keep evil away; or *ereike*, a heath, possibly in reference to the natural habitat of some species. Rock and border plants and shrubs. *Hypericaceae.*

　androsaemum, an-dros-E-mum, old generic name from Gr. *aner*, man; *haima*, blood, the berry being red. The Tutsan.
　auruem, see *H. monogynum.*
　balearicum, bal-e-AR-ik-um, of the Balearic Isles.
　calycinum, kal-is-E-num, from L. *calyx*, a cup, probably in allusion to the large cup-shaped calyx.
　coris, KOR-is, the leaves resembling *Coris.*
　empetrifolium, em-pet-rif-O-le-um, with leaves resembling *Empetrum.*
　fragile, FRAJ-il-e, fragile.

hircinum, her-SE-num, from L. *hircus*, he-goat, pertaining to the smell.

hookerianum, hook-er-e-A-num, after Sir William Jackson Hooker (1785–1865), professor of botany, director of the Royal Botanic Gardens, Kew.

humifusum, hu-me-FEW-sum, spread over the ground.

hyssopifolium, his-sup-e-FOH-le-um, leaves resemble *Hyssopus*.

kalmianum, kal-me-A-num, after Peter Kalm (1715–1779), Finnish naturalist, pupil of Linnaeus and traveller in North America, who discovered it.

lysimachioides, lis-im-ak-e-OY-dees, resembling *Lysimachia* (Loosestrife).

monogynum, mon-O-jin-um, having a single pistil.

× *moserianum*, mo-ser-e-A-num, hybrid developed by Jean-Jacques Moser, Versailles.

patulum, PAT-u-lum, spreading.

polyphyllum, pol-if-IL-lum, many-leaved.

repens, RE-penz, creeping and rooting.

reptans, REP-tans, creeping.

Hypolepis, hi-po-LEP-is; from Gr. *hypo*, under; *lepis*, a scale, the position of the sori. Greenhouse ferns. *Dennstaedtiaceae*.

distans, DIS-tanz, distant, the frond divisions.

millefolium, mil-le-FO-le-um, thousand-leaved.

repens, RE-penz, creeping.

Hyssopus, his-SO-pus; applied to this plant from a very ancient name used by the Greeks, probably of Hebrew origin. A pot herb. The Hyssop. *Lamiaceae*.

officinalis, of-fis-in-A-lis, of the shop (apothecary's), applied to plants always kept "in stock" by herbalists.

Iberis, I-ber-is; from Iberia, the ancient name for Spain, were many of the species are common. Rock and border plants. *Brassicaceae*.

carnosa, kar-NO-sa, fleshy.

corifolia, kor-if-OL-e-a, with leathery leaves.

coronaria, kor-on-AR-e-a, crown flowering. The Rocket Candytuft.

pruitii, see *I. carnosa*.

saxatilis, saks-A-til-is, inhabiting rocks.

semperflorens, sem-per-FLOR-enz, always flowering.

sempervirens, sem-per-VEER-enz, always green.

tenoreana, see *I. carnosa*.

umbellata, um-bel-LA-ta, flowers in an umbel. Annual Candytuft.

Idesia, i-DE-ze-a; named after E.Y. Ides, a German or Dutch explorer, who travelled in China in the seventeenth century for Tzar Peter the Great. Tree. *Salicaceae*.

polycarpa, pol-ik-AR-pa, many-fruited.

Ilex, I-leks; from the old Latin name *ilex*, an evergreen oak (Holm Oak), to which the Holly was supposed to bear some resemblance. Many of the hollies in cultivation are forms of *I. aquifolium*. Evergreen trees and shrubs. *Aquifoliaceae*.

× *altaclarensis*, al-ta-kla-REN-sis, raised at Highclere Castle in 1835 (*I. aquifolium* × *I. perado*).

aquifolium, ak-we-FO-le-um, old name, meaning pointed leaves. Possibly from L. *acus*, needle or pin; *folia*, leaf, on account of its prickly leaf.

cornuta, kor-NU-ta, horned or horn shaped.

crenata, kre-NA-ta, cut in round scallops; leaves crenate.

perado, per-A-do, introduced by James Gordon in 1760.

perado subsp. *platyphylla*, plat-e-FIL-la, broadleaves.

pernyi, PER-ne-i, after Paul Hubert Perny (1818–1907), French missionary in China.

platyphylla, see *I. perado* subsp. *platyphylla*.

Illicium, il-LIS-e-um; from L. *illicio*, to attract or allure, referring to the aromatic perfume. The Aniseed Tree. Shrubs and trees. *Schisandraceae*.

anisatum, an-is-A-tum, anise-scented.

floridanum, flor-id-A-num, of Florida.

Imantophyllum, im-ant-of-IL-lum; from Gr. *imas*, a leather thong; *phyllon*, a leaf, alluding to the leaves which are strap-like in form and texture. An excellent name dropped in favour of the merely complimentary one of *Clivia* (which see). Both names were published on the same date, namely, October 1, 1828.

Impatiens, im-PA-she-enz (or im-PAT-e-enz); from L. *impatiens*, impatient or hasty, in allusion to the manner in which the pods of some species explode and scatter their seed when touched. Annuals and biennials. *Balsaminaceae*.

balsamina, bawl-sa-ME-na, Balsam, old name for the group.

glandulifera, glan-dul-IF-er-a, gland-bearing – the leaves.

longicornuta, long-e-KOR-nu-ta, long horned, that is, the flowers.

noli-tangere, no-li-TAN-ger-e, pop, 'touch me not', in reference to the expulsive action of the seed pods.

roylei, see *I. glandulifera*.

sultani, see *I. walleriana*.

walleriana, wall-er-e-AN-a, named in honour of Rev. Horace Waller (1833–1896), who collected impatiens on a Zambezi expedition in 1864 with Scottish explorer David Livingstone. Busy-Lizzies.

Incarvillea, in-kar-VIL-le-a; commemorating Pierre d'Incarville (1706–1757), French Jesuit missionary to China, correspondent of M. Jussieu. Herbaceous perennials. *Bignoniaceae*.

brevipes, see *I. mairei*.

delavayi, de-la-VA-i, after Père Jean Marie Delavay (1834–1895), missionary and plant collector in Yunnan province, China.

mairei, MAIR-e-i, in honour of Edouard Ernest Maire (1848–1932), missionary in Yunnan, West China, who made large collections of herbarium specimens between 1905 and 1916.

olgae, OL-gay-e, named after Olga Fedtschenko (1845–1921), Russian botanist.

Indigofera, in-dig-OF-er-a; from indigo, the blue dye (L. *indicum*, indigo); *fero*, to bear, or produce. Shrubs. *Leguminosae*.

gerardiana, see *I. heterantha*.

heterantha, het-e-RAN-tha, from Gr. *heteros*, varying; *anthos*, flower, in allusion to the diverse flowers.

Inula, IN-u-la; believed to be a corruption of helenium, *I. helenium* (Elecampane) being the *Inula campana* of Medieval Latin. Herbaceous perennials. *Compositae*.

ensifolia, en-sif-OL-e-a, leaves in the shape of a sword.

glandulosa, see *I. orientalis*.

helenium, hel-E-ne-um, old generic name, meaning Helen-flower.

macrocephala, mak-ro-SEF-a-la, large headed.

montana, mon-TA-na, of mountains.

oculus-christi, OK-u-lus-KRIS-te, Christ's eyes, presumably the appearance of the blossom.

orientalis, or-e-en-TA-lis, Eastern.

royleana, roy-le-A-na, named for John Forbes Royle (1798–1858), British botanist and physician, in India 1819–1831, then professor of material medica in London 1837–1856.

salicina, sal-is-E-na, resembling *Salix* (willow), the leaves.

Ionopsidium, misapplied see below.

acaule, see *Cochlearia acaulis*.

Ipomoea, ip-o-ME-a; from Gr. *ips*, worm, used by Linnaeus for bindweed; *homoios*, like, referring to the twining habit. Mostly annuals. *Convolvulaceae*.

batatas, bat-A-tas, the vernacular Carib (Haitian) Indian name for sweet potato. From it derives the English word potato.

coccinea, see *I. rubriflora*.

hederacea, see *I. nil*.

lobata, lo-BA-ta, lobed.

nil, NIL, possibly taken from *hub-al-nil* or *granum nil*, the Arabic for Ipomoea.

purpurea, pur-PUR-e-a, purple coloured.

quamoclit, kwa-MOK-lit, *Quamoclit*, the native name.

rubriflora, roo-bree-FLOR-a, red flowered.

rubro-coerula, see *I. tricolor*.

tricolor, TRIK-o-lor, three coloured.

versicolor, see *I. lobata*.

Iresine, i-res-IN-e; from Gr. *eiros*, wool, alluding to the flowers and seeds. Tender annuals and herbaceous perennials. *Amaranthaceae*.

herbstii, HERB-ste-i, after Hermann Herbst, nursery and seedsman of Herbst and Stenger, Kew Nursery, Kew Road, Richmond.

lindenii, LIN-den-e-i, after Jean Jules Linden (1817–1898), Luxembourg botanical explorer in South America, later nurseryman in Belgium.

Iris, I-ris; from Gr. *iris*, a rainbow, presumably in reference to the many colours of the flowers. Bulbous, rhizomatous and herbaceous perennials. *Iridaceae*.

brevicaulis, brev-e-KAW-lis, short-stemmed.

bulleyana, bul-le-A-na, after Arthur Kilpin Bulley (1861–1942), founder of Bees nursery, Neston, Cheshire.

chamaeiris, see *I. lutescens*.

chrysographes, kris-o-GRAF-es, veined with gold.

cristata, kris-TA-ta, crested.

delavayi, de-la-VA-i, after Père Jean Marie Delavay (1834–1895), missionary and plant collector in Yunnan province, China.

douglasiana, dug-las-e-A-na, after David Douglas (1799–1834), botanist and explorer who introduced North American plants to Europe.

ensata, en-SAR-ta, resembling a sword.

filifolia, fil-if-OL-e-a, three-leaved, narrow foliage.

florentina, flor-en-TE-na, of Florence, Italy.

foetidissima, fet-id-IS-sim-a, most fetid – the leaf colour.

foliosa, see *I. brevicaulis*.

forrestii, for-RES-te-i, after George Forrest (1873–1932), Scottish plant collector. Forrest collected in China between 1904 and 1932.

fulva, FUL-va, tawny.

× *germanica*, jer-MAN-ik-a, of Germany.

gracilipes, gras-IL-e-pez, slender stalked.

graminea, gram-IN-e-a, grassy, the foliage.

hexagona, heks-ag-O-na, the ovary being six-angled.

histrio, HIS-tre-o, from L. *histrio*, an actor, the flowers being dramatic.

hoogiana, hoo-ge-A-na, dedicated to the brothers Johannes Marius Cornelius Hoog (1865–1950) and Thomas Marinus Hoog (1873–1948), of C.G. van Turbergen nursery Haarlem, Dutch bulb growers.

japonica, jap-ON-ik-a, of Japan.

juncea, JUN-se-a, a rush, the plant having rush-like leaves.

kaempferi, see *I. ensata*.

lacustris, la-KUS-tris, a lake, found by the Great Lakes.

laevigata, lev-e-GA-ta, smooth.

latifolia, lat-if-O-le-a, broad-leaved.

lutescens, lu-TES-senz, becoming yellow.

missouriensis, mis-soor-e-EN-sis, found at the source of the River Missouri, Rocky Mountains.

monnieri, see *I. orientalis*.

ochroleuca, see *I. orientalis*.

orientalis, or-e-en-TA-lis, Eastern.

pallida, PAL-lid-a, pale, the flowers paler in colour than those of the commoner *I.* × *germanica*.

pseudacorus, sued-ak-OR-us, false acorus so named to distinguish it from *Acorus calamus*, true Acorus.

pumila, PU-mil-a, dwarf or diminutive.

reticulata, re-tik-ul-A-ta, netted – the bulb.

ruthenica, roo-THEN-ik-a, Russian.

siberica, si-BIR-ik-a, of Siberia.

spuria, SPU-re-a, illegitimate, considered a hybrid by Linnaeus.

stylosa, see *I. unguicularis*.

tectorum, tek-TOR-um, on roofs, this iris being grown on thatched roofs in Japan.

tenax, TE-naks, tough, the fibres of the leaves.

tingitana, ting-e-TA-na, of Tangiers.

unguicularis, un-gwik-ul-AR-is, furnished with a claw, narrowing to the base.

versicolor, ver-SIK-o-lor, variable coloured.

xiphioides, see *I. latifolia*.

xiphium, ZIF-e-um, old Greek name for *Gladiolus segetum*, from *xiphos*, sword.

Isatis, i-SA-tis; classical name for a healing herb. Biennials. *Brassicaceae.*

glauca, GLAW-ka, blue-green, the foliage.

tinctoria, ting-TOR-e-a, of dyers. Woad. The blue dye used by ancient Britons to stain their bodies.

Ismelia, iz-MEL-e-a; origin obscure named by Henri Cassini in 1826. Annual. *Compositae.*

carinata, ka-ri-NA-ta, keeled.

Ismene, is-ME-ne; after *Ismene*, daughter of Oedipus and Jocasta in Greek legend. Bulbous plants. *Amaryllidaceae.*

longipetala, long-e-PET-a-la, long petalled.

narcissiflora, nar-sis-i-FLOR-ra, narcissus flowered.

Isoetes, is-o-EE-tez; from Gr. *isos*, equal; *etos*, year – the plant does not alter with the seasons. Submerged aquatic. The Quillwort. *Isoetaceae.*

lacustris, la-KUS-tris, found in lakes.

Isolatocereus, i-so-la-toh-SE-re-us; from L. *isolato*, remote or isolated; *cereus*, wax taper (a candle), describing the sparseness of plants in habitat. Cacti. *Cactaceae.*

dumortieri, do-mor-TE-ayr-e, in honour of Barthélemy Charles Joseph Dumortier (1797–1878), Belgian botanist and member of parliament.

Isolepis, is-o-LEP-is; from Gr. *isos*, equal; *lepis*, a scale, the scales of the perianth are equal. Greenhouse dwarf sedge. *Cyperaceae.*
  cernua, SER-nu-a, drooping.
  gracilis, see *I. cernua.*
  setacea, se-TA-se-a, bristly.

Isoloma, is-o-LO-ma; from Gr. *isos*, equal; *loma*, a border, the lobes of the corolla are equal. Herbaceous plants. *Gesneriaceae.*
  digitaliflorum, see *Kohleria digitaliflora.*
  hondense, see *Kohleria hondensis.*

Isopyrum, is-o-PI-rum; from Gr. *isos*, equal; *pyros*, wheat, the seeds resemble those of wheat. Perennial herbs. *Ranunculaceae.*
  fumarioides, see *Leptopyrum fumarioides.*
  thalictroides, thal-ik-TROY-dees, resembling *Thalictrum.*

Itea, I-te-a; the old Greek name for a willow, alluding to the pendulous racemes looking similar to willow catkins. Trees and shrubs. *Iteaceae.*
  ilicifolia, il-is-if-OL-e-a, *Ilex* (holly) leaved.

Ixia, IKS-e-a; from the Gr. name *ixia*, birdlime, in reference to the sticky nature of the sap. Half-hardy bulbs. *Iridaceae.*
  campanulata, kam-pan-u-LAH-ta, bell-shaped.
  crateroides, see *I. campanulata.*
  viridiflora, ver-id-if-LO-ra, green-flowered.

Ixiolirion, iks-e-o-LIR-e-on; from Gr. *ixia*, birdlime; *leirion*, a lily, literally the ixia like Lily. Bulbs. *Ixioliriaceae.*
  montanum, see *I. tartaricum.*
  tataricum, tah-TAR-ik-um, from Central Asia, formerly called Tartary.

Ixoca, iks-O-ka; the name is a shortened form of the obsolete genus *Ixocaulon*. Perennial herbs. *Caryophyllaceae.*
  quadrifida, kwod-RIF-id-a, petals four-notched.

Ixora, iks-OR-a; after *Iswara*, a Malabar deity to whom the flowers were offered. Tropical flowering plants. *Rubiaceae.*
  coccinea, kok-SIN-e-a, scarlet.
  macrothyrsa, ma-kro-THER-sa, large compact cylindrical panicle.

Jacaranda, jak-ar-AN-da; the vernacular Brazilian name. Tropical trees grown as ornamental foliage pot plants. *Bignoniaceae.*
  caerulea, se-RU-le-a, sky-blue.
  mimosifolia, mim-O-see-FOL-e-a, *Mimosa* leaved.

Jacobaea, jay-ko-BE-a; from its medieval name St James's (*Jacobus*) Wort. Herbaceous perennials. *Compositae.*
  adonidifolia, ad-on-id-if-O-le-a, resembling *Adonis* leaves.
  incana, in-KA-na, hoary or grey, the leaves.
  maritima, mar-IT-im-a, of sea coasts. The Dusty Miller.

Jacobinia, jak-o-BIN-e-a; derivation unknown, possibly named for the town of Jacobina near Bahia, Brazil. Tender perennials. *Acanthaceae.*
  chrysostephana, kris-OS-tef-A-na, golden crowned.
  coccinea, see *Pachystachys coccinea.*
  ghiesbreghtiana, Gheez-brek-te-A-na, after Auguste Boniface Ghiesbreght (1810–1893), Belgium plant collector.

Jamesia, JAME-se-a; in honour of Dr. Edwin James (1797–1861), American botanist, who first discovered it in 1820 on Major Long's expedition to the Rocky Mountains. Shrub. *Hydrangeaceae.*
  americana, a-mer-ik-A-na, of America.

Jasione, jas-e-O-ne; Ancient Greek name for another shrub. Rock plants. *Campanulaceae.*
  crispa, KRIS-pa, finely waved; closely curled.
  humilis, see *J. crispa.*
  laevis, LE-vis, smooth, polished.
  perennis, see *J. laevis.*

Jasminum, jaz-MIN-um; said to be derived from the Persian name *yasmin*, or *yasamin*. Shrubby flowering climbers. *Oleaceae.*
  beesianum, bee-ze-A-num, in honour of the nursery firm Bees who introduced it.
  fruticans, FRUT-ik-anz, from L. *frutex*, a shrub; shrubby or bushy.
  mesnyi, mez-NE-i, in honour of William Mesny (1842–1919), from Jersey.
  nudiflorum, nu-dif-LO-rum, naked flowered, the shrub blooming when the branches are leafless. The Winter Jasmine.

officinale, of-fis-in-A-le, of the shop (herbal). The Jessamine or Jasmine.

Jeffersonia, jef-fer-SO-ne-a; commemorating Thomas Jefferson (1743–1826), President of the United States from 1801–1809. Woodland herb. *Berberidaceae*.
   diphylla, dif-IL-la, two-leaved, that is in pairs.

Juglans, JUG-lanz; old Latin name for the walnut. From *jovis*, of Jupiter; *glans*, an acorn. The nut of Jupiter in mythology. Trees. *Juglandaceae*.
   nigra, NY-gra, black.
   regia, RE-je-a, royal, princely, application uncertain. The Walnut.

Juncus, JUN-kus; from L. *jungo*, to tie or bind, the stems being used as cord. Aquatic grasses. *Juncaceae*.
   effusus, ef-FEW-sus, spread out, the leaves.
   zebrinus, see *J. effusus*.

Juniperus, ju-NIP-er-us; old Latin name for the Juniper tree. Evergreen trees and shrubs. *Cupressaceae*.
   chinensis, tshi-NEN-sis, of China.
   communis, kom-MU-nis, common, that is, in groups or communities. The Juniper.
   drupacea, droo-PA-se-a, alluding to the drupe-like fruits.
   deppeana, dep-e-A-na, after Ferdinand Deppe (1794–1861), German botanist.
   excelsa, eks-SEL-sa, tall.
   pachyphlaea, see *J. deppeana*.
   procumbens, pro-KUM-benz, prostrate.
   sabina, sa-BI-na, old Latin name for the Savin.
   virginiana, vir-jin-e-A-na, of Virginia.

Jussiaea, jus-SE-e-a; after Bernard de Jussieu (1699–1777), pioneer French botanist. Bog aquatics. *Onagraceae*.
   longifolia, see *Ludwigia longifolia*.
   repens, see *Ludwigia adscendens*.
   scabra, SKA-bra, rough, the bark.
   sprengeri, see *Ludwigia peruviana*.

Justicia, jus-TIS-e-a; after James Justice F.R.S. (fl. 1730–1763), a noted Scottish horticulturist. Greenhouse flowering shrubs. *Acanthaceae*.
   calycotricha, see *Schaueria calycotricha*.
   carnea, KAR-ne-a, flesh-coloured.

carthaeginensis, kar-tha-jin-EN-sis, of Cartagena, Columbia.
   flavicoma, flav-e-KO-ma, yellow-haired.
   floribunda, flor-e-BUN-da, abundant or free flowering.

Kaempferia, keep-FEER-e-a; after Engelbert Kaempfer (1651–1716), physician. Kaempfer joined the Dutch East India Company and travelled widely throughout the East and settled in Nagasaki, Japan for two years. Tropical foliage plants. *Zingiberaceae*.
   gilbertii, GIL-bert-e-i, origin obscure possibly after Mr. Gilbert of Moulmein (in present day Burma), who sent plant specimens to Joseph Hooker.
   rotunda, ro-TUND-a, round, the tuberous roots.

Kalanchoe, kal-an-KO-e; corrupted from the native Chinese name for one of the species. Greenhouse succulents. *Crassulaceae*.
   carnea, KAR-ne-a, flesh coloured.
   dinklagei, dink-large-e-i, named after Max Julius Dinklage (1864–1935), botanist and collector.
   dyeri, see *K. dinklagei*.
   flammea, FLAM-me-a, flame coloured.
   kewensis, kew-EN-sis, of Kew Gardens, where first raised.
   marmorata, mar-mor-A-ta, marbled-leaved.

Kalmia, KAL-me-a; named after Pehr Kalm (1716–1779), Finnish pupil of Linnaeus, who was sent by the Royal Swedish Academy of Sciences in 1748 to report on the natural resources of North America. Flowering shrubs. *Ericaceae*.
   angustifolia, an-gus-tif-O-le-a, narrow-leaved.
   glauca, GLAW-ka, sea-green – the foliage.
   latifolia, lat-if-O-le-a, broad-leaved.

Kalosanthes, kal-os-AN-theez; from Gr. *kalos*, beautiful; *anthos*, flower, in reference to floral beauty. Greenhouse succulent. *Crassulaceae*.
   coccinea, kok-SIN-e-a, scarlet.

Kaulfussia, misapplied see below.
   amelloides, see *Felicia heterophylla*.

Kennedia, ken-NED-e-a; after John Kennedy (1759–1842), a partner of Lee and

Kennedy, nursery men of Hammersmith, London. Woody and herbaceous perennials. *Leguminosae.*
  coccinea, kok-SIN-e-a, scarlet.
  prostrata, pros-TRA-ta, prostrate, lying flat.

Kentia, misapplied see below.
  belmoreana, see *Howea belmoreana.*
  forsteriana, see *Howea forsteriana.*

Kerria, KER-re-a; named after William Kerr (d. 1814), plant collector of Kew, who introduced *K. japonica.* Flowering shrubs. *Rosaceae.*
  japonica, jap-ON-ik-a, of Japan.

Kirengeshoma, kir-en-ge-SHOW-ma; Japanese name for a yellow-flowered perennial, from *ki,* yellow; *renge,* lotus blossom; *shoma,* hat. Herbaceous perennial. *Hydrangeaceae.*
  palmata, pal-MA-ta, palmate, like a hand – the leaves.

Kitaibelia, kit-a-BE-le-a; after Paul Kitaibel (1757–1817), Hungarian botanist, professor of botany at Pest. Border and woodland plants. *Malvaceae.*
  vitifolia, vi-tif-OL-e-a, *Vitis* or vine-leaved.

Kleinia, KLY-ne-a; after Jacob Theodor Klein (1685–1759), German botanist. Perennial succulents. *Compositae.*
  articulata, ar-tik-u-LA-ta, jointed.
  galpinii, GAL-pin-e-i, after Ernest Edward Galpin (1858–1941), South African plant collector.
  repens, RE-penz, creeping and rooting.

Knautia, NOOR-te-a; in honour of Christoph Knaut (1638–1694), German doctor and botanist. Annuals and herbaceous perennials. *Caprifoliaceae.*
  arvensis, ar-VEN-sis, growing in cultivated fields. The Field Scabious.
  macedonica, mas-e-DON-ik-a, of Macedonia. The Macedonian Scabious.

Kneiffia, nif-FEE-a; in honour of Friedrich Gotthard Kneiff (1785–1832), of Strasbourg, pharmacist, botanist and botanical author. Herbaceous plants. *Onagraceae.*
  pumila, PU-mil-a, dwarf.

Kniphofia, nif-O-fe-a; after Johann Hieronymous Knipof (1704–1763), professor of medicine at Erfurt and author. Herbaceous perennials. *Xanthorrhoeaceae.*
  alooides, see *K. uvaria.*
  burchellii, see *K. uvaria.*
  caulescens, kaw-LES-scenz, long-stemmed.
  ensifolia, en-sif-OL-e-a, leaves in the shape of a sword.
  macowanii, see *K. triangularis.*
  nelsonii, see *K. triangularis.*
  northiae, NOR-the-e, in honour of Marianne North (1830–1890), prolific English botanical artist and traveller.
  rufa, ROO-fa, reddish.
  triangularis, try-an-goo-LAR-is, with three angles.
  tuckii, see *K. ensifolia.*
  tysonii, TI-so-ne-i, after William Tyson (1851–1920), plant collector active in South Africa.
  uvaria, u-VAR-e-a, from L. *uva,* bunch of grapes, old generic name meaning clustered. The Red-hot Poker.

Kochia, KOK-e-a; after Wilhelm Daniel Josef Koch (1771–1849), professor of botany at Erlangen. Foliage annuals. *Amaranthaceae.*
  scoparia, see *Bassia scoparia.*
  trichophylla, trik-of-IL-la, hairy-leaved. Summer Cypress.

Koelreuteria, kol-roy-TEER-e-a; after Joseph Gottlieb Koelrueter (1733–1806), professor of natural history at Karlsruhe, pioneer in plant hybridisation. Deciduous flowering tree. *Sapindaceae.*
  paniculata, pan-ik-ul-A-ta, flowers in panicles.

Kohleria, koh-LER-e-a; after Johann Michael Kohler (1812–1884), lecturer in natural history at Zurich. Herbs and shrubs. *Gesneriaceae.*
  amabilis, am-A-bil-is, lovely.
  digitaliflora, DIJ-it-al-if-LO-ra, the flowers resembling *Digitalis* (foxgloves).
  hondensis, HON-den-sis, of Honda, New Granada a port town, on the Magdelena river, in present day Columbia.

Kolkwitzia, kol-KWIT-zee-a; named for Richard Kolkwitz (1873–1956), professor of botany in Berlin. Flowering shrub. *Caprifoliaceae.*
  amabilis, am-A-bil-is, lovely.

Koniga, KONE-ig-a; after Charles Koenig. Hardy annual. *Brassicaceae*.
  maritima, see *Lobularia maritima*.

Lablab, LAB-lab; Egyptian name adopted by Linnaeus. Perennial herbs. *Leguminosae*.
  purpureus, pur-PUR-re-us, purple.

+ *Laburnocytisus*, la-BUR-no-si-TIS-us; an intergeneric graft-chimaera between *Laburnum* and *Cytisus*. Small tree. *Leguminosae*.
  adamii, ad-AM-e-i, horticultural curiosity raised by Jean Louis Adam, French nurseryman, in 1825.

Laburnum, la-BUR-num; the old Latin name for the tree. Trees and shrubs. *Leguminosae*.
  alpinum, al-PINE-um, alpine.
  anagyroides, an-a-JI-roy-dees, resembling *Anagyris*.
  vulgare, see *L. anagyroides*.

Lachenalia, lak-en-A-le-a; named after Werner de la Chenal (1736–1800), Swiss botanist and author. Greenhouse bulbs. *Asparagaceae*.
  aloides, al-OY-dees, resembling *Aloe*.
  aloides var. aloides, al-OY-dees, resembling *Aloe*.
  aloides var. aurea, AW-re-a, golden.
  bulbifera, bul-BIF-er-a, bearing bulblets.
  nelsonii, see *L. aloides* var. *aloides*.
  pendula, see *L. bulbifera*.
  tricolor, see *L. aloides* var. *aloides*.

Lactuca, lak-TU-ka; from L. *lac*, milk, in reference to the white juice. Perennials and salad vegetables. *Compositae*.
  bourgaei, BOOR-je-i, after Eugene Bourgeau (1813–1877), French plant collector.
  plumieri, ploo-me-AIR-i, after Charles Plumier (1646–1704), French botanist.
  sativa, SAT-iv-a, cultivated. The Lettuce.

Laelia, LA-le-a; from Laelia, the name of a vestal virgin. Tropical orchids. *Orchidaceae*.
  albida, AL-bid-a, nearly white.
  anceps, AN-ceps, two-edged, flattened.
  autumnalis, aw-tum-NA-lis, autumn flowering.
  cinnabarina, see *Cattleya cinnabarina*.
  crispa, see *Cattleya crispa*.
  × elegans, see *Cattleya × elegans*.
  pumila, see *Cattleya pumila*.
  purpurata, see *Cattleya purpurata*.

× *Laeliocattleya*, LA-le-o-KAT-le-a; name for intergeneric hybrids between *Laelia* and *Cattleya*. Orchids. *Orchidaceae*.

Lagarosiphon, la-ga-ro-SI-fon; from Gr. *lagaros*, narrow; *siphon*, tube. Aquatic plants. *Hydrocharitaceae*.
  major, MA-jor, greater.

Lagenaria, lag-en-AR-e-a; from Gr. *lagenos*, a bottle, referring to the shape of the fruit. Tender annuals. The Bottle Gourd. *Cucurbitaceae*.
  siceraria, sis-e-RA-re-a; possibly from L. *sicera*, intoxicating drink.
  vulgaris, see *L. siceraria*.

Lagerstroemia, la-ger-STRO-me-a; after Magnus von Lagerstroem (1691–1759), Swedish merchant, a friend of Linnaeus. Shrubs or trees. *Lythraceae*.
  indica, IN-di-ka, of India.

Lagurus, lag-UR-us; from Gr. *lagos*, a hare; *oura*, a tail, alluding to the tail-like inflorescence. Annual ornamental grass. *Poaceae*.
  ovatus, o-VA-tus, egg-shaped – the leaves.

Lamarckia, lam-ARK-e-a; after Jean-Baptiste Pierre Antoine de Monet, Chevalier de Lamarck (1744–1829), French naturalist. Annual ornamental grass. *Poaceae*.
  aurea, AW-re-a, golden, the inflorescence.

Lamium, LA-me-um; from Gr. *laimos*, the throat, alluding to the throat-like appearance of the blossoms. Herbaceous perennials. *Lamiaceae*.
  album, AL-bum, white – the flowers.
  galeobdolon, ga-le-OB-do-lon, old generic name, meaning a weasel and a bad smell.
  maculatum, mak-ul-A-tum, spotted.

Lampranthus, lam-PRAN-thus; from Gr. *lampros*, bright, shining; *anthos*, a flower, in allusion to the brilliant flowers. Shrubs. *Aizoaceae*.
  aureus, AW-re-us, golden.
  blandus, BLAND-us, mild.
  brownii, BROWN-e-i, after Nicholas Edward Brown (1849–1934), English plant taxonomist and an authority on succulents.
  coccineus, kok-SIN-e-us, scarlet.

deltoides, del-TOY-dees, triangular shaped – the leaves.

multiradiatus, mul-te-RA-de-a-tus, many-rayed.

roseus, see *L. multiradiatus.*

spectabilis, spek-TAB-il-is, notable.

violaceus, vy-o-LA-se-us, violet.

Lamprocapnos, lam-pro-KAP-nos; from Gr. *lampros*, bright, shining; *kapnos*, smoke, the genus being in the Fumitory subfamily. One species of herbaceous perennial. *Papaveraceae.*

spectabilis, spek-TAB-il-us, showy. The Bleeding Heart.

Lantana, lan-TA-na; an ancient name for *Viburnum*, the foliage of the two shrubs being similar. Greenhouse flowering shrubs. *Verbenaceae.*

camara, ka-MAR-a, the South American vernacular name.

Lapageria, lap-a-JEER-e-a; commemorating Joséphine Tascher de la Pagerie (1763–1818), the wife of Napolean Bonaparte. Greenhouse climbers. *Philesiaceae.*

rosea, RO-ze-a, rose-coloured.

Lapeirousia, lap-a-ROO-se-a; after Philippe-Isidore Picot de Lapeyrouse, Baron de Lapeyrouse (1744–1818), French naturalist. Hardy bulbous flowering plants. *Iridaceae.*

anceps, AN-ceps, two-edged, flattened.

cruenta, see *Freesia laxa.*

Lardizabala, lar-diz-AB-a-la; commemorating Miguel de Lardizábal y Uribe (1744–1824), Spanish patron of botany. Monotypic genus. Hardy flowering climber. *Lardizabalaceae.*

biternata, BIT-ter-na-ta, twice ternate – the leaves.

Larix, LAR-iks; the classical name for the Larch, the English name being derived from it. Deciduous conifers. *Pinaceae.*

decidua, de-SID-u-a, deciduous.

europea, see *L. decidua.*

kaempferi, KEM-fer-i, after Engelbert Kaempfer (1651–1716), German physician and traveller.

leptolepis, see *L. kaempferi.*

Lasiandra, las-e-AN-dra; from Gr. *lasios*, woolly; *aner*, an anther, alluding to the

woolly stamens. Greenhouse flowering shrubs. *Melastomataceae.*

macrantha, mak-RANTH-a, large-flowered.

Lasianthaea, las-e-AN-the-a; from Gr. *lasios*, woolly; *anthos*, a flower. Herbaceous perennials. *Compositae.*

aurea, AW-re-a, golden – the flower.

Lasthenia, las-THE-ne-a; said to be the name of a girl pupil of Plato. Hardy annuals. *Compositae.*

californica, kal-if-OR-nik-a, of California.

glabrata, glab-RA-ta, smooth – the leaves.

Lastrea, LAS-tre-a; named after Charles Jean Louis Delastre (1792–1859), French botanist. Hardy ferns. *Dryopteridaceae.*

aemula, EM-u-la, to rival, this fern rivalling others in possessing fragrance. The Hay-scented Buckler Fern.

cristata, kris-TA-ta, crested. In this case the word refers to the fringed margins of the fronds.

filix-mas, see *Dryopteris filix mas.*

montana, mon-TA-na, of mountains.

spinulosa, spi-nul-O-sa, spiny – the margins of lobes and pinnacles.

thelypteris, see *Thelypteris confluens.*

Latania, lat-A-ne-a; from the Mauritius native name *Latanier*. Greenhouse palms. *Arecaceae.*

borbonica, see *L. lontaroides.*

lontaroides, lon-ta-ROY-dees, resembling *Lontarus.*

Lathyrus, LATH-e-rus; Ancient Greek name for some leguminous plant. Annuals and perennials. *Leguminosae.*

grandiflorus, gran-dif-LO-rus, large flowered.

latifolius, lat-if-O-le-us, broad-leaves.

magellanicus, maj-el-LAN-ik-us, from the Straits of Magellan. Lord Anson's Pea.

nervosus, ner-VO-sus, large-nerved.

odoratus, od-o-RA-tus, sweet smelling.

tingitanus, ting-e-TA-nus, of Tangiers.

vernus, VER-nus, vernal or Spring, time of flowering.

Laurus, LAW-rus; old Latin name for a Bay tree, the true 'Laurel' of the ancients, perhaps derived from the Celtic, *laur*, green. Evergreen shrub. *Lauraceae.*

nobilis, NO-bil-is, large or noble. The Bay Tree.

Lavandula, lav-AN-du-la; said to be derived from L. *lavo*, to wash, the Romans and Greeks having used Lavender in their baths. Sub-shrub. *Lamiaceae*.
　angustifolia, an-gus-tif-O-le-a, narrow-leaved.
　angustifolia subsp. *pyrenaica*, pir-en-A-ik-a, Pyrenean.
　spica, see *L. angustifolia*.
　stoechas, STO-kas, from Gr. *stoechas* in a row.
　vera, see *L. angustifolia* subsp. *pyrenaica*.

Lavatera, la-VA-ter-a; commemorating the Lavater brothers, Johann Heinrich Lavater (1611–1691), Swiss physician and professor of medicine and natural history, and Johann Jacob Lavater (1594–1636), Swiss physician and naturalist. Biennials and perennials; some sub-shrubby. *Malvaceae*.
　arborea, see *Malva arborea*.
　olbia, olb-E-a, rich.
　trimestris, tri-MES-tris, maturing in three months.

Layia, LA-e-a; after George Tradescant Lay (c.1800–1845), British naturalist and explorer. Hardy annuals. Annual herbs. *Compositae*.
　elegans, EL-e-ganz, elegant.
　glandulosa, glan-dul-O-sa, glandular.
　platyglossa, plat-e-GLOS-sa, broad-tongued.

Lechenaultia, le-shen-AULT-e-a; after Jean-Baptiste Leschenault de La Tour (1773–1826), French botanist. Greenhouse flowering shrubs. *Goodeniaceae*.
　biloba, bi-LO-ba, two-lobed, the foliage.
　formosa, for-MO-sa, handsome.

Ledum, LE-dum; probably from Gr. *ledon*, *Cistus ledon*, which it resembles. Shrubs. *Ericaceae*.
　groenlandicum, see *L. palustre* subsp. *groenlandicum*.
　latifolium, lat-if-O-le-um, broad leaved.
　palustre, pal-US-tree, marsh loving.
　palustre subsp. *groenlandicum*, green-LAND-e-kum, of Greenland.

Leea, LEE-a; after James Lee (1715–1795), a noted Hammersmith nurseryman. Tropical foliage plants. *Vitaceae*.
　amabilis, am-A-bil-is, lovely.

Leiophyllum, li-o-FIL-lum; from Gr. *leios*, smooth; *phyllon*, a leaf, the foliage being glossy. Shrub. *Ericaceae*.
　buxifolium, buks-if-O-le-um, resembling *Buxus* (Box), the leaf.

Lemaireocereus, le-mair-e-o-SE-re-us; after Charles Lemaire (1801–1871), a French cactus (*cereus*) specialist. Greenhouse cacti. *Cactaceae*.
　candelabrum, see *Isolatocereus dumortieri*.
　hystrix, see *Cereus hystrix*.

Lemna, LEM-na; the Greek name for a water plant. Floating aquatics. The Duck Weed. *Araceae*.
　minor, MY-nor, dwarf.
　trisulca, TRIS-ul-ka, in threes – the appearance of leafy growths.

Leonotis, le-on-O-tis; from Gr. *leon*, a lion; *ous*, an ear, the flower having a fancied resemblance to a lion's ear. Greenhouse flowering shrub. *Lamiaceae*.
　leonurus, le-o-NU-rus, lion's tail, the flower spike.

Leontopodium, le-on-to-PO-de-um; from Gr. *leon*, a lion; *pous*, a foot, the flowers and leaves being supposed to resemble a lion's paw. Hardy perennials. *Compositae*.
　alpinum, see *L. nivale* subsp. *alpinum*.
　nivale, niv-A-le, snowy.
　nivale subsp. *alpinum*, al-PINE-um, alpine. The Edelweiss.

Leonurus, le-on-U-rus; from Gr. *leon*, a lion; *oura*, a tail, the tufted flowerhead suggesting a lion's tail. Herbaceous perennials. *Lamiaceae*.
　cardiaca, kar-DI-a-ka, of the heart, ancient medicine.

Leopoldia, le-o-POL-de-a; commemorating Leopoldo Giovanni Giuseppe Francesco Ferdinando Carlo (1797–1870), Grand Duke of Tuscany, patron of Filippo Parlatore. Bulbous perennials. *Asparagaceae*.
　comosa, ko-MO-sa, hairy-tufted. The Tassel Hyacinth.

Lepidium, lep-ID-e-um; from Gr. *lepis*, a scale, the shape of the pods. The garden or salad cress. *Brassicaceae.*
  sativum, SAT-iv-um, cultivated. Salad Cress.

Lepismium, lep-IS-me-um; from Gr. *lepis*, a scale, the small scales attached to the areoles. Greenhouse cacti. *Cactaceae.*
  commune, kom-MU-ne, common.
  cruciforme, kru-se-FOR-me, in the shape of a cross.

Leptopteris, lep-to-TER-is; from Gr. *leptos*, slender; *pteris*, a fern. Ferns. *Osmundaceae.*
  hymenophylloides, hi-men-of-il-LOY-dees, resembling *Hymenophyllum*.

Leptopyrum, lep-to-PI-rum; from Gr. *leptos*, slender; *pyros*, wheat, in allusion to the fruits. Herbaceous perennials. *Ranunculaceae.*
  fumarioides, fu-mar-e-OY-dees, resembling *Fumaria*.

Leptosiphon, lep to SI fon; from Gr. *leptos*, slender; *siphon*, a tube, referring to the flower of some species. Annuals and rock plants. *Polemoniaceae.*
  androsaceus, see *Linanthus androsaceus.*
  densiflorus, den-sif-LO-rus, the flowers clustered.

Leptospermum, lep-to-SPER-mum; from Gr. *leptos*, slender; *sperma*, a seed, the latter being very thin, almost threadlike. Shrubs. *Myrtaceae.*
  scoparium, sko-PAR-e-um, resembling broom, *Cytisus scoparium*. Manuka.

Leptosyne, lep-TOS-in-e; from Gr. *leptos*, slender, mainly annuals of slender growth. Annuals and perennials. *Compositae.*
  douglasii, see *Coreopsis douglasii.*
  maritima, see *Coreopsis maritima.*
  stillmannii, see *Coreopsis stillmannii.*

Lespedeza, les-pe-DE-za; named in honour of Vicente Manuel de Céspedes (1721–1794), Spanish governor of East Florida. He gave André Michaux permission to explore East Florida in search of new plants. The genus name is a result of a misspelling in print. Hardy flowering shrubs. *Leguminosae.*
  bicolor, BIK-ol-or, two-coloured.
  capitata, kap-it-A-ta, flowers in a head.

Leucanthemella, lew-KAN-the-mel-la; diminutive form of *Leucanthemum*, which see. Perennial herbs. *Compositae.*
  serotina, ser-o-TIN-a, late in starting spring growth.

Leucanthemum, lew-KAN-the-mum; from Gr. *leukos*, white; *anthemon*, a flower. Perennial herbs. *Compositae.*
  × *superbum*, su-PER-ba, superb.
  vulgare, vul-GAR-e, common. The Oxeye Daisy.

Leuchtenbergia, look-ten-BER-ge-a; in honour of the Duke of Leuchtenberg, name adopted by Hooker by which this plant was said to be known upon the continent; although he was unable to find any records. Greenhouse cacti. *Cactaceae.*
  principis, prin-SIP-is, noble, princely.

Leucocoryne, lew-ko-KOR-rin-e; from Gr. *leukos*, white; *coryne*, a club, referring to the white protruding sterile stamens of the type species. Bulbous perennials endemic to Chile. *Amaryllidaceae.*
  ixioides, iks-e-OY-dees, resembling *Ixia.*

Leucojum, lew-KO-e-um; from Gr. *leukos*, white; *ion*, a violet, referring to the colour and possibly the fragrance to the flower. Hardy bulbs. The Snowflake. *Amaryllidaceae.*
  aestivum, ES-tiv-um, summer – season of flowering.
  vernum, VER-num, spring – season of flowering.

Leucophyta, lew-KO-fy-ta; from Gr. *leukos*, white; *phyton*, plant, in allusion to the colour of the plant. Subshrub. *Compositae.*
  brownii, BROWN-e-i, after Robert Brown (1773–1858), Scottish botanist, who first described the genus in 1817.

Leucothoe, lew-KO-tho-e; said to be called after Leucothea, daughter of a Babylonian king (Grecian mythology), who, on being buried by her father, was transformed into a shrub by Apollo. Shrubs. *Ericaceae.*
  axillaris, aks-il-LAR-is, the flowers in axillary racemes.
  catesbaei, KATS-be-i, after Mark Catesby (1683–1749), author of 'A Natural History of Carolina'.

davisiae, da-VIS-e-e, collected by Nancy Jane Davis (1833–1921), American plant collector, one of the founders of Birmingham School, Pennsylvania and for over sixty years its principal.

Lewisia, lew-IS-e-a; after Captain Meriwether Lewis (1774–1809), explorer, of the Lewis and Clark expedition 1804–1806. Rock plants. *Montiaceae*.

cotyledon, kot-e-LE-don, old name meaning cup-shaped (leaf).

cotyledon var. *howellii*, HOW-el-e-i, after Thomas Howell (1842–1912), collector of the flora of Washington and Oregon.

rediviva, red-iv-I-va, reviving, the plant suddenly flowering, although appearing lifeless.

tweedyi, TWEED-e-i, after James Tweedie (1775–1862), plant collector in South America.

Leycesteria, lay-ses-TEER-e-a; commemorating William Leycester (1775–1831), the last of the East India Company's judges in Bengal to be designated Chief Judge. Shrubs. *Caprifoliaceae*.

formosa, for-MO-sa, handsome.

Liatris, li-a-tris; derivation unknown. Herbaceous perennials. Perennial herbs. *Compositae*.

elegans, EL-e-ganz, elegant.

pycnostachya, pik-no-STAK-e-a, densely spiked.

Libertia, li-BER-te-a; after Marie-Anne Libert (1782–1865), Belgian botanist. Rhizomatous perennial herbs. *Iridaceae*.

chilensis, chil-EN-sis, Chilean.

formosa, see *L. chilensis*.

grandiflora, gran-dif-LO-ra, large-flowered.

ixioides, iks-e-OY-dees, resembling *Ixia*.

Libocedrus, lib-o-CED-rus; from Gr. *libanos*, incense; *kedros*, a cedar. Coniferous trees. *Cupressaceae*.

decurrens, see *Calocedrus decurrens*.

plumosa, plu-MO-sa, from L. *plumeus*, feathery.

Libonia, le-BO-ne-a; after Joseph Libon (1821–1861), Belgian plant collector and botanist, active in Brazil. Greenhouse shrubby flowering plants. *Acanthaceae*.

× *penrhosiensis*, pen-rhos-e-EN-sis, of Penrhos Hall, Wales.

Ligularia, lig-U-lar-e-a; from L. *ligula*, a little tongue; referring to the shape of the ray florets. Perennial herbs. *Compositae*.

dentata, den-TA-ta, toothed, the leaves.

veitchiana, veech-e-A-na, first collected by Dr. A Henry in the province of Hupeh and exhibited by James Veitch and Sons.

wilsoniana, wil-so-ne-A-na, in honour of Ernest Henry Wilson (1876–1930), English plant collector in China.

Ligustrum, li-GUS-trum; Latin name for Privet, possibly from L. *ligo*, to bind, the twigs having been used for tying. Shrubs. *Oleaceae*.

coriaceum, see *L. japonicum*.

japonicum, jap-ON-ik-um, of Japan.

ovalifolium, o-val-if-O-le-um, oval-leaved.

vulgare, vul-GAR-e, common. Common Privet.

Lilium, LIL-e-um; Latin name for Lily and common to almost all European languages. Hardy bulbs. *Liliaceae*.

auratum, aw-RA-tum, golden-rayed.

bulbiferum, bul-BIF-er-um, bulbil-bearing.

candidum, KAN-did-um, white. The White Lily.

chalcedonicum, kal-se-DON-ik-um, of Chalcedon, Asia Minor.

croceum, see *L. bulbiferum*.

davidii, DA-vid-e-i, after Pere Armand David (1826–1900), French missionary and plant collector in China.

davidii var. *willmottiae*, wil-MOT-e-e, after Ellen Ann Wilmott (1858–1934), English gardener at Warley Place, Essex.

× *elegans*, EL-e-ganz, elegant.

hansonii, han-SO-ne-i, after Peter Hanson (1821–1887), Danish-American landscape painter and noted authority on tulips.

henryi, HEN-re-i, after Dr. Augustine Henry (1857–1930), Irish plantsman and pioneer collector in China.

lancifolium, lan-sif-OL-e-um, lance-shaped leaves.

longiflorum, long-e-FLOR-um, long-flowered.

martagon, MAR-ta-gon, old name of obscure origin.

monadelphum, mon-a-DEL-fum, monadelphous, having the stamens united.

pardalinum, par-da-LE-num, panther-spotted.

parryi, PAR-re-i, after Charles Christopher Parry (1823–1890), British-American botanist.

philippinense, fil-ip-e-NEN-see, of Philippine Islands.

pomponium, pom-PO-ne-um, meaning obscure, possibly of much splendour. The Scarlet Pompone.

regale, re-GA-le, royal, alluding to the magnificent flowers.

speciosum, spes-e-O-sum, showy.

superbum, su-PER-bum, superb.

× *testaceum*, tes-TA-se-um, pale brown or apricot, the colour of the flowers.

tigrinum, see *L. lancifolium*.

willmottiae, see *L. davidii* var. *willmottiae*.

Limnanthemum, lim-NAN-the-mum; from Gr. *limne*, marsh; *anthemon*, a blossom, a reference to the plants being found in marshland or aquatic. Greenhouse and hardy aquatics. *Menyanthaceae*.

humboldtianum, see *Nymphoides indica*.

nymphoides, nim-FOY-dees; resembling *Nyphaea*.

peltatum, see *Nymphoides peltata*.

Limnanthes, lim-NAN-thes; from Gr. *limne*, a marsh; *anthos*, a flower, some of these annuals inhabiting moist places. *Limnanthaceae*.

douglasii, dug-LAS-e-i, after David Douglas (1799–1834), Scottish plant collector.

Limnobium, lim-NO-be-um; from Gr. *limne*, a marsh; *bios*, life, living in marshy pools. Greenhouse submerged aquatic. *Hydrocharitaceae*.

bogotense, see *L. laevigatum*.

laevigatum, lev-e-GA-tum, smooth.

stoloniferum, see *L. laevigatum*.

Limnophila, lim-NO-fil-a; from Gr. *limne*, a marsh; *philos*, loving, in reference to the place of growth. Submerged aquatic. *Plantaginaceae*.

gratioloides, see *L. indica*.

indica, IN-di-ka, of India.

sessiliflora, SES-sil-e-FLOR-a, flowers without a foot stalk.

Limonium, lim-ON-ne-um; from Gr. *leimon*, a meadow, the plants found growing in salt marshes. Greenhouse and hardy perennials. *Plumbaginaceae*.

bonducellii, bon-du-KEL-le-i, common in the deserts of Algeria, whence it was reported by M. Bonduelle, adjunct surgeon.

bourgeaui, boor-JE-i, after Eugène Bourgeau (1813–1877), French naturalist, who collected plants on the Canary Islands.

eximium, see *Goniolimon eximium*.

gmelinii, mel-E-ne-i, after Johann Georg Gmelin (1709–1755), German naturalist, botanist and geographer.

latifolium, see *L. platyphyllum*.

minutum, min-EW-tum, small, minute.

ovalifolium, o-val-if-O-le-um, oval-leaved.

platyphyllum, plat-e-FIL-lum, broad-leaves.

profusum, pro-FU-sum, profusely flowering.

sinuatum, sin-u-A-tum, with a wavy margin, scalloped-leaved.

suworowii, see *Psylliostachys suworowi*.

vulgare, vul-GAR-e, common. The Sea Lavender.

Linanthus, lin-AN-thus; from Gr. *linon*, flax; *anthos*, a flower. The flowers resembling *Linum*. Annual and perennial herbaceous plants. *Polemoniaceae*.

androsaceus, an-dro-SA-se-us, resembling *Androsace*.

Linaria, lin-AR-e-a; from L. *linum*, flax, which some species resemble in growth. Rock plants and annuals. *Plantaginaceae*.

aequitriloba, see *Cymbalaria aequitriloba*.

alpina, al-PINE-a (or al-PIN-a), of the Alps or alpine.

bipartita, see *L. incarnata*.

cymbalaria, see *Cymbalaria muralis*.

dalmatica, dal-MAT-e-KA, of Dalmatia.

dalmatica subsp. *macedonica*, mas-e-DON-ik-a, of Macedonia.

hepaticifolia, hep-at-ik-e-FO-le-a, leaves resembling *Hepatica*.

incarnata, in-kar-NA-ta, flesh-coloured.

macedonica, see *L. dalmatica* subsp. *macedonica*.

maroccana, mar-ok-KA-na, of Morocco.

purpurea, pur-PUR-e-a, purple coloured.

reticulata, re-tik-ul-A-ta, netted or lined.

tristis, TRIS-tis, square leaved.

vulgaris, vul-GAR-is, common. The Common Toadflax.

Linnaea, lin-NE-a; named after Carl Linnaeus (1707–1778), by Jan Frederik Gronovius at Linnaeus' request. The Twinflower, *L. borealis*, a woodland plant, being a great favourite of his. Evergreen shrub. *Caprifoliaceae.*

borealis, bor-e-A-lis, northern.

Linum, LI-num; the Latin name for flax (Gr. *linon*). Herbaceous, rock plants and annuals. *Linaceae.*

alpinum, al-PINE-um, alpine.

arboreum, ar-bor-E-um, tree like.

flavum, FLA-vum, yellow – the flowers.

grandiflorum, gran-dif-LO-rum, large flowered.

monogynum, mon-O-jin-um, having a single pistil.

narbonense, nar-bon-EN-se, of Narbonne.

perenne, per-EN-ne, perennial.

suffruticosum, suf-frut-ik-O-sum, having a woody base.

suffruticosum subsp. *salsoloides*, sal-sol-OY-dees, like *Salsola* (Saltwort).

usitatissimum, u-sit-a-TIS-sim-um, most useful. The Flax Plant.

Lippia, LIP-pe-a; after Augustus Lippi (1678–1701), Italian naturalist and botanist, who travelled in Egypt and Abyssinia. Herbs, shrubs and small trees. *Verbenaceae.*

citriodora, see *Aloysia citriodora.*

Liquidambar, lik-wid-AM-bar; from L. *liquidus*, liquid; *ambar*, amber, in reference to the gum (storax) yielded by some species. Trees. *Altingiaceae.*

styraciflua, ster-ak-IF-lu-a, storax-flowing, hence the popular name, Sweet Gum.

Liriodendron, lir-e-o-DEN-dron; from Gr. *lirion*, a lily; *dendron*, a tree. Trees. *Magnoliaceae.*

chinense, tshi-NEN-se, of China.

tulipifera, tew-lip-IF-er-a, tulip bearing. The Tulip Tree.

Liriope, li-RE-o-pee; after the Greek woodland nymph, Liriope, the mother of Narcissus. Rhizomatous herbs. *Asparagaceae.*

graminifolia, gram-in-if-O-le-a, grass-leaved.

muscari, mus-KAR-e, from Gr. *moschos*, musk, the flowers having a musky odour.

Lithops, LITH-ops; from Gr. *lithos*, stone; *ops*, face, on account of the resemblance to the stones (pebbles) among which the plants grow. Greenhouse succulents. The Pebble Plants. *Aizoaceae.*

bella, BEL-la, beautiful or pretty.

fulviceps, FUL-ve-seps, from L. *fulvi*, tawny; ceps, head.

lesliei, LES-le-i, after Thomas Nicholas Leslie (1858–1942), plant collector and meteorologist.

turbiniformis, ter-bin-if-OR-mis, shaped like a spinning top or cone.

Lithospermum, lith-o-SPER-mum; from Gr. *lithos*, a stone; *sperma*, a seed, the latter being extremely hard. Sub-shrubby rock plants. *Boraginaceae.*

graminifolium, see *Moltkia suffruticosa.*

officinale, of-fis-in-A-le, of shops (herbal).

prostratum, see *Glandora prostrata.*

purpurocaeruleum, see *Buglossoides purpurocaerulea.*

Littorella, lit-tor-EL-la; from L. *littus*, the shore, inhabits sandy pools. Hardy aquatic. *Plantaginaceae.*

lacustris, see *L. uniflora.*

uniflora, uni-FLOR-a, one flowered, the blooms on single stems.

Livistona, liv-is-TO-na; after Patrick Murray (1634–1671), Baron of Livingston, near Edinburgh. His plant collection became the foundation of Edinburgh Botanic Garden. Greenhouse palms. *Arecaceae.*

chinensis, tshi-NEN-sis, of China.

humilis, HUM-il-is, low or dwarf.

rotundifolia, see *Saribus rotundifolius.*

Loasa, lo-A-sa; native South American name, meaning and derivation unknown. Greenhouse annual climbing plants. *Loasaceae.*

lateritia, lat-er-IT-e-a, from Latin meaning brick-red, the colour of the flowers.

Lobelia, lo-BE-le-a; after M. Matthias de L'Obel (1538–1616), a Fleming, physician to James I of England, traveller, plant collector and botanical author. Hardy and half-hardy herbaceous annuals and perennials. Many garden varieties. *Campanulaceae.*

angulata, ang-ul-A-ta, angled, presumably the growths.

cardinalis, kar-din-A-lis, scarlet, cardinal red.

erinus, e-RI-nus, meaning obscure, an old generic name. The bedding lobelia.

fulgens, see *L. cardinalis*.

nummularia, num-mul-AR-e-a, from L. *nummus*, a coin, the shape of the leaf.

siphilitica, sif-il-IT-ik-a, alluding to the disease, for which the plant was once used as a remedy.

tenuior, TEN-u-e-or, more slender.

tupa, TEW-pa, the old generic name of native Chilean origin.

Lobivia, lob-IV-e-a; an anagram of Bolivia, where the species are found. Greenhouse cacti. *Cactaceae*.

bruchii, BROOK-e-i, after Carlos Bruch (1869–1943), German photographer and scientific illustrator who moved to Argentina.

caespitosa, see *Echinopsis maximiliana* subsp. *caespitosa*.

densispina, den-se-SPY-na, densely spined.

ferox, see *Echinopsis ferox*.

grandis, see *L. bruchii*.

grandiflora, gran-dif-LO-ra, large-flowered.

haageana, see *L. marsoneri* var. *iridescens*.

marsoneri, mar-SO-ne-rye, after Oreste Marsoner, Argentine cacti collector.

marsoneri var. *iridescens*, ir-id-ES-senz, appearing to change colour from different angles.

pentlandii, see *Echinopsis pentlandii*.

rebutioides, see *L. densispina*.

Lobularia, lob-u-LAR-e-a; diminutive of L. *lobus*, alluding to the small fruit. Annual and perennial herbs. *Brassicaceae*.

maritima, mar-IT-im-a, of sea coasts. The Sweet Alyssum.

Loiseleuria, loys-el-EUR-e-a; after Jean Louis Auguste Loiseleur-Deslongchamps (1774–1849), a French physician and botanist. One species of trailing flowering small evergreen shrub. *Ericaceae*.

procumbens, pro-KUM-benz, lying down.

Lomaria, lo-MAR-e-a; from Gr. *loma*, a margin, in reference to the position of the sori. Greenhouse and hardy ferns. *Blechnaceae*.

alpina, see *Blechnum penna-marina*.

gibba, GIB-ba, gibbous or humped.

spicant, see *Blechnum spicant*.

Lomatia, lo-MA-te-a; from Gr. *loma*, edge, referring to the winged edge of the seeds. Greenhouse foliage shrubs. *Proteaceae*.

elegantissima, el-e-gan-TIS-sim-a, most elegant.

longifolia, long-if-OL-e-a, long leaves.

Lomelosia, lo-me-LO-se-a; the border (Gr. *loma*) being membranous. Annuals and perennials. *Caprifoliaceae*.

caucasica, kaw-KAS-ik-a, Caucasian.

Lonicera, lon-IS-er-a; named after Adam Lonicer (1528–1586), German botanist. Climbers and shrubs. *Caprifoliaceae*.

aureoreticulata, AW-re-o-ret-ik-ul-A-ta, golden veined.

caprifolium, kap-rif-O-le-um, herbalist name, a plant which climbs like a goat.

fragrantissima, fra-gran-TIS-sim-a, most fragrant.

involucrata, in-vol-u-KRA-ta, from L. *involucrum*, roll in, envelop, referring to the bracts covering the inflorescence.

ligustrina, li-GUS-tre-na, resembling *Ligustrum* (Privet).

ligustrina var. *pileata*, pil-e-A-ta, having a cap, the berry being topped by a curious outgrowth of the calyx.

ligustrina var. *yunnanensis*, yun-nan-EN-sis, of Yunnan, west China.

nitida, see *L. ligustrina* var. *yunnanensis*.

periclymenum, per-ik-LIM-en-um, Greek name, *periklymenon* for the Woodbine or Honeysuckle.

pileata, see *L. ligustrina* var. *pileata*.

rupicola, roo-PIK-o-la, of rocks.

rupicola var. *syringantha*, sir-ing-AN-tha, the flowers resembling *Syringa* (lilac).

sempervirens, sem-per-VEER-enz, from L. *semper*, ever; *virens*, green. Always green.

setifera, set-IF-e-ra, bearing bristles.

standishii, stan-DISH-e-i, after John Standish (1814–1875), English nurseryman, who raised Robert Fortune's Chinese and Japanese plant introductions.

syringantha, see *L. rupicola* var. *syringantha*.

xylosteum, zy-LOS-te-um, a disused generic name from Gr. *xylon*, wood; *osteon*, bone – the woody stems.

Lophocereus, LOF-o-se-RE-us; from Gr. *lophos*, a crest; *cereus*, wax taper, referring to the bristly top of the stem when flowering. Greenhouse cacti. *Cactaceae*.

schottii, SHOT-te-i, after Arthur Carl Victor Schott (1814–1875), German-American cartographer and botanist, who mapped the US Mexican border.

Lophophora, lof-OF-or-a; from Gr. *lophos*, a crest; *phoreo*, to bear, the reference is the hairs borne at the areoles. Greenhouse cacti. *Cactaceae*.
   lewinii, see *L. williamsii*.
   williamsii, WILL-yams-e-i, after Williams.

Lotus, LO-tus; old name adopted by Greek naturalists for a trefoil-like plant. Greenhouse and hardy perennials. *Leguminosae*.
   corniculatus, kor-nik-ul-A-tus, a little horn, the shape of the flower. Bird's foot Trefoil.
   peliorhynchus, pel-e-or-IN-kus, stork's beak.

Luculia, lu-KU-le-a; from *Luculi Swa*, the native Nepalese name for *Luculia gratissima*. Greenhouse evergreen flowering shrub. *Rubiaceae*.
   gratissima, gra-TIS-sim-ma, most welcome or very grateful, the sweet fragrance.
   pinceana, PIN-se-a-na, after Robert Taylor Pince (1804–1871), nurseryman of Lucombe and Pince Co. Exeter.

Ludwigia, lud-VIG-e-a; after Kristian Gottlieb Ludwig (1709–1773), German botanist and professor of medicine. Bog plants and submerged aquatics. *Onagraceae*.
   adscendens, ad-SEN-denz, ascending, mounting.
   longifolia, long-if-O-le-a, long-leaved.
   mulerttii, mul-ERT-te-i, after Mullert.
   palustris, pal-US-tris, found in marshy places.
   peruviana, pe-ru-ve-A-na, of Peru.

Luma, LEU-ma; old name of Chilean origin for a related species *Amomyrtus luma*. Shrubs and small trees. *Myrtaceae*.
   apiculata, ap-ik-ul-A-ta, the leaves pointed.

Lunaria, loon-AIR-e-a; from L. *luna*, the moon, alluding to the round and silvery seed vessels. Hardy biennial or perennial herbs. *Brassicaceae*.
   annua, ann-U-a, annual.
   biennis, see *L. annua*.
   rediviva, red-iv-I-va, reviving, the plant being perennial.

Lupinus, lu-PE-nus (or lu-PY-nus); from L. *lupus*, a wolf (destroyer), the mistaken belief that some species devastated land by their abundance. Annual or perennial herbs and shrubs. *Leguminosae*.

arboreus, ar-BOR-e-us, tree-like. The Tree Lupin.
   hartwegii, hart-VE-ge-i, after Karl Theodor Hartweg (1812–1871), German plant hunter, who collected for the Horticultural Society of London in Mexico and California.
   mutabilis, mu-TA-bil-is, variable in colour or form.
   nootkatensis, noot-kat-EN-sis, of Nootka Sound, Vancouver Island.
   paynei, PA-ne-i, after Theodore Payne (1872–1963), English born Californian nurseryman who discovered it.
   polyphyllus, pol-if-IL-lus, many-leaved. The Common Lupin.
   pubescens, pew-BES-senz, downy.
   subcarnosus, sub-kar-NO-sus, somewhat fleshy.

Luronium, lu-row-NE-um; ancient name used by Dioscorides. Aquatic herb. *Alismataceae*.
   natans, NA-tanz, floating.

Lycaste, ly-KAS-tee; after Lycaste, a Sicilian beauty, mother of Eryx. Lycaste on account of her beauty is sometimes referred to as Venus. Greenhouse orchids. *Orchidaceae*.
   aromatica, ar-o-MAT-ik-a, aromatic.
   deppei, DEP-pe-i, after Ferdinand Deppe (1794–1861), German naturalist, who travelled to Mexico and California.
   skinneri, see *L. virginalis*.
   virginalis, ver-JIN-a-lis, white, virginal.

Lychnis, LIK-nis; from Gr. *lychnos*, a lamp, in reference to the brilliantly coloured flowers. Herbaceous border and rock plants. *Caryophyllaceae*.
   alpina, see *Silene suecica*.
   chalcedonica, see *Silene chalcedonica*.
   coeli-rosa, see *Silene coeli-rosa*.
   coronaria, see *Silene coronaria*.
   dioica, see *Silene dioica*.
   diurna, di-UR-na, day-flowering. Double kind chiefly cultivated.
   flos-cuculi, see *Silene flos-cuculi*.
   flos-jovis, see *Silene flos-jovis*.
   × *haageana*, ha-ag-e-A-na, after Friedrich Adolph Haage (1796–1866), German nurseryman, or Johann Nicolaus Haage (1826–1878), German nurseryman.
   vespertina, see *Silene latifolia*.
   viscaria, see *Silene viscaria*.

Lycium, LY-se-um; said to be from Gr. *lykion*, a thorny medicinal plant, from Lycia, in Asia Minor. Shrubs. *Solanaceae*.
barbarum, BAR-bar-um, foreign.
barbatum, bar-BA-tum, bearded.
chinense, tshi-NEN-se, of China.

Lycopersicon, lik-o-PER-sik-on (or LY-co-PER-se-kon); from Gr. *lykos*, a wolf; *persicon*, a peach, a belief when first cultivated as an ornamental in Europe of supposed poisonous qualities. See also *Solanum lycopersicum*. Greenhouse annual fruit-bearing plant. *Solanaceae*.
esculentum, es-kul-EN-tum, edible. The Wild Tomato.

Lycoris, ly-KOR-is; after Lycoris, a Roman beauty and the subject of Cornelius Gallus' love poetry. Bulbous plants. *Amaryllidaceae*.
aurea, AW-re-a, golden.
radiata, rad-e-A-ta, rayed – radiating from the centre.
squamigera, skwam-IG-er-a, scale-bearing.

Lygodium, ly-GO-de-um; from Gr. *lygodes*, flexible, referring to the twining stems. Greenhouse climbing ferns. *Lygodiaceae*.
japonicum, jap-ON-ik-um, of Japan. Japanese Climbing Fern.
palmatum, pal-MA-tum, leaves palmate, like a hand. American Climbing Fern.
scandens, SKAN-denz, climbing.

Lyonia, ly-O-ne-a; after John Lyon (1765–1814), Scottish plant collector, who introduced North American plants into Europe. Shrubs and trees. *Ericaceae*.
ligustrina, lig-us-TRIN-a, resembling *Ligustrum* (privet).

Lysichiton, lis-e-KI-ton; from Gr. *lysis*, loosing; *chiton*, a tunic, alluding to the wide open spathe which is released from the spadix as the fruits ripen. Skunk Cabbage. Herbaceous perennials. *Araceae*.
americanus, a-mer-e-KAY-nus, of the Americas. From Alaska to California.
camtschatcensis, kams-kat-KEN-sis, of the Kamchatka Peninsula in the Russian Far East. The range extends to Japan.

Lysimachia, lis-e-MAK-e-a; probably from Gr. *luo*, to loose; *mache*, strife, hence Loos-

estrife. Some authorities state that the genus is named after Lysimachus, King of Thrace (306 BC.) who, it is said, was the first to discover the Loosestrife's supposed soothing properties. Herbaceous perennials. *Primulaceae*.
clethroides, kleth-ROY-dees, the flowers resembling the genus *Clethra* (White Alder).
europaea, u-ro-PE-a, European.
nummularia, num-mul-AR-e-a, from L. *nummus*, a coin, the shape of the leaf. The Creeping Jenny.
punctata, punk-TA-ta, the flowers being dotted.
verticillata, ver-tis-il-LA-ta, whorled – the foliage.
vulgaris, vul-GAR-is, common. The Yellow Loosestrife.

Lythrum, LITH-rum; from Gr. *lythron*, blood, in allusion to the colour of the flowers. Herbaceous perennials. *Lythraceae*.
alatum, al-A-tum, winged, the stalks.
salicaria, sal-ik-AR-e-a, the leaves willow-like, or the flower spikes willow-herb like. The Purple Loosestrife.
virgatum, ver-GA-tum, twiggy.

Lytocaryum, li-to-KAR-ee-um; from the Gr. *lysis*, loosen or break down; *karyo*, nut. Palm. *Arecaceae*.
weddellianum, wed-del-le-A-num, after Hugh Algernon Weddell (1819–1877), physician and botanist, active in South America.

Machaerocereus, misapplied please see below.
eruca, see *Stenocereus eruca*.

Mackaya, mak-KAY-a; after James Townsend Mackay (1775–1862), Scottish botanist, curator of the Trinity College Gardens, Dublin. Greenhouse flowering shrub. *Acanthaceae*.
bella, BEL-la, beautiful or pretty.

Macleaya, ma-CLAY-a; after Alexander Macleay (1767–1848), Scottish entomologist, who was elected a fellow of the Linnean Society of London in 1794. Perennial herbs. *Papaveraceae*.
cordata, kor-DA-ta, heart shaped, the leaves.

Magnolia, mag-NO-le-a; named by Linnaeus in commemoration of Pierre Magnol (1638–1715), a professor of botany and director of Montpellier Botanic Gardens, France. Shrubs and trees. *Magnoliaceae.*

conspicua, see M. denudata.

denudata, de-nu-DA-ta, uncovered or not hairy.

grandiflora, gran-dif-LO-ra, large-flowered.

kobus, KO-bus, a Japanese name.

× *lennei,* see M. × soulangeana.

obovata, ob-ov-KA-ta, egg-shaped, the broadest part near the tip.

× *soulangeana,* soo-lan-je-A-na, after Etienne Soulange-Bodin (1774–1846), French horticulturist, of Fromont, who raised this hybrid in his gardens.

stellata, stel-LA-ta, starry, the flowers.

Mahonia, ma-HO-ne-a; after Bernard McMahon (1775–1816), Irish-American horticulturist, who produced the first published seed list in the United States. Shrubs. *Berberidaceae.*

aquifolium, see Berberis aquifolium

bealei, bee-LE-i, after Thomas Chaye Beale (1805–1857), Scottish merchant in Shanghai, in whose garden Fortune preserved his specimens prior to despatch to England.

japonica, jap-ON-ik-a, of Japan.

Maianthemum, ma-AN-the-mum; from Gr. *Maia,* the mother of Mercury (Gr. mythology), to whom the month of May was dedicated; *anthemon,* a flower. Rock and woodland plants. *Asparagaceae.*

bifolium, bi-FO-le-um, twin leaved.

convallaria, see M. bifolium.

racemosum, ra-se-MO-sum, with flowers in racemes.

stellatum, stel-LA-tum, starry.

Malacocarpus, mal-a-ko-KAR-pus; from Gr. *malakos,* soft; *karpos,* fruit, referring to the soft fleshy fruits. Greenhouse cacti. *Cactaceae.*

corynodes, kor-e-NO-dees, the stigmas being club-like.

erinaceus, see Parodia erinacea.

Malcolmia, mal-KO-me-a; after William Malcolm (d. 1820), London nurseryman, botanist and associate of Robert Sweet. Hardy annuals. *Brassicaceae.*

maritima, mar-IT-im-a, of the sea. The Virginian Stock.

Malope, MAL-o-pe; ancient Gr. name used by Pliny for a kind of mallow; Gr. *malos,*

meaning soft or soothing, from the leaf texture or medicinal properties. Hardy annuals. *Malvaceae.*

grandiflora, gran-dif-LO-ra, large-flowered.

trifida, TRIF-id-a, the leaves being three-cleft.

Malus, MAY (or MAL)-us; from Gr. *melon,* an apple, also applied to other fruits. *Rosaceae.*

baccata, bak-KAR-ta, berried.

coronaria, kor-on-AR-e-a, crowned.

domestica, do-MES-tik-a, domestic – from its various uses.

× *eleyi,* EE-ley-i, hybrid cross named after Charles Eley, the raiser.

floribunda, flor-e-BUN-da, abundant or free flowering. Japanese Flowering Crabapple.

× *prunifolia,* proo-nif-O-le-a, *Prunus* (Plum) leaved.

sikkimensis, sik-kim-EN-sis, of Sikkim, India.

× *spectabilis,* spek-TAB-il-is, showy.

toringo, tor-IN-go, a Japanese name.

trilobata, try-lo-BA-ta, leaves with three lobes.

Malva, MAL-va; from L. *malva,* mallow, from Gr. *malakos,* soothing, probably alluding to an emollient yielded by the seeds. Annuals and herbaceous perennials. *Malvaceae.*

alcea, al-SEE-a; from Gr. *alkaia,* a kind of mallow.

arborea, ar-BOR-e-a, tree-like.

crispa, see M. verticillata.

moschata, mos-KA-ta, musky, the leaves slightly fragrant. The Musk Mallow.

verticillata, ver-tis-il-LA-ta, whorled – the leaves.

Malvastrum, mal-VAS-trum; from *Malva* and L. *aster,* a star. Rock plants and hardy perennials. *Malvaceae.*

coccineum, see Sphaeralcea coccinea.

gilliesii, gil-LEEZ-e-i, after John Gillies (1792–1834), Scottish surgeon, plant collector in South America.

lateritium, lat-er-IT-e-um, brick-red.

Mammillaria, mam-mil-LAR-e-a; from L. *mammilla,* a nipple, in reference to the teat-like tubercles characteristic of many species. Greenhouse cacti. *Cactaceae.*

applanata, see M. heyderi subsp. hemisphaerica.

chionocephala, ki-on-o-SEF-a-la, snowy-headed.

cirrifera, sir-RIF-er-a, bearing tendrils.

dolichocentra, see M. polythele.

echinata, ek-in-A-ta, spines resembling a hedge-hog.

elegans, see *M. haageana* subsp. *elegans*.

geminispina, gem-e-ni-SPI-na, twin spines.

gracilis, GRAS-il-is, slender.

haageana, ha-ag-e-A-na, after Friedrich Adolph Haage (1796–1866), German nurseryman, or Johann Nicolaus Haage (1826–1878), German nurseryman.

haageana subsp. *elegans*, EL-e-ganz, elegant.

heyderi, HED-er-i, after Edward Heyder (1808–1884), German cacti specialist.

heyderi subsp. *hemisphaerica*, hem-e-SFER-ik-a, the form of half a sphere.

longimamma, long-im-AM-ma, long tubercled.

magnimamma, mag-ne-MAM-ma, large tubercled.

microthele, mi-kro-THE-le, small-nippled.

nivea, see *M. geminispina*.

polythele, po-le-THE-le, many nippled.

prolifera, pro-LIF-er-a, numerous white spines.

pusilla, see *M. prolifera*.

sempervivi, sem-per-VI-ve, like a *sempervivum*.

stella-aurata, see *Cactus stella-aurata*.

tetracantha, see *M. polythele*.

uncinata, un-sin-NA-ta, hooked.

villifera, see *Neomammillaria villifera*.

vivipara, see *Escobaria vivipara*.

Mandevilla, man-de-VIL-la; after Henry John Mandeville (1773–1861), British Minister in Buenos Aires and plant collector. Greenhouse evergreen climber. *Apocynaceae*.

boliviensis, bol-iv-e-EN-sis, Bolivian.

laxa, LAKS-a, loose.

sauveolens, see *M. laxa*.

Mandragora, man-dra-GOR-a; from Gr. *mandragoros* (Mandrake), a herb possessing narcotic properties. Hardy perennials. *Solanaceae*.

officinarum, of-fis-in-AR-um, of the shop, herbal.

Manettia, man-ET-te-a; after Xavirio Manetti (1723–1785), Prefect of Botanic Garden at Florence. Climbing shrubs. *Rubiaceae*.

bicolor, see *M. luteorubra*.

luteorubra, LOO-te-o-ROO-bra, yellow and red.

Maranta, mar-AN-ta; after Bartolomeo Maranti (1500–1571), Italian botanist,

student of Ghini at Pisa. Tropical foliage perennials. *Marantaceae*.

arundinacea, ar-un-din-A-se-a, resembling *Arundo* (reed).

bellula, see *Calathea bellula*.

bicolor, see *Micristata*.

cristata, kris-TA-ta, crested.

gratiosa, gra-ti-O-sa, favoured, the beautiful leaf colour. Advertised in W. Bull's catalogue 1884. Species obscure.

insignis, see *Calathea lancifolia*.

leopardina, see *Calathea concinna*.

leuconeura, lu-ko-NEU-ra, white veined – the leaves.

massangeana, see *M. leuconeura*.

musaica, see *Calathea bella*.

picta, see *Calathea warszewiczii*.

polita, see *Calathea makoyana*.

roseo-picta, see *Calathea roseopicta*.

wagneri, see *Calathea roseopicta*.

warscewiczi, see *Calathea warszewiczii*.

zebrina, see *Calathea zebrina*.

Margyricarpus, mar-ge-re-KAR-pus; from L. *margarita*, pearl; Gr. *karpos*, a berry. Half-hardy shrub. *Rosaceae*.

pinnatus, pin-NA-tus, foliage pinnate.

setosus, see *M. pinnatus*.

Marica, misapplied see below.

brachypus, see *Neomarica brachypus*.

caerulea, see *Neomarica caerulea*.

northiana, see *Neomarica northiana*.

Marrubium, mar-ROO-be-um; believed to be the Hebrew name, *marrob*, bitter juice. One of the five bitter herbs used in the Jewish Passover rites. It is possible Linnaeus derived the word from L. *marruvium* or *marrubium*; a town in the province of L'Aquila, Italy. Aromatic herbs. *Lamiaceae*.

vulgare, vul-GAR-e, common. The Horehound.

Marsdenia, mars-DE-ne-a; after William Marsden (1754–1836), First secretary to the Admiralty and plant collector. Greenhouse and hardy shrubs. *Apocynaceae*.

erecta, see *Cionura erecta*.

flavescens, see *Pergularia flavescens*.

floribunda, flor-e-BUN-da, abundant or free flowering.

macrophylla, mak-rof-IL-a, with large leaves.

maculata, see *M. macrophylla*.

Marshallia, mar-SHAL-le-a; after Humphry Marshall (1722–1801), American botanist. Half-hardy perennials. *Compositae*.
  lanceolata, lan-se-o-LA-ta, the leaves spear-shaped.

Marsilea, mar-SE-le-a; after Luigi Ferdinando, Count de Masigli (1658–1730), Italian botanist. Aquatic ferns. *Marsileaceae*.
  quadrifolia, kwad-rif-OL-e-a, four lobes to the leaves.

Martynia, mar-TIN-e-a; after Dr. John Martyn (1699–1768), professor of botany at Cambridge. Half-hardy annuals. *Martyniaceae*.
  annua, AN-u-a, annual.
  fragrans, see *Proboscidea fragrans*.
  proboscidea, see *Proboscidea louisianica*.

Masdevallia, maz-dev-AL-le-a; after Jose Masdevall (c.1740–1801), Spanish botanist and physician. Greenhouse orchids. *Orchidaceae*.
  amabilis, am-A-bil-is, lovely.
  bella, see *Dracula bella*.
  caudata, kaw-DA-ta, tailed.
  chimaera, see *Dracula chimaera*.
  coccinea, kok-SIN-e-a, scarlet.
  harryana, see *M. coccinea*.
  ignea, IG-ne-a, fiery – colour of flowers.
  lindenii, see *M. coccinea*.
  tovarensis, to-var-EN-sis, of Tovar, Columbia.
  veitchiana, veech-e-A-na, introduced by James Veitch and Sons.

Matricaria, mat-re-KAR-e-a; from L. *matrix*, the womb; once used medicinally in uterine disorders. Hardy perennials. *Compositae*.
  eximia, eks-IM-e-a, excellent, choice.
  inodora, see *Tripleurospermum inodorum*.

Matteuccia, mat-TEW-ke-a; after Carlo Matteucci (1811–1868), Italian physicist and neurophysiologist, a pioneer in the field of bioelectromagnetism. Hardy Ferns. *Onocleaceae*.
  struthiopteris, stru-the-OP-ter-is, from Gr. *strouthion*, an ostrich; *pteris*, a fern, and the fronds being supposed to resemble ostrich's feather. Hardy ferns.

Matthiola, mat-TE-o-la; after Pietro Andrea Gregorio Mattioli (1501–1577), Italian physician and botanist. Half-hardy annuals and biennials. Stock-gilli-flower, Ten-week Stock, Brompton Stock, etc. of hybrid origin, have their parentage in this genus. *Brassicaceae*.
  annua, see *M. incana*.
  bicornis, see *M. longipetala* subsp. *bicornis*.
  incana, in-KA-na, hoary, the leaves. The Brompton Stock.
  longipetala, long-e-PET-a-la, long petalled.
  longipetala subsp. *bicornis*, bik-OR-nis, two-horned, the seed pod. The Night-scented Stock.
  sinuata, sin-u-A-ta, scalloped-leaved.

Maurandya, maw-RAN-de-a; named in 1797 by Gomez Ortega in honour of Catalina Pancracia Maurandy, Spanish botanist, of Cartagena who published scientific papers. Half-hardy twiners. *Plantaginaceae*.
  barclayana, bar-KLA-ar-na, after Robert Barclay (1757–1830), English botanist and horticulturist.
  scandens, SKAN-denz, climbing.

Maxillaria, maks-il-LAR-e-a; from L. *maxilla*, the jaw; referring to the appearance of the column and lip to the jaws of an insect. Greenhouse orchids. *Orchidaceae*.
  grandiflora, gran-dif-LO-ra, large-flowered.
  harrisoniae, see *Bifrenaria harrisoniae*.
  picta, see *Brasiliorchis picta*.
  sanderiana, san-der-e-A-na, discovered in Ecuador by Klaboch and cultivated by Sander's nursery, St Albans, England.
  tenuifolia, see *Maxillariella tenuifolia*.
  venusta, ven-US-ta, charming.

Maxillariella, maks-il-LA-re-EL-la; a diminutive of *Maxillaria* (which see), in reference to the much smaller flowers. Greenhouse orchids. *Orchidaceae*.
  tenuifolia, ten-u-if-OL-e-a, narrow-leaved.

Mazus, MA-zus; from Gr. *mazos*, a teat, in reference to the tubercles at the mouth of the flowers. Creeping rock plants. *Phrymaceae*.
  pumilio, pew-MIL-e-o, dwarf.
  pumilus, pew-MIL-us, dwarf.
  reptans, REP-tans, creeping and rooting.
  rugosus, see *Mazus pumilus*.

Meconopsis, mek-on-OP-sis; from Gr. *mekon*, a poppy; *opsis*, like. Biennials and perennials. *Papaveraceae*.

baileyi, BA-le-i, after Lieutenant-Colonel Frederick Marshman Bailey (1882–1967), British army officer.

betonicifolia, bet-on-ik-e-FO-le-a, betony leaved.

cambrica, see *Papaver cambricum*.

grandis, GRAN-dis, of great size.

integrifolia, in-teg-rif-OL-e-a, leaves entire, not divided.

prattii, PRAT-te-i, collected by Antwerp Edgar Pratt (1852–1924), British naturalist and explorer.

quintuplinervia, kwin-tup-lin-ER-ve-a, five nerved – the leaves.

simplicifolia, sim-plis-if-OL-e-a, leaves simple, that is, not divided.

villosa, vil-LO-sa, shaggy, with fine hairs.

wallichii, wol-LICH-e-i, after Nathaniel Wallich (1786–1854), Danish surgeon and botanist, who worked for the East India Company and became superintendent of the Calcutta Botanic Garden.

Medeola, med-E-o-la; called after *Medea*, the Greek sorceress. Low growing herbaceous perennial. *Liliaceae*.

asparagoides, see *Asparagus asparagoides*.

virginiana, vir-jin-e-A-na, of Virginia, U.S.A.

Medicago, med-ik-A-go; Medik indirectly from Media, the country whence Alfalfa was supposed to have been derived. Herbaceous perennials and fodder plants. *Leguminosae*.

echinus, see *M. intertexta*.

falcata, fal-KA-ta, sickle-shaped.

intertexta, in-ter-TEX-ta, intertwined.

sativa, SAT-iv-a, cultivated. Alfalfa; Lucerne.

scutellata, skew-tel-LA-ta, a little shield.

Medinilla, me-din-IL-la; after José de Medinilla y Pineda, Spanish governor of the Marianas in the 1820's. Tropical flowering shrubs. *Melastomataceae*.

curtisii, ker-TIS-e-i, after William Curtis (1746–1799), English botanist and author.

magnifica, mag-NIF-ik-a, magnificent.

Megasea, misapplied see below.

ciliata, see *Bergenia ciliata*.

cordifolia, see *Bergenia crassifolia*.

crassifolia, see *Bergenia crassifolia*.

stracheyi, see *Bergenia stracheyi*.

Melaleuca, mel-a-LEW-ka; from Gr. *melas*, black; *leukos*, white, the colours of the old and new bark. Greenhouse shrubs. *Myrtaceae*.

ericifolia, er-ik-if-O-le-a, leaves resembling *Erica*.

fulgens, FUL-jenz, shining or glowing.

leucadendra, loo-ka-DEN-dra, white-leaved like *Leucadendron*.

scabra, SKA-bra, rough – the leaves.

thymifolia, ty-mif-OL-e-a, *Thymus* (Thyme) leaved.

Melianthus, me-li-AN-thus; from Gr. *mele*, honey; *anthos*, a flower, the blooms yielding plentiful amounts of nectar. Half-hardy perennials. *Melianthaceae*.

comosus, kom-O-sus, tufted with hairs.

major, MA-jor, greater.

pectinatus, pek-tin-A-tus, like a comb.

Melicytus, mel-e-SY-tus; from Gr. *mele*, honey; *kytos*, a hollow jar, the staminal nectaries being hollow. Trees and shrubs. *Violaceae*.

crassifolius, kras-sif-OL-e-us, thick-leaved.

Melinis, ME-lin-is; from Gr. *meline*, millet. Grasses. *Poaceae*.

repens, RE-penz, creeping.

Meliosma, mel-i-OZ-ma; from Gr. *mele*, honey; *osme*, a smell, the scent of the flowers. Deciduous trees and shrubs. *Sabiaceae*.

myriantha, mir-e-AN-tha, myriad flowers.

veitchiorum, veech-e-OR-um, after Veitch Nurseries.

Melissa, mel-IS-sa; from Gr. *melissa*, a bee, the plants being attractive to bees. Perennial herbs. *Lamiaceae*.

officinalis, of-fis-in-A-lis, of the shop (apothecary's), applied to plants always kept "in stock" by herbalists.

Melittis, mel-IT-tis; same derivation as *Melissa*. Aromatic herb. *Lamiaceae*.

melissophyllum, mel-is-sof-IL-lum, leaves resembling *Melissa*.

Melocactus, mel-o-KAK-tus; from L. *melo*, a melon; *cactus*, descriptive of the globular form of these cacti. Greenhouse cacti. *Cactaceae*.

communis, see *M. intortus.*
intortus, in-TOR-tus, twisted.

Menispermum, me-nis-PER-mum; from Gr. *mene*, the crescent moon; *sperma*, seed, the latter being crescent-shaped. Hardy climbing shrub. *Menispermaceae.*
  canadense, kan-a-DEN-se, of Canada.

Mentha, MEN-tha; named to honour the Greek nymph, Minthe, supposedly turned into this aromatic plant by Persephone. Herbaceous perennials and carpeting plants. *Lamiaceae.*
  aquatica, a-KWAT-ik-a, growing in water. The Bergamot Mint.
  gibraltarica, see *M. pulegium.*
  × *piperita*, pi-per-E-ta, pepper. The Peppermint.
  pulegium, pu-LE-je-um, from L. *pulex*, a flea, which the plant was supposed to eradicate. The Pennyroyal.
  requienii, re-KWE-en-e-i, after Esprit Requien (1788–1851), French naturalist.
  spicata, spe-KA-ta, spiked. Spearmint.
  viridis, see *M. spicata.*

Mentzelia, ment-ZE-le-a; in honour of Christian Mentzel (1622–1701), German botanist. Mainly annuals and biennials. *Loasaceae.*
  aurea, AW-re-a, golden yellow.
  bartonioides, bar-to-ne-OY-dees, resembling *Bartonia.*
  lindleyi, LIND-le-i, after John Lindley (1799–1865), British botanist, appointed first chair of botany at University College London.

Menyanthes, men-e-AN-thes; possibly from Gr. *men*, month; *anthos*, a flower, the flowering period of the Bogbean, being supposed to last a month. Hardy aquatic. *Menyanthaceae.*
  crista-galli, see *Nephrophyllidium crista-galli.*
  nymphoides, see *Limnanthemum nymphoides.*
  trifoliata, trif-ol-e-A-ta, leaves in three. The Bogbean.

Menziesia, men-ZE-ze-a; or men-E-se-a, named after Archibald Menzies (1754–1842), Scottish surgeon and botanist on Vancouver's expedition 1790–1795. Dwarf ericaceous shrubs. *Ericaceae.*
  coerulea, se-RU-le-a, blue.

empetrifolia, see *Phyllodoce empetriformis.*
  ferruginea, fer-ru-JIN-e-a, rusty.
  polifolia, pol-if-OL-e-a, Polium leaved, that is, *Teucrium polium.*

Mertensia, mer-TEN-se-a; named after Francis Karl Mertens (1764–1831), professor of botany at Bremen. Hardy perennials. *Boraginaceae.*
  alpina, al-PINE-a (or al-PIN-a), of the Alps or alpine.
  ciliata, sil-e-A-ta, an eyelash, fringed with hair.
  echioides, see *Pseudomertensia echioides.*
  primuloides, prim-ul-OY-dees, resembling *Primula.*
  sibirica, si-BIR-ik-a, of Siberia.
  virginica, vir-JIN-ik-a, of Virginia.

Mesembryanthemum, mes-em-bre-AN-the-mum; from Gr. *mesembria*, midday; *anthemon*, a flower, in reference to the first recorded species opening at noon. Annuals and biennials. *Aizoaceae.*
  acinaciforme, see *Carpobrotus acinaciformis.*
  aurantiacum, aw-RAN-te-ak-um, orange-coloured.
  aureum, AW-re-um, golden.
  barbatum, bar-BA-tum, bearded, having hooked hairs.
  blandum, BLAND-um, pleasing.
  bolusiae, BO-lus-e-e, after Harriet Margaret Louisa Bolus (1877–1970), South African botanist and taxonomist.
  brownii, BROWN-e-i, after Nicholas Edward Brown (1849–1934), English plant taxonomist and an authority on succulents.
  coccineum, see *Lampranthus coccineus.*
  cooperi, see *Delosperma cooperi.*
  cordifolium, kor-dif-O-le-um, heart-shaped leaves.
  criniflorum, see *Stigmatocarpum criniflorum.*
  crystallinum, kris-tal-LE-num, crystalline – the foliage. The Ice Plant.
  cymbifolium, kim (or sim)-bif-OL-e-um, boat shaped leaves.
  deltoides, see *Lampranthus deltoides.*
  densum, DEN-sum, close, dense.
  dolabriforme, dol-A-brif-OR-me, axe or hatchet shaped leaves.
  echinatum, see *Delosperma echinatum.*
  edule, see *Carpobrotus edulis.*
  inclaudens, see *Erepsia inclaudens.*
  polyanthum, pol-e-ANTH-um, many flowered.

pomeridianum, see *Carpanthea pomeridiana*.
pugioniforme, see *Conicosia pugioniformis*.
pyropeum, py-ro-PE-um, flame coloured.
roseum, see *Lampranthus multiradiatus*.
spectabile, see *Lampranthus spectabilis*.
tigrinum, see *Faucaria tigrina*.
tricolorum, see *Cephalophyllum tricolorum*.
turbiniforme, ter-bin-if-OR-me, shaped like a spinning top or cone.
uncinatum, un-sin-A-tum, hooked at the end – the leaves.
violaceum, vi-o-LA-se-um, violet-coloured.

Mespilus, MES-pil-us; from Gr. *mesos*, half; *pilos*, a bullet or ball, referring to the half-ball shape of the fruit. Fruit bearing tree. *Rosaceae*.
germanica, jer-MAN-ik-a, of Germany. The Medlar.

Metasequoia, met-a-se-KWOY-a; from Gr. *meta*, with; *sequoia* (which see), a fossil genus rediscovered on the border between the Szechuan and Hupeh provinces, China 1945. Evergreen tree. *Cupressaceae*.
glyptostroboides, glip-toh-stro-BOY-dees, resembling *Glyptostrobus*.

Metrosideros, me-tros-id-E-ros; from Gr. *metra*, heart of a tree; *sideros*, iron, alluding to the hardness of the wood. Greenhouse flowering shrubs. *Myrtaceae*.
floribunda, see *Angophora floribunda*.
speciosa, see *Callistemon speciosus*.

Meum, ME-um; from Gr. *meion*, small, in allusion to the fineness of the foliage. Hardy aromatic herb. *Apiaceae*.
athamanticum, ath-am-AN-tik-um, resembling *Athamanta*, this genus being named after Mount Athamas, Sicily.

Meyenia, mey-EN-e-a; after Franz Julius Ferdinand Meyen (1804–1840), German naturalist, professor of botany in Berlin. Greenhouse flowering shrub. *Solanaceae*.
erecta, see *Thunbergia erecta*.

Michauxia, me-SHO-se-a; after André Michaux (1746–1802), French botanist. Biennials. *Campanulaceae*.
campanuloides, kam-pan-ul-OY-dez, resembling *Campanula*.

Microglossa, mi-kro-GLOS-a; from Gr. *mikros*, small; *glossa*, a tongue, referring to the short segments of the corolla. Shrub. *Compositae*.
albescens, see *Aster albescens*.

Microlepia, mi-kro-LE-pe-a; from Gr. *mikros*, small; *lepis*, a scale, the appearance of the spore cases. Greenhouse ferns. *Dennstaedtiaceae*.
hirta cristata, see *Davallia hirta*.

Micromeria, mi-kro-MEER-e-a; from Gr. *mikros*, small; *meris*, a part, referring to the small flowers and leaves of these plants. Half-hardy shrubby perennials. *Lamiaceae*.
croatica, kro-AT-ik-a, of Croatia.
marginata, mar-jin-A-ta, margined with another colour.
piperella, see *M. marginata*.
rupestris, see *Clinopodium thymifolium*.

Microsperma, misapplied please see below.
bartonioides, see *Eucnide bartonioides*.

Microstegium, mi-kro-STE-ge-um; from Gr. *mikros*, small; *stege*, a roof, to cover over, presumably the small lemmas. Grasses. *Poaceae*.
glabratum, GLAB-ra-tum, somewhat glabrous (smooth).

Mikania, mik-AN-e-a; after Joseph Mikan (1743–1814), professor of botany at Prague. Greenhouse flowering shrubs. *Compositae*.
scandens, SKAN-denz, climbing.

Mila, MIL-a; anagram of Lima, capital of Peru, in the neighbourhood of which the species is found. Greenhouse cacti. *Cactaceae*.
caespitosa, ses-pit-O-sa, growing in tufts.

Milla, MIL-la; named by Cavanilles to honour Julian Milla, head gardener in the Royal Garden, Madrid, 18th century. Half-hardy bulbs. *Asparagaceae*.
biflora, bif-LO-ra, two-flowered, that is, in pairs.
laxiflora, see *Triteleia laxa*.
uniflora, see *Tristagma uniflorum*.

Millettia, mil-LET-te-a; after Charles Millett (c. 1825), plant collector and official with the British East India Company. Climbers and trees. *Leguminosae.*

japonica, jap-ON-ik-a, of Japan.

Miltonia, mil-TO-ne-a; after Charles Wentworth-Fitzwilliam (1786–1857), Viscount Milton then later the 5th Earl Fitzwilliam, patron of natural science and lover of orchids. Epiphytic orchids. *Orchidaceae.*

× *bleuana*, see *Miltoniopsis* × *bleuana*.

clowesii, KLOWES-e-i, after Rev. John Clowes (1777–1846), orchid grower, of Broughton Hall, Manchester (now Clowes Park), he gifted his orchid collection to the Royal Botanic Gardens, Kew.

phalaenopsis, see *Miltoniopsis phalaenopsis.*

roezlii, see *Miltoniopsis roezlii.*

spectabilis, spek-TAB-il-is, notable.

vexillaria, see *Miltoniopsis vexillaria.*

Miltoniopsis, mil-to-ne-OP-sis; from *Miltonea* (which see); *opsis*, resembling. Orchids. *Orchidaceae.*

× *bleuana*, blu-A-na, the first *Miltoniopsis* cross by Alfred Bleu, French orchid breeder, in 1883, from *M. vexillaria* and *M. roezlii.*

phalaenopsis, fal-e-NOP-sis, resembling a moth.

roezlii, ROEZ-le-i, in honour of Benedikt Roezl (1824–1885), Czech botanist and plant collector.

vexillaria, veks-il-LA-re-a, standard bearing – the conspicuous labellum.

Mimosa, mi-MO-sa; from Gr. *mimos*, imitator, referring to the sensitivity of the leaves to touch or injury. Greenhouse plants. Sensitive plant. *Leguminosae.*

pudica, PUD-ik-a, humble, bashful.

sensitiva, sen-sit-IV-a, sensitive to touch.

Mimulus, MIM-ul-us; from L. *mimus*, a mimic, the flowers being supposed to resemble a mask, or a monkey's face, hence Monkey-flower; or from L. *mimo*, an ape. Herbaceous perennials, most kinds in cultivation are cultivars of *M. luteus.* *Phrymaceae.*

cardinalis, kar-din-A-lis, scarlet, cardinal red.

cupreus, KU-pre-us, copper-coloured.

guttatus, gut-TA-tus, covered with small spots.

harrisonii, cultivar of *M. moschatus.*

luteus, LU-te-us, yellow. The Common Monkey-flower.

moschatus, mos-KA-tus, musk. The Musk Plant.

ringens, RIN-gens, the flowers gaping.

Mina, misapplied see below.

lobata, see *Ipomoea lobata.*

Minuartia, min-u-AR-te-a; in honour of Jaun Minuart (1693–1768), Spanish apothecary and botanist at Barcelona, then Madrid. Mostly perennial herbs. *Caryophyllaceae.*

laricifolia, lar-is-if-o-le-a, *Larix* (Larch) like leaves.

verna, VER-na, spring – time of flowering.

villarsii, vil-LAR-se-i, after Dominique Villars (1745–1814), professor of botany at Grenoble, whose worked for his work on the flora of the Dauphiné region, France.

Mirabilis, mir-AB-il-is; from L. *mirabilis*, wonderful or to be admired. Tender perennials. *Nyctaginaceae.*

jalapa, jal-A-pa, old name. The Jalap or Marvel of Peru.

longiflora, long-if-LO-ra, long-flowered.

Miscanthus, mis-KAN-thus; from Gr. *miskos*, a stem; *anthos*, a flower, referring to the tall flowering stems. Ornamental and economic grasses. *Poaceae.*

× *giganteus*, ji-GAN-te-us, gigantic. Hybrid cross between *M. sacchariflorus* and *M. sinensis.* Elephant Grass.

sacchariflorus, sak-kar-e-FLOR-us, sugary flowered.

sinensis, si-NEN-sis, Chinese.

Mitchella, mit-CHEL-a; named by Linnaeus for Dr. John Mitchell (1711–1768), a botanist, of Virginia. Rock or woodland herb. *Rubiaceae.*

repens, RE-penz, creeping.

Mitella, mit-EL-la; the diminutive of L. *mitra*, a mitre (a little mitre), in allusion to the two-cleft seed pod. Small woodland plants. *Saxifragaceae.*

diphylla, dif-IL-la, two-leaved.

Mitraria, mit-RAH-re-a; from L. *mitra*, mitre, referring to the shape of the fruit. Greenhouse shrub. *Gesneriaceae.*

coccinea, kok-SIN-e-a, scarlet.

Molinia, mol-EE-ne-a; after Juan Molina (1740–1829), a writer on Chilean natural history. Hardy grass. *Poaceae.*
  caerulea, se-RU-le-a, sky-blue.

Moltkia, MOLT-ke-a; named after Count Joachim Godske Moltke (1746–1818), a Danish nobleman and patron of the sciences. Shrubby perennial. *Boraginaceae.*
  petraea, pet-RE-a, of rocks.
  suffruticosa, suf-frut-ik-O-sa, having a woody base.

Momordica, mo-MOR-dik-a; from L. *mordeo*, to bite, in allusion to the jagged seeds as though bitten. Tender annual fruiting climbers. *Cucurbitaceae.*
  balsamina, bawl-sa-ME-na, balsam scented.
  charantia, kar-AN-te-a, *Charantia* the pre-Linnean name for this plant.
  elaterium, see *Ecballium elaterium.*

Monanthes, mo-NAN-thez; from Gr. *monos*, single; *anthos*, a flower, one-flowered. Given in error as the type species (*M. polyphylla*) was thought to be one-flowered; it is few flowered. Greenhouse succulents. *Crassulaceae.*
  laxiflora, laks-if-LOR-a, with loose flowers.
  muralis, mu-RA-lis, from L. *muralis*, of walls; found on walls.
  polyphylla, pol-if-IL-la, many-leaved.

Monarda, mon-AR-da; after Nicolás Bautista Monardes (1493–1588), a physician and botanist of Seville. Herbaceous perennials. *Lamiaceae.*
  didyma, DID-im-a, double or twin, the flowers having stamens in pairs of different sizes.
  fistulosa, fis-tul-O-sa, stem hollow.

Monilaria, mo-nil-AR-e-a; from L. *monilla*, a necklace, the stems constricted into bead-like sections. Greenhouse succulents. *Aizoaceae.*
  moniliformis, mo-ne-le-FOR-mis, necklace like.

Monstera, mon-STE-ra; derivation unclear although it is possible that it is a latinised French equivalent of *Dracontium*, it being typical to associate aroids with snakes,

dragons and monsters. Perennial climbers. *Araceae.*
  deliciosa, de-lis-e-O-sa, delicious.

Montbretia, misapplied see below.
  × *crocosmiiflora*, see *Crocosmia x crocosmiiflora.*
  pottsii, see *Crocosmia pottsii.*

Montiopsis, mon-te-OP-sis; resembling *Montia*. Annuals and perennials. *Montiaceae.*
  umbellata, um-bel-LA-ta, flowers in an umbel. Annual Candytuft.

Monvillea, mon-VIL-e-a; dedicated to Baron Hippolyte Boissel de Monville (1794–1863), French collector and authority on cactus. Greenhouse cacti. *Cactaceae.*
  cavendishii, kav-en-DISH-e-i, commemorating William Spencer Cavendish (1790–1858), 6th Duke of Devonshire, cactus collector.
  spegazzinii, see *Cereus spegazzinii.*

Moraea, mor-EE-a; after Robert More (1703–1780), a keen botanist and natural historian. Originally spelt Morea, however Linnaeus amended it to Moraea in 1762, to honour his father-in-law J. Moraeus, a Swedish physician. Bulbous plants. *Iridaceae.*
  aristata, ar-is-TA-ta, bristled.
  bicolor, see *Dietes bicolor.*
  collina, kol-LE-na, found on hills.
  robinsoniana, see *Dietes robinsoniana.*
  unguiculata, un-gwik-ul-A-ta, narrow-clawed, the lower end of the petal.

Morella, mo-REL-la; alluding to the fruits being a similar colour to Morello Cherries. Evergreen. *Myricaceae.*
  cerifera, ser-IF-er-a, wax-bearing, the fruits yielding a candle-wax. Wax Myrtle.

Morina, mor-E-na; named after Louis Morin (1635–1714), a French plant collector and botanist. Herbaceous perennials. *Caprifoliaceae.*
  coulteriana, kol-ter-e-A-na, in honour of Thomas Coulter (1793–1843), Irish botanist.
  longifolia, long-if-OL-e-a, long leaves.

Morisia, mor-IS-e-a; after Giuseppe Giacinto Moris (1796–1869), Italian botanist, professor at the University of Turin. Rock plant. *Brassicaceae*.

hypogaea, see *M. monanthos*.

monanthos, mon-AN-thos, one-flowered.

Morus, MOR-us; ancient L. name. Tree cultivated for its edible fruit and leaves for silkworm forage. Trees. *Moraceae*.

alba, AL-ba, from the L. *alba*, white, the fruits.

nigra, NY-gra, black. The Mulberry.

rubra, ROO-bra, red.

Moschosma, misapplied see below.

riparium, see *Tetradenia riparia*.

Muehlenbeckia, muhl-en-BEK-e-a; after Henri Gustave Muehlenbeck (1798–1845), German physician and plant collector, remembered for his works on Bryophytes. Slender trailing shrubs. *Polygonaceae*.

complexa, kom-PLEKS-a, the branches interwoven, entangled. The Wire Vine.

Mulgedium, mul-GE-de-um; probably from L. *mulgeo*, to milk, the juice of the plants being white. Annuals and biennials. *Compositae*.

plumieri, see *Lactuca plumieri*.

Musa, MU-za; said to be in honour of Antonius Musa, a freedman of Emperor Augustus, whose physician he became; the Arabic name *mouz*, is considered by some to be the basis of the Latin *musa*. Tropical fruiting plants. *Musaceae*.

acuminata, a-ku-min-A-ta, long-pointed, the leaves.

basjoo, BA-shou, the Japanese vernacular name from the Chinese vernacular name *Ba jiao*, for banana.

cavendishii, see *M. acuminata*.

ensete, see *Ensete ventricosum*.

× *paradisiaca*, par-a-DIS-e-ak-a, of paradise. The Plantain.

× *sapientum*, see *M.* × *paradisiaca*.

Muscari, mus-KAR-e; from Gr. *moschos*, musk, the flowers of some species having a musky odour. Hardy bulbs. *Asparagaceae*.

armeniacum, ar-me-ne-AK-um, of Armenia.

botryoides, bot-re-OY-dez, from Gr. *botrus*, grapes, like a bunch of grapes. The Grape Hyacinth.

comosum, see *Leopoldia comosa*.

conicum, see *M. armeniacum*.

moschatum, see *M. racemosum*.

racemosum, ra-se-MO-sum, with flowers in racemes.

Mussaenda, mus-SEN-da; Latinized version of the Sinhalese name for *M. frondosa*. Tropical flowering shrubs. *Rubiaceae*.

erythrophylla, er-ith-ROF-il-la, red-leaved.

frondosa, fron-DOZ-a, leafy.

macrophylla, mak-rof-IL-a, with large leaves.

Mutisia, mew-TIS-e-a; named after José Celestino Mutis (1732 –1808), Spanish botanist who settled in South America. Greenhouse climbers. *Compositae*.

clematis, see *M. orbignyana*.

decurrens, de-KUR-rens, running down – the leaves clasping the stems.

orbignyana, or-bin-YA-na, commemorating Alcide Charles Victor Marie Dessalines d'Orbigny (1802–1857), French naturalist.

Myosotidium, my-o-so-TID-e-um; from *Myosotis* (see below) and Gr. *eidos*, an appearance, the flowers resembling those of *Myosotis*. One species a perennial herb. *Boraginaceae*.

hortensium, hor-TEN-se-um, belonging to gardens.

nobile, see *M. hortensium*.

Myosotis, my-o-SO-tis; from Gr. *mus*, a mouse; *otos*, an ear, the foliage resemblance. The plant to which the name was originally given by the ancient Greeks was not a forget-me-not. Hardy biennials and perennials. *Boraginaceae*.

alpestris, al-PES-tris, alpine.

azorica, az-OR-ik-a, of the Azores.

dissitiflora, dis-sit-if-LO-ra, the flowers far apart. The garden Forget-me-not.

palustris, see *M. scorpioides*.

scorpioides, skor-pe-OY-dees, from Gr. *skorpios*, resembling a scorpion.

Myrica, mer-IK-a; from Gr. *myrike*, tamarisk. Shrubs. *Myricaceae*.

cerifera, see *Morella cerifera*.

gale, gale, old name for Bog Myrtle (Sweet Gale), probably from *Gagel*, an Anglo-Saxon term for the same shrub.

Myriophyllum, mer-e-of-IL-lum; from Gr. *myrios*, a myriad; *phyllon*, a leaf, in reference to the many divisions in the leaves. Submerged aquatics. Water Milfoil and Feather-foil. *Haloragaceae*.
  aquaticum, a-KWAT-ik-um, aquatic.
  heterophyllum, het-er-o-FIL-um, variously leaved, those emerged differing from those submerged.
  proserpinacoides, see *M. aquaticum*.
  spicatum, spe-KA-tum, spiked.
  verticillatum, ver-tis-il-LA-tum, whorled – the foliage.

Myrrhis, MER-ris; from Gr. *myrrha*, fragrant. Sweet Cicely. True myrrh is *Commiphora myrrha*. Aromatic herb. *Apiaceae*.
  odorata, od-o-RA-ta, sweet smelling.

Myrsiphyllum, misapplied see below.
  asparagoides, see *Asparagus asparagoides*.

Myrtus, MER-tus; from Gr. *murtos*, the ancient name for Myrtle. Half-hardy shrubs. *Myrtaceae*.
  communis, kom-MU-nis, common.
  luma, see *Amomyrtus luma*.
  ugni, see *Ugni molinae*.

Naegelia, misapplied see below.
  cinnabarina, see *Smithiantha cinnabarina*.
  fulgida, see *Smithiantha fulgida*.
  multiflora, see *Smithiantha multiflora*.
  zebrina, see *Smithiantha zebrina*.

Nananthus, nan-AN-thus; from Gr. *nanos*, dwarf; *anthos*, a flower, alluding to the dwarf habit of the plants. Greenhouse succulents. *Aizoaceae*.
  pole-evansii, pole-EV-anz-e-i, after Illtyd Buller Pole-Evans (1879–1968), Welsh born South African botanist and plant collector.
  vittatus, vit-TA-tus, ribbon-striped.

Nandina, nan-DY-na; from Japanese name *nandin*. Shrubs. *Berberidaceae*.
  domestica, do-MES-tik-a, domestic – from its various uses in Japanese households.

Narcissus, nar-SIS-sus; a classical L. name derived from the Gr. *narke*, numbness, torpor, in allusion to its narcotic qualities. Hardy bulbs. *Amaryllidaceae*.

bulbocodium, bul-bo-KO-de-um, probably from Gr. *bolbus*, a bulb; *kodion*, a little fleece, the covering of the bulb. The Hoop Petticoat Daffodil.
cyclamineus, sik-la-MIN-e-us, like a *Cyclamen* flower.
flavus, FLA-vus, pure yellow.
hispanicus, his-PAN-ik-us, of Spain.
× *incomparabilis*, in-kom-par-A-bil-is, incomparable.
jonquilla, jon-KWIL-la, variant of Spanish *jonquillo*, from L. *juncus*, a rush, referring to the rush-like leaves. The Jonquil.
juncifolius, see *N. flavus*.
major, see *N. hispanicus*.
maximus, see *N. hispanicus*.
minor, see *N. psuedonarcissus* subsp. *minor*.
× *odorus*, od-OR-us, sweet-scented.
poeticus, po-ET-ik-us, the Poet's Narcissus.
pseudonarcissus, SUED-o-nar-SIS-sus, the false narcissus. The English Daffodil.
p. subsp. *minor*, MI-nor, smaller.
tazetta, taz-ET-ta, old name from the Italian vernacular name *tazza*, used for *Narcissus*, meaning small cup; from the form of the corona. Polynesian Narcissus.
triandrus, tre-AN-drus, having three stamens.

Nassella, NA-sel-la; from L. *nassa*, a basket with a narrow neck, in allusion to the inflorescence. Grasses. *Poaceae*.
  cernua, SER-nu-a, drooping – the flowers. Nodding Needlegrass.
  pulchra, PUL-kra, pretty. Purple Needlegrass. The State Grass of California.

Nasturtium, nas-TUR-she-um; from L. *nasi-tortium*, distortion of the nose, in reference to the pungency of some of the species. Aquatic salad herb. The garden plant popularly called Nasturtium is *Tropaeolum majus*, which see. *Brassicaceae*.
  officinale, of-fis-in-A-le, of shops (herbal). The Watercress.

Neillia, ne-IL-le-a; named after Dr. Patrick Neill (1776–1851), Scottish naturalist and Secretary of the Caledonia Horticultural Society. Shrubs. *Rosaceae*.
  amurensis, see *Physocarpus amurensis*.
  opulifolia, see *Physocarpus opulifolius*.

Nelumbo, ne-LUM-bo; Sinhalese name for *N. nucifera*. Aquatic herbs. *Nelumbonaceae*.
  lutea, LU-te-a, yellow.
  nucifera, nu-SIF-e-ra, bearing nuts.

Nemesia, nem-e-ZE-a; from Gr. *nemesion*, an old name used by Dioscorides for some sort of snapdragon. Half-hardy annuals used for bedding. *Scrophulariaceae*.
  floribunda, flor-e-BUN-da, abundant or free flowering.
  strumosa, stroo-MO-sa, having cushion like swellings.
  versicolor, ver-SIK-ol-or, changeable colour.

Nemophila, nem-OF-il-a; from Gr. *nemos*, grove or glade; *phileo*, to love, the plants inhabiting such places. Hardy annuals. *Boraginaceae*.
  insignis, see *menziesii* subsp. *insignis*.
  maculata, mak-ul-A-ta, blotched.
  menziesii, men-ZE-se-i, after Archibald Menzies (1754–1842), the Scottish botanist. The Baby Blue-eyes.
  m. subsp. *insignis*, in-SIG-nis, showy.

Neomammillaria, ne-O-mam-mil-LAR-e-a; from Gr. *neo*, new; *mammillaria* from L. *mammilla*, a nipple. Greenhouse cacti. *Cactaceae*.
  villifera, vil-LIF-er-a, bearing shaggy hair.

Neomarica, ne-o-MAR-ik-a; from Gr. *neo*, new; *Marica*, the genus. Greenhouse perennials. *Iridaceae*.
  brachypus, brak-IP-us, stalks short.
  caerulea, se-RU-le-a, sky-blue.
  northiana, north-e-A-na, after Marianne North (1830–1890), English biologist and botanical artist, whose collection of paintings is housed at the Royal Botanic Gardens, Kew.

Nepenthes, ne-PEN-thez; from Gr. meaning without care, in allusion to the passage in the Odyssey where Helen so drugged the wine cup that its contents freed man from grief and care. The Pitcherplant. Tropical perennials. *Nepenthaceae*.
  curtisii, KER-tis-e-i, after Curtis.
  distillatoria, dis-til-la-TOR-e-a, distilling. The first introduced species.
  mirabilis, mir-A-bil-is, wonderful.

northiana, north-e-A-na, after Marianne North (1830–1890), botanical illustrator.
rafflesiana, raf-les-e-A-na, after Sir Thomas Stamford Raffles (1781–1826), patron of science and founder of Singapore.
ventricosa, ven-trik-O-sa, swollen or bellied.

Nepeta, NEP-e-ta (or nep-E-ta); name used by Pliny, possibly after Nepi in Italy. Hardy and half-hardy herbaceous plants. *Lamiaceae*.
  cataria, ka-TAR-e-a, pertaining to cats.
  glechoma, see *Glechoma hederacea*.
  mussinii, see *N. racemosa*.
  racemosa, ra-se-MO-sa, with flowers in racemes.

Nephrodium, nef-RO-de-um; from Gr. *nephros*, a kidney, the shape of the indusium covering the spore cases. Greenhouse ferns. *Dryopteridaceae*.
  molle, see *Christella dentata*.
  multifidum, mul-TIF-id-um, many times divided.
  richardsii, RICH-ards-e-i, possibly after Louis Claude Marie Richards (1754–1821), French botanist and collector.

Nephrolepis, nef-rol-EP-is; from Gr. *nephros*, a kidney; *lepis*, a scale, referring to the shape of the indusium covering the spore cases. Ferns. *Nephrolepidaceae*.
  bausei, BAUS-e-i, after Christian Frederick Bause (d. 1895), German born British hybridiser of indoor plants.
  biserrata, bi-ser-RAY-ta, double-toothed, that is the teeth on the leaves being themselves toothed.
  cordifolia, kor-dif-OL-e-a, heart shaped.
  davallioides, dav-al-le-OY-dees, resembling *Davallia*.
  exaltata, eks-al-TA-ta, elevated or tall. The Boston Fern.
  rufescens, see *N. biserrata*.
  todeaoides, TO-de-a-OY-dees, resembling *Todea*.

Nephrophyllidium, nef-ro-fi-LID-e-um; from Gr. *nephros*, a kidney; *phyllon*, leaf. Perennial herb. *Menyanthaceae*.
  crista-galli, kris-ta-GAL-le, cock's crest.

Nerine, ne-RI-ne; from Gr. *nereis*, the water nymph of that name, in allusion to the myth that bulbs of *N. sarniensis* (Guernsey Lily) were cast on to the shore of Guernsey after a shipwreck. Bulbs. *Amaryllidaceae*.

bowdenii, bow-DEN-e-i, collected by Athelstan Cornish-Bowden (1871–1942), in South Africa and introduced into British gardens in 1902.

flexuosa, see *N. undulata*.

fothergillii, see *N. sarniensis*.

pumila, PU-mil-a, dwarf.

sarniensis, sar-ne-EN-sis, of Guensey (ancient name Sarnia).

undulata, un-du-LA-ta, waved – the leaves.

Nerium, NE-re-um; name used by Dioscorides. Tender shrubs. *Apocynaceae*.

oleander, O-le-AN-der, from Italian *oleandro*, referring to the olive-like leaves.

Nertera, NER-ter-a; from Gr. *nerteros*, lowly, the plant being very prostrate. Half-hardy herbaceous perennial. *Rubiaceae*.

depressa, see *N. granadensis*.

granadensis, gran-a-DEN-sis, of Columbia (New Granada).

Nicandra, nik-AN-dra; after Nikander of Colophon, Greek botanist and medical writer, c. 150 BC. Hardy annual. *Solanaceae*.

physalodes, FY-sal-OY-dees, resembling *Physalis* – the seed vessels.

Nicotiana, nik-o-te-A-na (or ne-ko-she-A-na); named after Jean Nicot (1530–1600), French Ambassador to Portugal who introduced tobacco into France. Annuals and perennials. *Solanaceae*.

affinis, see *N. alata*.

alata, al-A-ta, winged – the petiole.

× *sanderae*, SAN-der-e, after Henry Frederick Conrad Sander (1847–1920), German born British nurseryman, St Albans, England.

suaveolens, SWA-ve-ol-enz, sweet smelling.

sylvestris, sil-VES-tris, sylvan or of woodland.

tabacum, tab-A-kum, tobacco, old name for the Virginian tobacco plant. Tobacco.

Nierembergia, ne-er-em-BER-ge-a; after Juan Eusebio Nieremberg (1595–1658), a Spanish Jesuit and author of a book on nature in 1635. Half-hardy perennials. *Solanaceae*.

coerulea, ser-U-le-a, blue.

frutescens, see *N. scoparia*.

hippomanica, hip-po-MAN-ik-a, from Gr. *hippomanes*, used for herbs which drive horses mad, are poisonous to them or of which they are madly fond.

rivularis, riv-u-LAR-is, of riversides.

scoparia, sko-PAR-e-a, Broom-like.

Nigella, ni-JEL-la; from L. *nigellus*, the diminutive of *niger*, black, referring to the seed. Hardy annuals. *Ranunculaceae*.

damascena, dam-as-SE-na, Damascus, but the word here probably means damask.

hispanica, his-PAN-ik-a, of Spain.

Niphobolus, misapplied see below.

lingua, see *Pyrrosia lingua*.

Nivenia, ni-VEN-e-a; after James Niven (1776–1827), Scottish gardener at Edinburgh and Syon House and collector in South Africa 1798–1812. Woody iris. *Iridaceae*.

corymbosa, kor-im-BO-sa, corymbose.

Nolana, no-LA-na; from L. *nola*, a little bell, the form of the flowers. Half-hardy trailing annuals. *Solanaceae*.

atriplicifolia, see *N. paradoxa*.

paradoxa, pa-ra-DOKS-a, paradoxical, contrary to exception.

Nonea, non-E-a; after Johann Philipp Nonne (1729–1772), a German botanist. Annual and perennial herbs. *Boraginaceae*.

echioides, ek-e-OY-dees, like an *Echium*. The Prophet's Flower.

lutea, LU-te-a, yellow.

Nopalea, no-PAL-e-a; from *Nopal*, the Mexican name for some species. Greenhouse cacti. *Cactaceae*.

cochenellifera, kok-chin-el-LIF-er-a, cochineal-bearing. The favourite food plant of the cochineal insect.

Nopalxochia, no-pal-ZOK-e-a; an Aztec name. Greenhouse cacti. *Cactaceae*.

phyllanthoides, see *Disocactus phyllanthoides*.

Nothofagus, noth-o-FA-gus; from Gr. *nothos*, false; L. *fagus*, beech, being similar to beech but from the Southern Hemisphere. Trees. *Nothofagaceae*.

antarctica, an-TARK-tik-a, of the Southern Polar region, used in botany for the region south of 45° S.

cunninghamii, kun-ning-HAM-e-i, after Allan Cunningham (1791–1839), collector of Australian plants.

dombeyi, DOM-bee-i, named after Joseph Dombey (1742–1794), French botanist, who travelled in Chile and Peru with Ruiz and Pavon.

menziesii, men-ZE-se-i, after Archibald Menzies (1754–1842), the Scottish botanist.

Notholaena, noth-o-LE-na; from Gr. *nothos*, spurious; *chlaena*, a cloak, referring to the imperfect indusium. Ferns. *Pteridaceae*.
  dealbata, see *Argyrochosma dealbata*.
  flavens, see *Argyrochosma nivea* var. *tenera*.
  nivea, see *Argyrochosma nivea*.
  sinuata, see *Astrolepis sinuata*.

Nuphar, NEW-far; from *naufar*, the Arabic name for this plant. Hardy aquatic. *Nymphaeaceae*.
  lutea, LU-te-a, yellow. The Yellow Water Lily.

Nuttallia, nut-TAL-le-a; after Thomas Nuttall (1786–1859), English botanist, who travelled extensively in the U.S.A. from 1810 to 1834. Deciduous flowering shrub. *Rosaceae*.
  cerasiformis, see *Oemleria cerasiformis*.

Nycterinia, nik-ter-IN-e-a; from Gr. *nykteros*, by night, in allusion to the night fragrance of the flowers. Half-hardy annuals. *Scrophulariaceae*.
  capensis, ka-PEN-sis, of the Cape of Good Hope.
  selaginoides, sel-ag-in-OY-dez, resembling *Selaginella*.

Nyctocereus (A.Berger) Britt. & Rose, NIK-to-SE-re-us; from Gr. *nyktos*, night; *cereus*, cactus, the species are night-blooming. Cacti. *Cactaceae*.
  serpentinus, see *Disocactus flagelliformis*.

Nymphaea, NIM-fe-a; from Gr. *Nymphe*, goddess of springs (water-nymph), referring to the habit. The Water-Lilies. *Nymphaeaceae*.
  alba, AL-ba, white.
  nouchali, new-KA-le, Burman in his *Flore Indica* cites this Indian name for the plant that is found on the Coramandel Coast and notable for oval leaves and blue flowers.

odorata, od-or-A-ta, sweet-scented.
odorata subsp. *tuberosa*, tu-ber-O-sa, tuberous.
pygmaea, see *N. tetragona*.
stellata, see *N. nouchali*.
tetragona, te-tra-GO-na, from Gr. *tetra*, four; *gonia*, an angle, the receptacle being four-angled.
tuberosa, see *N. odorata* subsp. *tuberosa*.

Nymphoides, nim-FOY-dees; resembling *Nyphaea*. Aquatics. *Menyanthaceae*.
  indica, IN-di-ka, of India.
  peltata, pel-TA-ta, shaped like a shield, the leaves.

Nyssa, NIS-sa; named for *Nyssa*, one of the water nymphs. *N. aquatica* grows in swamps. Trees. *Cornaceae*.
  aquatica, a-KWAT-ik-a, growing in or near water. Tupelo.
  sylvatica, sil-VAT-ik-a, inhabiting woods.

Ochna, OK-na; from Gr. ochne, the wild pear, Ochna leaves resemble those of the pear. Tropical flowering shrub. *Ochnaceae*.
  kirkii, KERK-e-i, after John Kirk (1832–1922), Scottish physician, explorer and naturalist.
  multiflora, mul-tif-LO-ra, many flowered.
  serrulata, ser-rul-A-ta, leaves finely toothed.

Ocimum, O-sim-um; from Gr. *okimon*, an aromatic herb, possibly this one. Annual aromatic herb. *Lamiaceae*.
  basilicum, ba-SIL-ik-um, princely, royal. The classical name for basil alluding to its healing qualities. The Sweet Basil.
  minimum, MIN-e-mum, small or least.

Odontadenia, o-don-ta-DE-ne-a; from Gr. *odontos*, a tooth; *aden*, a gland. In reference to the toothed glands. Shrubs. *Apocynaceae*.
  macrantha, mak-RANTH-a, large-flowered.

× *Odontioda*, o-don-te-O-da; a name compounded from *Odontoglossum* and *Cochlioda*, the species being hybrids between members of these two genera. The first hybrid being registered in 1904. See *Oncidium*.
  bradshawiae, see *Oncidium* 'Bradshawiae'.

Odontoglossum, o-don-to-GLOS-um; from Gr. *odontos*, a tooth; *glossa*, a tongue, alluding to the shape of the lip. Greenhouse orchids. *Orchidaceae*.
  alexandrae, see *Oncidium alexandrae*.

bictonense, see *Rhynchostele bictoniensis*.
cervantesii, see *Rhynchostele cervantesii*.
citrosmum, see *Cuitlauzina pendula*.
crispum, see *Oncidium alexandrae*.
grande, see *Rossioglossum grande*.
hallii, see *Oncidium hallii*.
harryanum, see *Oncidium harryanum*.
luteopurpureum, see *Oncidium luteopurpureum*.
pescatorei, see *Oncidium nobile*.
rossii, see *Rhynchostele rossii*.
triumphans, see *Oncidium spectatissimum*.

Odontonema, o-don-to-NE-ma; from Gr.
odontos, a tooth; *nema*, a thread, alluding
to the peduncles of one species. Shrubs and
herbaceous perennials. *Acanthaceae*.
   rutilans, ROO-til-anz, reddish – the flowers.

Oemleria, em-LEER-e-a; named for Augustus Gottlieb Oemler (1773–1852), German-American pharmacist and naturalist, a
friend of Nuttall, Elliott and Torrey. Shrub.
Rosaceae.
   cerasiformis, ser-as-if-OR-mis, cherry-like –
      cerasus.

Oenanthe, ee-NAN-thee; from Gr. *oinos*,
wine; *anthos*, a flower, having a vinous odour.
Aquatics. *Apiaceae*.
   fistulosa, fis-tul-O-sa, stem hollow between the
      joints or nodes. The Water Dropwort.
   fluviatilis, floo-ve-A-til-is, found in rivers.

Oenothera, ee-NOTH-e-ra (or en-oth-E-ra);
possibly a corruption from Gr. *oinos*, wine;
thera, pursuing or imbibing. The roots of the
ancient plant from which the name derives
being regarded as an incentive to drinking. Herbaceous perennials, biennials and
annuals. *Onagraceae*.
   biennis, bi-EN-nis, biennial.
   cespitosa, ses-pit-O-sa, growing in tufts.
   fruticosa, frut-ik-O-sa, shrubby.
   lamarckiana, lam-ARK-e-A-na, after Jean Baptiste de Monet Lamarck (1744–1829),
      French naturalist and botanical author.
   missouriensis, mis-soor-e-EN-sis, of Missouri,
      U.S.A.
   pumila, see *Kneiffia pumila*.
   speciosa, spes-e-O-sa, showy.
   taraxacifolia, tar-aks-a-sif-O-le-a, *Taraxacum*
      (Dandelion) leaved.

Olea, OL-e-a; Classical Latin name for the
olive (the same derivation as Gr. *elaio*). Economically important fruit. *Oleaceae*.
   europaea, u-ro-PE-a, European. The Olive Tree.

Olearia, ol-e-A-re-a; named in memory of
Johann Olschlager (1635–1711), German
horticulturist. The latinised version of the
family name is *Olearius*. Herbs, shrubs or
small trees. *Compositae*.
   gunniana, gun-ne-A-na, after Ronald Campbell
      Gunn (1808–1881), Tasmanian magistrate
      and botanist.
   haastii, ha-AST-e-i, after Julius von Haast (1822–
      1887), German born geologist and plant collector who settled in New Zealand.
   macrodonta, mak-ro-DON-ta, long toothed, the
      leaves.
   nummariifolia,   num-mul-AR-e-e-FO-le-a,
      resembling *Lysimachia nummularia* (Creeping Jenny).
   stellulata, stel-lew-LA-ta, a little star, the flowers.

Olsynium, ol-SIN-e-um; from Gr. *ol*, whole;
syn, together, referring to the stamens being
hardly united. Perennial herbs. *Iridaceae*.
   douglasii, dug-LAS-e-i, after David Douglas
      (1799–1834), Scottish plant collector.
   filifolium, fil-if-O-le-um, thread-like foliage.

Omphalodes, om-fa-LO-dees; from Gr.
omphalos, a naval; *eidos*, like, the shape of the
seeds. The Navelwort. Annuals and perennials. *Boraginaceae*.
   cappadocica, kap-pa-DO-sik-a, of Cappadocia,
      Asia Minor.
   linifolia, lin-e-FO-le-a, resembling *Linum* (flax)
      leaves.
   luciliae, lu-SIL-e-e, after Mme. Lucile Boissier
      (1822–1849), wife of Pierre Edmond Boissier, she died whilst accompanying him on an
      expedition in Spain.
   nitida, NIT-id-a, shining – the leaves.
   verna, VER-na, spring, spring-flowering.

Oncidium, on-SID-e-um; from Gr. *onkos*, a
tumour. Alluding to the swellings on the lip.
Orchids. *Orchidaceae*.
   alexandrae, al-ex-AN-dra, after Princess Alexandra of Denmark.
   bicallosum, see *Trichocentrum bicallosum*.
   'Bradshawiae', Hybrid cross *O. andersonianum*
      × *O. harryanum*.

concolor, see *Gomesa concolor*.

flexuosum, see *Cyrtochilum flexuosum*.

forbesii, see *Gomesa forbesii*.

hallii, HAL-le-i, after Col. Francis Hall (d.1834), plant collector in Ecuador during 1831 and 1832.

harryanum, har-ry-A-num, after Sir Harry Veitch (1840–1924), horticulturist who sent collectors out for the firm of James Veitch & Sons.

kramerianum, see *Psychopsis krameriana*.

luteopurpureum, LU-te-o-pur-PUR-e-um, yellow and purple.

macranthum, see *Cyrtochilum macranthum*.

nobile, NO-bil-e, notable, renowned.

ornithorhynchum, or-ni-thor-IN-kum, bird's bill or beak.

papilio, see *Psychopsis papilio*.

rogersii, see *Gomesa varicosa*.

spectatissimum, spek-ta-TIS-sim-um, most spectacular.

sphacelatum, sfak-el-A-tum, scorched.

splendidum, see *Trichocentrum splendidum*.

tigrinum, tig-RE-num, tiger-striped.

varicosum, see *Gomesa varicosa*.

Onoclea, on-OK-le-a; from Gr. *onos*, vessel; *kleio*, to close, a plant with leaves rolled up into the semblance of berries, referring to the capsule-like fructification. Ferns. *Onocleaceae*.

germanica, see *Matteuccia struthiopteris*.

sensibilis, sen-SIB-il-is, sensitive. The Sensitive Fern.

Ononis, on-O-nis; ancient Gr. name used by Theophrastus. Rock and border perennials. *Leguminosae*.

fruticosa, frut-iK-O-sa, shrubby.

hircina, see *O. spinosa* subsp. *hircina*.

minutissima, min-u-TIS-sim-a, very small.

natrix, NAT-riks, goat-root.

rotundifolia, ro-tun-dif-O-le-a, round-leaved.

spinosa, spi-NO-sa, spiny.

spinosa subsp. *hircina*, her-SE-na, with goat smell.

Onopordum, on-op-OR-dum; Latinized version of an old Gr. name, *onopordon*, from *onos*, an ass; *porde*, fart, possibly alluding to the effect on donkeys. Ornamental thistles. *Compositae*.

acanthium, ak-ANTH-e-um, resembling *Acanthus*. The Cotton Thistle.

illyricum, il-LER-ik-um, of Illyria.

Onosma, on-OZ-ma; from Gr. *onos*, an ass; *osme*, a smell, reference obscure. Rock plants. *Boraginaceae*.

albo-roseum, AL-bo-ro-ZE-um, white and rosy.

taurica, TAW-rik-a, of the Crimean peninsula known as Taurica. The Golden Drop.

Onychium, on-IK-e-um; from Gr. *onychion*, a little claw, in allusion to the shape of the fertile segments. Greenhouse ferns. *Pteridaceae*.

japonicum, jap-ON-ik-um, of Japan.

Ophiopogon, off-e-o-PO-gon; from Gr. *ophis*, a serpent; *pogon*, a beard. Perennial plants. *Asparagaceae*.

jaburan, jab-U-ran, oriental name.

japonicus, jap-ON-ik-us, of Japan.

planiscapus, plan-e-SKA-pus, flat flowering stem.

spicatus, see *Liriope graminifolia*.

Ophrys, OFF-ris; the Gr. name for a plant with two leaves possibly from Gr. *ophrys*, eyebrows, in allusion to the fringe of the inner sepals. Terrestrial orchids. *Orchidaceae*.

apifera, ap-IF-er-a, bee-bearing. The Bee Orchid.

aranifera, see *O. sphegodes*.

insectifera, in-sek-TIF-er-a, insect-bearing.

muscifera, see *O. insectifera*.

sphegodes, sfeg-O-dees, wasp-like.

tenthredinifera, ten-three-din-IF-er-a, saw-fly-bearing.

Oplismenus, op-LIS-me-nus; from Gr. *hoplismenos*, weapon (armed), referring to the awned glumes in the inflorescence. Greenhouse ornamental foliage grass. *Poaceae*.

burmannii, bur-MAN-ne, after Nicolaas Laurens Burman (1734–1793), Dutch botanist and author of Flora Indica (1768).

Opuntia, o-PUN-te-a; from Opuntus (or Opus), a town in Greece; it is said the word is derived from Latin not applicable to the plants now named. Cactus plants. *Cactaceae*.

engelmannii, en-gel-MAN-e-i, after Georg Engelmann (1809–1884), German-born botanist and physician. Engelmann moved to St. Louis where he was respected as an author on Cactaceae.

ficus-indica, FI-kus-IN-dik-a, Indian fig. The Indian Fig.

humifusa, hum-e-FU-sa, spread over the ground.

leucotricha, lu-ko-TRIK-a, White-haired.

macrorhiza, mak-rorh-E-za, large rooted.

mesacantha, see *O. humifusa*.

microdasys, mi-KROD-as-is, Gr. compound word, small and thick.

missouriensis, see *O. polycantha*.

monacantha, mon-ak-ANTH-a, one-spined.

papyracantha, pap-y-rak-ANTH-a, papery spines.

polycantha, pol-e-KANTH-a, many spines.

rafinesquei, see *O. humifusa*.

tuna, TU-na, native name.

vulgaris, see *O. ficus-indica*.

Orbea, OR-be-a; from L. *orbis*, disc, in reference to the opening of the corolla. Succulents. *Apocynaceae*.

variegata, var-e-eg-A-ta, variegated – the flowers.

Orchis, OR-kis; ancient Gr. name, referring to the two oblong tubers at the root of many species. Hardy terrestrial orchids. *Orchidaceae*.

anthropophora, an-thro-POF-o-ra, resembling a man. The Green Man Orchid.

foliosa, see *Dactylorhiza foliosa*.

hircina, see *Himantoglossum hircinum*.

laxiflora, see *Anacamptis laxiflora*.

maculata, see *Dactylorhiza maculata*.

mascula, MAS-ku-la, male, probably referring to its earliness and vigour.

purpurea, pur-PUR-e-a, purple coloured.

pyramidalis, see *Anacamptis pyramidalis*.

sambucina, see *Dactylorhiza sambucina*.

Oreocereus, OR-e-o-SE-RE-us; from Gr. *oros*, a mountain; *cereus*, wax taper. Greenhouse cacti. *Cactaceae*.

celsianus, kel-se-A-nus, named after Jacques Martin Cels (1740–1806), French botanist who created a botanical garden in Paris. Cel's Hair Candle Cactus.

trollii, TROL-e-i, dedicating Wilhelm Troll (1897–1978), German botanist, a specialist in plant morphology. The Old Man of the Andes cactus.

Origanum, or-IG-a-num; from Gr. *oros*, a mountain; *ganos*, gladness, the usual habitat and attractiveness of the plants. Herbaceous and sub-shrubby perennials. *Lamiaceae*.

dictamnus, dik-TAM-nus, old generic name. The Dittany of Crete.

marjorana, mar-jor-A-na, marjoram, old name. The Sweet Marjoram.

onites, on-E-tez, onites. The Pot Marjoram.

vulgare, vul-GAR-e, common. The Common Marjoram.

Ornduffia, orn-DUF-e-a; in commemoration of Robert Ornduff (1932–2000), botanist who studied *Villarsia*. Aquatic plants. *Menyanthaceae*.

reniformis, ren-if-OR-mis, kidney-shaped, the leaves.

Ornithogalum, or-nith-OG-a-lum; from Gr. *ornis*, bird; *gala*, milk, 'bird's milk' was said to be a current expression among the ancient Greeks for some wonderful thing. Bulbous plants. *Asparagaceae*.

arabicum, ar-AB-ik-um, of Arabia.

candicans, KAN-dik-ans, white. The Spire Lily.

conicum, KON-e-kum, from Gr. *konicos*, cone-shaped.

lacteum, see *O. conicum*.

longibracteatum, see *Albuca bracteata*.

narbonense, nar-bon-EN-se, of Narbonne.

nutans, NU-tanz, drooping or nodding.

pyramidale, pir-am-ID-al-e, pyramidal, the flower spikes.

pyrenaicum, pir-en-A-ik-um, Pyrenean.

thyrsoides, ther-SOY-dees, flowers in a thyrse-like spike.

umbellatum, um-bel-LA-tum, umbelled, the flower stalks all arising from the same point.

Ornus, misapplied see below.

vulgaris, see *Sorbus aucuparia*.

Orobus, OR-o-bus; old Gr. name, said to be derived from Gr. *oro*, to excite; *bous*, ox, the vetches being tempting fodder. Herbaceous perennials and rock plants. Unresolved. *Leguminosae*.

vernus, see *Lathyrus vernus*.

Orontium, or-ON-te-um; adopted old Gr. name for a plant that grew on the banks of the river Orontes. Aquatic perennial. *Araceae*.

aquaticum, a-KWAT-ik-um, aquatic.

Osmanthus, oz-MAN-thus; from Gr. *osme*, perfume; *anthos*, a flower, the blossoms being very fragrant. Shrubs. *Oleaceae*.

aquifolium, see *O. heterophyllus*.

delavayi, de-la-VA-i, after Père Jean Marie Delavay (1834–1895), missionary and plant collector in Yunnan province, China.

fragrans, FRA-granz, fragrant.

heterophyllus, het-er-o-FIL-us, variously leaved.

Osmunda, oz-MUN-da; various derivations have been offered in explanation for this name. One explanation is from Osmunder, the Saxon name for the Nordic God Thor; alternatively said to be named for Osmundus, c. 1025, a Scandinavian clergyman favoured by the King; or from L. *os*, mouth, and *mundare*, to clean. Hardy ferns. *Osmundaceae.*

cinnamomea, see *Osmundastrum cinnamomeum.*

claytoniana, kla-to-ne-A-na, after John Clayton (1686–1773), English born American botanist.

regalis, re-GA-lis, Royal, stately. The Royal Fern.

Osmundastrum, os-mun-DAS-trum, from *Osmunda* and *astrum*, indicating incomplete resemblance. Hardy Fern. *Osmundaceae.*

cinnamomeum, sin-na-MO-me-um, cinnamon, the colour of the fructification.

Osteospermum, oss-tee-o-SPUR-mum; a blended word from Gr. *osteon*, bone, and L. *spermum*, seed. Shrubs, subshrubs or annual to perennial herbs. *Compositae.*

ecklonis, ek-LON-is, in honour of Christian Friedrich Ecklon (1795–1868), Danish botanist.

Ostrowskia, os-TROW-ske-a; named after Michael Nicholazewitsch von Ostrowsky, Russian patron of botany. Hardy perennial. *Campanulaceae.*

magnifica, mag-NIF-ik-a, magnificent.

Ostrya, OS-tre-a; from Gr. *ostrys*, the name given by Theophrastus for this tree. Deciduous trees. *Betulaceae.*

carpinifolia, kar-pi-nif-O-le-a, resembling *Carpinus* (hornbeam) leaves.

Othonna, oth-ON-na; Ancient Greek name for another plant. Possibly from Gr. *othone*, linen, the leaves of many of these ragworts having a soft downy covering. Greenhouse herbaceous perennials and shrubs. *Compositae.*

arborescens, ar-bor-ES-senz, tree-like.

coronopifolia, kor-on-op-e-FO-le-a, leaves resembling *Coronopus.*

crassifolia, kras-sif-OL-e-a, thick-leaved.

denticulata, den-tik-u-LA-ta, toothed, the leaves.

digitata, dij-e-TA-ta, fingered, the leaves.

filicaulis, fil-e-KAW-lis, thread-stemmed.

heterophylla, het-er-of-IL-la, diversely leaved.

perfoliata, per-fo-le-A-ta, the leaf-stem pierced.

Othonnopsis, oth-on-NOP-sis; from *Othonna* (which see) and *opsis*, resemblance. Half-hardy sub-shrub. Unresolved. *Compositae.*

cheirifolia, see *Hertia cheirifolia.*

Ourisia, owr-IS-e-a; after Governor Ouris of the Falkland Islands. Hardy rock plants. *Plantaginaceae.*

coccinea, kok-SIN-e-a, scarlet.

Oxalis, OX-a-lis; from Gr. *oxys*, acid, alluding to the acidity of the leaves of many species. Rock garden and woodland perennials. *Oxalidaceae.*

acetosella, as-eto-o-SEL-la, old generic name, from L. *acetum*, vinegar or sour, the leaves. The Wood Sorrel.

adenophylla, ad-en-OF-il-la, with glandular leaves.

bowiei, BO-e-i, named after James Bowie (1789–1869), botanist and Kew gardener who collected in Brazil with Alan Cunningham and was sent to the Cape, South Africa in 1817.

cernua, see *O. pes-caprae.*

corniculata, kor-nik-ul-A-ta, horned.

deppei, DEP-pe-i, after Ferdinand Deppe (1794–1861), a botanist and collector in South America.

enneaphylla, en-ne-AF-il-la, from Gr. for nine-leaved, that is nine divisions to each leaf.

floribunda, flor-e-BUN-da, abundant or free flowering.

lasiandra, las-e-AN-dra, woolly stamened.

lobata, see *O. perdicaria.*

oregana, or-e-GA-na, from Oregon.

perdicaria, per-dee-kar-E-a, from Chilean *Yerba de la perdiz*, partridge herb.

pes-caprae, pez-KA-pre, from L. goat's foot, referring to the leaflet.

tetraphylla, tet-raf-IL-la, four-leaved (leaflets).

valdiviana, see *O. valdiviensis.*

valdiviensis, val-div-e-EN-sis, from the Valdivian rainforests in Chile.

Oxera, ox-E-ra; from Gr. *oxys*, acid, referring to the sour taste. Warm-house climber. *Lamiaceae*.
  pulchella, pul-KEL-la, pretty (diminutive).

Oxycoccos, misapplied see below.
  macrocarpus, see *Vaccinium macrocarpon*.
  palustris, see *Vaccinium oxycoccos*.

Oxypetalum, ox-e-PET-a-lum; blended from Gr. *oxys*, sharp; L. *petalum*, a petal – the petals being sharp pointed. Warm-house climbers. *Apocynaceae*.
  coeruleum, se-RU-le-um, blue.

Oxytropis, ox-e-TRO-pis; from Gr. *oxys*, sharp; *tropis*, a keel, the keel petals ending in a sharp point. Hardy herbaceous perennials. *Leguminosae*.
  jacquinii, jak-kwin-E-i, named after Nicholas Joseph von Jacquin (1727–1817), Dutch born botanist.
  montana, see *O. jacquinii*.
  neglecta, nee-GLEK-ta, from L. *neglectus*, overlooked.
  pyrenaica, see *O. neglecta*.
  uralensis, u-ra-LEN-sis, from the Ural Mountains.

Ozothamnus, o-zo-THAM-nus; possibly from Gr. *ozos*, twiggy; *thamnos*, shrub, alluding to the form. Flowering shrub. *Compositae*.
  leptophyllus, lep-to-FY-lus, from Gr. *leptos*, slender; *phyllon*, a leaf.
  rosmarinifolius, roz-mar-in-if-OL-e-us, leaves resembling *Rosmarinus* (rosemary).

Pachycereus, PAK-e-SE-re-us; from Gr. pachys, thick; cereus, (which see). Cacti. *Cactaceae*.
  pringlei, PRIN-gl-e, after Cyrus Guernsey Pringle (1838–1911), American plant collector active in Mexico.

Pachysandra, pak-e-SAN-dra; from Gr. *pachys*, thick; *aner*, a man, alluding to the unusually thick stamens. Woodland shrubs. *Buxaceae*.
  procumbens, pro-CUM-benz, procumbent, growing along the ground without rooting.
  terminalis, ter-min-A-lis, flowers terminal.

Pachystachys, pak-e-STAK-is; from Gr. pachys, thick; *stachys*, a spike, the flowers in dense clusters. Herbaceous perennials and shrubs. *Acanthaceae*.
  coccinea, kok-SIN-e-a, scarlet.

Paeonia, pe-O-ne-a (English rendering Peony, PE-o-ne); named after Paeon, a physician of the gods in Ancient Greece, who used the plant medicinally. Most of the garden peonies are varieties or hybrids. *Paeoniaceae*.
  albiflora, see *P. lactiflora*.
  corallina, see *P. mascula*.
  delavayi, de-la-VA-i, after Père Jean Marie Delavay (1834–1895), missionary and plant collector in Yunnan province, China.
  lactiflora, lak-tif-LO-ra, flowers are milk-white.
  lutea, see *P. delavayi*.
  mascula, MAS-ku-la, male, probably referring to its vigour.
  × *moutan*, see *P* × *suffruticosa*.
  officinalis, of-fis-in-A-lis, of the shop (apothecary's), applied to plants always kept "in stock" by herbalists.
  × *suffruticosa*, suf-frut-ik-O-sa, having a woody base.

Palaua, PAL-u-a; after Antonio Palau y Verdera (1734–1793), Spanish professor of botany, who introduced Spain to Linnaeus' system of plant classification. Half-hardy annual. *Malvaceae*.
  dissecta, dis-SEK-ta, cut – the leaves.
  flexuosa, see *P. dissecta*.

Paliurus, pal-e-U-rus; the Greek name used by Theophrastus. Flowering shrubs. *Rhamnaceae*.
  aculeatus, see *P. spina-christi*.
  spina-christi, SPY-na-KRIS-te, Christ's thorn.

Panax, PAN-aks; from Gr. *pan*, all; *akos*, a remedy, in allusion to the medicinal attributes of *P. ginseng*. Tropical ornamental foliage plants. *Araliaceae*.
  balfourii, see *Polyscias balfouriana*.
  filicifolium, see *Polyscias filicifolia*.
  guilfoylei, see *Polyscias guilfoylei*.
  victoriae, see *Polyscias guilfoylei*.

Pancratium, pan-KRA-te-um; from Gr. *pan*, all; *kratos*, potent, name used by Dioscorides for a bulbous plant used medicinally. Bulbs. *Amaryllidaceae*.
  fragrans, see *Hymenocallis caribaea*.

illyricum, il-LIR-ik-um, of Illyria, on the Adriatic.
maritimum, mar-IT-im-um, maritime, coastal; in reference to the sea.

Pandanus, PAN-dan-us; latinised from Malay *pandang*, the vernacular name. Tropical foliage plants. The Screw Pine. *Pandanaceae*.
  baptistii, see *P. tectorius*.
  sanderi, see *P. tectorius*.
  tectorius, tek-TOR-e-us, of roofs.
  variegatus, see *P. tectorius*.
  veitchii, see *P. tectorius*.

Panicum, PA-nik-um; the Latin name for a kind of millet used for bread making. Ornamental grasses. *Poaceae*.
  capillare, kap-il-LAR-e, hair-like, that is, slender.
  plicatum, see *Setaria palmifolia*.
  variegatum, var-e-eg-A-tum, variegated.

Papaver, pap-A-ver; Latin name for a poppy, of doubtful origin. Annuals and perennials. *Papaveraceae*.
  alpinum, al-PINE-um, alpine.
  cambricum, KAM-brik-um, of Wales. The Welsh Poppy.
  glaucum, GLAW-kum, glaucous or blue-green, the foliage. The Tulip Poppy.
  nudicaule, nu-di-KAW-le, naked-stemmed.
  orientale, or-e-en-TA-le, Eastern. The Oriental Poppy.
  pavoninum, pa-vo-NE-num, a peacock. The Peacock Poppy.
  rhoeas, RE-as, old generic name, possibly from Gr. *rhoia*, a pomegranate, which the flower and fruits of the field poppy were supposed to resemble. The Corn Poppy. Shirley strain developed from this species.
  rupifragum, roo-pe-FRAG-um, rock breaking.
  somniferum, som-NIF-er-um, causing sleep. The Opium Poppy. The Carnation and other garden strains developed from this.
  umbrosum, um-BRO-zum, growing in shady places.

Paphiopedilum, pa-fe-o-PED-il-um; from Gr. *paphia*, an epithet of Aphrodite (Venus); *pedilon*, slipper. Venus' Slipper Orchid. *Orchidaceae*.
  bellatulum, bel-LAT-u-lum, pretty.
  insigne, in-SIG-ne, striking.
  spicerianum, spi-ser-e-A-num, after Mrs Spicer of Wimbledon whose son, a tea-planter, sent back specimens from Bhutan.

superbiens, su-PERB-e-enz, superb.
venustum, ven-US-tum, charming.
villosum, vil-LO-sum, shaggy, hairy.

Papilionanthe, pa-pil-e-o-NAN-thee; from L. *papilio*, butterfly; Gr. *anthos*, a flower. Orchids. *Orchidaceae*.
  teres, TER-ees, *terete*, that is, circular in cross section – the leaves and stems.

Papyrus, misapplied see below.
  antiquorum, see *Cyperus papyrus*.

Paradisea, par-a-DIS-e-a; commemorates Giovianni Paradisi, an Italian. Hardy herbaceous plants. *Asparagaceae*.
  liliastrum, lil-e-as-trum, star Lily. St. Bruno's Lily.

Parahebe, par-er-HEE-bee; from Gr. *para*, near, alongside; *Hebe*, from which genus this has been removed. Subshrubs. *Plantaginaceae*.
  cataractae, kat-ar-RAK-te, it appears to be from a local name, its flower sprays suggesting a waterfall.

Paris, PAR-is; from L. *par*, equal, referring to the regularity of the parts. Hardy perennial. *Melanthiaceae*.
  quadrifolia, kwad-rif-O-le-a, four leaved.

Parnassia, par-NAS-se-a; named after Mount Parnassus, a sacred mountain of the ancient Greeks, from which these waterside plants were fabulously supposed to have sprung. *Celastraceae*.
  palustris, pal-US-tris, found in marshy places. The Grass of Parnassus.

Parochetus, from Gr. *para*, near; *ochetus*, a brook; the plant delighting in watersides. Carpeting herb. *Leguminosae*.
  communis, kom-MU-nis, common, that is, growing in groups or communities.

Parodia, pa-row-DE-a; Spegazzini dedicated it to the memory of Dr. Domingo Parodi (1823–1890), one of the first investigators of Paraguayan flora. Cactus. *Cactaceae*.
  erinacea, er-in-A-se-a, from L. *erinaceus*, a hedgehog, the branches being spiny.

Paronychia, par-o-NIK-e-a; from Gr. *paronychia*, a whitlow, which these plants were

supposed to cure, hence English names Nailwort and Whitlow-wort. *Caryophyllaceae.*
argentea, ar-JEN-te-a, silvery, the foliage.
capitata, kap-it-A-ta, growing in a dense head.
kapela, ka-PE-la, of the mountainous region of Velika Kapela, Croatia.
kapela subsp. *serpyllifolia*, ser-pil-if-O-le-a, leaves like wild thyme, *Thymus serpyllum.*
serpyllifolia, see *P. kapela* subsp. *serpyllifolia.*

Parrotia, par-RO-te-a; named after Johann Jacob Friedrich Wilhelm Parrot (1791–1841), German naturalist and traveller. Trees. *Hamamelidaceae.*
persica, PER-sik-a, of Persia.

Parthenocissus, par-thee-no-SIS-us; from Gr. *parthenos*, a virgin; *kissos*, ivy; described by Planchon as 'hermaphrodite flowers which are actually physiologically polygamo-monoecious with many psuedo-hermaphrodite male flowers...'. Climbing plants. *Vitaceae.*
henryana, hen-re-A-na, after Dr. A. Henry (1857–1930), physician, plant collector and dendrologist.
inserta, IN-sir-ta, insert, introduce.
quinquefolia, kwin-kwe-FO-le-a, leaflets in five. The Virginia Creeper.
tricuspidata, try-kusp-e-DA-ta, three-pointed, the older or larger leaves with three tailed divisions.

Passiflora, pas-e-FLOR-a; from L. *passus*, suffering; *flos*, flower, literally the Flower of the Passion (Passion Flower), the early Spanish Roman Catholic priests in South America finding in the plant features they regarded as symbols of the Cruxifixion. Thus the five stamens were the five wounds; the three stigmas, the three nails; the style of the pistil, the flogging column; the corona, the crown of thorns, or the halo of glory; the digitate or fingered leaves, the hands of the multitude; the coiled tendrils, the flogging cords; the five sepals and five petals, the disciples (Peter and Judas being omitted in the count). Tender climbers. *Passifloraceae.*
alata, al-A-ta, winged – the stalks.
antioquiensis, an-te-o-kwe-EN-sis, from Antioquia, Columbia.
caerulea, se-RU-le-a, sky-blue.
coccinea, kok-SIN-e-a, scarlet.

edulis, ed-U-lis, edible, the fruit.
incarnata, see *P. edulis.*
manicata, man-ik-A-ta, collared or sleeved.
princeps, see *P. racemosa.*
quadrangularis, kwod-ran-gul-A-ris, square-stalked.
racemosa, ras-em-O-sa, resembling a raceme.
vitifolia, vi-tif-O-le-a, *Vitis* (Vine) leaved.

Pastinaca, pas-te-NAK-a; from L. *pastus*, food; referring to the edible root. Herbaceous perennials. *Apiaceae.*
sativa, SAT-iv-a, cultivated. The Parsnip.

Patrinia, pat-RIN-e-a; commemorating Eugène Louis Melchior Patrin (1742–1815), French mineralogist and naturalist, who traveled in Siberia. Herbaceous biennials and perennials. *Caprifoliaceae.*
palmata, pal-MA-ta, palmate, like a hand – the leaves.
scabiosifolia, ska-be-O-se-FO-le-a, scabious-leaved.
villosa, vil-LO-sa, shaggy, hairy.

Paullinia, paul-LIN-e-a; after a Danish botanist Simon Paulli (1603–1680), professor of anatomy, surgery and botany at Copenhagen. Tender flowering climber. *Sapindaceae.*
thalictrifolia, thal-ik-trif-OL-e-a, leaves resembling *Thalictrum.*

Paulownia, paw-LO-ne-a; named after Princess Anna Paulowna (1795–1865), daughter of Czar Paul I of Russia. Princess of Orange later Queen consort of the Netherlands. Flowering and foliage tree. *Paulowniaceae.*
imperialis, see *P. tomentosa.*
tormentosa, to-men-TO-sa, felted, the leaf underparts.

Pavia, PA-ve-a; named after Pieter Pauw (1564–1617), Dutch botanist and anatomist. Unresolved see *Aesculus.* Trees. *Sapindaceae.*
californica, see *Aesculus californica.*
carnea, see *Aesculus glabra.*

Pavonia, pav-O-ne-a; after José Antonio Pavón y Jiménez (1754–1840), Spanish botanist and traveller, who collaborated with Hipólito Ruiz López. Tropical flowering plants. *Malvaceae.*

coccinea, kok-SIN-e-a, scarlet.
multiflora, mul-tif-LO-ra, many flowered.

Pedicularis, ped-ik-u-LAR-is; from L. *pediculus*, a louse, the plant (Lousewort) being supposed to cause lice to appear on sheep which browsed upon it. Rock plants. *Orobanchaceae*.
   dolichorrhiza, dol-ik-orh-E-za, long rooted.
   flammea, FLAM-me-a, flame coloured.
   megalantha, meg-al-ANTH-a, large-flowered.
   sceptrum-carolinum, SEP-trum-kar-o-LIN-um, Charles' Sceptre (King Charles XII of Sweden).

Pediocactus, PED-e-o-KAK-tus; from Gr. *pedion*, a plain; *Cactus*, referring to the habitat, the Great Plains of Colorado, U.S.A. Hardy or greenhouse cacti. *Cactaceae*.
   simpsonii, SIM-son-e-i, after James Hervey Simpson (1813–1883), an employee of the Topographical Engineers.

Pelargonium, pel-ar-GO-ne-um; from Gr. *pelargos*, a stork, the ripe seed head being supposed to resemble the head and beak of that bird, hence Storksbill. Most kinds commonly grown are of garden origin and are popularly spoken of as 'Geraniums'. *Geraniaceae*.
   capitatum, kap-it-A-tum, flowers clustered in a head.
   citriodorum, sit-re-o-DOR-um, lemon scented.
   crispum, KRISP-um, curly – the leaves waved.
   echinatum, ek-in-A-tum, the spines resembling a hedgehog.
   grandiflorum, gran-dif-LO-rum, large flowered.
   graveolens, GRAV-e-ol-enz, strong smelling.
   inquinans, IN-kwe-nans, dyed or stained.
   peltatum, pel-TA-tum, shaped like a shield. The Ivy-leaved Pelargonium.
   radula, rad-U-la, rasp-leaved.
   tomentosum, to-men-TO-sum, felted – the leaves.
   zonale, zo-NA-le, zoned or banded. The Zonal Pelargonium.

Pelecyphora, pel-ek-if-OR-a; from Gr. *pelekys*, hatchet; *phoreo*, to bear, hatchet-bearing, the shape of the tubercles suggesting hatchets. Greenhouse cacti. *Cactaceae*.
   aselliformis, as-EL-lif-OR-mis, resembling a Woodlouse, the tubercles.

Pellaea, pel-LE-a; from Gr. *pellos*, dark coloured, referring to the black stalks or stipes of the fronds. Greenhouse ferns. *Pteridaceae*.
   atropurpurea, atro-pur-PUR-e-a, deep purple.
   calomelanos, kal-o-MEL-an-os, beautiful black, stalks or stipes.
   flexuosa, see *P. ovata*.
   geraniifolia, jer-a-ne-e-FO-le-a, leaves resembling *Geranium*.
   hastata, see *P. calomelanos*.
   ovata, o-VA-ta, egg-shaped – the leaves.
   rotundifolia, ro-tun-dif-O-le-a, round-leaved, the pinnae.
   ternifolia, ter-ne-FO-le-a, leaves in threes, the pinnae.

Peltandra, pel-TAN-dra; from Gr. *pelte*, a little shield; *aner*, a man, hence *andros*, a stamen. The united stamens having the form of a shield. Aquatics. *Araceae*.
   virginica, vir-JIN-ik-a, of Virginia.

Peltoboykinia, pel-to-boy-KIN-e-a; from Gr. *pelte*, a little shield; *Boykinia*, in allusion to resembling this genus. Herbaceous perennials. *Saxifragaceae*.
   tellimoides, tel-li-MOY-dees, resembling *Tellima*.

Pennisetum, pen-nis-E-tum; from L. *penna*, a feather; *seta*, a bristle; the hairs attached to the flower plumes being feathered in some species. Ornamental grasses. *Poaceae*.
   longistylum, long-e-STY-lum, long-styled.
   polystachion, pol-e-STAK-e-on, many-spiked.
   setaceum, se-TA-se-um, bristly.
   setosum, see *P. polystachion*.

Penstemon, pen-STE-mon; from Gr. *pente*, five; *stemon*, a stamen, alluding to five (four fertile and one rudimentary) stamens. Hardy perennials; many hybrids. *Plantaginaceae*.
   barbatus, bar-BA-tus, bearded with hooked hairs.
   barbatus subsp. *torreyi*, TOR-re-i, after John Torrey (1796–1873), American botanist, co-author with Asa Gray of the 'Flora of North America'.
   bridgesii, brid-JE-se-i, after Bridges, an American collector.
   campanulatus, kam-pan-u-LAH-tus, bell-shaped.
   centranthifolius, sen- (or ken-) tran-the-FO-le-us; leaves resembling *Centranthus* (Red Valerian).

cobaea, KO-be-a, resembling *Cobaea*, the flowers.

confertus, kon-FER-tus, closely crowded, the flowers.

cordifolius, kor-de-FO-le-us, heart-shaped leaves.

diffusus, dif-FEW-sus, spreading, the habit.

fruticosus, frut-ik-O-sus, shrubby.

fruticosus var. *scouleri*, SKOOL-er-i, after John Scouler (1804–1871), Scottish naturalist.

glaber, GLA-ber, smooth.

glaucus, GLAW-kus, sea-green, the foliage.

hartwegii, hart-VE-ge-i, after Karl Theodor Hartweg (1812–1871), German plant hunter, who collected for the Horticultural Society of London in Mexico and California.

heterophyllus, het-er-o-FIL-us, variously leaved.

humilis, HUM-il-is, low or dwarf.

isophyllus, i-so-FIL-lus, with equal-sized leaves.

menziesii, men-ZE-se-i, after Archibald Menzies (1754–1842), the Scottish botanist.

roezlii, REZ-le-i, after Benedikt Roezl (1824–1885) Austrian gardener, traveller and botanist.

rostriflorus, ros-tre-FLO-rus, beak-flowered.

rupicola, roo-PIK-o-la, of rocks.

scouleri, see *P. fruticosus* var. *scouleri*.

secundiflorus, se-kun-de-FLOR-us, a one-sided flower spike.

spectabilis, spek-TAB-il-is, notable.

torreyi, see *P. barbatus* subsp. *torreyi*.

Pentaglottis, pent-a-GLOT-is; from Gr. *penta*, five; *glotta*, tongue, the five pubescent scales of the corolla. Perennial herb. *Boraginaceae*.

sempervirens, sem-per-VEER-enz, from L. *semper*, ever; *virens*, green. Always green. Alkanet.

Pentas, PEN-tas; from Gr. *pente*, five; the parts of the flower being in fives. Tropical evergreen flowering shrubs. *Rubiaceae*.

carnea, see *P. lanceolata* subsp. *cymosa*.

lanceolata, lan-se-o-LA-ta, the leaves lance-shaped.

lanceolata subsp. *cymosa*, si-MO-sa, from Gr. *cyma*, young sprout, the flowers in the centre of the cymes opening first.

Peperomia, pep-er-O-me-a; from Gr. *peperi*, pepper; *homoios*, similar; flowers and foliage similar to those of Piper, the pepper plant. Tropical ornamental foliage plants. *Piperaceae*.

argyreia, ar-ger-I-a, silver-striped.

marmorata, mar-mor-A-ta, marbled.

nummularifolia, see *P. rotundifolia*.

rotundifolia, ro-tun-dif-O-le-a, round-leaved.

sandersii, see *P. argyreia*.

Pereskia, per-ESK-e-a; commemorating Nicholas Claude Fabry de Peiresc (1580–1637), French patron of botany. Greenhouse cacti. *Cactaceae*.

aculeata, ak-u-le-A-ta, prickly.

bleo, BLE-o, Brazilian vernacular name.

Perezia, pe-RE-se-a; after Lorenzo Perez, apothecary of Toledo, author of the 'Book of Theriaca' (1575). Half-hardy bedding annual. *Compositae*.

multiflora, mul-tif-LO-ra, many flowered.

Pergularia, per-gu-LAR-e-a; from L. *pergula*; plants fit for a pergola. Perennial climbers. *Apocynaceae*.

flavescens, fla-VES-sens, yellowish.

Pericallis, per-e-KAL-lis; from Gr. *peri*, around; *kallos*, beauty. Perennial herbs and shrubs. *Compositae*.

cruenta, kru-EN-ta, bloody, referring to the purple colour of the back of the leaf.

Perilla, per-IL-la; derivation obscure, possibly from the Hindu vernacular name. Half-hardy bedding annual. *Lamiaceae*.

nankinensis, see *Plectranthus scutellarioides*.

Periploca, per-IP-lo-ka; from Gr. *periploke*, an intertwining, the habit of the plant. Hardy twiner. *Apocynaceae*.

graeca, GRE-ka, of Greece.

Peristeria, per-is-TEER-e-a; from Gr. *peristera*, a dove, in allusion to the form of the column. Warm-house orchids. *Orchidaceae*.

elata, e-LA-ta, tall.

Pernettya, per-NET-e-a; named after Antoine Joseph Pernety (1716–1801), author of a book on the Falkland Islands. Berry-bearing ornamental shrubs. *Ericaceae*.

mucronata, see *Gaultheria mucronata*.

Perovskia, per-OV-ske-a; after Count Vasily Alekseevich Perovsky (1794–1857) once Governor of Russian province of Orenburg. Sub-shrubby perennial. *Lamiaceae*.

atriplicifolia, at-rip-lis-e-FO-le-a, leaves resembling *Atriplex*.

Persea, PER-se-a; ancient name for an Egyptian tree (*Cordia myxa*). Tropical fruiting shrub. *Lauraceae*.
   americana, a-mer-ik-A-na, of America.
   gratissima, see *P. americana*.

Persica, misapplied see below.
   davidiana, see *Prunus davidiana*.
   vulgaris, see *Prunus persica*.
   vulgaris var. *laevis*, see *Prunus persica* var. *nucipersica*.

Persicaria, per-se-KAR-e-a; from *Persica*, peach, referring to the leaf shape. Annuals and herbaceous perennials. *Polygonaceae*.
   bistorta, bis-TOR-ta, twice-turned, the twisted root; old generic name for the Bistort.
   campanulata, kam-pan-u-LA-ta, resembling *Campanula* (bellflower).
   capitata, kap-it-A-ta, growing in a dense head.
   wallichii, wol-LICH-e-i, after Nathaniel Wallich (1786–1854), Danish surgeon and botanist, who worked for the East India Company and became superintendent of the Calcutta Botanic Garden.

Petasites, pet-a-SE-tes; from Gr. *petasos*, a broad-brimmed hat, or sunshade, in reference to the large leaves of some species. Herbaceous perennials. *Compositae*.
   fragrans, FRA-granz, fragrant.

Petrea, pet-RE-a; after Robert James, Lord Petre (1713–1742), a patron of botany. Greenhouse flowering shrubs. *Verbenaceae*.
   volubilis, vol-U-bil-is, twisting round; the twining stems.

Petrocallis, pe-tro-KAL-lis; from Gr. *petros*, rock; *kallos*, beauty; from its habitat and beautiful flowers. Alpine perennial herb. *Brassicaceae*.
   pyrenaica, pir-en-A-ik-a, Pyrenean.

Petrorhagia, pe-tro-RAG-e-a; from Gr. *petra*, rock; *rhagas*, a fissure; breaking rock. Annual or perennial herbs. *Caryophyllaceae*.
   saxifraga, sax-e-FRA-ga, from L. *saxum*, a rock (or stone); *frango*, to break.

Petroselinum, pet-ros-el-EE-num; from Gr. *petros*, a rock; *selinon*, parsley. The Garden Parsley. *Apiaceae*.
   crispum, KRISP-um, curly – the leaves waved.

Petunia, pe-TU-ne-a; from Brazilian *petun*, tobacco, petunias being allied to the Tobacco Plant. Greenhouse and bedding plants. *Solanaceae*.
   nyctaginiflora, nik-ta-gin-e-FLOR-a, flowers resembling *Nyctaginia*.
   violacea, vi-o-LA-se-a, violet-coloured.

Peucedanum, pu-SED-a-num; the Greek name used by Hippocrates. Perennial and biennial herbs or shrubs. *Apiaceae*.
   graveolens, see *Anethum graveolens*.
   sativum, see *Pastinaca sativa*.

Phacelia, fa-SE-le-a; from Gr. *phakelos*, a bundle, alluding to the disposition of the flowers. Annuals and perennials. *Boraginaceae*.
   campanularia, kam-pan-u-LAR-e-a, bell-shaped, the flowers.
   grandiflora, gran-dif-LO-ra, large-flowered.
   minor, MY-nor, dwarf.
   minor var. *whitlavia*, whit-LA-ve-a, named after Francis Whitla (1783–1855), an Irish botanist.
   parryi, PAR-re-i, after Charles Christopher Parry (1823–1890), British-American botanist.
   tanacetifolia, tan-a-set-if-O-le-a, *Tanacetum* or tansy-leaved.
   viscida, VIS-kid-a, viscid or sticky, the stems and leaves.
   whitlavia, see *P. minor* var. *whitlavia*.

Phaius, FA-us; from Gr. for dark and swarthy, from colour of flowers of original species. Warm-house terrestrial orchids. *Orchidaceae*.
   blumei, see *P. tankervilleae*.
   × *cooksoniae*, kook-SO-ne-a, after Norman Charles Cookson (1842–1909), Lead manufacturer and Orchid grower, who raised this hybrid.
   grandifolius, see *P. tankervilleae*.
   tankervilleae, tan-kar-VIL-e-a; in 1788 Joseph Banks named it in commemoration of Lady Emma Tankerville, in whose greenhouse it flowered.
   tuberculosus, see *Gastrorchis tuberculosa*.

Phalaenopsis, fal-a-NOP-sis; from Gr. *phalaina*, moth; *opsis*, resemblance, in allusion to the flowers. Warm-house Orchids. *Orchidaceae*.

amabilis, am-A-bil-is, lovely.

grandiflora, see *P. amabilis*.

lowii, LOW-e-i, after Sir Hugh Low (1824–1905), British colonial administrator and plant collector in Borneo.

sanderiana, san-der-e-A-na, in commemoration of Henry Frederick Conrad Sander (1847–1920), nurseryman and orchid specialist, brought into cultivation by Sander's nursery, St Albans, England.

schilleriana, shil-ler-e-AN-a, after Consul Gustav Wilhelm Schiller (1803–1870), Shipping company owner and orchid collector.

Phalaris, FAL-ar-is; Ancient Greek name, possibly from *phalaros*, shining, referring to the polished seeds. Ornamental grasses. *Poaceae*.

arundinacea, ar-un-din-A-se-a, resembling *Arundo* (reed).

canariensis, ka-nar-e-EN-sis, of the Canary Islands.

Phaseolus, FAS-e-o-lus; ancient name from L. *faseolus*; Gr. *phaselos*, the name of a bean. A wide range of annuals and perennials including climbing and dwarf beans. *Leguminosae*.

coccineus, kok-SIN-e-us, scarlet.

multiflorus, see *P. coccineus*.

vulgaris, vul-GAR-is, common.

Phedimus, fed-E-mus; a mythological name. Succulents. *Crassulaceae*.

middendorffianus, mid-den-dor-fe-A-nus, after Alexander Theodor von Middendorff (1815–1894), Russian zoologist and introducer of many Siberian plants.

Phegopteris, feg-O-ter-is; from Gr. *phegos*, now considered the Beech but possibly the Sweet Chestnut; *pteris*, fern. The Beech Fern. *Thelypteridaceae*.

connectilis, kon-NEK-til-is, from L. *conecto*, to join together, in reference to the pinnae.

Philadelphus, fil-a-DEL-fus; according to Sweet, Linnaeus named this in honour of an Egytian King Ptolemy Philadelphus. Fragrant flowering shrubs. *Hydrangeaceae*.

coronarius, kor-on-AIR-e-us, crown or wreath-like.

delavayi, de-la-VA-i, after Père Jean Marie Delavay (1834–1895), missionary and plant collector in Yunnan province, China.

gordonianus, gor-DON-e-a-nus, after James Gordon (1708–1780), nurseryman of Mile End, London, correspondent of Linnaeus.

grandiflorus, gran-dif-LO-rus, large flowered.

incanus, in-KA-nus, hoary or grey, the leaf underside.

inodorus, in-o-DOR-us, having no fragrance.

microphyllus, mi-kro-FIL-lus, small-leaved.

satsumi, sat-SU-me, Japanese name.

tomentosus, to-men-TO-sus, felted, the leaves.

Philesia, fil-E-ze-a; from Gr. *philein*, to love, in reference to the Lily-like flowers. Dwarf shrub. *Philesiaceae*.

buxifolia, see *P. magellanica*.

magellanica, maj-el-AN-ik-a, of the area of the Straits of Magellan.

Phillyrea, fil-LER-e-a; the ancient Gr. name of the plant. Evergreen shrubs or small trees. *Oleaceae*.

angustifolia, an-gus-tif-O-le-a, narrow-leaved.

latifolia, lat-if-O-le-a, broad-leaved.

Phlebodium, fleb-O-de-um; from Gr. *phlebos*, a vein, referring to the strong venation or veining of the fronds, and *odous*, a tooth, the shape of the areoles. Warm-house ferns. *Polypodiaceae*.

aureum, AW-re-um, golden – the sori or rhizome scales.

sporodocarpum, spor-o-do-KAR-pum, spore-fruited, the prominent sori.

Phlomis, FLO-mis; from Gr. *phlomos*, a mullein, or some other woolly plant, which this subject resembled. Herbaceous perennials and shrubs. *Lamiaceae*.

fruticosa, frut-ik-O-sa, shrubby.

herba-venti, HERB-a-VEN-ti, herb of the wind.

samia, SA-me-a, of Samos.

Phlox, floks; from Gr. *phlego*, to burn, or *phlox*, a flame, doubtless in allusion to the brightly coloured flowers. Herbaceous perennials and annuals. *Polemoniaceae*.

amoena, am-E-na, lovely, pleasing.

canadensis, kan-a-DEN-sis, of Canada.

decussata, dek-us-SA-ta, divided crosswise, presumably the leaf arrangement.

divaricata, di-var-e-KAR-ta, spreading.

drummondii, drum-MON-de-i, after Thomas Drummond (1780–1835), plant collector in Canada and the United States of America for the Veitch nursery.

ovata, o-VA-ta, egg-shaped – the leaves.

paniculata, pan-ik-ul-A-ta, flowers in a panicle or branching inflorescence.

pilosa, pil-O-sa, hairy.

× *stellaria*, stel-LAIR-e-a, old name; star-shaped.

stolonifera, sto-lon-IF-er-a, having stolons, or rooted runners.

subulata, sub-u-LA-ta, awl-like, the leaves.

Phoenix, FE-niks; the Greek name for Date Palm, used by Theophrastus. Greenhouse and room palms. *Arecaceae*.

canariensis, ka-nar-e-EN-sis, of the Canary Islands.

dactylifera, dak-til-IF-er-a, furnished with fingers. The Date Palm.

roebelenii, ro-BEL-in-e-i, after Carl Roebelin (1855–1927), Swiss plant collector, in the service of Frederick Sander.

rupicola, roo-PIK-o-la, rock loving.

Phormium, FOR-me-um; from Gr. *phormos*, a basket, the fibres of the leaves used for basket-making. Evergreen perennial herbs. *Xanthorrhoeaceae*.

colensoi, kol-EN-so-i, after William Colenso (1811–1899) New Zealand missionary and botanist.

cookianum, see *P. colensoi*.

tenax, TE-naks, tough, the leaf-fibres. The New Zealand Flax.

Photinia, fo-TIN-e-a; from Gr. *photeinos*, shining, referring to the glossy leaves. Trees and shrubs. *Rosaceae*.

arbutifolia, ar-bew-tif-OL-e-a, resembling *Arbutus* leaves.

× *fraseri*, FRA-sir-i, discovered by Oliver Fraser of Fraser's Nursery, Birmingham, Alabama c. 1940.

japonica, jap-ON-ik-a, of Japan.

serrulata, ser-rul-A-ta, leaves finely toothed.

Phragmipedium, frag-my-pe-DE-um; from Gr. *phragma*, a fence; *pedilon*, a slipper. Lady Slipper Orchid. *Orchidaceae*.

caudatum, kaw-DA-tum, tailed.

× *dominianum*, dom-in-e-A-num, after John Dominy (1816–1891), British horticulturist,

who was noted for plant hybridisation, he worked for Veitch Nurseries.

× *sedenii*, sed-E-ne-i, after John Seden (1840–1921), British hybridiser, trained by John Dominy at Veitch Nurseries.

Phragmites, frag-MY-teez; from Gr. *phragma*, a fence, alluding to the fence or hedge-like habit of growth, also Gr. name for reed. Waterside perennial. *Poaceae*.

australis, aws-TRA-lis, southern.

communis, see *P. australis*.

Phrynium, FRY-ne-um; from Gr. *phrynos*, a toad, the plants inhabit marshes. Tropical herbaceous foliage plants. *Marantaceae*.

variegatum, see *Calathea variegata*.

Phuopsis, fu-OP-sis; from *Phu*, old Greek name for Valerian; *opsis*, like, the flowers resembling those of Valerian. Rock garden trailer. *Rubiaceae*.

stylosa, sty-LO-sa, the inflorescence having many and prominent styles.

Phygelius, fy-JE-le-us; from Gr. *phyge*, flight, according to William Jackson Hooker referring to avoidance, 'in consequence of its so long escaped the researches of botanists'. Tender perennials. *Scrophulariaceae*.

capensis, ka-PEN-sis, of the Cape of Good Hope.

Phyllanthus, fil-LAN-thus; from Gr. *phyllon*, a leaf; *anthos*, a flower, the flowers being produced along the edges of the leaf-like phyllodes. Tropical shrubby plants. *Phyllanthaceae*.

disticha, DIS-tik-a, leaves in two rows.

disticha f. *nivosa*, niv-O-sa, snowy white – the leaves.

glaucescens, see *P. grandifolius*.

grandifolius, gran-de-FO-le-us, large-leaved.

mimosoides, mim-o-SOY-dees, resembles *Mimosa*.

nivosus, see *Breynia disticha*.

nivosus var. *roseopictus*, see *P. disticha* f. *nivosa*.

pulcher, PUL-ker, beautiful.

Phyllocactus, fil-lo-KAK-tus; from Gr. *phyllon*, a leaf; and *cactus*. Greenhouse cacti. *Cactaceae*.

ackermanni, see *Disocactus ackermannii*.

crenatus, see *Epiphyllum crenatum*.

grandis, see *Epiphyllum oxypetalum*.

latifrons, see *Epiphyllum oxypetalum*.
phyllanthoides, see *Disocactus phyllanthoides*.

Phyllodoce, fil-LO-do-ke (fil-o-DO-se);
name of the sea nymph in Greek classics.
Dwarf ericaceous shrubs. *Ericaceae*.
  empetriformis, em-pet-rif-OR-mis, resembling
    Empetrum (the crowberry).

Phyllostachys, fil-LOS-tak-is; from Gr.
phyllon, a leaf; *stachys*, a spike, the flowers in
leafy spikes. Hardy bamboos. *Poaceae*.
  aurea, AW-re-a, golden, the stems.
  nigra, NY-gra, black, the stems.
  viridiglaucescens, ver-id-e-glaw-SES-senz, glau-
    cous green.

Phymatodes, fy-mat-O-dees; from Gr.
phymata, tubercles, the impressed sori (fructification) looking like tubercles on the
upper side of the fronds. Greenhouse ferns.
Dipteridaceae.
  albosquamata, AL-bo-skwa-MA-ta, white scaly –
    white dots on the fronds.
  billardierei, bil-LAR-de-ai-i, after Jacques-Ju-
    lien Houtou de Labillardière (1755–1834),
    French explorer and botanist.
  nigrescens, see *Phymatosorus membranifolium*.

Phymatosorus, fy-mat-O-sor-us; from Gr.
phymata, tubercles; *soros*, stack; pile; heap,
impressed sori (fructification) looking like
tubercles on the upper side of the fronds.
Greenhouse ferns. *Polypodiaceae*.
  membranifolium, mem-bran-e-FO-le-um, foliage
    resembling skin.
  pustulatus, pus-tu-LA-tus, covered with blad-
    der-like excrescences – the seats of the sori.

Physalis, FY-sa-lis; from Gr. *physa*, a bladder,
in allusion to the inflated calyx. Herbaceous
perennials. *Solanaceae*.
  alkekengi, al-ke-KEN-ge, probably a corruption
    from the Gr. *halikakabos*, in reference to the
    bladder shape.
  alkekengi var. *franchetii*, fran-SHET-e-i, after
    Adrien René Franchet (1834–1900), French
    botanist at the Muséum national d'histoire
    naturelle in Paris.
  ixocarpa, ix-o-KAR-pa, viscid – the fruits. The
    Tomatillo or Jamberry.
  peruviana, pe-ru-ve-A-na, of Peru. The Cape
    Gooseberry or Goldenberry.

Physaria, fy-SAR-e-a; from Gr. *physa*, a
bladder, bellows, in allusion to the inflated
fruit. Bladderpod. Herbaceous perennials.
Brassicaceae.
  gracilis, GRAS-il-is, slender.
  mendocina, men-dos-E-na, of Mendoza, Chile.

Physocarpus, fy-so-KAR-pus; from Gr.
physa, a bladder; *karpos*, fruit, in allusion to
the inflated follicles. Shrubs. *Rosaceae*.
  amurensis, am-oor-EN-sis, the region of the
    Amur river.
  opulifolius, op-ul-if-O-le-us, leaves like *Viburnum
    opulus*, the Guelder-rose.

Physoplexis, fy-so-PLEK-sis; from Gr. *physa*,
bladder; *plexis*, plaiting, weaving, in reference to the joining together of the divisions
of the swollen corolla. Rock plant. *Campanulaceae*.
  comosa, kom-O-sa, with hairy tufts. The Tufted
    Horned Rampion.

Physoptychis, fy-so-TIK-is; from Gr. *physa*, a
bladder; *ptyche*, fold, in allusion to the blad-
der-like silicles. Perennial herbs. *Brassicaceae*.
  caspica, KAS-pi-ka, from the region of the
    Caspian Sea.

Physostegia, fy-so-STE-je-a; from Gr. *physa*,
a bladder; *stege*, a covering, in reference to
the formation of the calyx. Herbaceous perennials. *Lamiaceae*.
  virginiana, vir-jin-e-A-na, of Virginia, U.S.A.

Phyteuma, fy-TEW-ma; possibly from Gr.
phyteuo, to plant, or Gr. *phyton*, vegetable
growth; used by Dioscorides and adapted by
Linnaeus. Herbaceous perennials and rock
plants. *Campanulaceae*.
  comosum, see *Physoplexis comosa*.
  halleri, see *P. ovatum*.
  orbiculare, or-bik-ul-AR-e, resembling an orb, the
    rounded flowers.
  ovatum, o-VA-tum, egg-shaped.
  sieberi, SI-ber-i, after Franz Wilhelm Sieber
    (1789–1844), botanist and plant collector.
  spicatum, spe-KA-tum, spiked – the flowers.

Phytolacca, fy-tol-AK-ka; from Gr. *phyton*,
a plant; *lacca*, lac, in allusion to the crimson
colour of the fruit juice. Herbaceous perennials. The Poke Weeds. *Phytolaccaceae*.

acinosa, ak-in-O-sa, full of kernels.

americana, a-mer-ik-A-na, of America.

decandra, see *P. americana*.

dodecandra, doe-dek-AN-dra, having twelve stamens.

Picea, PI-se-a; ancient L. name. Conifers. The Spruce. *Pinaceae.*

abies, A-beez, resembling *Abies* (firs). The Norway Spruce.

× *albertiana*, al-ber-te-A-na, the Alberta Spruce. Compact growing cross.

breweriana, brew-er-e-A-na, after William Henry Brewer (1828–1910), American botanist, first Chair of Agriculture at Sheffield Scientific School, Yale University.

engelmannii, en-gel-MAN-ne-i, after George Engelmann (1809–1884), German-American botanist, a pioneer of western North American Flora.

excelsa, see *P. abies*.

mariana, MA-re-a-na, introduced from Maryland (*terra mariana*).

morinda, see *P. smithiana.*

nigra, see *P. mariana.*

omorika, om-OR-ik-a, local name for Serbian spruce.

orientalis, or-e-en-TA-lis, eastern – Eastern Asia (China).

pungens, PUN-jenz, sharp – the pointed leaves.

sitchensis, sit-KEN-sis, of Sitka.

smithiana, smith-e-A-na, in honour of Sir James Edward Smith (1759–1828), founder and first president of the Linnean Society of London.

Pieris, PY-er-is; mythological name. Evergreen shrubs belonging to the Heath family. Shrubs. *Ericaceae.*

floribunda, flor-e-BUN-da, abundant or free flowering.

formosa, for-MO-sa, handsome.

japonica, jap-ON-ik-a, of Japan.

Pilea, PY-le-a; from *pileus*, the Roman felt cap, because of the calyx covering of the achene. Greenhouse foliage perennial. *Urticaceae.*

microphylla, mi-krof-IL-la, small leaved.

muscosa, see *P. microphylla.*

Pilocereus, py-lo-SE-re-us; from L. *pilosus*, shaggy and *cereus* (which see), alluding to the long hairs on the spine cushions. Greenhouse cacti. *Cactaceae.*

senilis, see *Cephalocereus senilis.*

Pilosella, py-lo-SEL-la; diminutive form of L. *pilosus*, shaggy, a little hairy. Perennial flowering plant. *Compositae.*

aurantiaca, aw-ran-te-A-ka, golden orange.

Pilularia, pil-ul-A-re-a; from L. *pilula*, a pill – referring to the round spore cases. Submerged aquatic ferns. *Marsileaceae.*

globulifera, see *Calamistrum globuliferum.*

Pimelea, py-MEEL-e-a; from Gr. *pimele*, fat, referring to the viscid matter on the leaves of some species and the oily seeds. Greenhouse flowering shrubs. *Thymelaeaceae.*

decussata, dek-us-SA-ta, divided crosswise.

ferruginea, fer-ru-JIN-e-a, rusty.

rosea, RO-ze-a, rose-coloured.

spectabilis, spek-TAB-il-is, notable.

Pimenta, py-MEN-ta; from Spanish *pimento*. Warm-house shrub. *Myrtaceae.*

acris, see *P. racemosa.*

dioica, di-OY-ka, literally two houses, that is, male and female parts being on separate plants, dioecious.

officinalis, see *P. dioica.*

racemosa, ras-em-O-sa, resembling a raceme.

Pinguicula, pin-GWIK-ul-a; from L. *pinguis*, fat or greasy, from the appearance of the leaves in common Butterwort. Herbaceous perennials. *Lentibulariaceae.*

grandiflora, gran-dif-LO-ra, large-flowered.

vulgaris, vul-GAR-is, common.

Pinus, PY-nus; ancient classical name for a pine tree. Coniferous trees. *Pinaceae.*

austriaca, see *P. nigra.*

cembra, SEM-bra, old name for the Arolla Pine.

coulteri, KOLE-ter-i, discovered in the Santa Lucia Mountains by Thomas Coulter (1793–1843), in 1831.

halepensis, al-ep-EN-sis, of Aleppo. Aleppo Pine.

jeffreyi, JEF-re-e, after John Jeffrey (1826–1854), Scotish botanist and plant collector in North America.

laricio, see *P. nigra* subsp. *laricio.*

monophylla, mon-o-FIL-a, with one leaf.

mugo, MEW-go, Italian for dwarf pine.

nigra, NY-gra, black.

nigra subsp. *laricio*, lar-IS-e-o, resembling *Larix* (larch); old botanical name.

pinaster, py-NAS-ter, old name for the Maritime Pine.

pinea, PY-ne-a, a Pine or Stone Pine. The Umbrella Pine (Fr. *Pin Parasol*).

ponderosa, pon-der-O-sa, large and heavy-wooded.

radiata, rad-e-A-ta, rayed – the form of the branches.

strobus, STRO-bus, from Gr. *strobilos*, an old generic name referring to cones. The Weymouth Pine i.e. Lord Weymouth's.

sylvestris, sil-VES-tris, of woods. The Scots Pine.

Piper, PY-per; the ancient name. Herbs, woody climbers, shrubs or small trees. *Piperaceae*.

betle, BE-tl, Betel – native name.

excelsum, ek-SEL-sum, tall or lofty.

nigrum, NI-grum, black. The Black Pepper.

Piptanthus, pip-TAN-thus; from Gr. *pipto*, to fall; *anthos*, a flower, alluding to the short duration of the blossoms. Flowering shrubs. *Leguminosae*.

nepalensis, nep-al-EN-sis, of Nepal.

Pistia, PIS-te-a; from Gr. *pistos*, aquatic. Floating aquatics. *Araceae*.

stratiotes, strat-e-O-tez, resembling *Stratiotes*. The Water Cabbage.

Pisum, PY-sum; the Classical Latin name, possibly related to the Celtic, *pis*, pea. Annuals. *Leguminosae*.

saccharatum, sak-kar-A-tum, sugar. The Sugar Snap.

sativum, SAT-iv-um, cultivated.

umbellatum, um-bel-LA-tum, bearing umbels. The Crown Pea.

Pitcairnia, pit-CAIRN-e-a; after William Pitcairn (1712–1791), English physician, who had a botanic garden in Islington. Tropical flowering perennials. *Bromeliaceae*.

andreana, an-dre-A-na, after Édouard-François André (1840–1911), French horticulturist and garden designer.

bifrons, BY-fronz, twin leaves.

bracteata, see *P. bifrons*.

fulgens, see *P. bifrons*.

Pittosporum, pit-TOS-por-rum; from Gr. *pitte*, tar; *sporos*, seed, the latter being coated with a resinous substance. Flowering shrubs. *Pittosporaceae*.

crassifolium, kras-sif-OL-e-um, thick-leaved.

mayi, see *P. tenuifolium*.

tenuifolium, ten-u-if-OL-e-um, narrow-leaved.

tobira, to-BI-ra, native Japanese name.

undulatum, un-du-LA-tum, waved – the leaves.

Pityrogramma, pit-e-row-GRAM-ma; from Gr. *pityron*, chaff; *gramma*, writing, from the white powdery covering on the lower surface of the fronds. Ferns. *Pteridaceae*.

calomelanos, cal-om-EL-an-os, beautiful black.

calomelanos var. *peruviana*, pe-ru-ve-A-na, of Peru.

dealbata, de-al-BA-ta, whitewashed – the silvery farina on the fronds.

ebenea, e-bee-NE-a, ebony black the mature stipes.

Plagianthus, pla-ge-AN-thus; from Gr. *plagios*, oblique; *anthos*, a flower, in allusion to the asymmetrical shape of the petals. Flowering trees. *Malvaceae*.

betulinus, bet-u-LE-nus, the leaves like *Betula* (birch).

lyallii, LI-al-e-i, after David Lyall (1817–1895), physician, botanist and collector.

Platanthera, pla-TAN-ther-a; from Gr. *platus*, broad; *anthera*, an anther, in allusion to the broad anthers on these flowers. Orchids. *Orchidaceae*.

bifolia, bi-FO-le-a, two-leaved.

blephariglottis, blef-ar-e-GLOT-is, eyelash-tongued, the lip ciliated.

grandiflora, gran-dif-LO-ra, large-flowered.

Platanus, PLAT-a-nus; the old Greek name, *platanos*, for the Plane tree, meaning broad (*platus*), in reference to the palmate leaves or wide-spreading branches. Trees. *Platanaceae*.

acerifolia, a-ser-if-O-le-a, leaves resembling *Acer*. The London Plane.

occidentalis, oks-se-den-TA-lis, western – North America.

orientalis, or-e-en-TA-lis, eastern – Eastern Asia (China).

Platycladus, plat-e-KLA-dus; from Gr. *platys*, broad or flat; *klados*, a branch, in reference to the flat branches. Conifer. *Cupressaceae.*

　orientalis, or-e-en-TA-lis, eastern – Eastern Asia (China).

Platycerium, plat-e-SER-e-um; from Gr. *platys*, broad; *keras*, a horn, in allusion to the broad horn-shaped fertile fronds. Greenhouse ferns. *Polypodiaceae.*

　aethiopicum, see *P. stemaria.*

　alcicorne, alk-ik-ORN-e, elk's horn. The Elkhorn Fern.

　grande, GRAN-de, large and fine.

　stemaria, ste-MA-re-a, stag's horn. The Staghorn Fern.

Platyclinis, misapplied see below.

　filiformis, see *Dendrochilum filiforme.*

　glumacea, see *Dendrochilum glumaceum.*

Platycodon, plat-ik-O-don; from Gr. *platys*, broad; *kodon*, a bell, in allusion to the large bell-shaped flowers. Herbaceous perennials. The Chinese Bellflower. *Campanulaceae.*

　grandiflorus, gran-dif-LO-rus, large flowered.

Platystemon, plat-e-STE-mon; from Gr. *platys*, broad; *stemon*, a stamen, in reference to the form of the flowers. Hardy annuals. *Papaveraceae.*

　californicus, kal-if-OR-nik-us, of California. Cream Cups.

Plectranthus, plek-TRAN-thus; from Gr. *plectron*, spur; *anthos*, flower. Annuals, herbaceous perennials and shrubs. *Lamiaceae.*

　scutellarioides, sku-tel-lar-e-OY-dees, resembling *Scutellaria.*

　thyrsoideus, thyr-so-ID-e-us, thyrse-like – the flower spikes.

　welwitschii, wel- (or vel-) VITS-ke-i, after Friedrich Martin Joseph Welwitsch (1806–1872), Austrian botanist and explorer.

Pleioblastus, pli-O-blast-us; from Gr. *pleios*, full; *blastos*, bud; in allusion to the many buds. Grasses. *Poaceae.*

　argenteostriatus, ar-jen-te-o-stri-A-tus, silvery striped.

　fortunei, for-TOO-ne-i, after Robert Fortune (1812–1880), Scottish plant collector in China.

　viridistriatus, vir-id-e-stri-A-tus, green striped.

Pleione, pli-O-ne; from Gr. mythology, Pleione, mother of Pleiades. Greenhouse orchids. *Orchidaceae.*

　humilis, HUM-il-is, low or dwarf.

　× *lagenaria*, lag-e-NA-re-a, bottle-shaped.

　maculata, mak-ul-A-ta, spotted.

　praecox, PRA-koks, early flowering.

Pleiospilos, pla-OS-pil-os; from Gr. *pleios*, full; *spilos*, a dot or spot, in allusion to the dotted leaves. Greenhouse succulents. *Aizoaceae.*

　bolusii, BO-lus-e-i, after Harry Bolus (1834–1911), South African botanist, who founded the Bolus Herbarium.

　roodiae, ROOD-e-e, after Mrs Petrusa Benjamina Rood (1861–1946), South African succulent plant collector, who sent plants and seed to N.E. Brown and Pole-Evans.

　simulans, SIM-u-lanz, simulating or looking like – in this case the stony surroundings.

Pleroma, ple-RO-ma; from Gr. *pleroma*, fullness – the cells in the capsules. Greenhouse flowering shrubs. *Melastomataceae.*

　macranthum, mak-RANTH-um, large-flowered.

Plumbago, plum-BA-go; from L. *plumbum*, lead, so called by Pliny, who attributed the curing of lead poisoning to the European species. Flowering shrubs. The Leadwort. *Plumbaginaceae.*

　auriculata, aw-rik-ul-A-ta, with an ear-shaped appendage.

　capensis, see *P. auriculata.*

　indica, IN-di-ka, of India.

　larpentae, see *Ceratostigma plumbaginoides.*

　rosea, see *P. indica.*

　willmottiana, see *Ceratostigma willmottianum.*

Plumeria, plu-MAIR-e-a; after Charles Plumier (1646–1704), French botanist. Warm house flowering shrubs. *Apocynaceae.*

　acutifolia, see *P. rubra.*

　bicolor, see *P. rubra.*

　rubra, ROO-bra, red. The Frangipani Tree.

Podophyllum, pod-o-FIL-lum; a contraction of *Anapodophyllum*; duck's-foot-leaved. Herbaceous perennials. *Berberidaceae.*

　emodi, see *Sinopodophyllum hexandrum.*

　peltatum, pel-TA-tum, shaped like a shield, the leaves.

Poinciana, misapplied see below.
    elata, see *Caesalpinia pulcherrima*.
    gilliesii, see *Caesalpinia gilliesii*.
    regia, see *Delonix regia*.

Polemonium, pol-e-MO-ne-um; derivation doubtful, possibly Gr. *polemos*, war, from the lance shaped leaflets, or, as Pliny suggested, because two kings went to war as to which of them had discovered the virtues of the plant. Other authorities state Dioscorides named it after King Polemon II of Pontus. Herbaceous perennials. *Polemoniaceae*.
    caeruleum, ser-U-le-um, sky-blue. Jacob's Ladder.
    carneum, KAR-ne-um, flesh-coloured.
    confertum, kon-FER-tum, crowed the flowers.
    hultenii, hul-TE-ne-i, after Oskar Eric Gunnar Hultén (1894–1981), Swedish botanist and plant geographer.
    humile, see *P. hultenii*.
    reptans, REP-tans, creeping.
    richardsonii, rich-ard-SO-ne-i, collected by Sir John Richardson (1787–1865), Scottish naval surgeon, naturalist and arctic explorer.

Polianthes, pol-e-AN-theez; from Gr. *polios*, grey, whitish; *anthos*, a flower. Perennial herbs. *Asparagaceae*.
    geminiflora, jem-in-if-LO-ra, twin-flowered.
    tuberosa, tu-ber-O-sa, bearing tubers.

Polygala, pol-IG-a-la; from Gr. *polys*, much; *gala*, milk, the supposition that the presence of these herbs in pasture increased the production of milk, hence Milkwort, the English name. Annuals, perennials, herbs and shrubs. *Polygalaceae*.
    chamaebuxus, kam-e-BUKS-us, from Gr. *chamai*, low growing; *Buxus*, box, from the resemblance of the leaves to those of *Buxus*.
    myrtifolia, mer-te-FO-le-a, leaves resembling *Myrtus* (Myrtle).

Polygonatum, pol-ig-on-A-tum; from Gr. *polys*, many; *gonu*, joints. Gerard states that the name alludes to the many knots, or joints, in the roots and not the stem, as is popularly supposed. Herbaceous perennials. *Asparagaceae*.
    hirtum, HER-tum, hairy.
    latifolium, see *P. hirtum*.

    multiflorum, mul-tif-LO-rum, many flowered. Solomon's Seal of gardens.
    odoratum, od-o-RA-tum, sweet-smelling.
    officinale, see *P. odoratum*.

Polygonum, pol-IG-on-um; from Gr. *polys*, many; *gonu*, joints; in reference to the stem formation. Annuals, herbaceous perennials and climbers. The Knotweeds. *Polygonaceae*.
    affine, af-FIN-ne, related or similar to.
    baldschuanicum, see *Fallopia baldschuanica*.
    bistorta, see *Persicaria bistorta*.
    campanulatum, see *Persicaria campanulata*.
    capitatum, see *Persicaria capitata*.
    compactum, see *Reynoutria japonica*.
    polystachyum, see *Persicaria wallichii*.
    sachalinense, see *Reynoutria sachalinensis*.
    vacciniifolium, vak-sin-e-i-FO-le-um, leaves resembling *Vaccinium*.

Polyphlebium, pol-e-FLE-be-um; from Gr. *poly*, many; *phlebos*, vein, in reference to fronds with prominent veins. Fern. *Hymenophyllaceae*.
    venosum, ve-NO-sum, veined.

Polypodium, pol-e-PO-de-um; from Gr. *polys*, many; *pous*, a foot (many little feet), in allusion to the furry foot-like divisions of the creeping stems. Hardy and greenhouse ferns. *Polypodiaceae*.
    albosquamatum, AL-bo-skwa-MA-tum, white scaly, dots on the fronds.
    alpestre, AL-pes-tre, of mountains.
    aureum, see *Phlebodium aureum*.
    billardierei, bil-LAR-de-air-i, after Jacques-Julien Houtou de Labillardière (1755–1834), French explorer and botanist.
    cambricum, KAM-bre-kum, of Wales. The Welsh Polypody.
    dryopteris, see *Gymnocarpium dryopteris*.
    phegopteris, see *Phegopteris connectilis*.
    pustulatum, see *Phymatosorus pustulatus*.
    vulgare, vul-GAR-e, common. The Polypody.

Polyscias, pol-e-SKI-as; from Gr. *polys*, many; *skias*, canopy, the flower being divided into lesser umbels. Evergreen shrubs and trees. *Araliaceae*.
    balfouriana, BAL-four-e-A-na, after John Hutton Balfour (1808–1884), Scottish botanist, Regis Keeper of the Royal Botanic Garden Edinburgh.

filicifolia, fil-is-if-O-le-a, fern-leaved.

guilfoylei, gwil-FOY-le-i, introduced in 1868 by William Guilfoyle (1840–1912), landscape and botanist, who later became curator of the Melbourne Botanic Gardens.

Polystichum, pol-IS-tik-um; from Gr. *poly*, many; *stichos*, a row, in reference to the several rows of sori. Greenhouse and hardy ferns. *Dryopteridaceae*.

  acrostichoides, ak-ROS-tik-OY-dees; resembling *Acrostichum*.

  aculeatum, ak-u-le-A-tum, prickly – the acute pinnae. The Prickly Shield Fern.

  angulare, see *P. setiferum*.

  chilense, chil-EN-se, Chilean.

  lonchitis, lon-KI-tis, spear-shaped. The Holly Fern.

  munitum, mu-NE-tum, armed with spines.

  setiferum, set-IF-e-rum, bearing bristles.

  tetragonum, te-tra-GO-num, from Gr. *tessara* four; *gonus* angle.

Pontederia, pon-te-DEER-e-a; named after J. Pontedera (1688–1757), once professor of botany at Padua. Hardy aquatic. *Pontederiaceae*.

  cordata, kor-DA-ta, heart shaped, the leaves.

Populus, POP-u-lus; the *arbor-populi* (tree of the people) of the Romans, the Italian or Lombardy Poplar being much planted in their cities. Trees. *Salicaceae*.

  alba, AL-ba, from the L. *alba*, white.

  balsamifera, bawl-sam-IF-er-a, balsam scented.

  × *canadensis*, kan-a-DEN-sis, of Canada.

  × *candicans*, KAN-dik-ans, shining white – the leaves.

  × *canescens*, kan-ES-sens, greyish-white, hoary.

  deltoides, del-TOY-dees, triangular, shape of the leaves.

  deltoides subsp. *monilifera*, mon-il-IF-er-a, neck-lace bearing – the long fruits.

  monilifera, see *P. deltoides* subsp. *monilifera*.

  nigra, NY-gra, black.

  nigra var. *italica*, it-AL-ik-a, of Italy. The Lombardy Poplar.

  serotina, see *P.* × *canadensis*.

  tremula, TREM-u-la, trembling, the quivering of the leaves. The Aspen.

  trichocarpa, trik-o-KAR-pa, with hairy fruits.

Portulaca, por-tu-LAK-a; an old L. name, possibly from L. *porto*, to carry; *lac*, milk,

alluding to the milky juice. Annuals. *Portulacaceae*.

  grandiflora, gran-dif-LO-ra, large-flowered.

  oleracea, o-ler-A-se-a, of the vegetable garden, a pot-herb. The Purslane.

Posoqueria, po-zo-KE-re-a; part of the native Guyanese name – *Aymara posoqueri* for *P. longifolia*. Tropical flowering shrubs. *Rubiaceae*.

  coriacea, ko-re-A-se-a, leathery, the leaves.

  coriacea subsp. *formosa*, for-MO-sa, beautiful.

  fragrantissima, fra-gran-TIS-sim-a, most fragrant.

  longiflora, long-if-LO-ra, long-flowered.

Potamogeton, pot-a-mog-E-ton; from Gr. *potamos*, a river; *geiton*, a neighbour, growing in rivers or ponds. Submerged aquatics. The Pondweeds. *Potamogetonaceae*.

  crispus, KRIS-pus, curly – the leaves waved.

  lucens, lu-SENZ, shining – the foliage.

  pectinatus, see *Stuckenia pectinata*.

  perfoliatus, per-fol-e-A-tus, perfoliate leaved – stem-clasping leaves.

  pusillus, pu-SIL-lus, small – the plant.

Potentilla, po-ten-TIL-la; from L. *potens*, powerful, some species having active medicinal properties. Rock plants, herbaceous perennials and shrubs. *Rosaceae*.

  argentea, ar-JEN-te-a, silvery, the foliage.

  argyrophylla, ar-ger-OF-il-la, silvery-leaved.

  aurea, AW-re-a, golden, the flowers.

  davurica, da-VOO-rik-a, of Davuria, Siberia.

  fragiformis, fraj-if-OR-mis, resembling *Fragaria* (strawberry).

  fruticosa, frut-ik-O-sa, shrubby.

  nepalensis, nep-al-EN-sis, of Nepal.

  nitida, NIT-id-a, shining – the leaves.

  purdomii, see *Coluria longifolia*.

  rupestris, roo-PES-tris, growing on rocks.

  tridentata, see *Sibbaldiopsis tridentata*.

Poterium, po-TEER-e-um; from Gr. *poterion*, a drinking-cup, the shape of the calyx in these herbs. The Burnets. *Rosaceae*.

  canadense, see *Sanguisorba canadensis*.

  obtusum, see *Sanguisorba obtusa*.

  sanguisorba, see *Sanguisorba minor*.

Pratia, misapplied see below.

  angulata, see *Lobelia angulata*.

  begonifolia, see *Lobelia nummularia*.

Primula, PRIM-u-la; from L. *primus*, first, referring to the early flowering of many of the primroses. Hardy and greenhouse herbaceous plants, some treated as annuals. *Primulaceae*.

acaulis, see *P. vulgaris*.

auricula, aur-IK-ul-a, from L. *auricula*, an ear – the ear-like leaves. The Auricula.

beesiana, beez-e-A-na, after Messrs. Bees Ltd. the nursery.

bulleyana, bul-le-A-na, after Arthur Kilpin Bulley (1861–1942), founder of Bees nursery, Neston, Cheshire.

capitata, kap-it-A-ta, growing in a dense head.

cashmeriana, kash-mer-e-A-na, of Kashmir.

chionantha, ki-on-AN-tha, snow-white flowers.

cockburniana, kok-burn-e-A-na, named by Antwerp Pratt for H. Cockburn of the Consular Service and Rev. George Cockburn of the Scotch Kirk Mission who assisted him in his travels in China.

denticulata, den-tik-u-LA-ta, toothed, the leaves.

elatior, e-LA-te-or, taller. The Oxlip.

farinosa, far-in-O-sa, mealy, the foliage and stems.

florindae, flor-IN-de, named for Florinda Kingdon-Ward.

forrestii, for-RES-te-i, after George Forrest (1873–1932), Scottish plant collector in China.

frondosa, fron-DO-za, leafy.

glaucescens, GLAW-ses-senz, somewhat blue.

glycyosma, see *P. wilsonii*.

helodoxa, hel-o-DOKS-a, the glory of the bog.

hirsuta, hir-SU-ta, hairy.

involucrata, in-vol-u-KRA-ta, from L. *involucrum*, roll in, envelop, referring to the flowers being ruffed.

japonica, jap-ON-ik-a, of Japan.

juliae, JU-le-e, after Julia Mlokosiewicz, who discovered it.

littoniana, see *P. vialii*.

malacoides, mal-ak-OY-dees, resembling mallow, presumably the flower colour.

marginata, mar-jin-A-ta, the leaves margined with another colour – white.

matthioli, mat-THE-ol-le, after Pietro Andrea Gregorio Mattioli (1501–1577), Italian physician and botanist.

microdonta, see *P. sikkimensis*.

obconica, ob-KON-ik-a, an inverted cone – the calyx.

× *polyantha*, pol-e-AN-tha, many-flowered. A naturally occurring hybrid between *P. veris* and *P. vulgaris*.

polyneura, pol-e-NOR-a, many veins, within the leaf.

pulverulenta, pul-ver-ul-EN-ta, powdered.

rosea, RO-ze-a, rose-coloured.

saxatalis, saks-A-til-is, haunting rocks.

secundiflora, sek-un-dif-LO-ra, the flowers of the cluster all turned one way.

sieboldii, se-BOLD-e-i, after Philipp Franz Balthasar von Siebold (1796–1866), German physician, botanist, and traveler.

sikkimensis, sik-kim-EN-sis, of Sikkim.

sinensis, si-NEN-sis, Chinese.

× *variabilis*, var-e-AB-il-is, variable.

veitchii, see *P. polyneura*.

veris, VE-ris, spring-flowering.

vialii, vi-AL-e-i, in honour of Paul Vial (1855–1917), French missionary, ethnographer and linguist in China.

villosa, vil-LO-sa, shaggy, the leaves hairy.

viscosa, see *P. hirsuta*.

vulgaris, vul-GAR-is, common.

wilsonii, wil-SO-ne-i, in honour of Ernest Henry Wilson (1876–1930), English plant collector in China.

winteri, WIN-ter-i, after Mr E.L. Winter, commissioner of Kumaon, who collected it.

Proboscidea, pro-bos-SID-e-a; the seed pods resembling a proboscis. Annual and perennial herbs. *Martyniaceae*.

fragrans, FRA-granz, fragrant.

louisianica, loo-e-se-AN-ik-a, of Louisiana, U.S.A.

Prospero, pro-SPE-ro; from L. *prosperus*, (*pro*, conform; *spes*, hope), prosper, to grow quickly. Some authorities make the connection with the character in 'The Tempest', Prospero, Duke of Milan. Hardy bulb. *Asparagaceae*.

autumnale, aw-tum-NA-le, autumnal.

Prostanthera, pros-tan-THE-ra; from Gr. *prostheke*, appendage; *anthera*, an anther – the connectives of the anthers are spurred. Tender flowering shrubs. *Lamiaceae*.

rotundifolia, ro-tun-dif-O-le-a, round-leaved.

Prosthechea, pros-thee-KEY-a; from Gr. *prostheke*, an appendage, in allusion to the appendage on the column. Appendage Orchid. *Orchidaceae.*

  fragrans, FRA-granz, fragrant.
  vitellina, vit-el-LE-na, yolk of egg colour.

Prumnopitys, prum-NOP-it-is; from Gr. *prumnos*, the last or extreme; *pitys*, a pine. Hardy conifer. The Plum Fir. *Podocarpaceae.*

  andina, an-DE-na, of the Andes.
  elegans, see *P. andina.*

Prunella, proo-NEL-la; from German *Bräune*, quinsy, which the plant was supposed to heal. Also spelt *Brunella* which the German herbalists used. Rock and border perennials. *Lamiaceae.*

  grandiflora, gran-dif-LO-ra, large-flowered.
  vulgaris, vul-GAR-is, common. The Self-heal.

Prunus, PROO-nus; classical name of the plum. Flowering and fruiting trees. *Rosaceae.*

  amygdaloides, am-IG-dal-OY-dees, resembling *amygdalus*, which see.
  amygdalus, am-IG-da-lus, from Gr. *amygdalos*, an almond, or from Gr. *amysso*, to lacerate, in reference to the fissures or channels in the 'stone'.
  avium, AV-e-um, L. *avis*, a bird. The Common Gean.
  cerasifera, ser-as-IF-er-a, cherry-bearing. The Cherry-Plum.
  cerasus, ser-A-sus, Gr. *kerasos*, a Cherry tree, said to have come from Cerasus in Pontus. The Cherry Tree.
  communis, see *P. dulcis.*
  cornuta, kor-NU-ta, horned – the shape of the fruits.
  davidiana, da-vid-e-A-na, after Père David (1826–1900).
  domestica, do-MES-tik-a, domestic – from its various uses.
  dulcis, DUL-cis, sweet. The Sweet Almond.
  incana, in-KA-na, woolly, the leaf undersides.
  incisa, IN-si-sa, deeply cut, the leaves.
  japonica, jap-ON-ik-a, of Japan.
  laurocerasus, LAW-ro-ser-A-sus, literally laurel cherry. The Cherry Laurel or 'Laurel' of gardens.
  lusitanica, loo-sit-A-nik-a, of Lusitania (Portugal). Portuguese Laurel.
  mahaleb, ma-A-leb, from Arabic, *mahleb* or *mahlab*, meaning the Mahalab cherry from which a spice is extracted.

  mume, MU-me, variant of the Japanese name, *ume*, for this species.
  padus, PA-dus, Gr. name for the true Bird-Cherry.
  persica, PER-sik-a, from *persicum*, the Latin name for peach, literally Persia, whence the tree reached Europe from China.
  persica var. *nucipersica*, nu-se-PER-sik-a, from L. *nuci*, a nut; persica, see above. The Nectarine.
  serrula, ser-RU-la, leaves with small saw-teeth margins.
  serrulata, ser-rul-A-ta, leaves finely toothed.
  spinosa, spi-NO-sa, spiny.
  subhirtella, sub-hir-TEL-la, slightly hairy – the leaves and young wood.
  triloba, tril-O-ba, the leaves usually three-lobed.

Pseuderanthemum, SUED-e-RAN-the-mum; false *Eranthemum*. Evergreen herbs and shrubs. *Acanthaceae.*

  albiflorum, al-bif-LOR-um, with white flowers.
  andersonii, an-der-SO-ne-i, probably after Thomas Anderson (1832–1870), botanist in India who collected with Joseph Hooker.
  cooperi, KOO-per-i, after Sir Daniel Cooper (1821–1902), who raised seed of the specimen which were sent to Vietch's nursery.

Pseudofumaria, sue-do-few-MAR-e-a; false *Fumaria*. Herbaceous perennials. *Papaveraceae.*

  lutea, LU-te-a, yellow.

Pseudolysimachion, SUE-do-lis-e-MAK-e-on; false *Lysimachia*. Herbaceous perennials. *Plantaginaceae.*

  linariifolium, le-nar-e-i-FO-le-um, resembling *Linaria* leaves.

Pseudomertensia, SUE-do-mer-TEN-se-a; the false *Mertensia*. Herbaceous perennials. *Boraginaceae.*

  echioides, ek-e-OY-dees, resembling *Echium*.

Pseudosasa, SUE-do-SA-sa; the false *Sasa*, allied to the true *Sasa* (which see). Bamboo. *Poaceae.*

  japonica, jap-ON-ik-a, of Japan.

Pseudotrillium, SUE-do-TRIL-le-um; false *Trillium*, proposed monotypic genus based on molecular evidence. Perennial herb. *Melanthiaceae.*

  rivale, re-VA-le, growing by brook-sides.

Pseudotsuga, SUE-do-SU-ga; the false *Tsuga*, allied to the true *Tsugas* (Hemlock Firs). Conifers. *Pinaceae*.

douglasii, see *Pseudotsuga menziesii*.

menziesii, men-ZE-se-i, after Archibald Menzies (1754–1842), Scottish naval officer, surgeon and botanist, who was appointed as naturalist on Vancouver's ship Discovery in 1790.

Psidium, SID-e-um; from Gr. *psidion*, a pomegranate. Tropical Fruiting Tree. The Guava. *Myrtaceae*.

guajava, gwa-JAR-va, from Sp. *gaujaba*.

guava, see *P. guajava*.

Psychopsis, SI-kop-sis; from Gr. *psyche*, butterfly; *opsis*, like, alluding to the shape of the flower. Epiphytic orchids. *Orchidaceae*.

krameriana, kra-mer-e-A-na, after Franz August Kramer (fl. 1852–1875), German gardener to Herr Senator Jenisch.

papilio, pa-PIL-e-o, the flower resembling a butterfly.

Psylliostachys, si-le-o-STAK-is; resembling *Plantago psyllium*; *stachys*, spike. Half hardy annuals. *Plumbaginaceae*.

suworowi, su-wor-O-i, after Ivan Petrovich Suvorov (1829–1880), Russian medical inspector of the Turkestan region.

Ptelea, TEL-e-a; from Gr. *ptelea*, the Greek name for elm, the similarity residing in the winged fruits. Ornamental Tree. *Rutaceae*.

trifoliata, trif-ol-e-A-ta, leaves in three.

Pteridium, ter-id-E-um; diminutive of Gr. *pteris*, a fern, from *pteron*, a wing. Bracken Fern. *Dennstaedtiaceae*.

aquilinum, ak-wil-E-num, an eagle, various explanations offered, most probable being the branched frond resembling a pair of outstretched wings. The Bracken.

Pteris, TER-is; from Gr. *pteron*, a wing, the branched frond resembling a pair of outspread wings. Greenhouse ferns. *Pteridaceae*.

aquilina, see *Pteridium aquilinum*.

cretica, KRE-tik-a, of Crete.

longifolia, long-if-OL-e-a, long leaves.

palmata, see *Doryopteris pedata* var. *palmata*.

serrulata, ser-rul-A-ta, finely toothed.

tremula, TREM-u-la, trembling.

umbrosa, um-BRO-za, growing in shady places. Shade loving.

wimsettii, possibly a variety of *P. cretica*.

Pterocactus, ter-o-KAK-tus; from Gr. *pteron*, a wing, and *cactus*, reference being to the winged seeds. Greenhouse cacti. *Cactaceae*.

pumilus, pew-MIL-us, dwarf.

tuberosus, tu-ber-O-sus, bearing tubers.

Pterocephalus, ter-o-SEF-a-lus; from Gr. *pteron*, wing; *kephale*, a head, signifying a winged head, alluding to the form of the flower. Annual or perennial herbs, subshrubs and shrubs. *Caprifoliaceae*.

perennis, per-EN-nis, perennial.

Ptilostemon, ty-lo-STE-mon; from Gr. *ptilon*, down; *stema*, stamen. Annual and perennial herbs. *Compositae*.

casabonae, kas-a-BO-ne, after Giuseppe Casabona (1515–1596), herbalist of Cosimo I of Florence and director of the Botanical Garden of Pisa.

diacantha, di-ak-AN-tha, two spined. The Fishbone Thistle.

Ptychosperma, ty-ko-SPER-ma; from Gr. *ptyche*, a fold; *sperma*, seed, in allusion to the fold within the seed. Palms. *Arecaceae*.

elegans, EL-e-ganz, elegant.

Pulmonaria, pul-mon-AIR-e-a; from L. *pulmo*, pertaining to the lungs, one species having being regarded as a remedy for diseases of the lungs, hence the common name Lungwort. Rock garden and woodland perennials. *Boraginaceae*.

angustifolia, an-gus-tif-O-le-a, narrow-leaved.

officinalis, of-fis-in-A-lis, of the shop (apothecary's), applied to plants always kept "in stock" by herbalists.

rubra, ROO-bra, red – the flowers.

saccharata, sak-kar-A-ta, sugared; application obscure but possibly alluding to the white-powdered leaves.

Punica, PU-ne-ka; from *Malum punicum*, Apple of Carthage, of Pliny. Flowering wall shrub. *Lythraceae*.

granatum, gra-NA-tum, from L. *granum*, grain; having many seeds.

Puschkinia, poos-KIN-e-a; after Apollo Mussin-Pushkin (1760–1805), Russian chemist and plant collector. Half-hardy bulbs. *Asparagaceae.*
  scilloides, sil-OY-dees, resembling *Scilla.*

Pyracantha, py-ra-KAN-tha; from Gr. *pyr*, fire; *akanthos*, a thorn, in reference to the brilliant berries and spiny branches. The Fire-Thorn. Evergreen shrubs. *Rosaceae.*
  angustifolia, an-gus-tif-O-le-a, narrow-leaved.
  atalantioides, a-ta-lan-te-OY-dees; resembling *Atalantia.*
  coccinea, kok-SIN-e-a, scarlet.
  gibbsii, see *P. atalantioides.*

Pyrethrum, py-RE-thrum; from Gr. *pyr*, fire, probably fever-heat, since the plant was used in ancient medicine to assuage fevers. Rock and herbaceous perennials. *Compositae.*
  parthenium, see *Tanacetum parthenium.*
  p. aureum, see *Tanacetum parthenium.*
  roseum, see *Tanacetum coccineum.*

Pyrola, PY-ro-la; from L. *pyrus*, a Pear Tree, in reference to the shape of the leaves. Herbaceous perennials. *Ericaceae.*
  rotundifolia, ro-tun-dif-O-le-a, round-leaved.

Pyrostegia, py-row-STE-je-a; from Gr. *pyr*, fire; *stege*, a roof; in reference to the colour of the corolla. Climbers. *Bignoniaceae.*
  venusta, ven-US-ta, lovely.

Pyrrosia, py-ROW-see-a; from Gr. *pyrros*, flame red, in allusion to the colour of the fronds. Ferns. *Polypodiaceae.*
  lingua, LING-wa, a tongue – the shape of the fronds.

Pyrus, PY-russ; the Latin name for pear. Trees. *Rosaceae.*
  amygdaliformis, am-ig-dal-if-OR-mis, resembling almond.
  aria, see *Sorbus aria.*
  aucuparia, see *Sorbus aucuparia.*
  baccata, see *Malus baccata.*
  calleryana, kal-le-re-A-na, named for Joseph-Marie Callery (1810–1862), missionary and interpreter who sent specimens to France from China.
  chamaemespilus, see *Sorbus chamaemespilus*

  communis, kom-MU-nis, common, that is, in groups or communities.
  cordata, kor-DA-ta, heart shaped, the leaves. The Plymouth Pear.
  coronaria, see *Malus coronaria*
  eleyi, see *Malus × eleyi*
  floribunda, see *Malus floribunda*
  malus, see *Malus domestica*
  melanocarpa, see *Aronia melanocarpa*
  nivalis, niv-A-lis, snowy. Snow Pear.
  prunifolia, see *Malus × prunifolia*
  pulcherrima, pul-KER-rim-a, most beautiful.
  pulcherrima var. *scheideckeri*, shi-DEK-er-i, after Peter Scheidecker, of Munich, who raised it.
  pyrifolia, py-re-fo-LE-a, Pear-leaved. Asian Pear.
  sikkimensis, see *Malus sikkimensis*
  sinensis, see *Chaenomeles sinensis*
  sorbus, see *Sorbus domestica*
  spectabilis, see *Malus × spectabilis*
  torminalis, see *Sorbus torminalis*
  toringo, see *Malus toringo*
  vilmorinii, see *Sorbus vilmorinii*

Quercus, KWER-kus; Latin name for an oak tree; some authorities derive word from Celtic, quer, fine and cuez, a tree. Evergreen and deciduous trees. *Fagaceae.*
  castaneifolia, kas-tan-e-i-FO-le-a, leaves resembling *Castanea* (Chestnut).
  cerris, SER-ris, old (Latin) name for this tree. The Turkey Oak.
  coccifera, kok-SIF-er-a, coccus-bearing, here alluding to the kermes insect parasitic on this tree, and which yields a scarlet dye, hence Kermes Oak.
  coccinea, kok-SIN-e-a, scarlet – the autumnal colour of the foliage. The Scarlet Oak.
  × *hispanica*, his-PAN-ik-a, of Spain.
  ilex, I-leks, ancient Latin name for the Holm Oak, now the generic name for the hollies which some evergreen oaks resemble. The Holm, Evergreen or Holly-leaved Oak.
  kelloggii, kel-LOG-e-i, after Albert Kellogg (1813–1887), pioneer Californian botanist.
  libani, LIB-an-e, of Lebanon.
  × *lucombeana*, see *Q. × hispanica.*
  palustris, pal-US-tris, found in marshy places.
  petraea, pet-RE-a, of rocks.
  phellos, FEL-los, willow. The Willow Oak.
  pontica, PON-tik-a, Pontic, the shores of the Black Sea.
  robur, RO-ber, classical L. for oak-wood also strength or applied to solid wood.
  rubra, ROO-bra, red – the autumnal leaf colour.

suber, SU-ber, cork, old Latin name for this tree. Cork Oak.

velutina, vel-u-TE-na, velvety – young wood and buds are downy.

Quesnelia, kwes-NEL-e-a; probably Martin Quesnel, French consul to French Guiana, who travelled and collected plants in South America. Quesnel introduced the genus to Europe. Bromeliads. *Bromeliaceae.*

liboniana, lib-o-ne-A-na, of Libon, Brazil.

marmorata, mar-mor-A-ta, marbled.

Ramonda, ra-MON-da; after Louis Francis Ramond (1753–1827), a French botanist. Rock plants. *Gesneriaceae.*

myconi, MY-ko-ne, after Francisco Mico, 16th century Spanish physician and botanist.

pyrenaica, see *R. myconi.*

serbica, SER-bik-a, of Serbia.

liboniana, lib-o-ne-A-na, of Libon, Brazil.

marmorata, mar-mor-A-ta, marbled.

Ranunculus, ra-NUN-kul-us; from L. *rana*, frog, some species inhabiting marshy places where frogs abound. Herbaceous, waterside and rock plants. *Ranunculaceae.*

aconitifolius, ak-on-e-tif-O-le-us, leaves resembling *Aconitum.*

acris, AK-ris, acrid, pungent.

amplexicaulis, am-pleks-e-KAW-lis, leaves clasping the stem.

anemonoides, see *Callianthemum anemonoides.*

asiaticus, a-she-AT-ik-us, Asian. The Persian Ranunculus.

crenatus, kre-NA-tus, leaves crenated or scalloped.

glacialis, glas-e-A-lis, from Alpine glacier regions.

gramineus, gram-IN-e-us, grass leaved.

lingua, lin-GWA, tongue-like, the leaves.

lyallii, LI-al-e-i, after David Lyall (1817–1895), physician, who collected in New Zealand.

nemorosus, see *Anemone nemorosa.*

nivalis, niv-A-lis, snowy.

nyssanus, nis-SA-nus, from Nyssa.

parnassifolius, par-nas-sif-O-le-us, leaves resembling *Parnassia.*

rutifolius, see *Callianthemum angustifolium.*

Raoulia, ra-OO-le-a; after Edouard Raoul (1825–1852), French naval surgeon who wrote on New Zealand plants when in New Zealand waters. Mat-forming rock plants. *Compositae.*

australis, aws-TRA-lis, southern.

glabra, GLAB-ra, smooth, or without hairs.

subsericea, sub-ser-IS-e-a, somewhat silky.

Raphanus, RAF-an-us; classical name used by Theophrastus. Radish. *Brassicaceae.*

caudatus, kaw-DA-tus, tailed, the shape of the inflorescence. The Rat-tailed Radish.

raphanistrum, raf-an-NIS-trum; from *Raphanus*, which see; *astrum*, indicating incomplete resemblance.

raphanistrum subsp. *sativus*, SAT-iv-us, cultivated. The Radish.

Rebutia, re-BUT-e-a; after Pierre Rebut (1827–1898), French wine-grower and trader in cacti. Greenhouse cacti. *Cactaceae.*

grandiflora, see *R. minuscula.*

minuscula, min-u-SKU-la, miniature.

Rehmannia, ra-MAN-e-a; named after Joseph Rehmann (1779–1831), a Russian doctor. Greenhouse perennials. *Plantaginaceae.*

angulata, see *R. piasezkii.*

elata, e-LA-ta, tall.

henryi, HEN-re-i, after Dr. Augustine Henry (1857–1930), Irish plantsman and pioneer collector in China.

piasezkii, pe-AS-ski-i, named after P.J. Piazki, who collected in China around 1875.

Reinwardtia, rin-WARDT-e-a; after Caspar Georg Carl Reinwardt (1773–1854), Dutch botanist, founding father of Bogor Botanical Gardens Indonesia. Greenhouse flowering shrub. *Linaceae.*

indica, IN-di-ka, of India.

tetragyna, tet-RA-ji-na, four styles.

trigyna, see *R. indica.*

Reseda, re-SE-da; from L. *resedo*, to heal, or assuage, the name being given by Pliny to a species of mignonette which was believed to possess certain medicinal virtues. Hardy annuals. *Resedaceae.*

odorata, od-o-RA-ta, sweet smelling or scented. The Mignonette.

Retinispora, misapplied see below.

obtusa, see *Chamaecyparis obtusa.*

pisifera, see *Chamaecyparis pisifera.*

plumosa, see *Chamaecyparis pisifera.*

Reynoutria, rey-NU-tre-a; in honour of Charles de Saint Omer (1533–1569), Lord of Reynoutre, patron of botany. Mostly herbaceous perennials. *Polygonaceae*.

japonica, jap-ON-ik-a, of Japan. Invasive Japanese Knotweed.

sachalinensis, sak-al-in-EN-sis, of Sakhalin Island, north of Japan.

Rhamnus, RAM-nus; ancient Gr. name, possibly from Gr. *rhamnos*, name for a thorny shrub. Deciduous or evergreen trees and shrubs. *Rhamnaceae*.

alaternus, al-a-TER-nus, an old generic name of doubtful origin.

cathartica, kath-AR-tik-a, cathartic. The Buckthorn.

costata, Kos-TA-ta, leaves conspicuously ribbed.

frangula, see *Frangula alnus*.

infectoria, in-fec-TOR-e-a, yielding dye.

purshiana, see *Frangula purshiana*.

Rhaphiolepis, raf-fe-O-lep-is; from Gr. *rhaphis*, needle; *lepis*, scale, the sharply pointed bracteoles surrounding the flower. Evergreen shrubs or small trees. *Rosaceae*.

indica, IN-di-ka, of India.

ovata, o-VA-ta, egg-shaped – the leaves.

Rhapis, RAP-is; from Gr. *rhaphis*, a needle, referring to the sharply pointed leaves. Greenhouse palms. The Ground Rattan Cane. *Arecaceae*.

excelsa, eks-SEL-sa, tall.

flabelliformis, see *R. excelsa*.

humilis, HUM-il-is, low or dwarf.

Rheum, RE-um; from the Gr. *rheon*, rhubarb, from *Rha*, imported roots from Iran. Herbaceous perennials. *Polygonaceae*.

emodi, em-O-de, Emodi Montes, Himalayas in Classical Greek.

officinale, of-fis-in-A-le, of the shop (herbal).

palmatum, pal-MA-tum, leaves palmate, like a hand.

rhaponticum, ra-PON-tik-um, *Rha* of Pontus. The Culinary Rhubarb.

Rhipsalis, RIP-sa-lis; from Gr. *rhips*, a willow or wickerwork, referring to the slender interlacing branches. Greenhouse cacti. *Cactaceae*.

baccifera, bak-sif-E-ra, bearing berries.

cassytha, see *R. baccifera*.

crispata, kris-PA-ta, curled.

houlletii, HOWL-let-e-i, after M. Houllet (1811–1890), French horticulturist, Orchid collector and later head of the Jardin des Plantes, Paris.

paradoxa, pa-ra-DOKS-a, paradoxical, contrary to exception.

Rhodanthe, ro-DAN-the; from Gr. *rhodon*, a rose; *anthos*, a flower, in reference to the deep-red colour. Half-hardy annuals. *Compositae*.

chlorocephala, klo-ro-SEF-a-la, from Gr. *chloros*, green; *kephale*, a head.

chlorocephala subsp. *rosea*, RO-ze-a, rosy coloured. The Everlasting.

maculata, mak-ul-A-ta, spotted.

manglesii, mang-LES-e-i, after James Mangles (1786–1867), British naval officer, naturalist and horticulturist.

Rhodiola, ROD-e-o-la; from L. *rhodia radix*, the rosy odour and tint of the root-stocks. The Rose-root. Perennial herbs. *Crassulaceae*.

hobsonii, hob-SO-ne-i, after Herbert Elgar Hobson (1844–1922), plant collector in Tibet.

primuloides, prim-u-LOY-dees, resembling *Primula*.

rosea, RO-ze-a, rose-coloured.

rosea var. *rosea*, RO-ze-a, rose-coloured.

Rhodochiton, ro-do-KY-ton; from Gr. *rhodo*, rose; *chiton*, a cloak, the calyx is red and swollen. Greenhouse flowering climber. *Plantaginaceae*.

volubile, vol-U-bil-e, twisting round.

Rhododendron, ro-do-DEN-dron; from Gr. *rhodon*, a rose; *dendron*, a tree. Trees and shrubs. *Ericaceae*.

ambiguum, am-BIG-u-um, uncertain, possibly alluding to the indefinite colour.

amoenum, am-E-num, pleasing, lovely.

arborescens, ar-bor-ES-cenz, tree like.

arboreum, ar-bor-E-um, tree like.

augustinii, aw-gus-TE-ne-i, after Dr. Augustine Henry (1857–1930), plant collector and dendrologist.

auriculatum, aw-rik-ul-A-tum, the leaves earshaped from L. *auricula*.

× *balsaminiflorum*, bawl-SAM-in-e-FLOR-um, balsam flowered.

calendulaceum, kal-en-du-LA-se-um, resembling *Calendula* (pot marigold), the brilliant colour.

calophytum, kal-o-FY-tum, beautiful plant.

calostrotum, kal-os-TRO-tum, literally beautiful covering, presumably the silvery leaves.

campanulatum, kam-pan-u-LA-tum, bell shaped flowers.

campylocarpum, kam-pi-lo-KAR-pum, bearing curved fruit.

campylogynum, kam-pi-lo-JIN-um, the style curved.

canadense, kan-a-DEN-se, of Canada.

catawbiense, kat-aw-be-EN-se, of Catawba, U.S.A.

caucasicum, kaw-KAS-ik-um, Caucasian.

ciliatum, sil-e-A-tum, fringed with bristles – the leaves.

cinnabarinum, sin-na-bar-E-num, cinnabar-red, the flowers.

dauricum, DAW-rik-um, of Dahuria, Siberia.

decorum, dek-OR-um, shapely or becoming.

dichroanthum, dik-ro-AN-thum, with bicoloured flowers.

discolor, DIS-ko-lor, variously coloured flowers.

falconeri, fal-KON-er-i, after Hugh Falconer (1808–1865), Scottish physician and botanist, superintendent of Calcutta Botanic Gardens.

fastigiatum, fas-tij-e-A-tum, fastigiate – erect branches tapering to a point.

ferrugineum, fer-ru-JIN-e-um, rusty – the leaf underside. The Alpine Rose.

flavidum, FLA-vid-um, pale yellow.

flavum, see *R. luteum*.

glaucum, GLAW-kum, glaucous or blue-green, the underside of the leaf.

griffithianum, grif-fith-e-A-num, after William Griffith (1810–1845), British botanist, plant collector in India and Afghanistan.

haematodes, hem-a-TO-dees, blood-like – colour of the flowers.

hippophaeoides, hip-po-fa-OY-dees, resembling *Hippophae* (sea buckthorn).

impeditum, im-ped-E-tum, tangled – the twiggy branches.

indicum, IN-dik-um, Indian – the familiar evergreen planted at Magnolia Plantation, South Carolina.

intricatum, in-trik-A-tum, web-like tangled.

lapponicum, lap-PON-ik-um, of Lapland.

ledifolium, see *R. mucronatum*.

ledoides, see *R. trichostomum* var. *ledoides*.

lepidotum, lep-id-O-tum, beset with scales.

luteum, LU-te-um, yellow.

molle, MOL-le, soft or velvety – the leaves.

moupinense, moo-pin-EN-se, of Mupin, Sichuan, West China.

mucronatum, moo-kro-NA-tum, pointed.

myrtilloides, see *R. campylogynum*.

neriiflorum, ne-re-i-FLO-rum, flowers resemble *Nerium* (Oleander).

nudiflorum, nu-de-FLOR-um, naked, the flowers coming before the leaves.

oleifolium, see *R. virgatum*.

orbiculare, or-bik-ul-AR-e, orbicular or round – the leaves.

oreotrephes, or-e-o-TRE-fez, mountain dweller.

polycladum, pol-e-KLA-dum, from Gr. *poly*, many; *klados*, a branch, in reference to the many branches.

ponticum, PON-tik-um, of the south shore of the Black Sea. Invasive species.

× *praecox*, PRA-koks, early – as to flowering.

primulinum, see *R. flavidum*.

punctatum, punk-TA-tum, dotted – the leaves.

racemosum, ra-se-MO-sum, flowers in raceme-like clusters.

rhodora, ro-DOR-a, old generic name signifying rosy-red.

russatum, rus-SA-tum, reddened – the foliage.

saluenense, sal-u--e-NEN-se, from the region of the Salween River of Burma and China.

schlippenbachii, schlip-pen-BACH-e-i, after Baron Alexander von Schlippenbach (1828-?), Russian naval officer and plant collector, he collected specimens of this plant from Korea in 1854.

scintillans, see *R. polycladum*.

serpyllifolium, ser-pil-if-OL-e-um, leaves like wild thyme, *Thymus serpyllum*.

souliei, SOO-le-i, discovered by Jean André Soulié (1858–1905), French missionary and plant collector in China. Murdered in Tibet.

thomsonii, tom-SON-e-i, after Thomas Thompson (1817–1878), Scottish physician, superintendent of Calcutta Botanic Garden.

trichostomum, trik-o-STO-mum, hairy mouthed, the throat of the flower.

trichostomum var. *ledoides*, led-OY-dees, resembling *Ledum*.

vaseyi, va-ZE-i, discovered by George Vasey (1822–1893), American physician and botanist.

virgatum, ver-GA-tum, twiggy.

viscosum, vis-KO-sum, sticky or viscid.

williamsianum, wil-yamz-e-A-num, after Mr. John Charles Williams (1861–1939), of

Caerhays Castle, Cornwall, the first amateur to appreciate the value of Rhododendrons.

yunnanense, yun-nan-EN-se, of Yunnan, west China.

Rhodophiala, ro-do-FY-a-la; from Gr. *rhodon*, rose; *phiale*, broad flat container, the flowers being funnel shaped. Bulbous perennials. *Amaryllidaceae*.

pratensis, pra-TEN-sis, of meadows.

Rhodora, misapplied see below.

canadensis, see *Rhododendron canadense*.

Rhodothamnus, ro-do-THAM-nus; Gr. *rhodo*, a rose; *thamnos*, a bush or shrub, the flowers rose-coloured. Flowering shrub. *Ericaceae*.

chamaecistus, kam-e-SIS-tus; from Gr. *chamai*, on the ground; *kistos*, an old generic name of misleading application. Ericaceous dwarf shrub.

Rhodotypos, ro-DO-tip-os; from Gr. *rhodon*, a rose; *typos*, type. The flowers suggesting a rose. Shrub. *Rosaceae*.

kerrioides, see *R. scandens*.

scandens, SKAN-denz, climbing.

Rhoeo, misapplied see below.

discolor, see *Tradescantia spathacea*.

Rhus, roos; from Gr. *rhous*, ancient name for the plant. Foliage shrubs with milky or resinous juice. Trees and shrubs. *Anacardiaceae*.

coppallinum, kop-al-LE-num, yielding copal (lacquer).

cotinoides, see *Cotinus obovatus*.

cotinus, see *Cotinus coggygria*.

glabra, GLAB-ra, smooth, destitute of hairs.

toxicodendron, see *Toxicodendron pubescens*.

typhina, TY-fe-na, the branches shaped like antlers. The Stag's Horn Sumach.

vernicifera, see *Toxicodendron verniciferum*.

Rhyncholaelia, rin-ko-LAY-le-a; from Gr. *rhyncos*, a beak and the genus *Laelia*. Orchids. *Orchidaceae*.

digbyana, dig-by-AN-a, sent in 1845 from British Honduras to Edward St. Vincent Digby (1809–1889), with whom it flowered in 1846.

Rhynchospermum, rin-kos-PER-mum; from Gr. *rhynchos*, a beak; *sperma*, a seed. Greenhouse climber. *Compositae*.

jasminoides, see *Trachelospermum jasminoides*.

Rhynchostele, rin-kos-TE-le; from Gr. *rhynchos*, beak; *stele*, pillar, possibly alluding to beak-like extension over the anther. Orchids. *Orchidaceae*.

bictoniensis, bik-ton-e-EN-sis, of Bicton Park Botanical Gardens, Devon.

cervantesii, ser-van-TE-see-i, after Cervantes.

rossii, ross-E-i, named for Sir John Ross (1777–1856), British naval officer and Arctic explorer, who collected orchids whilst in Mexico in 1830.

Rhynchostylis, rin-kos-TIE-lis; from Gr. *rhynchos*, beak; *stylos*, column, referring to the appearance of the type species flower column. Foxtail Orchids. *Orchidaceae*.

gigantea, ji-GAN-te-a, unusually tall or big.

retusa, re-TEW-sa, a rounded leaf with a slight notch to the tip.

Ribes, RY-bees; origin uncertain, possibly from Arabic *Ribas*, an acid plant used by Arabian physicians and known to science as *Rheum ribes*. Flowering and fruiting shrubs. *Grossulariaceae*.

aureum, AW-re-um, golden – the flowers.

grossularia, see *R. uva-crispa*.

nigrum, NI-grum, black – the fruit. The Black Currant.

rubrum, ROO-brum, red. The Red Currant.

sanguineum, san-GWIN-e-um, blood red, the flowers.

speciosum, spes-e-O-sum, showy. The Fuchsia Currant.

uva-crispa, u-va-KRIS-pa, curled bunch of grapes. The Gooseberry.

vulgare, see *R. rubrum*.

v. album, see *R. rubrum*.

viburnifolium, vi-bur-nif-O-le-um, resembling *Viburnum* leaves.

Riccia, RICH-e-a; after Pietro Francisco Ricci, a florentine botanist. Greenhouse floating cryptogamic plants known as Crystalworts. *Ricciaceae*.

fluitans, FLU-it-anz, floating.

Richardia, rik-AR-de-a; named after Richard Richardson (1663–1741), English physician. Greenhouse herbaceous perennials. *Rubiaceae*.

aethiopica, see *Zantedeschia aethiopica*.
africana, see *Zantedeschia aethiopica*.
albomaculata, see *Zantedeschia albomaculata*.
elliottiana, see *Zantedeschia elliottiana*.
pentlandii, see *Zantedeschia pentlandii*.
rehmannii, see *Zantedeschia rehmannii*.

Ricinus, RIS-in-us; classical L. name, possibly from L. *ricinus*, a tick or bug which the seed resembles. Foliage plants. *Euphorbiaceae*.

communis, kom-MU-nis, common or social. The Castor Oil Plant.

Rimaria, misapplied see below.
heathii, see *Gibbaeum heathii*.
roodiae, see *Vanheerdea roodiae*.

Rivina, riv-EE-na; after A.Q. Rivinus (1652–1723), professor of botany at Leipzig. Warm house fruiting shrub. *Phytolaccaceae*.
humilis, HUM-il-is, low or dwarf.

Robinia, rob-IN-e-a; named after Jean Robin (1550–1629), a French botanist and herbalist to Henry IV of France. Shrubs and trees. *Leguminosae*.

hispida, HIS-pid-a, bristly.
hispida var. *kelseyi*, kel-SE-i, after Harlan P. Kelsey (1872–1958), American nurseryman who introduced it in 1901.
inermis, in-ER-mis, unarmed, that is, not thorny. The Mop-headed Acacia.
pseudoacacia, SUE-da-a-KA-she-a; false *Acacia*.
viscosa, vis-KO-sa, viscid or gummy.

Rochea, RO-she-a; named after Daniel de la Roche (1743–1812), Swiss physician. Greenhouse succulents. *Crassulaceae*.
coccinea, see *Crassula coccinea*.
falcata, fal-KA-ta, sickle-shaped – the leaves.
jasminea, see *Crassula obtusa*.

Rodgersia, rod-JER-se-a; named after Admiral Rodgers (1812–1882), USA naval officer who commanded the expedition in which *R. podophylla* was discovered. Hardy perennials. *Saxifragaceae*.

aesculifolia, es-ku-le-FO-le-a; *Aesculus* (Horse-chestnut) leaved.
pinnata, pin-NA-ta, pinnated – the divided leaves.
podophylla, pod-o-FIL-la, foot-stalked leaves.
sambucifolia, sam-bu-kif-O-le-a, *Sambucus* (Elder) leaved.
tabularis, see *Astilboides tabularis*.

Roella, ro-EL-la; in honour of Willem Roelle (1700–1775), professor of anatomy Amsterdam, curator of the Hortus Amsterdam, who sent seeds of this plant, amongst others to Linnaeus. Greenhouse flowering shrubs. *Campanulaceae*.
ciliata, sil-e-A-ta, an eyelash, fringed with hair.
elegans, EL-e-ganz, elegant.

Romneya, ROM-ne-a; after Rev. John Thomas Romney Robinson (1792–1882), Irish astronomer and friend of Coulter. Sub-shrubby perennials. *Papaveraceae*.
coulteri, KOLE-ter-i, after Thomas Coulter (1793–1843), Irish physician and botanist. Coulter undertook botanical explorations in Mexico and California.
trichocalyx, trik-O-ka-liks, hairy-calyxed.

Romulea, rom-U-le-a; named after Romulus, the founder of Rome. Half-hardy bulbs. *Iridaceae*.
bulbocodium, bul-bo-KO-de-um, from L. *bulbus*, a globular root (bulb); *kodion*, wool, with which the bulbs are covered.

Rondeletia, RON-del-EE-te-a; after Guillaume Rondelet (1507–1566), French physician and author. Warm-house flowering shrubs. *Rubiaceae*.
odorata, od-o-RA-ta, sweet smelling.
speciosa, see *R. odorata*.

Rosa, RO-za; the ancient Latin name for the Rose, perhaps from Celtic *rhod*, red. Experts claim the Latins pronounced the word ROS-a – short 'o'. Flowering shrubs. *Rosaceae*.
acicularis, a-sik-ul-AR-is, needle-shaped, the thorns.
alba, AL-ba, from the L. *alba*, white, the flowers.
alpina, see *R. pendulina*.
arvensis, ar-VEN-sis, growing in cultivated fields.

banksiae, BANKS-se-e, named for Lady Banks (1758–1828), The Banksian Rose.

bracteata, brak-te-A-ta, having bracts, or modified leaves, at bases of leaf stalks.

californica, kal-if-OR-nik-a, of California.

canina, kan-I-na, dog, probably signifying common or worthless, that is, scentless. The Dog Rose.

carolina, ka-ro-LI-na, from Carolina, USA.

centifolia, sen- (or Ken-) tif-O-le-a, hundred-leaved in reference to the numerous petals. The Cabbage Rose.

cinnamomea, see *R. majalis*.

× *damascena*, dam-as-SE-na, damask. *R. gallica* × *R. moschata*. The Damask Rose.

ecae, EK-e, adapted from "E.C.A." Mrs Aitchison's initials, her husband having introduced the species.

ferox, FE-roks, from L. *ferox*, fierce, very prickly.

foetida, FET-id-a, bad-smelling.

gallica, GAL-ik-a, French.

glauca, GLAW-ka, sea-green, the foliage.

hugonis, see *R. xanthina*.

humilis, HUM-il-is, low or dwarf.

indica, IN-dik-a, the Chinese Rose probably brought back by the East India Company.

laevigata, lev-ig-GA-ta, smooth, the leaves.

luciae, LU-se-e, after Lucy Savatier, wife of Paul Amédée Ludovic Savatier.

lucida, LU-sid-a, shining or bright the glossy foliage.

lutea, see *R. foetida*.

macrophylla, mak-rof-IL-a, with large leaves.

majalis, maj-A-lis, May – the time of flowering.

microphylla, see *R. roxburghii* f. *normalis*.

moschata, mos-KA-ta, musk.

moyesii, moy-EEZ-e-i, after Rev. James Moyes of the China Inland Mission.

multiflora, mul-tif-LO-ra, many flowered.

nitida, NIT-id-a, shining – the leaves.

× *noisettiana*, noy-set-te-A-na, after M. Louis Claude Noisette (1772–1849), French botanist, nurseryman and specialist rose grower.

nutkana, nut-KA-na, takes its name from the Nuu-chah-nulth people.

pendulina, pen-du-LE-na, drooping.

polyantha, see *R. multiflora*.

pomifera, see *R. villosa*.

roxburghii, roks-burg-E-i, after William Roxburgh (1751–1815), Scottish physician and botanist, working predominantly in India.

roxburghii f. *normalis*, NOR-ma-lis, in conformity with rule.

rubiginosa, roo-be-gin- (or jin-)O-sa, rusty – the foliage. The Sweet Briar.

rubrifolia, see *R. glauca*.

rugosa, roo-GO-sa, wrinkled, the leaves.

sericea, ser-IS-e-a, silky – the leaves.

setigera, set-IJ-er-a, bearing bristles.

sicula, SIK-ul-a, of Sicily, whence it comes.

spinosissima, spin-no-SIS-sim-a, most spiny. The Burnet or Scotch Rose.

tomentosa, to-men-TO-sa, downy foliage.

villosa, vil-LO-sa, shaggy, hairy.

wichuraiana, see *R. luciae*.

xanthina, zan-THE-na, from Gr. *xanthos*, yellow.

Roscoea, ros-KO-e-a; after William Roscoe (1753–1831), founder of Liverpool Botanic Garden. Hardy perennials. *Zingiberaceae*.

cautleyoides, kawt-le-OY-dees, resembling *Cautlea*.

humeana, hu-m-e-AN-a, in honour of David Hume – gardener at RBG Edinburgh who died in WW1.

Rosmarinus, ros-mar-E-nus; from L. *ros*, dew (spray); *marinus*, sea. Often inhabiting sea-cliffs in Southern Europe. Woody shrub. *Lamiaceae*.

officinalis, of-fis-in-A-lis, of the shop (apothecary's), applied to plants always kept "in stock" by herbalists.

Rossioglossum, ross-e-o-GLOS-sum; named for Sir John Ross (1777–1856), British naval officer and Arctic explorer, who collected orchids whilst in Mexico in 1830. Orchids. *Orchidaceae*.

grande, GRAN-de, magnificent.

Rosularia, ros-u-LAR-e-a; forming rosettes. Succulents and rock plants. *Crassulaceae*.

sempervivoides, sem-per-viv-OY-dees, resembling *Sempervivum*.

Rubus, ROO-bus; old Roman name, probably derived from L. *ruber*, red, the colour of the fruits of many species. Climbing or trailing and upright – stemmed shrubby plants; fruiting and ornamental. *Rosaceae*.

biflorus, bif-LO-rus, two-flowered.

cockburnianus, kok-burn-e-A-nus, in recognition of the Cockburn family who resided in China.

deliciosus, de-lis-e-O-sus, delicious – referring to the beauty of the blossoms.

fruticosus, frut-ik-O-sus, shrubby. The Blackberry.

giraldianus, see *R. cockburnianus*.

idaeus, id-A-us, of Mount Ida. The Raspberry.

laciniatus, las-in-e-A-tus, leaves jagged or deeply cut. The Parsley-leaved Bramble.

loganobaccus, lo-GAN-o-BAK-kus. after Judge James Harvey Logan (1841–1928). The Loganberry.

nutkanus, see *R. parviflorus*.

odoratus, od-o-RA-tus, sweet smelling.

parviflorus, par-vif-LOR-us, from L. *parvus*, small; *flor*, flower.

phoenicolasius, fen-IK-ol-AS-e-us, purple-haired – the stems. The Wineberry.

rosifolius, ro-za-FOL-e-us, rose-leaved.

thibetanus, the-bet-A-nus, of Tibet.

Rudbeckia, rood-BEK-e-a; named after Olof Rudbeck (1630–1702), a Swedish botanist, founder of Uppsala Botanic Garden. Herbaceous perennials. *Compositae*.

californica, kal-if-OR-nik-a, of California.

hirta, HER-ta, hairy.

laciniata, las-in-e-A-ta, slashed or torn into narrow divisions.

maxima, MAKS-im-a, greatest.

newmani, NEW-man-e, after Newman.

pinnata, pin-NA-ta, pinnated – the divided leaves.

purpurea, see *Echinacea purpurea*.

speciosa, spes-e-O-sa, showy.

Ruellia, roo-EL-le-a; after Jean de la Ruelle (1474–1537), botanist and physician to Francis I of France. Warm-house flowering shrub. *Acanthaceae*.

macrantha, mak-RANTH-a, large-flowered.

Rumex, ROO-meks; old Latin name for a kind of sorrel, from L. *rumo*, to suck, from the habit of Romans sucking sorrel leaves to allay thirst. Border and aquatic perennials. *Polygonaceae*.

acetosa, as- (or ak-) et-O-sa, acid. The Garden Sorrel.

hydrolapathum, hid-rol-a-PATH-um, growing in water. The Water Dock.

patientia, pat-e-EN-te-a, patience. The Herb Patience.

scutatus, skew-TA-tus, resembling a shield. The French Sorrel.

Ruscus, RUS-kus; said to be a corruption of *bruscus*, the old herbalists' name for Butcher's Broom; possibly from Celtic *brus*, a box; *kelen*, holly, hence the name Box Holly. Evergreen shrubby plants. *Asparagaceae*.

aculeatus, ak-u-le-A-tus, prickly.

hypoglossum, hi-po-GLOS-sum, literally under tongue, in reference to the leaf-like bract on the underside.

Russelia, rus-SEL-e-a; named after Alexander Russell (1715–1768), Scottish physician and traveller. Greenhouse evergreens. *Plantaginaceae*.

equisetiformis, ek-we-se-te-FOR-mis, resembling Equisetum.

juncea, see *R. equisetiformis*.

sarmentosa, sar-men-TO-za, bearing runners.

Ruta, ROO-ta; ancient name for Rue, from L. *ruta*, from Gr. *ryte*, unpleasant or bitterness. *Rutaceae*.

graveolens, GRAV-e-ol-enz, strong smelling. Rue.

Sabatia, sab-A-te-a; after Liberato Sabbati (1714–1779), Italian botanist and gardener, Keeper of the botanical garden in Rome. Biennials. *Gentianaceae*.

campestris, kam-PES-tris, growing in fields.

Saccharum, SAK-ka-rum; from Gr. *sakcharon*, sugar. Tropical Grass. *Poaceae*.

officinarum, of-fis-in-AR-um, of the shops or economic. The Sugar Cane.

Saccolabium, sak-ko-LA-be-um; from L. *saccus*, a bag; *labium*, a lip, the labellum or lip is like a bag. Tropical orchids. *Orchidaceae*.

ampullaceum, see *Ascocentrum ampullaceum*.

blumei, see *Rhynchostylis retusa*.

giganteum, see *Rhynchostylis gigantea*.

Sagina, sa-GE-na; ancient name of spurrey, meaning fodder, which was originally regarded as a species of this genus. Pearlwort. Carpet bedding plants. *Caryophyllaceae*.

boydii, see *S. procumbens*.

glabra, GLAB-ra, smooth – the leaves.

pilifera, pil-IF-er-a, bearing hair.

procumbens, pro-CUM-benz, procumbent, growing along the ground without rooting.

Sagittaria, saj-it-TAIR-e-a; from L. *sagitta*, an arrow, in reference to the arrowhead form of the leaves in some species. Aquatics. *Alismataceae*.

latifolia, lat-if-O-le-a, broad-leaved.

montevidensis, mon-tev-e-DEN-sis; of Montevideo.

sagittifolia, saj-it-tif-O-le-a, arrow-leaved. The Arrowhead.

variabilis, see *S. latifolia*.

Saintpaulia, saint-PAW-le-a; after Baron Walter von Saint Paul-Ilaire (1860–1940), German district commissioner in Tanganyika, who discovered *S. ionantha*. Warmhouse perennial. *Gesneriaceae*.

ionantha, i-on-AN-tha, violet-flowered.

Salix, SA-liks; Latin name for willow, possibly from Celtic, *sal*, near; *lis*, water. Trees and shrubs. *Salicaceae*.

alba, AL-ba, from the L. *alba*, white.

alba var. *caerulea*, se-RU-le-a, blue, underparts of the leaves. The Bat Willow.

alba var. *vitellina*, vit-el-LE-na, orange-yellow – the twigs.

arbuscula, ar-BUS-ku-la, a small tree or shrub.

babylonica, bab-e-LON-ik-a, Babylonian. The Weeping Willow. Though not a native of Babylon, it is accepted that this tree was introduced to England (1692) from Asia Minor.

caprea, KAP-re-a, a goat. The Goat Willow.

cinerea, sin-er-E-a, ash-coloured.

eleagnos, el-e-AG-nos, resembling olive, the leaves.

× *fragilis*, FRAJ-il-is, brittle, hence Crack Willow.

herbacea, her-BA-se-a, herbaceous.

incana, see *S. eleagnos*.

lanata, lan-A-ta, woolly-leaves and young wood.

pentandra, pent-AN-dra, five-stamened.

repens, RE-penz, creeping.

retusa, re-TEW-sa, a rounded leaf with a slight notch to the tip.

viminalis, vim-e-NA-lis, slender or twiggy. The Osier.

Salpiglossis, sal-pe-GLOS-sis; from Gr. *salpinx*, a tube; *glossa*, a tongue, refers to the style in the tube of the corolla. Tender annual. *Solanaceae*.

sinuata, sin-u-A-ta, having a deeply waved leaf margin. The Scalloped Tube-Tongue.

Salvia, SAL-ve-a; from L. name used by Pliny, derived from L. *salvus*, meaning safe, unharmed, referring to the medicinal properties. Shrubs and herbaceous perennials. *Lamiaceae*.

argentea, ar-JEN-te-a, silvery, the foliage.

azurea, a-ZOR-e-a, Sky-blue, azure.

barrelieri, bah-rel-E-er-i, after Jacques Barrelier (1606–1673), French botanist and Dominican monk.

canescens, kan-ES-senz, more or less grey or hoary.

carduacea, kar-du-A-se-a, thistle-like.

coccinea, kok-SIN-e-a, scarlet.

dichroa, see *S. barrelieri*.

elegans, EL-e-ganz, elegant.

farinacea, far-in-A-se-a, mealy.

glutinosa, glu-tin-O-sa, sticky.

grahamii, see *S. microphylla*.

heerii, hee-RE-i, after Oswald Heer (1809–1883), Swiss geologist and naturalist, professor of botany at Zurich.

horminum, see *S. viridis*.

involucrata, in-vol-u-KRA-ta, from L. *involucrum*, roll in, envelop.

microphylla, mi-krof-IL-la, small leaved.

officinalis, of-fis-in-A-lis, of the shop (apothecary's), applied to plants always kept "in stock" by herbalists.

patens, PA-tenz, spreading.

pitcheri, see *S. azurea*.

rutilans, see *S. elegans*.

sclarea, SKLAR-e-a, clary, old name for sage, L. word meaning clear – its use in eye lotions.

splendens, SPLEN-denz, splendid.

turkestanica, see *S. sclarea*.

uliginosa, u-lij-in-O-sa, growing in swamps.

virgata, vir-GA-ta, with willowy twigs.

viridis, VIR-id-is, green.

Salvinia, sal-VIN-e-a; after Antonio Salvini (1653–1729), professor of Greek at Florence. Greenhouse aquatics. *Salviniaceae*.

auriculata, aw-rik-ul-A-ta, with an ear-shaped appendage.

natans, NA-tanz, floating.

Sambucus, sam-BU-kus; ancient Latin name of elder, said to be derived from L. *sambuca*, the name of a musical instrument which was made of Elder wood. Foliage and fruiting shrubs. *Adoxaceae*.

nigra, NY-gra, black – the fruits. The Elder.

racemosa, ras-em-O-sa, resembling a raceme.

Samolus, SA-mo-lus; name used by Pliny; several derivations suggested; possibly from Celtic, *san*, health; *mos*, a pig, alluding to its value as a food for pigs. Herbaceous perennial. *Primulaceae*.
repens, RE-penz, creeping.

Sanchezia, san-KE-ze-a; in honour of José Sanchez (d.1797), professor of botany at the College of Surgery, Cadiz; formerly at the Royal Botanical Gardens, Madrid. Perennial herbs. *Acanthaceae*.
nobilis, NO-bil-is, large or noble, of fine appearance.

Sanguinaria, san-gwin-AIR-e-a; from L. *sanguis*, blood, the sap being a red colour. Tuberous perennials. *Papaveraceae*.
canadensis, kan-a-DEN-sis, of Canada. The Bloodroot.

Sanguisorba, san-gwe-SOR-ba; from L. *sanguis*, blood; *sorbeo*, to soak, in allusion to the styptic qualities of the root, an infusion of which was used to prevent bleeding. Herbaceous perennials and small shrubs. *Rosaceae*.
canadensis, kan-a-DEN-sis, of Canada.
minor, MY-nor, dwarf.
obtusa, ob-TU-sa, blunt.

Sansevieria, san-se-VEER-e-a; after Raimondo di Sangro (1710–1771), Prince of San Severo and patron of horticulture. Greenhouse and room foliage plants. Bowstring Hemp. *Asparagaceae*.
cylindrica, sil-IN-drik-a, cylindrical.
guineensis, see *S. hyacinthoides*.
hyacinthoides, hy-a-sinth-OY-dees, resembling *Hyacinthus* (hyacinth).
trifasciata, tri-fas-see-A-ta, three-banded.
zeylanica, zey-LAN-ik-a, of Sri Lanka (formerly known as Ceylon).

Santolina, san-tol-E-na; from L. *sanctum linum*, holy flax, a Pre-Linnaean name for *S. virens*. Aromatic shrubs. *Compositae*.
chamaecyparissus, kam-e-sip-ar-IS-sus, an old name meaning ground cypress.
decumbens, de-KUM-benz, prostrate.
incana, see *S. decumbens*.
virens, VY-renz, green. The Cotton Lavender.

viridis, VIR-id-is, green, in comparison to the other species.

Sanvitalia, san-vit-A-le-a; after the Italian house of Sanvitali, of Parma. Hardy annual. *Compositae*.
procumbens, pro-CUM-benz, procumbent, growing along the ground without rooting.

Saponaria, sap-on-AIR-e-a; from L. *sapo*, soap, the bruised leaves of *S. officinalis* producing a lather, once used as a soap substitute. Annuals and herbaceous perennials. *Caryophyllaceae*.
caespitosa, ses-pit-O-sa, growing in tufts.
calabrica, kal-AB-rik-a, of Calabria.
ocymoides, o-sim-OY-dees, resembling *Ocymum*.
officinalis, of-fis-in-A-lis, of the shop (apothecary's), applied to plants always kept "in stock" by herbalists.
pulvinaris, pul-vin-AR-is, cushioned.
vaccaria, see *Vaccaria hispanica*.

Sarcococca, sar-ko-KOK-ka; from Gr. *sarx*, flesh; *kokkos*, a berry, the fruits being fleshy. Shrubs. *Buxaceae*.
confusa, kon-FU-sa, uncertain.
hookeriana, see *S. pruniformis*.
pruniformis, pru-ne-FOR-mis, from L. *prunus*, plum; *formis*, having the form of.
ruscifolia, rus-ke-FO-le-a, leaves resembling *Ruscus*.
saligna, see *S. pruniformis*.

Saribus, sa-RE-bus; native Indonesian name, possibly from *sariboe*, one thousand, in reference to the many spines which look like shark's teeth. Greenhouse Palms. *Arecaceae*.
rotundifolius, ro-tun-dif-O-le-us, round-leaved.

Sarmienta, sar-me-EN-ta; dedicated to Martín Sarmiento (1695–1772), Spanish scholar and Benedictine monk, whose writings included botany. Greenhouse trailer. *Gesneriaceae*.
repens, RE-penz, creeping.

Sarracenia, sar-ra-SE-ne-a; after Michel Sarrasin (1659–1734), a physician of Quebec, who sent the plants to Tournefort. Carnivorous perennial herbs. *Sarraceniaceae*.

drummondii, drum-MON-de-i, in honour of Thomas Drummond (1780–1835), who collected across North America.

flava, FLA-va, yellow.

purpurea, pur-PUR-e-a, purple coloured.

variolaris, var-e-o-LAR-is, pimpled.

Sasa, SA-sa; the Japanese name for dwarf bamboo. Bamboo. *Poaceae*.

palmata, pal-MA-ta, palmate, like a hand – the leaves.

veitchii, VEECH-e-i, introduced from Japan by Charles Maries (1851–1902), plant collector, who collected for the James Veitch & Sons Nursery.

Satureja, sat-u-RE-ja; old Latin name for savory, possibly from the Arabic *sattar*, a name applied to labiates in general. Herbs. *Lamiaceae*.

hortensis, hor-TEN-sis, belonging to gardens.

montana, mon-TA-na, of mountains.

Satyrium, sat-ER-e-um; from an old Gr. *satyrion*, orchid; from their connection to the satyrs. Orchids. *Orchidaceae*.

carneum, KAR-ne-um, flesh-coloured.

coriifolium, kor-e-if-OL-e-um, resembling *Correa* leaves.

Sauromatum, saw-ROM-a-tum; from Gr. *sauros*, lizard, in reference to the spotted spathe. Tuberous perennial. *Araceae*.

guttatum, see *S. venosum*.

venosum, ve-NO-sum, veined.

Saururus, sau-RU-rus; from Gr. *sauros*, a lizard; *oura*, a tail – the form suggested by the inflorescence. Aquatics. *Saururaceae*.

cernuus, SER-nu-us, nodding or drooping – the flowers. The Lizard's Tail.

chinensis, tshi-NEN-sis, of China.

Saussurea, saus-SU-re-a; in honour of Swiss father and son H.B. de Saussure (1740–1799), philosopher and naturalist, and N.T. de Saussure (1767–1845), botanist and chemist. Herbaceous perennials. *Compositae*.

alpina, al-PINE-a (or al-PIN-a), of the Alps or alpine.

pygmaea, PIG-me-a, dwarf.

Saxegothaea, saks-GO-the-a; named in honour of Prince Albert (1819–1861), consort of Queen Victoria, who was Prince of Saxe-Coburg and Gotha. Conifers. Prince Albert's Yew. *Podocarpaceae*.

conspicua, kon-SPIK-u-a, conspicuous or remarkable.

Saxifraga, sax-e-FRA-ga; from L. *saxum*, a rock (or stone); *frango*, to break; the belief being its capability of breaking rock as it grew in crevices. Annuals and herbaceous perennials. *Saxifragaceae*.

aizoides, ay-ZOY-dees, resembling *Aizoon*.

aizoon, see *S. paniculata*.

altissima, see *S. hostii*.

× *andrewsii*, AN-drews-e-i, after William Andrews (1802–1880), Irish plant collector, noted for his work on *Saxifraga*.

aretioides, ar-et-e-OY-dees, resembling *Aretia*.

aspera, AS-per-a, rough that is the leaves.

biflora, bif-LO-ra, two-flowered, that is, in pairs.

burseriana, bur-sir-e-A-na, commemorating Joachim Burser (1583–1639), German physician and botanist.

caesia, SE-se-a, grey-leaved.

callosa, kal-LO-sa, calloused, with a thick skin.

ceratophylla, see *S. trifurcata*.

cernua, SER-nu-a, drooping – the flowers.

cespitosa, ses-pit-O-sa, growing in tufts.

cochlearis, kok-le-AR-is, shell-like – the foliage.

cordifolia, see *Bergenia crassifolia*.

cortusifolia, see *S. serotina*.

cotyledon, kot-e-LE-don, old name meaning cupshaped (leaf), usually applied to the lobe of a seed.

crassifolia, see *Bergenia crassifolia*.

crustata, krus-TA-ta, encrusted, with silvery scales.

cuneata, ku-ne-A-ta, wedge-shaped, the leaves.

cuneifolia, ku-ne-i-FO-le-a, wedge-leaved.

cymbalaria, sim-bal-AR-e-a, old generic name from L. *cymbalum*, cymbal, in reference to the leaf shape.

diapensioides, di-a-pen-se-OY-dees, resembling *Diapensia*, a very small Lapland shrub.

exarata, ex-a-RA-ta, furrowed.

exarata subsp. *moschata*, mos-KA-ta, musky.

federici-augusti, fred-er-E-ki-aw-GUS-ti, in honour of Frederick Augustus I of Saxony (1750–1827), King of Saxony.

federici-augusti subsp. *grisebachii*, grise-BACH-e-i, after August Heinrich Rudolf Grisebach

(1814–1879), professor of botany at Göttingen.

ferdinandi-coburgi, fer-din-AN-di-KO-bur-gi, in honour of Prince Ferdinand Georg August of Saxe-Coburg and Gotha (1785–1851).

florulenta, flor-u-LEN-ta, full of flower.

fortunei, for-TOO-ne-i, after Robert Fortune (1812–1880), Scottish plant collector in China.

fragilis, FRAJ-il-is, fragile.

fragilis subsp. *paniculata*, pan-ik-ul-A-ta, panicled.

geranioides, jer-a-ne-OY-dees, resembling *Geranium*.

× *geum*, JE-um, to stimulate (ancient medicine).

globulifera, glob-ul-IF-er-a, globe bearing, the gem-buds being a distinctive feature.

granulata, gran-u-LA-ta, granulated – the small grain-like root tubers.

grisebachii, see *S. federici-augusti* subsp. *grisebachii*.

hostii, HOST-e-i, after Nicholas Thomas Host (1761–1834), botanist and physician to the Emperor of Austria.

hypnoides, hip-NOY-dees, moss-like.

imbricata, see *S. retusa*.

incrustata, see *S. crustata*.

juniperifolia, jew-nip-er-if-O-le-a, leaves resembling *Juniperus* (juniper).

laevis, see *S. pseudolaevis*.

ligulata, see *S. stolonifera*.

lingulata, see *S. callosa*.

longifolia, long-if-OL-e-a, long leaves.

marginata, mar-jin-A-ta, the leaves margined with white.

maweana, maw-e-A-na, after George Maw (1832–1912), plant collector.

media, ME-de-a, medium, in allusion to the altitude of the plant's natural range, or its stature.

moschata, see *S. exarata* subsp. *moschata*.

muscoides, mus-KOY-dees, fly-like.

nivalis, niv-A-lis, snowy.

oppositifolia, op-pos-it-if-O-le-a, leaves opposite.

paniculata, pan-ik-ul-A-ta, panicled.

pedemontana, ped-e-mon-TA-na, from Piedmont.

peltata, see *Darmera peltata*.

pseudolaevis, sued-o-LE-vis, from Gr. *pseudo*, false; *laevis*, smooth.

purpurascens, see *Bergenia purpurascens*.

retusa, re-TEW-sa, a rounded leaf with a slight notch to the tip.

rotundifolia, ro-tun-dif-O-le-a, round-leaved.

sancta, SANG-ta, sacred, holy; application obscure.

sarmentosa, see *S. stolonifera*.

serotina, ser-o-TIN-a, late in starting spring growth.

sibthorpii, sib-THORP-e-i, after John Sibthorp (1758–1796), professor of botany at Oxford.

spathulata, see *S. hypnoides*.

squarrosa, skwar-RO-sa, scales projecting outwards – the foliage.

stellaris, stel-LAR-is, starry – the flowers.

stolonifera, sto-lon-IF-er-a, having stolons, or rooted runners.

stracheyi, see *Bergenia stracheyi*.

taygetea, tay-GE-te-a, from Taygetus a mountain range in Southern Greece.

tellimoides, see *Peltoboykinia tellimoides*.

tenella, ten-EL-la, delicate, fine in texture.

tombeanensis, tom-be-an-EN-sis, of Tombea, Italy.

tricuspidata, try-kusp-e-DA-ta, three-toothed, the leaf lobes.

trifurcata, try-fur-KA-ta, three forked, the divisions of the leaves.

umbrosa, um-BRO-za, shade-loving.

valdensis, val-DEN-sis, from Mount Baldo, Northern Italy.

valentina, see *S. fragilis* subsp. *paniculata*.

vandellii, van-DEL-le-i, after Domingo Vandelli (1735–1816), Portuguese botanist.

Scabiosa, skay-be-O-sa; from L. *scabies*, itch, the plant once being regarded as a remedy for skin diseases. Annual and perennial herbs. Pincushion Flower. *Caprifoliaceae*.

atropurpurea, atro-pur-PUR-e-a, deep purple.

caucasica, see *Lomelosia caucasica*.

columbaria, kol-um-BAR-e-a, old name meaning dove-coloured.

ochroleuca, OK-ro-LOO-ka, yellowish white.

pterocephala, see *Pterocephalus perennis*.

Scadoxus, sca-DOKS-us; from Gr. *scadion*, umbel; *doxa*, glory. Bulbs and rhizomatous herbs. *Amaryllidaceae*.

multiflorus, mul-tif-LO-rus, many flowered.

multiflorus subsp. *katharinae*, kath-ar-EE-ne, collected by Katherine Saunders (1824–1901), English born plant collector and botanical illustrator in Natal, South Africa.

puniceus, pu-NIK-e-us, reddish-purple.

Schaueria, show-ER-e-a; in honour of Johannes Conrad Schauer (1813–1848),

German botanist, professor of botany at Greifswald. Perennial herbs and subshrubs. *Acanthaceae.*

calicotricha, kal-ik-O-trik-a, beautiful haired.

Schefflera, shef-LER-a; for Johann Peter Ernst von Scheffler (1739–1809), German physician and botanist from Danzig, who contributed plants to Reyger's *Florae Gedanensis.* Tree, shrubs, subshrubs and vines. *Araliaceae.*

elegantissima, el-e-gan-TIS-sim-a, most elegant.

veitchii, VEECH-e-i, introduced, in 1866, by John Gould Veitch (1839–1870), plant collector.

Schellolepis, skell-lo-LEP-is; from Gr. *schello*, skeleton; *lepis*, scale; the character of the scale surrounding the sori. Ferns. *Polypodiaceae.*

subauriculata, sub-aw-rik-ul-A-ta, rather ear-shaped.

Schivereckia, shiv-er-EK-e-a; after Suibart Burchard Schivereck (1742–1806), professor of botany at the University of Lemberg. Rock Plants. *Brassicaceae.*

podolica, pod-OL-ik-a, of Podolia, South West Russia.

Schisandra, ski-ZAN-dra; from Gr. *schizo*, to cut; *aner*, a man; in reference to the split stamens. Twining shrubs. *Schisandraceae.*

chinensis, tshi-NEN-sis, of China.

Schizanthus, skiz-AN-thus; from Gr. *schizo*, to cut; *anthos*, a flower, the petals deeply fringed. Greenhouse annuals. *Solanaceae.*

grahamii, GRA-am-e-i, after Robert Graham (1786–1845), Scottish physician and botanist a founding father of Glasgow Botanic Garden.

pinnatus, pin-NA-tus, foliage pinnate the best known species.

retusus, see *S. grahamii.*

wisetonensis, wis-ton-EN-sis, of Wiseton Hall, Nottinghamshire seat of Joseph Frederick Laycock.

Schizocodon, skiz-ok-O-don; from Gr. *schizo*, to cut; *codon*, a bell, the bell-shaped flowers being deeply cut or fringed. Rock or woodland plant. *Diapensiaceae.*

soldanelloides, sol-dan-el-LOY-dees, resembling *Soldanella.*

Schizopetalon, skiz-o-PET-a-lon; from Gr. *schizo*, to cut; *petalon*, a petal, the fringed flowers. Annual. *Brassicaceae.*

walkeri, WAW-ker-i, after John Walker, who sent seed back from Chile.

Schizophragma, skiz-o-FRAG-ma; from Gr. *schizo*, to cut; *phragma*, wall of an enclosure, in reference to the curious splitting of the seed capsules. Shrubs. *Hydrangeaceae.*

hydrangeoides, hy-dran-je-OY-dees, resembling *Hydrangea.*

Schizostylis, misapplied see below.

coccinea, see *Hesperantha coccinea.*

Schlumbergera, sklum-BER-ger-a; after Frederick Schlumberger, Belgian horticulturist and cactus breeder. *Cactaceae.*

gaertneri, see *Hatiora gaertneri.*

russelliana, rus-sel-e-A-na, in honour of John Russell (1766–1839), 6th Duke of Bedford, patron of botany. Christmas cactus.

truncata, trun-KA-ta, ending bluntly – the stem segments.

Schoenoplectus, sken-o-PLEK-tus; from Gr. *schoinos*, rush; *pleko*, plait, in allusion to the mat forming rhizomes. Annual and perennial rhizomatous herbs. *Cyperaceae.*

lacustris, lak-US-tris, of lakes.

tabernaemontani, tab-er-na-MON-ta-ne, after Jacob Theodore (1525–1590), called *Tabernaemontanus* from his birthplace; German physician, herbalist and early botanist.

triqueter, tre-KWE-ter, stems three-angled.

Schubertia, shu-BER-te-a; after Gotthilf Heinrich von Schubert (1780–1860), German physician and botanist. Twinning shrubs. *Apocynaceae.*

grandiflora, gran-dif-LO-ra, large-flowered.

Sciadopitys, si-a-DOP-it-is; from Gr. *skias*, a parasol or sunshade; *pitys*, a fir tree, the whorled leaves like the ribs of an umbrella. Conifer. *Sciadopityaceae.*

verticillata, ver-tis-il-LA-ta, whorled – the leaves. The Umbrella Pine.

Scilla, SIL-la; ancient Gr. or L. name for another plant. Hardy and tender bulbs. *Asparagaceae.*

× *allenii*, AL-len-e-i, after James Allen, Park House, Shepton Mallet, who noticed the hybrids freely seeding.

amoena, am-E-na, pleasing.

autumnalis, see *Prospero autumnale.*

bifolia, bi-FO-le-a, two-leaved.

campanulata, see *Hyacinthoides hispanica.*

festalis, see *Hyacinthoides non-scripta.*

hispanica, see *Hyacinthoides hispanica.*

hyacinthoides, hy-a-sinth-OY-dees, resembling *Hyacinthus* (hyacinth).

italica, see *Hyacinthoides italica.*

leucophylla, see *Alrawia bellii.*

lingulata, see *Hyacinthoides lingulata.*

litardierei, li-tar-DEER-e-i, after René Verriet de Litardière (1888–1957), French botanist, director of the botanical institute Grenoble.

luciliae, lu-SIL-e-e, after Mme. Lucile Boissier.

patula, see *Hyacinthoides hispanica.*

peruviana, per-u-ve-A-na, misleading, for this species is from the Mediterranean region and brought back to Britain on HMS Peru.

pratensis, see *S. litardierei.*

puschkinioides, see *Fessia puschkinioides.*

sardensis, sar-DEN-sis, Sardinian.

siberica, si-BIR-ik-a, of Siberia.

verna, VER-na, spring, spring-flowering.

Scirpus, SKER-pus; old L. name for a rush or a reed. Bog plants. *Cyperaceae.*

cernuus, see *Isolepis cernua.*

lacustris, see *Schoenoplectus lacustris.*

setaceus, see *Isolepis setacea.*

tabernaemontani, see *Schoenoplectus tabernaemontani.*

tabernaemontani zebrinus, cultivar of *Schoenoplectus tabernaemontani.*

triqueter, see *Schoenoplectus triqueter.*

Sclerocactus, skler-o-KAK-tus; from Gr. *scleros*, hard (cruel) and cactus – the spines being hooked. Greenhouse cacti. *Cactaceae.*

polyancistrus, pol-e-an-SIS-trus; many angles or hooks.

Scolopendrium, skol-o-PEN-dre-um; from Gr. *scolopendra*, a centipede, a name originally applied to the Ceterach Fern, which resembled that creature. The ripe sori are very suggestive of centipedes. Hardy evergreen ferns. *Aspleniaceae.*

vulgare, see *Asplenium scolopendrium.*

v. crispum, recognised as a group of cultivars of *Asplenium scolopendrium.*

Scolymus, SKOL-im-us; old Gr. name used by Hesiod, possibly from Gr. *skolos*, a thorn, these plants being spiny. Herbaceous perennials. *Compositae.*

hispanicus, his-PAN-ik-us, of Spain.

maculatus, mak-ul-A-tus, blotched – the leaves.

Scorzonera, skor-zon-E-ra; from old Fr. *scorzon*, a serpent, the plant once being regarded as a remedy for snake-bite. Edible-rooted perennial. *Compositae.*

hispanica, his-PAN-ik-a, of Spain. The Scorzonera.

Scutellaria, sku-tel-LAR-e-a; from L. *scutella*, a dish, referring to the form of the persistent calyx. Greenhouse and hardy perennials. The Skull-caps. *Lamiaceae.*

alpina, al-PINE-a (or al-PIN-a), of the Alps or alpine.

baicalensis, bi-kal-EN-sis, from Baikalia, Russia.

coccinea, kok-SIN-e-a, scarlet.

galericulata, gal-er-ik-ul-A-ta, small helmet shaped.

indica, IN-di-ka, of India.

indica var. *parvifolia*, par-ve-FO-le-a, with small leaves.

Seaforthia, misapplied see below.

elegans, see *Ptychosperma elegans.*

Securigera, see-cur-e-JE-ra; from L. *securis*, an axe; *gero*, to bear, in allusion to the shape of the pods. Low growing vines. *Leguminosae.*

orientalis, or-e-en-TA-lis, from the Orient; Eastern.

varia, VAR-e-a, varying in colour.

Sedum, SE-dum; Tournefort was the first to describe it as from L. *sedendo*, sitting; or *sedando*, settling, in allusion to the characteristic of some species growing on the rocks. Tournefort identifies some species as having healing properties, L. *inflammationes sedant*, inflammation and aches. Succulent greenhouse and hardy evergreen and deciduous rock plants. *Crassulaceae.*

acre, AK-re, biting or sharp to the taste. The Common Stonecrop.

aizoon, ay-ZO-on, ever living.

album, AL-bum, white. The White Stonecrop.

altissimum, see *S. sediforme*.

amplexicaule, am-pleks-e-KAW-le, leaves clasping the stem.

anacampseros, an-a-KAMP-ser-os, an old generic name, meaning "to cause love to return" (Greek mythology).

anglicum, ANG-lik-cum, of England.

anopetalum, see *S. ochroleucum*.

brevifolium, brev-if-O-le-um, with short leaves.

caeruleum, ser-U-le-um, sky-blue.

carneum, see *S. lineare*.

compactum, kom-PAK-tum, compact – the habit of growth.

dasyphyllum, das-e-FIL-lum, with thick leaves.

dendroideum, den-dro-ID-e-um, resembling a tree.

divergens, di-VER-jens, spreading.

ellacombeanum, see *S. kamtschaticum*.

ewersii, ew-ERS-e-i, in honour of Johann Gustav von Ewers (1779–1830), rector of the University of Dorpat (now Tartu).

farinosum, far-in-O-sum, mealy, the foliage.

glaucum, see *S. dasyphyllum*.

hispanicum, his-PAN-ik-um, from Spain.

humifusum, hu-me-FEW-sum, spread over the ground.

kamtschaticum, kams-KAT-ik-um, of the Kamchatka Peninsula in the Russian Far East.

liebmannianum, leeb-man-E-a-num, after Frederik Michael Liebmann (1813–1856), Danish botanist and collector, director of the University of Copenhagen Botanic Garden.

lineare, lin-e-AR-e, with narrow leaves.

lydium, lid-E-um, old name, possibly alluding to Lydia, Asia Minor.

magellense, maj-el-EN-se, of Monte Majellla, Italy.

maximum, MAKS-e-mum, largest.

middendorffianum, see *Phedimus middendorffianus*.

moranense, mor-an-EN-se, from Real de Moran, Mexico.

multiceps, MUL-te-seps, with many heads.

nevii, NE-ve-i, after Reuben Denton Nevius (1827–1913), who discovered it.

obtusatum, ob-tew-SA-tum, the leaves are obtuse or blunt.

ochroleucum, OK-ro-LOO-kum, yellowish white.

oreganum, or-e-GA-num, Oregon, first found by the River Oregon.

palmeri, PAH-mer-i, after Edward Palmer (1829–1911), British born botanist, who emigrated to the United States and undertook fieldwork in North and South America.

pilosum, pil-O-sum, the leaves are hairy.

populifolium, pop-u-lif-O-le-um, leaves resembling *Populus* (Poplar).

praealtum, pre-AL-tum, the growth very high.

praegerianum, see *Rhodiola hobsonii*.

primuloides, see *Rhodiola primuloides*.

pulchellum, pul-KEL-um, beautiful but small.

reflexum, see *S. rupestre*.

rhodiola, see *Rhodiola rosen* var. *rosea*.

roseum, RO-ze-um, the fragrance of the fleshy rootstock, hence Rose-root (*Rhodiola*).

rupestre, roo-PES-tre, rock-breaking.

sediforme, sed-i-FORM-e, the appearance of Sedum.

sempervivoides, see *Rosularia sempervivoides*.

sexangulare, seks-ang-ul-AR-e, the leaves in six rows.

sieboldii, se-BOLD-e-i, after Philipp Franz Balthasar von Siebold (1796–1866), German physician, botanist, and traveler.

spectabile, spek-TAB-il-e, showy.

spurium, SPEW-re-um, false or doubtful, possibly in reference to its many false names.

stahlii, STAH-le-i, after Christian Ernst Stahl (1848–1919), German botanist, professor of botany at Jena.

stoloniferum, sto-lon-IF-er-um, bearing runners – the creeping stems.

telephium, te-LEF-e-um, old name derived from Telephus, son of Heracles.

ternatum, ter-NA-tum, leaves in threes.

Selaginella, sel-a-jin-EL-la; diminutive of *Selago*, an ancient name of a Lycopodium. Moss-like branching herb. *Selaginellaceae*.

apus, A-pus, stalkless.

caesia, see *S. uncinata*.

cuspidata, see *S. pallescens*.

denticulata, see *S. kraussiana*.

grandis, GRAN-dis, of great size.

kraussiana, kraus-se-A-na, after Christian Ferdinand Friedrich von Krauss (1812–1890), German botanist, who collected in South Africa.

lepidophylla, lep-id-OF-il-la, scaly leaves. The Resurrection Plant.

martensii, mar-TEN-se-i, after Martin Martins (1797–1863), Belgium Botanist, who with Galeotti collected in Mexico.

pallescens, pal-LESS-enz, rather pale.

uncinata, un-sin-NA-ta, end of leaves hooked.

willdenowii, wil-den-O-ve-i, after Carl Ludwig Wildenow (1765–1812), German botanist, director of the Botanical garden of Berlin.

Selenicereus, sel-en-e-SE-re-us; from Gr. *selene*, the moon; and *cereus* – the flowers opening at night. Greenhouse climbing cacti. *Cactaceae.*

coniflorus, ko-nif-LOR-us, cone-like flower buds.

grandiflorus, gran-dif-LOR-us, large flowered. The Queen of the Night.

macdonaldiae, mak-don-ald-E-e, received from Honduras by favour of Mrs MacDonald, possibly the wife of the late General Alexander MacDonald, Governor of Honduras.

Selenipedium, sel-en-e-PED-e-um; from Gr. *selenis*, a little crescent; *pedilon*, a slipper, the shape of the labellum. Greenhouse terrestrial orchids. *Orchidaceae.*

caudatum, see *Phragmipedium caudatum.*

× *dominianum*, see *Phragmipedium* × *dominianum.*

sedenii, see *Phragmipedium* × *sedenii.*

Sempervivum, sem-per-VI-vum; from L. *semper*, always; *vivus*, alive, alluding to the tenacity of life common to these plants. Greenhouse and hardy succulents. *Crassulaceae.*

arachnoideum, ar-ak-NOY-de-um, cob-webbed.

arboreum, see *Aeonium arboreum.*

arenarium, see *S. globiferum* subsp. *arenarium.*

caespitosum, ses-pit-O-sum, tufted.

calcaratum, kal-kar-A-tum, spurred.

calcareum, kal-KAR-e-um, chalk-loving.

canariense, see *Aeonium canariense.*

comollii, kom-OL-le-i, after Giuseppe Comolli (1780–1849), Italian botanist and professor of philosophy of mathematics at Pavia.

domesticum, see *Aichryson* × *aizoides* var. *domesticum.*

× *funckii*, FUNK-e-i, after Heinrich Christian Funck (1771–1839), German apothecary and bryologist.

globiferum, glob-IF-e-rum, globe bearing or spherical clusters.

globiferum subsp. *arenarium*, ar-en-A-re-um, sand-loving.

haworthii, see *Aeonium haworthii.*

heuffelii, HUF-fel-e-i, after Janos A. Heuffel (1800–1857), Hungarian botanist.

holochrysum, hol-o-KRY-sum, wholly golden.

montanum, mon-TA-num, mountain.

ruthenicum, ru-THEN-ik-um, Russian.

soboliferum, see *S. globiferum.*

spathulatum, see *Aeonium spathulatum.*

tabuliforme, see *Aeonium tabuliforme.*

tectorum, tek-TOR-um, of roofs. The Houseleek.

tectorum var. *glaucum*, GLAW-kum, sea-green.

Senecio, sen-E-se-o; from L. *senex*, old (an old man), in allusion to the grey and hoary seed pappus. Annuals, hardy and greenhouse perennials, and shrubs. *Compositae.*

abrotanifolius, ab-ROT-an-if-O-le-us, resembling *Artemisia abrotanum* leaves.

adonidifolius, see *Jacobaea adonidifolia.*

cineraria, see *Jacobaea maritima.*

clivorum, see *Ligularia dentata.*

cruentus, kru-EN-tus, dark blood-red.

doronicum, dor-ON-ik-um, old generic name for this or similar plant.

elegans, EL-e-ganz, elegant.

greyi, see *Brachyglottis greyi.*

incanus, see *Jacobaea incana.*

kaempferi, see *Farfugium japonicum.*

lanatus, lan-A-tus, woolly.

laxifolius, see *Brachyglottis laxifolia.*

macroglossus, mak-ro-GLOS-sus, large tongued. The Cape Ivy.

maritimus, mar-IT-im-us, of the sea.

pulcher, PUL-ker, beautiful.

tanguticus, see *Sinacalia tangutica.*

veitchianus, see *Ligularia veitchiana.*

wilsonianus, see *Ligularia wilsoniana.*

Senna, SEN-na; from Arabic *sana*. Trees, shrubs and herbs. *Leguminosae.*

corymbosa, kor-im-BO-sa, corymbose, flowers in corymbs.

marilandica, ma-ry-LAND-ik-a, native of the State of Maryland.

Sequoia, se-KWOY-a; named in honour of Sequoyah (1770–1843), inventor of the Cherokee syllablary. The Redwood. Coniferous trees. *Cupressaceae.*

gigantea, see *Sequoiadendron giganteum.*

sempervirens, sem-per-VEER-enz, from L. *semper*, ever; *virens*, green. Always green.

Sequoiadendron, se-kwoy-a-DEN-dron; from *Sequoia*, (which see), and Gr. *dendron*,

tree. The Giant Redwood. Coniferous trees. *Cupressaceae*.
  giganteum, ji-GAN-te-um, gigantic.

Serapias, ser-A-pe-as; the name of an Egyptian deity, Serapis, and used by Pliny for this plant or an ally. Hardy terrestrial orchids. *Orchidaceae*.
  cordigera, kor-DIG-er-a, heart-bearing.
  lingua, lin-GWA, tongue-like, the leaves.
  longipetala, see *S. vomeracea*.
  vomeracea, vom-er-A-se-a, from L. *vomeris*, ploughshare, in allusion to the shape of the labellum. The Ploughshare Orchid.

Sericographis, ser-ik-o-GRAF-is; from Gr. *serikos*, silk; *grapho*, to write. Greenhouse flowering shrubs. *Acanthaceae*.
  ghiesbreghtiana, see *Jacobinia ghiesbreghtiana*.

Serratula, ser-RA-tu-la; from L. *serrula*, a saw (literally a little saw), in allusion to the toothed leaf-margins. Hardy herbaceous perennials. *Compositae*.
  coronata, kor-on-A-ta, crowned, the tufted flower-heads.

Setaria, se-TA-re-a; from L. *seta*, a bristle, in allusion to the bristly inflorescence. Annual and perennial grasses. *Poaceae*.
  palmifolia, pal-me-FO-le-a, resembling palm leaves.

Shepherdia, shep-HER-de-a; after John Shepherd (1764–1836), curator of the Liverpool Botanic Gardens. Shrub. *Elaeagnaceae*.
  argenta, ar-JEN-te-a, silvery, the foliage.

Shortia, SHOR-te-a; after Dr. Charles Short (1794–1863), botanist of Kentucky. Woodland and rock garden plants. *Diapensiaceae*.
  galacifolia, ga-las-if-O-le-a, the leaves resembling *Galax*.
  uniflora, uni-FLOR-a, one flowered, that is blooms solitary.

Sibbaldiopsis, sib-bal-de-OP-sis; resembling *Sibbaldia*. Evergreen perennial plant. *Rosaceae*.
  tridentata, trid-en-TA-ta, three-lobed, the leaves.

Sibiraea, si-BIR-e-a; Siberian, the geographical distribution. Shrubs. *Rosaceae*.
  laevigata, lev-e-GA-ta, smooth-leaved.

Sibthorpia, sib-THOR-pe-a; after Humphry Sibthorpe (1713–1797), professor of botany at Oxford from 1747 to 1783. Trailing plants. *Plantaginaceae*.
  europaea, u-ro-PE-a, European.

Sidalcea, si-dal-SE-a; a combined word from *Sida* and *Alcea*, related genera. Herbaceous perennials. *Malvaceae*.
  candida, KAN-did-a, white.
  malviflora, mal-ve-FLOR-a, the flowers resemble *Malva* (Mallow).

Silene, si-LE-ne; the Greek name for another plant *Viscaria*, probably from Gr. *sialon*, saliva, the gummy exudations on the stems which ward off insects. Catchfly or campion. Annuals and herbaceous perennials. *Caryophyllaceae*.
  acaulis, a-KAW-lis, stemless.
  alpestris, al-PES-tris, alpine.
  armeria, ar-MEER-e-a, old generic name meaning "near the sea".
  chalcedonica, kal-se-DON-ik-a, of Chalcedonia, an ancient region that stretched along the Anatolian shore of the Bosphorus. The major town being Chalcedon.
  coeli-rosa, kee-le-RO-za, Rose of Heaven.
  compacta, kom-PAK-ta, the flower heads are compact.
  coronaria, kor-o-NA-re-a, used for garlands.
  dioica, di-OY-ka, literally two houses, that is male and female parts being on separate plants, dioecious.
  elisabethae, el-iz-a-BE-the, dedicated to Princess Elizabeth of Savoy (1800–1856), the wife of the Viceroy of the Lombardo-Veneto.
  flos-cuculi, flos-KUK-ul-e, cuckoo flower, that is, blooming around the time of cuckoos.
  flos-jovis, flos-JO-vis, Jove's flower, name of ancient origin.
  hookeri, HOOK-er-i, named in 1838 after William Jackson Hooker (1785–1865), then professor of botany at the University of Glasgow, who assisted with the layout of the Glasgow Botanic Gardens.
  laciniata, las-in-e-A-ta, the petals cut or fringed.
  latifolia, lat-if-O-le-a, broad-leaved.
  maritima, see *S. uniflora*.
  pendula, PEN-du-la, pendulous or weeping.
  quadrifida, see *Ixoca quadrifida*.
  schafta, SHAF-ta, derived from the vernacular Caspian name for this plant.

suecica, su-E-sik-a, of Sweden.
uniflora, uni-FLOR-a, one flowered.
viscaria, vis-KAR-e-a, sticky, the stems gummy.

Silphium, SIL-fe-um; ancient name transferred to this genus referring to the resinous juice. Herbaceous perennials. *Compositae.*
laciniatum, las-in-e-A-tum, leaves cut into narrow fringe-like segments. The common name Compass Plant refers to the North-South orientation of the leaves.
perfoliatum, per-fo-le-A-tum, the leaves perfoliate or stem clasping.

Silybum, SIL-ib-um; name applied by Dioscorides to some thistle-like plants. Annual and biennial herbs. *Compositae.*
marianum, mar-e-A-num, St. Mary's, in reference to the white spots on the leaves.

Sinacalia, si-na-KA-le-a; genus of Chinese plants related to *Cacalia*. Perennial herbs. *Compositae.*
tangutica, tan-GU-te-ka, Tangusian, Siberia.

Sinningia, sin-NING-e-a; after Wilhelm Sinning (1792–1874), head gardener to the Bonn University, where it was raised in 1825 from seed. Greenhouse tuberous perennials. *Gesneriaceae.*
cardinalis, kar-din-A-lis, scarlet, cardinal red.
speciosa, spes-e-O-sa, showy.

Sinofranchetia, si-no-fran-SHET-e-a; from *sino*, China; and Adrien René Franchet (1834–1900), French botanist and authority on Chinese plants. One species a climbing shrub. *Lardizabalaceae.*
chinensis, tsh-NEN-sis, of China.

Sinopodophyllum, si-no-pod-o-FIL-lum; from prefix *sino*, China and *Anapodophyllum*; duck's-foot-leaved. Herbaceous perennials. *Berberidaceae.*
hexandrum, heks-AN-drum, with six stamens.

Sinowilsonia, si-no-wil-SO-ne-a; prefix *sino*, China; and after Ernest Henry Wilson (1876–1930), plant collector in China. Genus of one shrub. *Hamamelidaceae.*
henryi, HEN-re-i, after Dr. Augustine Henry (1857–1930), Irish plantsman and pioneer collector in China.

Sisyrinchium, sis-e-RINK-e-um; old Gr. name first applied to another plant. Small herbaceous perennials with grass-like tufted leaves. Blue-eyed Grass. *Iridaceae.*
angustifolium, an-gus-tif-O-le-um, having narrow leaves.
bellum, BEL-lum, pretty.
bermudiana, ber-mu-de-A-na, of Bermuda.
californicum, kal-if-OR-nik-um, native habitat California.
filifolium, see *Olsynium filifolium*.
graminifolium, gram-in-if-OL-e-um, grass-leaved.
grandiflorum, see *Olsynium douglasii*.
striatum, stri-A-tum, striped, the leaves channelled or grooved.

Sium, SEE-um; old Gr. name for a marsh plant. The root vegetable, Skirret. *Apiaceae.*
sisarum, SIS-ar-um, from the Arabic *dgizer*, a carrot. The shape of the roots.

Skimmia, skim-e-a; from *skimmi*, a Japanese name for *S. japonica*. Berry-bearing shrubs. *Rutaceae.*
arborescens, ar-bor-ES-cenz, tree like.
fortunei, see *Ilex cornuta.*
japonica, jap-ON-ik-a, of Japan.
laureola, LAW-re-o-la, a little laurel.
melanocarpa, mel-an-ok-AR-pa, black-fruited.
multinervia, mul-te-NER-ve-a, many-nerved.
repens, RE-penz, creeping.

Smilacina, misapplied see below.
racemosa, see *Maianthemum racemosum.*
stellata, see *Maianthemum stellatum.*

Smilax, SMI-laks; ancient Gr. name of obscure meaning. Tendril climbing vines. The Greenbriar. *Smilacaceae.*
argyrea, ar-gy-RE-a, silvery.
aspera, AS-per-a, rough.
officinalis, of-fis-in-A-lis, of the shops. The Sarsaparilla.

Smithiantha, smith-e-AN-tha; commemorating Matilda Smith (1854–1926), botanical artist. Bulbous plants. *Gesneriaceae.*
cinnabarina, kin- (or sin-) nab-ar-EE-na, vermillion.
fulgida, FUL-jid-a, shining.
multiflora, mul-tif-LO-ra, many flowered.
zebrina, ze-BRY-na, zebra-striped.

Sobralia, sob-RA-le-a; dedicated to Don Francisco Martinez Sobral (fl. 1798), Spanish physician to the Royal Court of King Charles IV, promoter of botany. Warmhouse terrestrial orchids. *Orchidaceae*.
  macrantha, mak-RANTH-a, large-flowered.

Solandra, so-LAN-dra; after Daniel Carlsson Solander (1733–1782), Swedish naturalist, Apostle of Linnaeus, companion of Sir Joseph Banks on Captain Cook's first voyage of exploration. Tropical flowering shrubs. *Solanaceae*.
  grandiflora, gran-dif-LO-ra, large-flowered.

Solanum, so-LA-num; name given by Pliny, the Roman naturalist, to one of the nightshades; possibly derived from L. *solamen*, solace, from medicinal virtues. Hardy and greenhouse annuals, herbaceous perennials, tuberous-rooted vegetable and shrubs. *Solanaceae*.
  betaceum, be-TA-ce-um, beet-like. The Tamarillo or Tree Tomato.
  capense, ka-PEN-se, of the Cape – Cape Colony.
  capsicastrum, see *S. pseudocapsicum* var. *diflorum*.
  crispum, KRISP-um, curly – the leaves waved.
  jasminoides, jaz-min-OY-dees, resembling *Jasminum* (jasmine).
  lobelii, lo-BEL-e-i, after M. Matthias de L'Obel (1538–1616), a Fleming, physician to James I of England, traveller, plant collector and botanical author.
  lycopersicum, lik-o-PER-sik-um (or LY-co-PER-se-kum); from Gr. *lykos*, a wolf; *persicon*, a peach, probably in reference to supposed poisonous qualities. Cultivated tomato.
  marginatum, mar-jin-A-tum, edged with white.
  melongena, mel-ON-je-na, old name referring to the large fruits of the Egg-plant.
  psuedocapsicum, SUE-do-KAP-sik-um, false capsicum.
  pseudocapsicum var. *diflorum*, di-FLOR-a, two-flowered, that is, in pairs.
  sisymbriifolium, sis-im-bre-i-FO-le-um, resembling *Sisymbrium* leaves.
  tuberosum, tu-ber-O-sum, bearing tubers. The Potato.
  wendlandii, wend-LAND-e-i, introduced into cultivation by Hermann Wendland (1825–1903), German botanist, director of the Royal Gardens of Herrenhausen, Hanover.

Soldanella, sol-dan-EL-la; said to be from *soldo*, an Italian coin, in allusion to the roundness of the leaf. Alpine. *Primulaceae*.
  alpina, al-PINE-a (or al-PIN-a), of the Alps or alpine.
  minima, MIN-e-ma, from L. *minimus*, smallest.
  montana, mon-TA-na, of mountains.

Soleirolia, so-le-RO-le-a; after Joseph-François Soleirol (1781–1863), army engineer and plant collector, who collected specimens in Corsica and Sardinia. Creeping herb. *Urticaceae*.
  soleirolii, so-le-RO-le-i, see above.

Solidago, sol-id-A-go; from L. *solido*, to make whole or to heal, in reference to supposed healing properties. Herbaceous perennials. *Compositae*.
  brachystachys, see *S. virgaurea*.
  canadensis, kan-a-DEN-sis, of Canada.
  missouriensis, mis-soor-e-EN-sis, of Missouri, U.S.A.
  virga-aurea, VIR-ga-AW-re-a, from L. *virga*, twig or rod; *aurea*, golden. An old name, signifying a golden twig, hence the English name Golden-rod.
  virgaurea, virg-AW-re-a, golden twigs.

Sollya, SOL-e-a; after Richard Horsman Solly (1778–1858), English naturalist. Tender twining shrubs. *Pittosporaceae*.
  heterophylla, see *Billardiera heterophylla*.
  parviflora, par-vif-LOR-a, from L. *parvus*, small; *flor*, flower.

Sonerila, son-er-IL-a; from *Soneri-ila*, the native Malabar name for one species. Tropical perennials, flowering and ornamental foliage plants. *Melastomataceae*.
  maculata, mak-ul-A-ta, spotted.
  margaritacea, mar-gar-it-A-se-a, pearl-spotted.
  speciosa, spes-e-O-sa, showy.

Sophora, SOF-or-a; from Arabic *sophera*, a tree with pea-shaped flowers. Shrubs or trees. *Leguminosae*.
  davidii, DA-vid-e-i, after Pere Armand David (1826–1900), French missionary and plant collector in China.
  japonica, see *Styphnolobium japonicum*.

tetraptera, tet-RAP-ter-a, from Gr. literally four-winged – the seed pods.

viciifolia, see *S. davidii*.

Sophronitis, sof-ron-I-tis; from *sophrona*, modest, referring to the miniature cattleya-like plants and flowers. Greenhouse orchids. *Orchidaceae*.

grandiflora, see *Cattleya coccinea*.

Sorbaria, sor-BAR-e-a; from L. resembling *Sorbus*. Shrubs. *Rosaceae*.

sorbifolia, sor-be-FO-le-a, leaves resembling *Sorbus*.

tomentosa, to-men-TO-sa, downy foliage.

Sorbus, SOR-bus; from L. *sorbum*, service-berry; sorb apple. Trees and shrubs. *Rosaceae*.

aria, A-re-a, old generic name for Whitebeams, probably Persian place name of origin.

aucuparia, aw-ku-PAR-e-a, old name for Mountain Ash, from L. *aucupium*, bird-catching; from the ancient belief that the berries intoxicated birds, rendering them easily caught. The Rowan Tree or Mountain Ash.

chamaemespilus, kam-e-MES-pil-us, literally ground medlar – its dwarf stature.

commixta, kom-MIX-sta, mixed together.

domestica, do-MES-tik-a, domestic – from its various uses. The Service Tree.

intermedia, in-ter-MED-e-a, between.

torminalis, tor-min-A-lis, against colic. The Wild Service Tree.

vilmorinii, vil-mor-E-ne-i, after Maurice de Vilmorin (1849–1918), French nurseryman, who raised it from seed sent by Père Delavey.

Sparaxis, spar-AKS-sis; from Gr. *sparasso*, to tear, in reference to the lacerated spathes. Half-hardy bulbs, now mostly under *Dierama* and *Ixia*. Perennial herbs. *Iridaceae*.

grandiflora, gran-dif-LO-ra, large-flowered.

pulcherrima, see *Dierama pulcherrimum*.

tricolor, TRIK-o-lor, three coloured.

Sparmannia, spar-MAN-ne-a; after Andreas Sparmann (1748–1820), Swedish naturalist, who accompanied Captain Cook on his second expedition. Greenhouse flowering shrub. *Malvaceae*.

africana, af-re-KA-na, of Africa.

Spartium, SPAR-te-um; from Gr. *spartion*, a rush, which the plant resembles. Flowering shrub. *Leguminosae*.

junceum, JUN-ke-um, a rush, the form of the twigs. The Spanish Broom.

Spathiphyllum, spath-e-FI-lum; from Gr. *spatha*, spath; *phyllon*, a leaf, in reference to the spathe resembling a leaf. Evergreen perennials. *Araceae*.

wallisii, wal-LIS-e-i, introduced in 1875 from Columbia by Gustav Wallis (1830–1878), German born plant collector, employed by James Veitch and Sons, Chelsea.

Specularia, spek-ul-AIR-e-a; derived from L. *speculum*, a mirror. Annual. *Campanulaceae*.

speculumveneris, SPEK-ul-um-VEN-er-is, Venus's Looking-glass.

Spergula, SPER-gu-la; from L. *spargo*, to scatter, alluding to the scattering of the seeds. Annual herbs. *Caryophyllaceae*.

arvensis, ar-VEN-sis, growing in cultivated fields. The Corn Spurrey, an annual weed and indicator plant for acidic soils.

pilifera, see *Sagina pilifera*.

Sphaeralcea, sfer-AL-se-a; from Gr. *sphaira*, a globe; *alcea*, mallow, alluding to the rounded form of the seed pods. Globe Mallow. Hardy perennial. *Malvaceae*.

coccinea, kok-SIN-e-a, scarlet.

munroana, mun-ro-A-na, discovered by David Douglas in 1826 and named in honour of Mr. Munro, head gardener to the Horticultural Society of London.

Sphenogyne, misapplied see below.

speciosa, see *Ursinia anthemoides*.

Spigelia, spi-JE-le-a; after Adriaan van der Spiegel (1578–1625), Dutch physician and botanist, professor of anatomy at Padua. Herbaceous perennials. *Loganiaceae*.

marilandica, mair-e-LAN-dik-a, of Maryland, U.S.A.

Spinacia, spe-NA-se-a; from L. *spina*, a prickle, in allusion to the prickly seeds of some forms. Culinary vegetable. *Amaranthaceae*.

oleracea, ol-er-A-se-a, of the vegetable garden, culinary or potherbs. Spinach.

Spiraea, spi-RE-a; probably from Gr. *speira*, a wreath. Herbaceous perennials and shrubs. *Rosaceae.*

aitchisonii, aitch-e-SO-ne-i, after Dr James Aitchison (1836–1898), British physician and botanist, who collected in India and Afghanistan.

× *arguta*, ar-GU-ta, sharp-toothed or serrated.

aruncus, see *Aruncus dioicus.*

astilboides, as-TIL-boy-dees, resembling *Astilbe.*

bella, BEL-la, beautiful or pretty.

betulifolia, bet-u-le-FO-le-a; leaves resembling *Betula* (birch) leaves.

betulifolia var. *corymbosa*, kor-im-BO-sa, flowers in corymbs.

bracteata, see *S. nipponica.*

bullata, see *S. japonica.*

× *bumalda*, bu-MALD-a, commemorating Ovidio Montalbani (1601–1671), who published works under the pseudonym Gio. Antonio Bumalda.

camschatica, see *Filipendula camschatica.*

cana, KA-na, hoary.

canescens, kan-ES-senz, more or less grey or hoary.

cantoniensis, kan-ton-e-EN-sis, of Canton.

crenata, kre-NA-ta, cut in round scallops; leaves crenate.

decumbens, de-KUM-benz, prostrate.

discolor, see *Holodiscus dumosus.*

douglasii, dug-LAS-e-i, after David Douglas (1799–1834), Scottish plant collector.

douglasii subsp. *menziesii*, men-ZE-se-i, after Archibald Menzies (1754–1842), the Scottish botanist.

filipendula, see *Filipendula vulgaris.*

gigantea, see *Filipendula vulgaris.*

japonica, jap-ON-ik-a, of Japan.

laevigata, see *Sibiraea laevigata.*

lindleyana, see *Sorbaria tomentosa.*

lobata, see *Filipendula rubra.*

media, ME-de-a, intermediate, the stature.

menziesii, see *S. douglasii* subsp. *menziesii.*

mollifolia, mol-le-FO-le-a, soft-leaved.

nipponica, nip-ON-ik-a, Japanese.

palmata, see *Filipendula rubra.*

prunifolia, proo-nif-O-le-a, plum-leaved.

reevesiana, see *S. cantoniensis.*

salicifolia, sal-is-if-O-le-a, *Salix* (willow) leaved.

sorbifolia, see *Sorbaria sorbifolia.*

thunbergii, thun-BER-ge-i, after Carl Peter Thunberg (1743–1828), Swedish botanist a student of Linnaeus.

trifoliata, trif-ol-e-A-ta, leaves in three.

trilobata, try-lo-BA-ta, leaves with three lobes.

ulmaria, see *Filipendula ulmaria.*

× *vanhouttei*, van-HOUT-te-i, after Louis Benoît van Houtte (1810–1876), Belgium horticulturist.

Sprekelia, sprek-E-le-a; after Johann Herman von Sprekelsen (1691–1764), who sent the plant to Linnaeus. Greenhouse bulbs. *Amaryllidaceae.*

formosissima, for-mos-IS-sim-a, most beautiful.

Stachys, STAK-is; from Gr. *stachus*, spike, alluding to the pointed inflorescences. Herbaceous perennials and tuberous vegetable. *Lamiaceae.*

affinis, af-FIN-is, allied. Chinese Artichoke.

byzantina, bi-zan-TE-na, Byzantine. The Lamb's Ear.

corsica, KOR-sik-a, of Corsica.

grandiflora, see *S. macrantha.*

lanata, see *S. byzantina.*

lavandulifolia, lav-an-dew-le-FO-le-a, the leaves resembling *Lavandula* (lavender).

macrantha, mak-RANTH-a, large-flowered.

officinalis, of-fis-in-A-lis, of the shop (apothecary's), applied to plants always kept "in stock" by herbalists. Betony.

tubifera, see *S. affinis.*

Stanhopea, Stan-HO-pe-a; after Philip Henry Stanhope, 4th Earl Stanhope (1781–1855), president of the Medico-Botanical Society of London. Warm-house Orchids. *Orchidaceae.*

bucephalus, see *S. oculata.*

graveolens, GRAV-e-ol-enz, strong smelling.

jenischiana, jen-is-SHE-a-na, named by Kramer gardener to Herr Senator Jenisch of Kleinflottbeck, Hamburg.

oculata, ok-ul-A-ta, eyed.

tigrina, tig-RE-na, tiger marked.

Stapelia, sta-PEL-e-a; after Johannes Bodaeus van Stapel (1602–1636), Dutch physician and botanist, who edited botanical works of Theophrastus. Succulents. *Apocynaceae.*

asterias, as-TEER-e-as, resembles a starfish.

bufonia, see *Stisseria bufonia.*

gigantea, ji-GAN-te-a, unusually tall or big.

grandiflora, gran-dif-LO-ra, large-flowered.

hirsuta, hir-SU-ta, hairy.

variegata, see *Orbea variegata.*

Staphylea, staf-e-LE-a; from Gr. *staphyle*, a cluster, the inflorescence resembling a cluster of grapes. Shrubs. *Staphyleaceae.*
colchica, KOL-chik-a, from Colchis.
× *coulomberi*, koo-lom-be-AIR-i, after Coulombier of Vitry, France in whose nursery it was first noticed in 1887. Considered by some authorities to be a hybrid of *S. colchica* and *S. pinnata* by others as a variety of *S. colchica.*
pinnata, pin-NA-ta, pinnated – the divided leaves.
trifolia, trif-O-le-a, three-leaved.

Statice, misapplied see below.
bonduelli, see *Limonium bonducellii.*
bourgaei, see *Limonium bourgeaui.*
dumosa, see *Goniolimon tataricum.*
eximia, see *Goniolimon eximium.*
gmelinii, see *Limonium gmelinii.*
latifolia, see *Limonium platyphyllum.*
limonium, see *Limonium vulgare.*
minuta, see *Limonium minutum.*
ovalifolia, see *Limonium ovalifolium.*
profusa, see *Limonium profusum.*
sinuata, see *Limonium sinuatum.*
suworowi, see *Psylliostachys suworowi.*
tatarica, see *Goniolimon tataricum.*

Stauntonia, staun-TO-ne-a; after Sir George Staunton (1737–1801), a traveller and botanist, who accompanied Lord Macartney on his mission to China in 1793. Shrub. *Lardizabalaceae.*
hexaphylla, heks-af-IL-la, having six leaflets to a leaf.

Steirodiscus, ste-row-DISK-us; from Gr. *steiros*, barren; *diskos*, disk, reference to sterile disk florets. Perennial herbs. *Compositae.*
tagetes, taj-E-tez, *Tagetes* (Marigold) like.

Stellaria, stel-LAR-e-a; from L. *stella*, a star, in reference to the star-shaped flowers. Rock plants. *Caryophyllaceae.*
graminea, gram-IN-e-a, grassy, the foliage.
holostea, hol-LO-ste-a, old generic name meaning "entire" and "a bone" used in ancient medicine for healing fractures. The Stitchwort.
media, ME-de-a, intermediate.

Stenanthium, sten-AN-the-um; from Gr. *stenos*, narrow; *anthos*, a flower, alluding to the finely cut segments of the corolla. Hardy perennial. *Melanthiaceae.*
densum, DEN-sum, close, dense.
gramineum, gram-IN-e-um, grassy, the foliage.
robustum, see *S. gramineum.*

Stenocereus, sten-o-SER-e-us; from Gr. *stenos*, narrow; L. *cereus*, a genus name for a cacti meaning tapering or candle. Cacti. *Cactaceae.*
eruca, er-OO-ka, resembling a caterpillar, the prostate stems. Commonly known as Creeping Devil.

Stenotaphrum, sten-o-TAF-rum; from Gr. *stenos*, narrow; *taphros*, a trench, the floral spikelets being situated in cavities in the stem. Grass. *Poaceae.*
secundatum, sek-un-DA-tum, one-sided flower spike.

Stephanandra, stef-an-AN-dra; from Gr. *stephanos*, a crown; *andros*, man or stamen, in allusion to the form of the stamens which persist around the capsule. Shrubs. *Rosaceae.*
flexuosa, see *S. incisa.*
incisa, IN-si-sa, deeply cut, the leaves.
tanakae, tan-A-ke, after Yoshio Tanaka (1838–1916), Japanese botanist.

Stephanotis, stef-an-O-tis; from Gr. *stephanos*, a crown; *otos*, an ear, referring to the auricles of the staminal crown. Tropical climbing flowering shrubs. *Apocynaceae.*
floribunda, see *Marsdenia floribunda.*

Sternbergia, stern-BER-ge-a; after Count Kaspar M. von Sternberg (1761–1838), Czech botanist. Bulbous plants. *Amaryllidaceae.*
clusiana, klew-ze-A-na, of Carolus Clusius (1526–1609), Flemish doctor and pioneering botanist.
colchiciflora, kol-tshe-se-FLOR-a, flowers resembling *Colchicum.*
fischeriana, see *S. vernalis.*
graeca, see *S. colchiciflora.*
lutea, LU-te-a, yellow.
macrantha, see *S. clusiana.*
vernalis, ver-NA-lis, of spring – time of flowering.

Stevia, STEVE-e-a; after Pedro Jaime Esteve (d.1566), botanist of Valencia. Herbaceous perennials. *Compositae*.
 serrata, ser-RA-ta, saw-toothed edge to the leaves.

Stewartia, stew-AR-te-a; named in honour of John Stuart, Earl of Bute (1713–1792), chief adviser to Augusta, Princess Dowager of Wales, when she founded the Royal Botanic Gardens, Kew, 1759–1760. Flowering shrubs. *Theaceae*.
 ovata, o-VA-ta, egg-shaped – the leaves.
 pentagyna, see *S. ovata*.
 psuedocamellia, SUE-do-kam-EL-le-a; false *Camellia*.

Stigmaphyllon, stig-maf-IL-lon; from Gr. *stigma*, the receptive top of the pistil; *phyllon*, a leaf – the stigma is leaf-like or foliaceous. Tropical flowering climbing shrub. *Malpighiaceae*.
 ciliatum, sil-e-A-tum, fringed with fine hairs.

Stigmatocarpum, stig-mat-o-KAR-pum; from Gr. *stigma*, stigma; *karpos*, fruit, the stigmas persisting on the capsule. Succulents. *Aizoaceae*.
 criniflorum, krin-if-LO-rum, the petals being hair-like.

Stipa, STY-pa; from L. *stuppa*, tow, in allusion to the silky inflorescence. Ornamental grasses. *Poaceae*.
 elegantissima, el-e-gan-TIS-sim-a, most elegant.
 pennata, pen-NA-ta, feathered. The Feather Grass.

Stisseria, sti-SEER-e-a; after Jean André Stisser (1657–1700), professor and founder of Helmstadt Botanical Garden. Succulents. *Sapotaceae*.
 bufonia, bu-FO-ne-a, toad-like.

Stokesia, STOKES-e-a; named after Jonathan Stokes (1755–1831), English physician and botanist. Herbaceous perennial. *Compositae*.
 cyanea, see *S. laevis*.
 laevis, LE-vis, smooth.

Stranvaesia, stran-VE-se-a; named by Lindley in honour of William Thomas Horner Fox-Strangeways (1795–1865),

4th Earl of Ilchester, English diplomat and plant collector. Some authorities include the genera within *Photinia*. Shrubs. *Rosaceae*.
 davidiana var. *undulata*, un-du-LA-ta, waved – the leaf margins. Unresolved name.
 glaucescens, see *S. nussia*.
 nussia, NEW-se-a, native Nepalese name for this specimen.
 undulata, see *S. davidiana* var. *undulata*.

Stratiotes, strat-e-O-tees; from Gr. *stratiotis*, a soldier, in allusion to the swordlike leaves. Aquatic. *Hydrocharitaceae*.
 aloides, al-OY-dees, resembling *Aloe*. The Water Soldier.

Strelitzia, stre-LITS-e-a; after Charlotte of Mecklenburg-Strelitz (1744–1818), wife of George III of England. Greenhouse perennials. *Strelitziaceae*.
 reginae, re-JI-ne, of the Queen – Queen Charlotte.

Streptocarpus, strep-to-KAR-pus; from Gr. *streptos*, twisted; *karpos*, a fruit, the latter being spiralled. Houseplants. *Gesneriaceae*.
 dunnii, DUN-ne-i; named for Edward John Dunn (1844–1937), Australian geologist, who collected seed for Kew in 1884 from the Transvaal, whilst surveying.
 polyanthus, pol-e-AN-thus, many-flowered.
 wendlandii, wend-LAND-e-i, introduced into cultivation by Carl Sprenger of Dammann & Co, Naples Italy in honour of Hermann Wendland (1825–1903), German botanist, director of the Royal Gardens of Herrenhausen, Hanover.

Streptosolen, strep-to-SO-len; from Gr. *streptos*, twisted; *solon*, tube, with reference to the form of the corolla tube. Greenhouse shrub. *Solanaceae*.
 jamesonii, jame-SO-ne-i, William Jameson (1796–1873), Scottish botanist, professor of chemistry and botany at the Central University of Ecuador in Quito.

Strobilanthes, strob-il-AN-thez; from Gr. *strobilos*, a pine cone; *anthos*, a flower, the flower head – especially in the bud stage, resembling a cone. Greenhouse flowering plants. *Acanthaceae*.
 anisophylla, see *S. persicifolia*.

dyeriana, dy-er-e-A-na, after William Thistle-ton-Dyer (1843–1928), director of the Royal Botanic Garden, Kew.
isophyllus, see *S. persicifolia*.
persicifolia, per-sis-if-O-le-a, resembling *Prunus persica* (peach) leaves.

Struthiopteris, stru-the-OP-ter-is; from Gr. *strouthion*, an ostrich; *pteris*, a fern, the fronds being supposed to resemble an ostrich's feather. Hardy ferns. *Blechnaceae*.
germanica, jer-MAN-ik-a, of Germany.

Stuckenia, stuk-E-ne-a; commemorating Wilhelm Adolf Stucken (1860–1901), German botanist, who collected plants in Australia. Aquatic. *Potamogetonaceae*.
pectinata, pek-tin-A-ta, feathered or comb-like, the arrangement of the leaves.

Stylophorum, sty-LO-for-um; from Gr. *stylos*, a style; *phoreo*, to bear, in allusion to the columnar style. Herbaceous perennial. *Papaveraceae*.
diphyllum, dif-IL-lum, two-leaved.

Styphnolobium, stif-no-LO-be-um; from Gr. Greek *styphno*, sour, astringent; *lobus*, pod, in reference to the sour tasting seed pod. Small trees and shrubs. *Leguminosae*.
japonicum, jap-ON-ik-um, of Japan.

Styrax, STY-raks; ancient Gr. name, derived from the Arabic for the shrub, yielding the resin known as storax. Shrubs. *Styracaceae*.
japonicus, jap-ON-ik-us, of Japan.
obassis, o-BAS-sis, latinised Japanese name.
odoratissimus, od-or-a-TIS-sim-us, very fragrant.
officinalis, of-fis-in-A-lis, of the shop (herbal).
veitchiorum, see *S. odoratissimus*.
wilsonii, wil-SO-ne-i, after Ernest Henry Wilson (1876–1930), English plant collector, who introduced it.

Sutherlandia, suth-er-LAN-de-a; named after James Sutherland (1639–1719), professor of botany at Edinburgh. Half-hardy shrubs. *Leguminosae*.
frutescens, fru-TES-senz, shrubby.

Swainsona, swain-SO-na; named for Isaac Swainson (1746–1812), physician, who kept a plant collection at Twickenham. Greenhouse shrubs. *Leguminosae*.
galegifolia, gal-e-gif-OL-e-a, resembles *Galega* foliage.

Swertia, SWER-te-a; after Emanuel Swert (1552–1612), a Dutch florist. Dwarf rock and bog plants. *Gentianaceae*.
perennis, per-EN-nis, perennial.

Syagrus, sy-AG-rus; a name used by Pliny for another plant. Greenhouse palms. *Arecaceae*.
weddelliana, see *Lytocaryum weddellianum*.

Symphoria, sim-FOR-e-a; from Gr. *symphoreo*, to accumulate; alluding to the racemes. Berry-bearing shrubs. *Caprifoliaceae*.
racemosa, ras-em-O-sa, flowers and fruits in racemes.

Symphoricarpos, sim-for-e-KAR-pus; from Gr. *symphoreo*, to accumulate; *karpos*, a fruit, alluding to the clustered fruits. Berry-bearing shrubs. *Caprifoliaceae*.
albus, AL-bus, white. The Snowberry.
occidentalis, oks-se-DEN-ta-lis, western – North America.
orbiculatus, or-bik-ul-A-tus, shaped like a disc, the leaves.
racemosus, see *Symphoria racemosa*.

Symphyandra, misapplied see below.
hofmannii, see *Campanula hofmannii*.
pendula, see *Campanula pendula*.

Symphyotrichum, sim-fe-o-TRIK-um; from Gr. *symphyio*, grow together; *thrix*, hair, in allusion to the hair-like flowers. Annuals and herbaceous perennials. *Compositae*.
cordifolium, kor-dif-O-le-um, heart-shaped leaves.
ericoides, er-ik-OY-dees, like *Erica* (heather).
novae-angliae, NO-vi-ANG-le-e, of New England, U.S.A.
novi-belgii, NO-vi-BEL-je-i, of New York, name of historical origin.
puniceum, pu-NIS-e-um, purple.

Symphytum, SIM-fy-tum; from Gr. *symphyo*, to make whole, or heal; *phyton*, plant, in allusion to the medicinal properties. Herbaceous perennials. *Boraginaceae*.

asperrimum, as-PER-re-mum, roughest.
caucasicum, kaw-KAS-ik-um, Caucasian.
officinale, of-fis-in-A-le, of the shop (herbal).

Symplocarpus, sim-plo-KAR-pus; from Gr. *symploke*, connected; *karpos*, fruit, the seed being united in a mass. Tuberous-rooted perennial. *Araceae*.
foetidus, FET-id-us, bad-smelling.

Synthyris, sin-THIR-is; from Gr. *syn*, together; *thyris*, a small aperture, referring to the formation of the seed vessel. Rock plants. *Plantaginaceae*.
pinnatifida, pin-na-TIF-id-a, leaves pinnately cut.
reniformis, ren-e-FOR-mis, kidney-shaped, the leaves.

Syringa, sy-RING-a; from Gr. *syrinx*, a tube, in allusion to the hollow stems sometimes used for pipe-stems. Flowering shrubs. *Oleaceae*.
chinensis, see *S. oblate*.
josikaea, jos-ik-E-a, named by Baron Jacquin to honour Baroness von Josika, who discovered it in Transylvania. Josika's Lilac.
oblata, o-BLA-ta, widened - the broad leaves.
pekinensis, see *S. reticulata* subsp. *pekinensis*.
persica, PER-sik-a, of Persia. The Persian Lilac.
reticulata, ret-ik-ul-A-ta, netted or lined.
reticulata subsp. *pekinensis*, pe-kin-EN-sis, first sent from Pekin.
villosa, vil-LO-sa, shaggy, with hairs, of no application to the plant so named.
vulgaris, vul-GAR-is, common.

Tabernaemontana, tab-er-na-MON-ta-na; after Jacob Theodore (1525–1590), called Tabernaemontanus from his birthplace; German physician, herbalist and early botanist. A large genus of tropical flowering trees and shrubs. *Apocynaceae*.
coronaria, see *T. divaricata*.
divaricata, de-var-ik-A-ta, wide spreading branches.
gratissima, see *T. divaricata*.

Tacsonia, tak-SO-ne-a; from *tacso*, a Peruvian name for one of the species. Greenhouse climbers. *Passifloraceae*.
× *exoniensis*, eks-on-e-EN-sis, of Exeter, Devon, England.
manicata, see *Passiflora manicata*.
vanvolxemii, see *Passiflora antioquiensis*.

Tagetes, ta-GE-tez; after Tages, an Etruscan deity. Half-hardy annuals. *Compositae*.
erecta, e-REK-ta, erect; upright. The African Marigold.
lunulata, loo-nu-LA-ta, in reference to the moon – crescent shaped.
minuta, min-U-ta, small, minute.
patula, see *T. erecta*.
signata, see *T. lunulata*.

Tamarix, TAM-ar-iks; from Tamaris (Tambro), a river in Spain, where some species abound. Flowering and hedge shrubs. *Tamaricaceae*.
anglica, see *T. gallica*.
chinensis, tshi-NEN-sis, of China.
gallica, GAL-ik-a, French.
hispida, HIS-pid-a, bristly.
pentandra, see *T. chinensis*.
tetrandra, tet-RAN-dra, four stamens.

Tanacetum, tan-a-SE-tum; derivation uncertain but said to be from Gr. *athanatos*, immortal, from its use in funeral cloths. Herbaceous perennials and rock plants. *Compositae*.
argenteum, ar-JEN-te-um, silvery-white – the foliage.
coccineum, kok-SIN-e-um, scarlet flowers.
herderi, see *Hippolytia herderi*.
parthenium, par-THEN-e-um, common pellitory. The Feverfew.
vulgare, vul-GAR-e, common. The Tansy.
v. crispum, see *T. vulgare*.

Tanakaea, tan-a-KE-a; in honour of Yoshio Tanaka (1838–1916), Japanese botanist. Rock plant. *Saxifragaceae*.
radicans, RAD-e-kanz, rooting i.e. the runners.

Taraxacum, ta-RAX-a-kum; through a native Arabian name to Persian *talkh charok*, bitter herb. Perennials. *Compositae*.
campylodes, kam-pe-LO-dees, having a curved appearance – the seed head.
officinale, see *T. campylodes*.

Tauscheria, towsh-E-re-a; after Ignatius J. Tauscher, professor of botany, Prague. Annual. *Brassicaceae*.
lasiocarpa, las-e-o-KAR-pa, hairy fruits.

Taxodium, taks-O-de-um; from L. *Taxus*, the yew; Gr. *oides*, resembling. Coniferous trees with yew-like foliage. *Cupressaceae*.
  distichum, DI-stik-um, the leaves in two rows. The Swamp Cypress.

Taxus, TAKS-us; Latin name for a yew tree; perhaps from Gr. *taxon*, a bow, the wood being once used for making bows. Evergreen trees. *Taxaceae*.
  baccata, bak-KAR-ta, berried. The Common Yew.
  brevifolia, brev-e-FO-le-a, short-leaved.
  cuspidata, kus-pid-A-ta, the leaves tipped with a short sharp point. The Japanese Yew.
  fastigiata, see *T. baccata*.

Tchihatchewia, ke-hatch-EW-e-a; in honour of the Russian botanist Tchihatcheff. Rock plants. *Brassicaceae*.
  isatidea, i-sa-TID-e-a, resembling *Isatis*.

Tecoma, te-KO-ma; said to be a contraction of the Mexican name *Tecomaxochtl*. Greenhouse and hardy trees and shrubs. *Bignoniaceae*.
  capensis, ka-PEN-sis, of the Cape of Good Hope.
  grandiflora, see *Campsis grandiflora*.
  radicans, see *Campsis radicans*.

Tecophilaea, te-KOF-e-le-a; after Tecophila Billotti, Italian botanical artist. Greenhouse flowering bulbs. *Tecophilaeaceae*.
  cyanocrocus, cy-AN-o-KRO-kus, referring to the colour (blue) and the shape (resembling a *Crocus*), literally the blue crocus.

Telanthera, tel-an-THE-ra; from Gr. *telios*, complete or perfect; *anthera*, an anther, the latter all being of equal lengths. Tender plants, for carpet bedding. *Amaranthaceae*.
  amabilis, see *Alternanthera ficoidea*.
  amoena, am-E-na, lovely, pleasing.
  bettzickiana, see *Alternanthera bettzickiana*.
  ficoidea, see *Alternanthera ficoidea*.
  versicolor, ver-SIK-o-lor, various or changeable colours.

Telekia, te-le-KE-a; in honour of Count Samuel Teleki de Szék (1739–1822), Hungarian patron of botany. Perennial herbs. *Compositae*.
  speciosa, spes-e-O-sa, showy.

Tellima, tel-LI-ma; said to be an anagram of *Mitella*, from which the genus was separated. Woodland perennials. *Saxifragaceae*.
  grandiflora, gran-dif-LO-ra, large-flowered.

Testudinaria, misplaced see below.
  elephantipes, see *Dioscorea elephantipes*.

Tetradenia, te-tra-DE-ne-a; from Gr. *tetra*, four; *aden*, a gland. Perennial shrubs. *Lamiaceae*.
  riparia, re-PAIR-e-a, frequenting river banks.

Tetragonia, tet-ra-GO-na; from Gr. *tetra*, four; *gonia*, an angle, the fruits being four angled. Hardy annual grown as spinach substitute in the vegetable garden. The New Zealand Spinach. *Aizoaceae*.
  expansa, see *T. tetragonioides*.
  tetragonioides, tet-ra-go-ne-OY-dees, resembling *Tetragonia*.

Tetraneuris, tet-ra-NU-ris; from Gr. *tetra*, four; *neura*, sinew. Annuals and perennial herbs. *Compositae*.
  acaulis, a-KAW-lis, stalkless, or apparently so.

Tetrapanax, tet-ra-PAN-ax; from Gr. *tetra*, four; *Panax*, in reference to the petals in the original description. Shrubs or small trees. *Araliaceae*.
  papyrifer, pap-e-RIF-er, papery.

Tetratheca, tet-ra-THE-ka; from Gr. *tetra*, four; *theke*, a box or cell, alluding to the anthers having four cells. Greenhouse flowering shrubs. *Elaeocarpaceae*.
  ericifolia, er-ik-e-FO-le-a; foliage resembling *Erica* (heath).
  hirsuta, hir-SU-ta, hairy.
  verticillata, ver-tis-il-LA-ta, whorled – the leaves.

Teucrium, TEW-kre-um; named after Teucher, a Trojan prince who first used one of the species in medicine. Annuals, herbaceous perennials, rock plants and shrubs. *Lamiaceae*.
  aureum, AW-re-um, golden – the flowers.
  chamaedrys, kam-E-dris, old name for germander signifying oak leaved and on the ground.
  fruticans, FRUT-ik-anz, from L. *frutex*, a shrub; shrubby or bushy.
  lucidum, LU-sid-um, shining – the foliage.

marum, MAR-um, old name for Cat Thyme, of uncertain origin. The Cat Thyme.

massiliense, mas-sil-e-EN-se, of Marseilles.

polium, PO-le-um, early name for Poly Germander, probably signifying grey – the foliage. The Poly Germander.

pyrenaicum, pir-en-A-ik-um, Pyrenean.

Thalia, THA-le-a; after Johannes Thal (1542–1583), German physician and botanist. Half-hardy perennials. *Marantaceae.*

dealbata, de-al-BA-ta, whitened, the foliage.

Thalictrum, thal-IK-trum; old Gr. name possibly from *thallo*, to flourish, or to abound in, referring to the numerous flowers. Herbaceous perennials. *Ranunculaceae.*

adiantifolium, cultivar see *T. minus.*

alpinum, al-PINE-um, alpine.

anemonoides, an-em-on-OY-dees, resembling *Anemone.*

aquilegiifolium, ak-wil-le-je-if-O-le-um, leaves resembling *Aquilegia.*

delavayi, de-la-VA-i, after Père Jean Marie Delavay (1834–1895), missionary and plant collector in Yunnan province, China.

dipterocarpum, see *T. delavayi.*

flavum, FLA-vum, yellow – the flowers.

glaucum, see *T. speciosissimum.*

minus, MI-nus, smaller.

speciosissimum, spes-e-o-SIS-se-mum, most showy.

Thelocactus, thel-o-KAK-tus; from Gr. *thele*, a nipple and *cactus*; refers to the tubercles of the plants. Greenhouse cacti. *Cactaceae.*

bicolor, BIK-ol-or, two-coloured.

hexaedrophorus, hex-a-DROF-or-us, having six sides – the tubercles.

setispinus, se-tis-PIN-us, spines resembling bristles.

subterraneus, see *Turbinicarpus subterraneus.*

Thelypteris, the-LIP-ter-is; from Gr. *thelus*, a female; *pteris*, a fern. The Female Fern. *Thelypteridaceae.*

confluens, kon-FLU-enz, from L. *confluo*, run together. Marsh Fern or Bog Fern.

Theobroma, the-o-BRO-ma; from Gr. *theos*, a god; *broma*, food. A name devised by Linneaus, food for the gods, referring to the fruit. The cocoa or chocolate. Warm house shrub. *Malvaceae.*

cacao, ka-KAY-o, Aztec name for the cocoa tree.

Thermopsis, ther-MOP-sis; from Gr. *thermos*, lupin; *opsis*, resemblance. Herbaceous perennials. *Leguminosae.*

caroliniana, see *T. villosa.*

fabacea, see *T. lupinoides.*

lupinoides, lu-pin-OY-dees, resembling *Lupinus* (lupin).

montana, mon-TA-na, of mountains.

villosa, vil-LO-sa, shaggy, hairy.

Thladiantha, thlad-e-AN-tha; from Gr. *thladias*, eunuch; *anthos*, a flower, in allusion to the suppressed anthers. Tender annual climbers. *Cucurbitaceae.*

dubia, DU-be-a, intermediate.

Thlaspi, THLAS-pe; from *thlaspis*, an old Greek name for a kind of cress. Rock plants. *Brassicaceae.*

bellidifolium, bel-lid-e-FO-le-um, foliage resembling *Bellis* (daisy).

rotundifolium, ro-tun-dif-O-le-um, round-leaved.

Thrinax, THRIN-aks; from Gr. *thrinax*, a trident, the shape of the leaves. Warmhouse palms. *Arecaceae.*

argentea, see *Coccothrinax argentea.*

excelsa, eks-SEL-sa, tall.

parviflora, par-vif-LOR-a, from L. *parvus*, small; *flor*, flower.

radiata, rad-e-A-ta, rayed – the leaf divisions.

Thuja, THEW-ya; classical name, possibly from Gr. *thuia*, ancient name for some resin bearing tree; or from Gr. *thuon*, a sacrifice, at which the resin would be burned as incense. Arbor-vitae. Coniferous trees. *Cupressaceae.*

dolabrata, see *Thujopsis dolabrata.*

gigantea, see *T. plicata.*

japonica, see *T. standishii.*

lobbii, see *T. plicata.*

occidentalis, oks-se-DEN-ta-lis, western – North America.

orientalis, see *Platycladus orientalis.*

plicata, pli-KA-ta, folded – the leaves.

standishii, stan-DISH-e-i, after John Standish (1814–1875), English nurseryman, who raised Robert Fortune's Chinese and Japanese plant introductions.

Thujopsis, thew-YOP-sis; from Gr. *Thuja*, and *opsis*, likeness, resembling *Thuja*. Coniferous tree. *Cupressaceae*.
  dolabrata, dol-a-BRA-ta, axe-shaped.

Thunbergia, thun- (or tun-) BER-ge-a; named after Karl Peter Thunberg (1743–1828), Swedish botanist, student of Linnaeus, and traveller in Japan and South Africa. Greenhouse climbers. *Acanthaceae*.
  alata, al-A-ta, winged – the leaf stalks.
  erecta, e-REK-ta, erect; upright.
  grandiflora, gran-dif-LO-ra, large-flowered.
  harrisii, HAR-ris-e-i, after Lord Harris, Governor of Madras, who first sent seeds to Kew.
  laurifolia, law-re-FO-le-a, foliage resembling *Laurus* (bay laurel).
  mysorensis, my-sor-EN-sis, from the Kingdom of Mysore, present day southern India.

Thunia, tu-NE-a; after Count Frank Graf von Thun of Tetschen (1786–1873), who had an important collection of orchids. Greenhouse terrestrial orchids. *Orchidaceae*.
  alba, AL-ba, from the L. *alba*, white.
  marshalliana, see *T. alba*.

Thymus, TY-mus; old Gr. name used by Theophrastus either for this plant or for savoury. Shrubby and trailing rock plants and culinary herbs. *Lamiaceae*.
  azoricus, see *T. serpyllum*.
  caespititius, ses-pit-it-E-us, growing closely, turf-like.
  carnosus, kar-NO-sus, flesh coloured – the leaves.
  × *citriodorus*, sit-re-o-DOR-us, lemon scented.
  erectus, see *T. carnosus*.
  herba-barona, HER-ba-bar-O-na, herb baron.
  lanuginosus, see *T. pulegioides*.
  micans, see *T. caespititius*.
  nitidus, see *T. richardii* subsp. *nitidus*.
  pulegioides, pu-le-je-OY-dees, resembling *Mentha pulegium*.
  richardii, rik-ARD-e-i, after Antoine Richard (1735–1807), royal gardener at the court of Louis XVI who introduced plants from the balearics.
  richardii subsp. *nitidus*, NIT-id-us, lustrous.
  serpyllum, ser-PIL-lum; old Gr. name *kerpyllos*, for the Wild Thyme.
  vulgaris, vul-GAR-is, common.

Thyrsacanthus, thir-sak-AN-thus; from Gr. *thyrsos*, a thyrse, and *acanthus* – thyrse-flowered *Acanthus*. Greenhouse flowering shrubs. *Acanthaceae*.
  rutilans, see *Odontonema rutilans*.

Tiarella, te-a-REL-la; from L. *tiara*, a little crown, alluding to the shape of the seed pod. Woodland plants. *Saxifragaceae*.
  cordifolia, kor-dif-OL-e-a, heart shaped.
  unifoliata, u-ne-fo-le-A-ta, one-leaved, that is, the leaves rising direct and singularly from the rootstock.

Tibouchina, tib-out-SHY-na; the native Guianan name. Greenhouse flowering shrubs. *Melastomataceae*.
  elegans, EL-e-ganz, elegant.
  semidecandra, sem-e-dek-AN-dra, with five anthers.

Tigridia, tig-RID-e-a; from Gr. *tigris*, a tiger; *eidos*, like, referring to the brightly spotted flowers. Half-hardy bulbs. *Iridaceae*.
  pavonia, pa-VO-ne-a, a peacock – the large showy flowers.

Tilia, TIL-e-a; old Latin name for Lime tree. Trees. *Malvaceae*.
  cordata, kor-DA-ta, heart shaped, the leaves.
  × *euchlora*, u-KLOR-a, dark green.
  × *europaea*, u-ro-PE-a, European.
  mongolica, mon-GOL-ik-a, Mongolian.
  petiolaris, see *T. tormentosa*.
  platyphyllos, plat-e-FIL-lus, broad-leaved.
  tormentosa, tor-men-TO-sa, felted, the leaf underparts.
  × *vulgaris*, see *T.* × *europaea*.

Tillandsia, til-LAND-se-a; after Elias Tillands (1640–1693), a Swedish botanist and physician, cataloguer of plants in Abo, Finland. Tropical epiphytes, flowering and ornamental foliage. *Bromeliaceae*.
  anceps, AN-ceps, two-edged, flattened.
  duvaliana, see *Vriesea duvaliana*.
  hieroglyphica, see *Vriesea hieroglyphica*.
  lindenii, LIN-den-e, after Jean Jules Linden (1817–1898), Belgium botanist and plant collector.
  regina, see *Vriesea regina*.
  tessalata, see *Vriesea gigantea*.

usneoides, us-ne-OY-dees, resembling *Usnea*, a genus of lichens, some pendulous. The Spanish Moss.

Tinantia, te-NAN-te-a; after François Auguste Tinant (1803–1853), Luxembourg botanist. Greenhouse or window herbaceous perennials. *Commelinaceae*.
erecta, e-REK-ta, erect habit.

Titanopsis, ti-tan-OP-sis; variant from late Middle English and Gr. *Titan*, the sun god; *opsis*, like; alluding to the round yellow flowers. Greenhouse succulent perennial. *Aizoaceae*.
calcarea, kal-kar-E-a, resembling limestone. Only found in limestone outcrops.

Todea, TO-de-a; after Heinrich Julius Tode (1733–1797), mycologist of Mecklenburg, Germany. Greenhouse ferns, coriaceous and filmy fronded. *Osmundaceae*.
africana, af-re-KA-na, of Africa.
barbara, BAR-bar-a, foreign.
hymenophylloides, see *Leptopteris hymenophylloides*.
pellucida, pel-LU-sid-a, pellucid or transparent.
superba, su-PER-ba, superb.

Tofieldia, to-FEEL-de-a; after Thomas Tofield (1730–1779), a friend of Hudson, the author of the genus. Herbaceous perennials. *Tofieldiaceae*.
calyculata, kal-ik-u-LA-ta, small-calyxed.
palustris, see *T. calyculata*.
pubens, see *Triantha racemosa*.

Tolmiea, TOL-me-a; after William Fraser Tolmie (1812–1886), Scottish surgeon of the Hudson Bay Company. Herbaceous perennial. *Saxifragaceae*.
menziesii, men-ZE-se-i, after Archibald Menzies (1754–1842), the Scottish botanist.

Tolpis, TOL-pis; derivation unexplained. Hardy annual. *Compositae*.
barbata, bar-BA-ta, bearded.

Torenia, tor-E-ne-a; after Reverend Olof Torén (1718–1753), an Apostle of Linnaeus, priest to the Swedish East India Company, he travelled to Surat, India and China. Greenhouse flowering annuals. *Linderniaceae*.
asiatica, aysh-e-AT-ik-a, Asiatic.
baillonii, bail-LO-ne-i, after Henri Ernest Baillon (1827–1895), French botanist.
flava, FLA-va, yellow.
fournieri, four-ne-AIR-i, after Eugène Pierre Nicolas Fournier (1834–1884), French botanist.

Torreya, tor-RE-a; after Dr. John Torrey (1796–1873), American botanist. Evergreen coniferous trees. *Taxaceae*.
californica, kal-if-OR-nik-a, of California.
nucifera, nu-SIF-er-a, nut-bearing.

Tournefortia, tourn-FOR-te-a; after Joseph Pitton de Tournefort (1656–1708), a notable systematic botanist whose labours laid the foundation for Linnaean plant classification. Greenhouse flowering shrubs. *Boraginaceae*.
bicolor, BIK-ol-or, two-coloured.
cordifolia, kor-dif-OL-e-a, heart shaped.
heliotropioides, see *Heliotropium nicotianifolium*.
laevigata, see *T. bicolor*.

Townsendia, town-SEND-e-a; after David Townsend (1787–1858), botanist of Pennsylvania, U.S.A. Rock plant. *Compositae*.
rothrockii, roth-ROK-e-i, after Joseph Rothrock (1839–1922), American plant collector on the Wheeler Expedition of 1875.
wilcoxiana, see *T. rothrockii*.

Toxicodendron, toks-ik-o-DEN-dron; from Gr. *toxicos*, poisonous; *dendron*, a tree. Trees. *Anacardiaceae*.
pubescens, pew-BES-senz, downy.
verniciferum, ver-nik-IF-er-a, yields varnish.

Toxicoscordion, toks-ik-o-SKOR-de-on; from Gr. *toxicos*, poisonous; *scordion*, a plant that smells like garlic. Bulbous plants. The Death Camas. *Melanthiaceae*.
nuttallii, nut-TAL-le-i, after Thomas Nuttall (1786–1859), English botanist, who travelled extensively in the U.S.A. from 1810 to 1834.

Trachelium, trak-E-le-um; from Gr. *trachelos*, the throat, in reference to the uses of the plant in ancient medicine. Herbaceous perennials. *Campanulaceae*.

caeruleum, ser-U-le-um, sky-blue. The Throat-wort.

Trachelospermum, trak-e-lo-SPER-mum; from Gr. *trachelos*, throat; *sperma*, seeds; application obscure. Greenhouse twining plants. *Apocynaceae.*

jasminoides, jaz-min-OY-dees, resembling Jasmine.

Trachycarpus, trak-e-KAR-pus; from Gr. *trachus*, rough; *karpus*, a fruit, the seeds of some species being hairy. Hardy palm. *Arecaceae.*

excelsus, see *Rhapis excelsa.*

fortunei, for-TOO-ne-i, after Robert Fortune (1812–1880), Scottish plant collector in China.

Trachymene, trak-e-ME-ne; from Gr. *trachus*, rough; *meninx*, a membrane, the channels in the fruit. Half-hardy annuals. *Araliaceae.*

coerulea, se-RU-le-a, blue.

Tradescantia, trad-e-SKAN-te-a; in honour of John Tradescant the Elder (c1570–1638), and John Tradescant the Younger (1608–1662), gardeners to Charles I. Greenhouse and hardy herbaceous perennials. *Commelinaceae.*

reginae, see *Dichorisandra reginae.*

rosea, see *Callisia rosea.*

spathacea, spath-A-se-a; with a spath, the spath-like bract surrounding the flower.

virginiana, vir-jin-e-A-na, of Virginia, U.S.A.

zebrina, ze-BRY-na, zebra-striped.

Tragopogon, trag-o-PO-gon; from Gr. *tragos*, a goat; *pogon*, a beard, referring to the long silky beards on the seeds. Culinary vegetable. *Compositae.*

porrifolius, por-rif-OL-e-us, foliage resembling *Allium porrum* (leek). The Salsafy.

Trapa, TRA-pa; from L. *calcitrapa*, an ancient four-pronged instrument once used in warfare for impeding cavalry horses. Word applied here in allusion to the four-horned seeds. Aquatic perennials. *Lythraceae.*

natans, NA-tanz, floating. The Water Chestnut.

Tremandra, tree-MAN-dra; from Gr. *trema*, aperture and *anthera*, the anthers burst open

through a hole. Greenhouse flowering shrub. *Elaeocarpaceae.*

stelligera, stel-LIG-er-a, star-bearing – refers to stellate down on the leaves.

Triantha, try-AN-tha; three-flowered. Herbaceous perennials. *Tofieldiaceae.*

racemosa, ras-em-O-sa, resembling a raceme.

Trichocentrum, tri-ko-SEN-trum; from Gr. *thrix*, a hair; *kentron*, spur, alluding to the long slender spur. Epiphytic orchids. *Orchidaceae.*

bicallosum, bik-al-LO-sum, two-warted.

splendidum, splen-DID-um, splendid.

Trichocereus, TRIK-o-SE-re-us; from Gr. *trichos*, a hair; *cereus*, cactus, the flowers having hairy tubes. Greenhouse cacti. *Cactaceae.*

macrogonus, see *Echinopsis macrogona.*

spachianus, see *Echinopsis spachiana.*

Trichodiadema, TRIK-o-di-a-DE-ma; from Gr. *trichos*, a hair; *diadema*, to bind round. Greenhouse succulent plants. *Aizoaceae.*

barbatum, bar-BA-tum, bearded.

densum, DEN-sum, close, dense.

stellatum, stel-LA-tum, starry.

stelligerum, stel-LIG-er-um, star-bearing.

Tricholaena, trik-ol-E-na; from Gr. *thrix*, a hair; *chlaina*, a cloak, referring to the shaggy spikelets. Half-hardy annual ornamental grass. *Poaceae.*

rosea, see *Melinis repens.*

Trichomanes, trik-OM-an-eez; from Gr. *thrix*, hair; *manos*, soft, the shining stems and soft, pellucid fronds. Greenhouse filmy ferns. *Hymenophyllaceae.*

bancroftii, ban-KROFT-e-i, after Edward Nathaniel Bancroft (1772–1842), English physician and botanist, active in Jamaica.

radicans, see *Vandenboschia radicans.*

reniforme, see *Cardiomanes reniforme.*

venosum, see *Polyphlebium venosum.*

Trichopilia, trik-op-E-le-a; from Gr. *thrix*, a hair; *pilion*, a cap, in allusion to three tufts of hair surmounting the column and hiding the anther bed. Greenhouse orchids. *Orchidaceae.*

crispa, see *T. marginata*.
marginata, mar-jin-A-ta, margined with another colour.
suavis, SWA-vis, sweet – the fragrance.
tortilis, TOR-til-is, twisted – the petals.

Trichosanthes, trik-os-AN-theez; from Gr. *thrix*, a hair; *anthos*, a flower, the edges of the corolla limbs are ciliated or fringed. Greenhouse ornamental gourd. *Cucurbitaceae*.
anguina, see *T. cucumerina*.
cucumerina, ku-ku-MER-e-na, resembling *Cucumis* (cucumber).

Trichostema, trik-o-STEM-a; from Gr. *thrix*, a hair; *stema*, stamen, in allusion to the hairlike slender filaments. Herbs and sub-shrubs. *Lamiaceae*.
lanatum, la-NA-tum, woolly.

Tricuspidaria, unresolved see below.
dependens, see *Crinodendron patagua*.
lanceolata, see *Crinodendron hookerianum*.

Tricyrtis, trik-ER-tis; from Gr. *treis*, three; *kyrtos*, humped, referring to the three outer sepals having swollen bases. Tender perennial. *Liliaceae*.
hirta, HER-ta, hairy – the plant is softly hairy.

Trientalis, tre-en-TA-lis; from L. *trien*, one-third of a foot, the height of the plant. Woodland herb. *Primulaceae*.
americana, a-mer-ik-A-na, of America.
europaea, see *Lysimachia europaea*.
latifolia, lat-if-O-le-a, broad-leaved.

Trifolium, tri-FO-le-um; from L. *tres*, three; *folium*, a leaf, the trefoil foliage. Trailing and other perennials and annuals. *Leguminosae*.
alpinum, al-PINE-um, alpine.
badium, BA-de-um, chestnut brown.
repens, RE-penz, creeping.
rubens, ROO-bens, red, usually means dark red.
uniflorum, u-nif-LO-rum, one-flowered.

Trillium, TRIL-le-um; from L. *triplum*, triple, alluding to the three-parted flowers. Tuberous perennials. The Wood Lilies. *Melanthiaceae*.
catesbaei, KATS-be-i, after Mark Catesby (1683–1749), author of 'A Natural History of Carolina'. Catesby's Trillium.
erectum, e-REK-tum, erect; upright.

grandiflorum, gran-dif-LO-rum, large flowered.
ovatum, o-VA-tum, egg-shaped, presumably the flower segments.
recurvatum, re-kur-VA-tum, recurved, the flowers.
rivale, see *Pseudotrillium rivale*.
sessile, SES-sil-e, stemless, the flowers.
stylosum, see *T. catesbaei*.

Tripleurospermum, tri-plu-ro-SPER-mum; from Gr. *tri*, three; *pleuron*, a rib; *sperma*, seed; in reference to the achene. Herbaceous perennials. *Compositae*.
inodorum, in-o-DOR-um, scentless. The Scentless Mayweed.

Tripodion, tri-POD-e-on; from Gr. *tri*, three; *podion*, a little foot. Herbaceous perennials. *Leguminosae*.
tetraphyllum, tet-raf-IL-um, from Gr. *tetra*, four; *phyllum*, leaf.

Tristagma, try-STAG-ma; from Gr. *tri*, three; *stagma*, that which drips, in reference to the three nectaries on the ovary. Bulbs. *Amaryllidaceae*.
uniflorum, u-nif-LO-rum, one-flowered.

Triteleia, try-tel-e-a; from Gr. *tri*, three; *telios*, perfect (complete), in allusion to the floral parts being in threes. Hardy bulbs. *Asparagaceae*.
bridgesii, brid-JEES-e-i, after Thomas Bridges (1807–1865), English botanist and collector. Bridges' Brodiaea.
grandiflora, gran-dif-LO-ra, large-flowered.
hendersonii, hen-der-SO-ne-i, after Louis Forniquet Henderson (1853–1942), American botanist and collector.
laxa, LAKS-a, loose – the flowers.
uniflora, see *Tristagma uniflorum*.

Tritoma, misapplied see below.
uvaria, see *Kniphofia uvaria*.

Tritonia, tri-TO-ne-a; from Gr. *triton*, a weathercock, in allusion to the variable positions of the anthers. Half-hardy bulbous plants. *Iridaceae*.
crocata, kro-KA-ta, saffron-yellow.
x crocosmiiflora, see *Crocosmia x crocosmiiflora*.
pottsii, see *Crocosmia pottsii*.

Trochodendron, trok-o-DEN-dron; from Gr. *trochos*, a wheel; *dendron*, a tree, the flowers being rayed like the spokes of a wheel. Evergreen tree. *Trochodendraceae*.

aralioides, ar-a-le-OY-dees, resembling *Aralia*.

Trollius, TROL-le-us; from the Swiss-German vernacular name *Trollblume*; some authorities give German *trol*, a globe, or something round. Herbaceous perennials. The Globe flower. *Ranunculaceae*.

altaicus, al-TA-ik-us, from the Altai Mountains in Central Asia.

asiaticus, a-she-AT-ik-us, of Asia.

chinensis, tshi-NEN-sis, of China.

europaeus, u-RO-pe-us, European.

ledebourii, led-e-BOUR-e-i, after Carl Friedrich von Ledebour (1785–1851), professor of science at the University of Tartu, Estonia.

ledebourii var. *polysepalus*, pol-e-SEP-a-lus, many sepals. Found only on the northern most Japanese Island of Rebun.

patulus, see *T. ranunculinus*.

pumilus, pew-MIL-us, dwarf.

ranunculinus, ra-nun-KUL-i-nus, resembling *Ranunculus* (buttercup).

Tropaeolum, trop-e-O-lum; from L. *tropaeum* (Gr. *tropaion*), a trophy, probably in allusion to the likeness of the flowers and leaves to the helmets and shields once displayed in Greece and Rome about scenes of victory. Annuals and herbaceous perennials. *Tropaeolaceae*.

aduncum, see *T. peregrinum*.

canariense, ka-nar-e-EN-se, of the Canary Islands.

lobbianum, see *T. peltophorum*.

majus, MA-jus, great. The Climbing Nasturtium.

minus, MI-nus, small. The Dwarf Nasturtium.

peltophorum, pel-to-FOR-um, from Gr. *pelte*, a little shield; *phoreo*, to bear. Shield Nasturtium.

pentaphyllum, pen-ta-FIL-lum, five-leaved or leaflets divided into five.

peregrinum, per-e-GRY-num, foreign or wandering, here probably means straggly in growth.

speciosum, spes-e-O-sum, showy.

tuberosum, tu-ber-O-sum, bearing tubers.

Tsuga, SU-ga; Japanese name for *Tsuga sieboldii*. Coniferous trees. *Pinaceae*.

albertiana, see *T. heterophylla*.

brunoniana, see *T. dumosa*.

canadensis, kan-a-DEN-sis, of Canada.

dumosa, du-MO-sa, bushy.

heterophylla, het-er-of-IL-la, variable leaf form.

mertensiana, mer-ten-se-A-na, after Franz Carl Mertens (1764–1831), German botanist.

sieboldii, se-BOLD-e-i, after Philipp Franz Balthasar von Siebold (1796–1866), German physician, botanist, and traveler.

Tulipa, TEW-lip-a; a corruption of the Persian word *thoulyban*, or *tulipant*, a turban, which the flower of the tulip is supposed to resemble. Hardy bulbs. The Tulip; most of the tulips in cultivation are hybrids. *Liliaceae*.

biflora, bif-LO-ra, two-flowered, that is, in pairs.

clusiana, klew-ze-A-na, of Carolus Clusius (1526–1609), pioneering botanist, remembered for his work on Tulip 'break' and plant breeding.

dasystemon, das-e-STE-mon, with hairy stamens.

elegans, see *T. gesneriana*.

gesneriana, ges-ner-e-A-na, after Conrad von Gessner (1516–1565), Swiss naturalist, who first described tulips growing at Augsburg.

greigii, GREG-e-i, after Major General Samuel Alexeyvich Greig (1827–1887), patron of botany, president of the Russian Horticultural Society.

kaufmanniana, kowf-man-ne-A-na, after Konstantin Petrovich von Kaufmann (1818–1882), the first Governor-General of Russian Turkestan.

orphanidea, or-fan-ID-e-a, after Theodoros G. Orphanides (1817–1886), professor of Botany at the National and Kapodistrian University of Athens.

persica, PER-sik-a, of Persia.

praecox, see *T. clusiana*.

praestans, PRE-stans, excelling, standing out.

sprengeri, spreng-ER-i, after Karl Sprenger (1846–1917), German nurseryman.

suaveolens, SWA-ve-ol-enz, sweetly scented.

sylvestris, sil-VES-tris, wild, pertaining to the woods.

tarda, TAR-da, late flowering.

vitelliana, see *T. gesneriana*.

Tunica, unresolved see below.

saxifraga, see *Petrorhagia saxifraga*.

Turbinicarpus, ter-bin-e-KAR-pus; with fruits shaped like a spinning top or cone. Cacti. *Cactaceae*.
  subterraneus, sub-ter-RAY-ne-us, underground in allusion to the fleshy tuberous root.

Tussilago, tus-sil-A-go; from L. *tussis*, a cough; *ago*, to act, its use in ancient medicine. Herbaceous perennials. Coltsfoot. *Compositae*.
  farfara, far-FAR-a, the ancient name for Coltsfoot.

Tweedia, TWEE-de-a; after James Tweedie (1775–1862), plant collector in South America. Greenhouse flowering twiners. *Apocynaceae*.
  coerulea, see *Oxypetalum coeruleum*.

Tydaea, unresolved see below.
  amabilis, see *Kohleria amabilis*.

Typha, TI-fa; ancient name, possibly from Gr. *typhe*, a cat's tail, or *typhos*, a fen, the usual habit of the reed-maces. Aquatics. *Typhaceae*.
  angustifolia, an-gus-tif-O-le-a, narrow-leaved.
  latifolia, lat-if-O-le-a, broad-leaved.
  laxmannii, lax-MAN-ne-i, after Erik Gustav Laxmann (1737-1796), Finnish-Swedish clergyman, explorer and naturalist.
  minima, MIN-e-ma, from L. *minimus*, smallest.

Ugni, UG-ne; derives from the Mapuche Native American name Uni, for Ugni molinae. Evergreen shrubs. *Myrtaceae*.
  molinae, mol-LIN-e, after Juan Ignacio Molina (1740–1829), a Chilean Jesuit Priest and botanist, who first described it.

Ulex, YU-leks; ancient L. name, used by Pliny for a type of heather. Thorny flowering shrub. *Leguminosae*.
  europaeus, u-RO-pe-us, European.
  gallii, GAL-le-i, of France (Gaul).
  minor, MY-nor, dwarf.
  nanus, see *U. minor*.

Ulmus, UL-mus; old L. name for an elm tree. The Romans used pollarded elms in vineyards over which to grow the vines. Trees. *Ulmaceae*.
  alata, al-A-ta, winged – branches having corky wings.
  campestris, see *U. glabra*.

carpinifolia, kar-pine-E-fo-le-a, resembling *Carpinus* (Hornbeam).
  fulva, see *U. rubra*.
  glabra, GLAB-ra, smooth, destitute of hairs.
  minor, MY-nor, dwarf.
  montana, see *U. glabra*.
  nitens, NIT-enz, shining or glossy – the leaves.
  procera, see *U. minor*.
  pumila, PU-mil-a, dwarf or diminutive.
  rubra, ROO-bra, red-coloured.
  stricta, see *U. minor*.

Umbellularia, um-bel-lu-lar-e-a; from L. *umbellula*, a little shade, in allusion to the flowers being in umbels, that is, parasol-shaped clusters. Shrubs. *Lauraceae*.
  californica, kal-if-OR-nik-a, of California.

Umbilicus, um-bil-E-kus; from L. *umbilicus*, the navel, referring to the rounded, concave leaves of some species. Succulent rock plant. *Crassulaceae*.
  pendulinus, see *U. rupestris*.
  rupestris, roo-PES-tris, rock loving.

Uniola, YU-ne-o-la; adopted L. name of an unknown plant. Grasses. *Poaceae*.
  paniculata, pan-ik-ul-A-ta, panicled.

Urceolina, ur-se-o-LE-na; from L. *urceolus*, a small cup or pitcher, alluding to the small size of the membranous floral cup or nectary. Greenhouse bulb. *Amaryllidaceae*.
  pendula, see *Urceolina urceolata*.
  urceolata, ur-se-o-LA-ta, urn-shaped.

Urospermum, u-ro-SPERM-um; from Gr. *oura*, a tail; *sperma*, seed, the latter having a tail-like protuberance. Border and rock plants. *Compositae*.
  dalechampii, da-le-SHAMP-e-i, after Jacques Daléchamps (1513–1588), French physician and botanist.
  picroides, pik-ROY-dees, resembling an ox-tongue.

Ursinia, ur-SE-ne-a; after Johann Ursinus of Regensburg (1608–1666), a German botanical author. Half-hardy annuals. *Compositae*.
  anethoides, an-eth-OY-dez, resembling *Anethum*.
  anthemoides, an-them-OY-dez, resembling *Anthemis*.
  pulchra, see *U. anthemoides*.

Utricularia, u-trik-u-LAIR-e-a; from L. *utriculus*, a small bladder, in allusion to the small insect-trapping sacs attached to the submerged leaves. Aquatic. *Lentibulariaceae*.

vulgaris, vul-GAR-is, common. The Bladderwort.

Uvularia, u-va-LAR-e-a; from L. *uvula*, the lobe hanging from the soft palate in man, because of the hanging flowers. Hardy perennials. *Colchicaceae*.

grandiflora, gran-dif-LO-ra, large-flowered.

perfoliata, per-fol-e-A-ta, perfoliate leaved – the leaves pierced by the stem.

Vaccaria, vak-KAR-re-a; old generic name from Latin meaning cow-herb. Annual Herb. *Caryophyllaceae*.

hispanica, his-PAN-ik-a, from Spain.

Vaccinium, vak-SIN-e-um; ancient Latin name, used by Virgil and Pliny, for the blueberry. Shrubs. *Ericaceae*.

angustifolium, an-gus-tif-O-le-um, having narrow leaves.

arctostaphylos, ark-tos-TAF-il-os, from Gr. *arktos*, a bear; *staphlye*, a bunch of grapes, old generic name meaning fruits eaten by bears.

corymbosum, kor-im-BO-sum, corymbs, in allusion to the cluster of flowers in which the outer stalks or pedicels are longer than the inner ones.

erythrocarpum, er-ith-ro-KAR-pum, having red fruit.

floribundum, flor-ib-UN-dum, abundant or free flowering.

glaucoalbum, GLAW-ko-AL-bum, blue-white, the underside of the leaf.

macrocarpon, mak-ro-KAR-pon, having large fruits.

mortinia, see *V. floribundum*.

myrtillus, mir-TIL-lus, myrtle, old name for Bilberry. The Bilberry or Whottleberry.

ovatum, o-VA-tum, egg-shaped, the leaves.

oxycoccos, oks-e-KOK-kos, from Gr. *oxys*, sharp or bitter; *kokkos*, a berry, in reference to the sourness of the fruits.

pennsylvanicum, pen-sil-VAN-ik-um, of Pennsylvania.

uliginosum, u-lij-in-O-sum, growing in swamps.

vitis-idaea, VI-tis-i-DE-a, old generic name, meaning vine of Mount Ida (Crete). The Cowberry.

Valeriana, va-leer-e-A-na; from L. *valeo*, to be healthy (ancient medicine); in reference to the plants associated medicinal use. Herbaceous perennials. *Caprifoliaceae*.

celtica, KEL-tik-a, Celtic.

dioica, di-OY-ka, literally two houses, that is, male and female parts being on separate plants, dioecious.

phu, few, Gr. *phou*, old name for Valerian, or Cretan Spikenard; said to mean evil smelling.

supina, su-PI-na, prostrate.

Valerianella, va-leer-e-a-NEL-la; diminutive of *Valeriana*, from the resemblance to these herbs. Salad vegetables. *Caprifoliaceae*.

locusta, low-KUS-ta, growing in an enclosed space.

olitoria, see *V. locusta*.

Vallisneria, val-lis-NEER-e-a; after Antonio Vallisnieri de Vallisnera (1661–1730), professor of Padua. Fresh-water aquatics. *Hydrocharitaceae*.

spiralis, spi-RA-lis, spiral, or coiled, the growths.

Vallota, misapplied see below.

purpurea, see *Cyrtanthus elatus*.

Vancouveria, van-koo-VEER-e-a; after Captain George Vancouver (1757–1798), Royal Navy, British explorer. Sailed with Captain Cook. He undertook a four year voyage (1791–1795) during which he carried out the first detailed survey of the Pacific coast of North America. Woodland herb. *Berberidaceae*.

hexandra, heks-AN-dra, with six stamens.

Vanda, VAN-da; the Sanskrit name of the first species introduced. Tropical orchids. *Orchidaceae*.

coerulea, ser- (or ker-) U-le-a, Sky-blue.

kimballiana, see *Holcoglossum kimballianum*.

suavis, see *V. tricolor* var. *suavis*.

teres, see *Papilionanthe teres*.

tricolor, TRIK-o-lor, three coloured.

tricolor var. *suavis*, SWA-vis, sweet.

Vandenboschia, van-den-BOSH-e-a; named in honour of Roelof Benjamin van den Bosch (1810–1862), Dutch botanist, specialising in ferns and mosses. Ferns. *Hymenophyllaceae.*

 radicans, RAD-e-kanz, creeping and rooting. The Killarney Fern.

Vanheerdea, van-HEER-dee-a; for Pieter Van Heerde (1893–1979), South African teacher and succulent plant collector. Succulents. *Aizoaceae.*

 roodiae, ROOD-e-e, after Mrs Petrusa Benjamina Rood (1861–1946), South African succulent plant collector, who sent plants and seed to N.E. Brown and Pole-Evans.

Vanilla, va-NIL-la; from Spanish *vaynilla,* a diminutive of *vaina,* signifying sheath, and bestowed because of the cylindrical seed pods suggesting the sheath of a knife. Tropical climbing orchid. The seed pods of *V. planifolia* are the vanilla of commerce. *Orchidaceae.*

 planifolia, plan-if-OL-e-a, flat-leaved.

Veltheimia, vel-TYM-e-a; after Count Veltheim (1741–1801), German patron of botany. Greenhouse flowering bulbs. *Asparagaceae.*

 bracteata, brak-te-A-ta, having bracts, or modified leaves, at bases of leaf stalks.
 capensis, ka-PEN-sis, of the Cape of Good Hope.
 glauca, see *V. capensis.*
 viridifolia, see *V. capensis.*

Venidium, ven-ID-e-um; from L. *vena,* vein; because of the ribbed fruits. South African half-hardy annuals and perennials. *Compositae.*

 calendulaceum, kal-en-du-LA-se-um, resembling *Calendula.*
 fastuosum, see *Arctotis fastuosa.*

Veratrum, ver-A-trum; ancient name of hellebore. False Hellebore. Herbaceous perennials. *Melanthiaceae.*

 album, AL-bum, white – the flowers.
 nigrum, NI-grum, black – the dark purple flowers.
 viride, VIR-id-e, green – the flowers.

Verbascum, ver-BAS-kum; classical L. name, possibly a corruption of L. *barbascum,* a hairy plant (*barba,* a beard), many of the mulleins having downy foliage. Herbaceous perennials. *Scrophulariaceae.*

 arcturus, ark-TU-rus, after Arcturus, a yellow star, the colour of the flowers.
 chaixii, SCHAY-ze-i, after Abbé Dominique Chaix (1730–1799), French cleric and botanist.
 creticum, KRE-tik-um, of Crete.
 cupreum, KU-pre-um, copper-coloured – the flowers.
 densiflorum, den-sif-LO-rum, many or dense flowers.
 olympicum, ol-IM-pik-um, of Olympia.
 pannosum, pan-NO-sum, roughly hairy, like wool cloth.
 phlomoides, flo-MOY-dees, like *Phlomis.*
 phoeniceum, fen-IK-e-um, reddish-scarlet.
 thapsiforme, see *V. densiflorum.*
 thapsus, THAP-sus, after Thapsus in ancient Africa (now Tunisia), or after Greek Thapsos Island.

Verbena, ver-BE-na; ancient L. name of the common vervain, *V. officinalis*; some authorities say it is derived from L. *verbenae,* the sacred branches of olive, laurel and myrtle used in religious ceremonies and also in medicine. Herbaceous perennials. *Verbenaceae.*

 bonariensis, bon-ar-e-EN-sis, of Bonaria, Buenos Ayres.
 chamaedryfolia, see *Glandularia peruviana.*
 erinoides, see *Glandularia laciniata.*
 hortensis, hor-TEN-sis, belonging to gardens.
 hybrida, hi-BRID-a, a Latinised form of hybrid, a cross between two plants.
 rigida, rij-ID-a, rigid; stiff.
 tenera, see *Glandularia tenera.*
 venosa, see *V. rigida.*

Verbesina, ver-be-SE-na; from the similarity of the foliage to *Verbena.* Half-hardy perennials. *Compositae.*

 encelioides, en-se-le-OY-dees, resembling *Encelia.*
 helianthoides, he-le-anth-OY-dees, resembling *Helianthus.*

Vernonia, ver-NO-ne-a; after William Vernon (circa 1666–1711), British botanist who collected in Maryland in 1698. Hardy perennials. *Compositae.*

 altissima, see *V. gigantea.*
 arkansana, ar-kan-SA-na, of Arkansas.

gigantea, ji-GAN-te-a, unusually tall or big.

noveboracensis, no-ve-bor-a-SEN-sis, of New York (*Novum Eboracum*, from the Roman name for York).

Veronica, ver-ON-ik-a; origin doubtful. Some authorities give it as a corruption of *Betonica*, the foliage of the plants being similar, others suggest it is a Latin form of the Greek word *Beronike*, yet others refer it to the Greek *hiera eicon*, sacred image, or the Arabic *viroo nikoo*, beautiful remembrance. Annuals, herbaceous perennials, aquatics and shrubs. *Plantaginaceae*.

amplexicaulis, am-pleks-e-KAW-lis, leaves clasping the stem.

anagallis, an-a-GAL-lis, old name for Water Pimpernel.

× *andersonii*, an-der-SO-ne-i, named after Anderson of Maryfield, Edinburgh, who crossed *V. speciosa* with *V. salicifolia* to develop this popular garden hybrid.

angustifolia, see *Psuedolysimachion linariifolium*.

armstrongii, arm-STRONG-e-i, found by J.F Armstrong in 1869.

austriaca, AWS-tre-ak-a, of Austria.

austriaca subsp. *teucrium,* TEW-kre-um, old generic name, which see.

balfouriana, bal-four-e-A-na, after Sir Isaac Bayley Balfour (1853–1922), professor of botany at the University of Edinburgh. Raised by seed from New Zealand around 1897.

beccabunga, bek-ka-BUNG-a, old name for Brooklime, meaning "mouth smart" that is, pungent.

bidwillii, bid-WIL-le-i, after John Bidwill (1815–1853)who discovered it.

buxifolia, buks-if-O-le-a, resembling *Buxus* (Box), the leaf.

canescens, kan-ES-senz, more or less grey or hoary.

carnosula, kar-NOS-u-la, somewhat fleshy – the foliage.

catarractae, see *Parahebe catarractae*.

chamaedrys, kam-E-dris, old name used by Theophrastus for Germander Speedwell, from Gr. *chamai*, on the ground; *drys*, oak; the plant's habit and shape of leaves.

chathamica, chat-HAM-ik-a, of Chatham Islands.

cinerea, see *V. wyomingensis*.

colensoi, kol-EN-so-i, after William Colenso (1811–1899), New Zealand missionary and botanist.

cuppressoides, ku-pres-OY-dees, the leaves resembling *Cupressus* (cypress).

darwiniana, dar-win-e-A-na, after Charles Darwin (1809–1882), geologist and naturalist who collected plants on the voyage of The Beagle.

decumbens, de-KUM-benz, lying on the ground with the tips upright.

elliptica, el-LIP-tik-a, elliptic, the leaves.

filiformis, fil-if-OR-mis, thread-like, the growths.

fruticans, FRUT-ik-anz, from L. *frutex*, a shrub; shrubby or bushy.

gentianoides, jen-te-an-OY-dees, resembling *Gentiana* – the tufted foliage.

hectori, hek-TOR-i, after Sir James Hector (1834–1907), New Zealand geologist and botanist of Scottish origin.

hulkeana, see *Heliohebe hulkeana*.

incana, see *V. spicata* subsp. *incana*.

longifolia, long-if-OL-e-a, long leaves.

lyallii, li-AL-e-i, after David Lyall (1817–1895), Scottish botanist and lifetime friend of Sir Joseph Dalton Hooker.

lycopodioides, li-ko-pod-e-OY-dees, resembling *Lycopodium* or club moss.

orientalis, or-e-en-TA-lis, from the Orient; Eastern.

parviflora, par-vif-LOR-a, from L. *parvus*, small; *flor*, flower.

pectinata, pek-tin-A-ta, from L. *pecten*, comb. Comblike – the leaves.

persica, PER-sik-a, of Persia.

pimeleoides, py-mel-e-OY-dees, resembling *Pimelia*.

pinguifolia, pin-gwe-FO-le-a, the leaves appearing fatty or greasy.

repens, RE-penz, creeping.

salicifolia, sal-is-if-O-le-a, leaves resembling *Salix* (willow).

salicornloides, sal-ik-orn-LOY-dees, resembling *Salicornia*.

saxatilis, see *V. fruticans*.

speciosa, spes-e-O-sa, showy.

spicata, spe-KA-ta, spiked – the inflorescence.

spicata subsp. *incana*, in-KA-na, covered in soft white hairs.

subsessilis, sub-SES-sil-is, partially sitting – the leaves having little or no stalk.

teucrium, see *austiaca* subsp. *teucrium*.

traversii, tra-VER-se-i, after William Thomas Locke Travers (1819–1903), solicitor, parliamentarian and botanist.

vernicosa, ver-nik-O-sa, shining as if varnished.

virginica, see *Veronicastrum virginicum*.

wyomingensis, wy-o-ming-EN-sis, in relation to the Algonquin name for large prairie place.

Veronicastrum, ver-on-e-KAS-trum; from *Veronica*, which see; *astrum*, indicating incomplete resemblance. Perennial herbs. *Plantaginaceae*.
  virginicum, ver-JIN-ik-um, of Virginia.

Vesalea, vee-sal-E-a; in honour of Andreas Vesalius (1514–1564), Brussels born Father of the Science of Anatomy, professor at the Univeristy of Padua. Shrubs. *Caprifoliaceae*.
  floribunda, flor-e-BUN-da, many-flowered.

Vesicaria, ves-e-KAIR-e-a; from L. *vesica*, a bladder, alluding to the inflated seed pods. Branched annuals or perennials. *Brassicaceae*.
  arctica, see *Physaria mendocina*.
  gnaphalodes, see *Physoptychis caspica*.
  gracilis, see *Physaria gracilis*.
  utriculata, see *Alyssoides utriculata*.

Viburnum, vi-BUR-num; old Latin name for one of the species of this genus, possibly *V. lantana*. Shrubs. *Adoxaceae*.
  acerifolium, a-ser-if-O-le-um, leaves resembling *Acer* (maple).
  atrocyaneum, at-row-sy-AN-e-um, very dark blue.
  atrocyaneum f. *harryanum*, har-re-A-num, after Sir Harry Veitch (1840–1924), horticulturist and head of the nursery firm James Veitch & Sons, Chelsea, London. Instrumental in promoting the Royal International Horticultural Exhibition of 1912 – the first Chelsea Flower Show.
  × *bodnantense*, bod-nan-TEN-see, referring to Bodnant Gardens, Talycafn, North Wales, largely created by the 2nd Lord Aberconway.
  carlesii, KAR-les-e-i, after William Richard Carles (1848–1929), consular and botanist, he collected plants in China, Japan and Korea sending specimens back to the Royal Botanic Garden Kew.
  davidii, DA-vid-e-i, after Père Armand David (1826–1900), French missionary and plant collector in China. Introduced by Wilson for Messrs. Veitch in 1904.
  farreri, FAR-rer-i, in honour of Reginald John Farrer (1880–1920), plant hunter and botanist.
  fragrans, FRA-granz, fragrant.

grandiflorum, gran-dif-LO-rum, large flowered. Introduced from Bhutan by Robert Cooper for A.K. Bulley in 1914.
  harryanum, see *V. atrocyaneum* f. *harryanum*.
  henryi, HEN-re-i, after Dr. Augustine Henry (1857–1930), Irish plantsman and pioneer collector in China.
  hessei, HES-se-i, after Hesse, a Hanoverian who introduced it.
  hupehense, hu-pe-EN-se, from Hupeh, China.
  kansuense, kan-su-EN-se, from Kansu, China.
  lantana, lan-TA-na, late Latin name of *Viburnum*. The Wayfaring Tree.
  macrocephalum, mak-ro-SEF-a-lum, large-headed, the flowers.
  odoratissimum, od-or-a-TIS-sim-um, sweetest-scented.
  opulus, OP-ul-us, once the generic name for the Guelder Rose; derived from an old Latin name for Maple – the leaves of both being somewhat similar. The Guelder Rose.
  prunifolium, pru-nif-O-le-um, *Prunus* (plum) leaved.
  rhytidophyllum, ry-tid-of-IL-lum, leaves deeply grooved.
  tinus, TI-nus, the old Latin name for the species, meaning obscure.
  tomentosum, to-men-TO-sum, felted – the leaves.
  utile, YU-til-e, useful.

Vicia, VIS-e-a; classical L. name, possibly from L. *vincio*, to bind, in reference to the clinging tendrils of many of the vetches. Annual and herbaceous perennials. *Leguminosae*.
  argentea, ar-JEN-te-a, silvery, the foliage.
  cracca, KRAK-a, old name for Tufted Vetch, possibly from Gr. *arachon*, a pea-like plant.
  faba, FA-ba, Faba – one-time generic name. The Broad Bean.
  orobus, OR-o-bus, once the generic name (q.v.) of the Bitter Vetch.
  pyrenaica, pir-en-A-ik-a, Pyrenean.
  unijuga, u-ne-JU-ga, in single pairs, the leaves.

Victoria, vik-TOR-e-a; after Queen Victoria. Tropical aquatic. *Nymphaeaceae*.
  amazonica, a-ma-ZON-ik-a, from the region of the Amazon.
  regia, RE-je-a, Royal.

Vieusseuxia, misapplied please see below.
  glaucopsis, see *Moraea aristata*.
  pavonia, see *Tigridia pavonia*.

Villarsia, vil-LAR-se-a; after Dominique Villars (1745–1814), professor of botany at Grenoble, who was noted for his work on the flora of the Dauphiné region, France. Herbaceous perennials and aquatics. *Menyanthaceae*.

chilensis, chil-EN-sis, Chilean.

nymphoidea, nim-FOY-de-a, resembling *Nyphaea*.

ovata, o-VA-ta, egg-shaped – the leaves.

reniformis, see *Ornduffia reniformis*.

Vinca, VIN-ka; old L. name, possibly from L. *vincio*, to bind, alluding to the long tough runners. Greenhouse and hardy shrubby plants. *Apocynaceae*.

difformis, dif-FOR-mis, of unusual form, probably alluding to the shape of flower segments.

herbacea, her-BA-se-a, herbaceous.

major, MA-jor, greater.

minor, MI-nor, lesser. The Lesser Periwinkle.

rosea, see *Catharanthus roseus*.

Viola, VI-o-la; the ancient Latin name for a violet (akin to Gr. *ion*, a violet). Annuals or perennial herbs and small shrubs. *Violaceae*.

arenaria, see *V. rupestris*.

biflora, bif-LO-ra, two-flowered, that is, in pairs.

bosniaca, see *V. tricolor* subsp. *macedonica*.

calcarata, kal-kar-A-ta, spurred.

canadensis, kan-a-DEN-sis, Canadian.

canina, kan-I-na, dog, probably signifying common or worthless, that is, scentless. The Dog Violet.

cenisia, sen-IS-e-a, from Mont Cenis, France.

cornuta, kor-NEW-ta, horned – the sepals are awl-shaped and suggest horns.

cucullata, see *V. obliqua*.

dichroa, dik-RO-a, two-coloured.

gracilis, GRAS-il-is, slender.

hederacea, hed-er-A-se-a, resembling *Hedera* (Ivy) – the shape of the leaves.

hirta, HER-ta, hairy.

hispida, HIS-pid-a, bristly.

lutea, LU-te-a, yellow.

munbyana, mun-be-A-na, after Giles Munby (1813–1876), botanist.

obliqua, ob-LEE-kwa, with unequal sides.

odorata, od-or-A-ta, sweet-scented. The Sweet Violet.

pedata, ped-A-ta, footed – the bird's claw-like leaves.

pedunculata, ped-ungk-ul-A-ta, peduncled – the long flower stalks.

pinnata, pin-NA-ta, pinnated – the divided leaves.

rothomagensis, see *V. hispida*.

rupestris, roo-PES-tris, growing on rocks.

tricolor, TRIK-o-lor, three coloured.

tricolor subsp. *macedonica*, mas-e-DON-ik-a, of Macedonia.

Viscaria, vis-KAIR-e-a; from L. *viscum*, birdlime. Rock and border plants. *Caryophyllaceae*.

oculata, ok-ul-A-ta, with an eye.

Viscum, VIS-kum; Latin name for Mistletoe. Parasitic shrubby plant. *Santalaceae*.

album, AL-bum, white – the berries. The Mistletoe.

Vitaliana, vit-al-e-A-na; in honour of Vitaliano Donati (1717–1762), Italian botanist. Perennial herb. *Primulaceae*.

primuliflora, prim-u-le-FLOR-a, Primrose-flowered.

Vitex, VI-teks; ancient L. name for *V. agnus-castus*. Hardy and greenhouse flowering shrubs. *Lamiaceae*.

agnus-castus, AG-nus-KAS-tus, chaste lamb tree – a classical name.

Vitis, VI-tis; old Latin name for grapevine. Climbing foliage and fruit plants. *Vitaceae*.

aestivalis, es-tiv-A-lis, summer.

amurensis, am-oor-EN-sis, the region of the Amur river.

arizonica, ar-i-ZON-ik-a, from Arizona.

armata, see *V. davidii*.

candicans, KAN-dik-ans, white – the shoots.

coignetiae, koyn-ET-e-e, first introduced from Japan to France by a Madame Coignet.

davidii, DA-vid-e-i, discovered in Shensi, in 1872, by Père Armand David (1826–1900), French missionary and plant collector in China. Plants in cultivation are probably derived from a re-introduction by Wilson for Messrs. Veitch in 1900.

flexuosa, fleks-u-O-sa, flexous, the growths curving in a wavy manner.

henryana, see *Parthenocissus henryana*.

heterophylla, see *Ampelopsis glandulosa* var. *heterophylla*.

inconstans, see *Parthenocissus tricuspidata*.

monticola, mon-TIK-o-la, growing on hills.

piasezkii, pi-a-ZET-ski-i, named after P.J. Piaszki, who collected in China around 1875.

quinquefolia, see *Parthenocissus quinquefolia*.

sinensis, see *V. piasezkii*.

striata, see *Cissus striata*.

thunbergii, thun-BERG-e-i, after Carl Peter Thunberg (1743–1828), Swedish botanist and student of Linnaeus.

vinifera, vin-IF-er-a, wine-producing. The Grape Vine.

vitacea, see *Parthenocissus inserta*.

Vittadinia, vit-ta-DIN-e-a; after Carlo Vittadini (1800–1865), Italian mycologist and physician. Perennial herbs with thick rootstocks, or branching sub-shrubs. *Compositae*.

australis, aws-TRA-lis, southern.

Vriesea, VRE-ze-a or VREEZ-e-a; after Willem Henrik de Vriese (1806–1862), Dutch botanist, professor of botany first at Amsterdam, then at Leiden. Perennial herbs. *Bromeliaceae*.

carinata, kar-in-A-ta, keeled.

duvaliana, du-val-e-A-na, after Henri Duval (1777–1814), French medical practitioner and author.

gigantea, ji-GAN-te-a, unusually tall or big.

hieroglyphica, hi-er-o-GLIF-ik-a, resembling hieroglyphics, the markings on the leaves.

psittacina, sit-tak-E-na, parrot-like - the floral colouring.

regina, re-JI-na, queen.

splendens, SPLEN-denz, splendid.

tessellata, see *V. gigantea*

Wahlenbergia, wah-len-BER-ge-a; named after Dr. Wahlenberg (1780–1851) of Uppsala, a botanical author. Rock-garden perennials. *Campanulaceae*.

albomarginata, AL-bow-mar-jin-A-ta, white margined.

dalmatica, see *Edraianthus dalmaticus*.

gracilis, GRAS-il-is, slender.

hederacea, hed-er-A-se-a, the leaves resembling *Hedera* (ivy).

kitaibelii, see *Edraianthus graminifolius*.

pumilio, see *Edraianthus pumilio*.

serpyllifolia, see *Edraianthus serpyllifolius*.

tasmanica, see *W. albomarginata*.

vinciflora, see *W. gracilis*.

Waitzia, WAIT-ze-a; after F.A.C. Waitz of Java, who corresponded with Wendland. Half-hardy annuals. *Compositae*.

aurea, see *Waitzia nitida*.

grandiflora, gran-dif-LO-ra, large flowered.

nitida, NIT-id-a, shining – the leaves.

Waldsteinia, wald- (or vald-) STI-ne-a; after Count Franz Adam Waldstein-Wartenburg (1759–1823), Austrian botanist, co-author of a book on Hungarian flora. Trailing perennials. *Rosaceae*.

fragarioides, fraj-air-e-OY-deez, resembling *Fragaria* (strawberry), the leaves.

ternata, ter-NA-ta, with three leaflets.

trifolia, see *W. ternata*.

Watsonia, wat-SO-ne-a; named after Sir William Watson (1715–1787), English medical practitioner and scientist. Half-hardy shrubs. *Iridaceae*.

ardernei, see *W. borbonica*.

borbonica, bor-bon-IK-a, in honour of the House of Bourbon of France.

borbonica subsp. *ardernei*, ar-DER-ne-i, after Henry Matthew Arderne (1834–1914), businessman and plantsman, who introduced it about 1890.

iridifolia, see *W. meriana*.

meriana, meer-e-A-na, after Maria Sybilla Merian (1647–1717), German-born naturalist and scientific illustrator.

Wedelia, wed- (or ved-) E-le-a; after George W. Wedel (1645–1721), professor of botany at Jena. Half-hardy perennials. *Compositae*.

aurea, see *Lasianthaea aurea*.

radiosa, rad-e-O-sa, rayed.

Weigela, we- (or ve-) JE-la; after Christian Ehrenfried von Weigel (1748–1831), a professor of botany at Griefswald. Flowering shrubs. *Caprifoliaceae*.

floribunda, flor-e-BUN-da, abundant or free flowering.

florida, FLO-rid-a, from L. *floridus*, flowery.

rosea, see *Diervilla florida*.

Weinmannia, ween- (or veen-) MAN-ne-a; after Johann Wilhelm Weinmann (1683–1741), of Regensburg, German apothecary. Greenhouse shrubs. *Cunoniaceae*.

reticulata, ret-ik-ul-A-ta, netted or lined.
trichosperma, trik-o-SPER-ma, hairy-seeded.

Wellingtonia, see *Sequoiadendron*.

Welwitschia, wel- (or vel-) VITS-ke-a; after Friedrich Welwitsch (1806–1872), Austrian botanist and explorer, who introduced this plant curiosity to Europe. Xerophyte. *Welwitschiaceae*.
mirabilis, mir-A-bil-is, wonderful.

Whitlavia, see *Phacelia*.

Widdringtonia, WID-ring-TO-ne-a; after Captain Widdrington, conifer botanist in the late 1700s & early 1800s. Tender conifers. *Cupressaceae*.
cupressoides, see *W. nodiflora*.
juniperoides, see *W. nodiflora*.
nodiflora, no-dif-LO-ra, flowering at the nodes.

Wigandia, wig- (or vig-) AN-de-a; after Johannes Wigand (1523–1587), Bishop of Pomernia, botanical author. Summer bedding foliage plants. *Boraginaceae*.
caracasana, see *W. urens*.
urens, U-rens, stinging; burning.
vigieri, VIG-e-air-e, dedicated to Achille Georges Hippolyte, Vicomte Vigier (1825–1883), who created a Botanic garden at Nice.

Wilcoxia, unresolved see below. *Cactaceae*.
tuberosus, see *Echinocereus poselgeri*.

Wisteria, wis-TEER-e-a; after Caspar Wistar (1761–1818), professor at University of Penn. Climbing flowering shrubs. *Leguminosae*.
chinensis, see *W. sinensis*.
floribunda, flor-e-BUN-da, abundant or free flowering.
japonica, see *Millettia japonica*.
multijuga, see *W. floribunda*.
sinensis, si-NEN-sis, Chinese.

Witsenia, wit-SEE-ne-a; after Nicholas Witsen eighteenth century Dutch patron of botany. Greenhouse flowering shrubs. *Iridaceae*.
corymbosa, see *Nivenia corymbosa*.

Wollemia, wol-EM-e-a; named after the Wollemi National Park, New South Wales.

Previously only found in fossil records until *Wollemia nobilis* was discovered in 1994. Trees. *Araucariaceae*.
nobilis, NO-bil-is, in honour of David Noble (born 1964), canyoner, member of the team that discovered it.

Woodsia, WOOD-se-a; named after Joseph Woods (1776–1864), English Architect and botanist. Greenhouse and hardy ferns. *Woodsiaceae*.
alpina, al-PINE-a (or al-PIN-a), of the Alps or alpine.
hyperborea, see *W. alpina*.
ilvensis, il-VEN-sis, from Ilva (Elba).
obtusa, ob-TU-sa, blunt.
polystichoides, pol-is-tik-OY-deez, resembling *Polystichum*.

Woodwardia, wood-WARD-e-a; after Thomas Jenkinson Woodward (1745–1820), English botanist. Greenhouse ferns. *Blechnaceae*.
areolata, ar-e-o-LA-ta, divided into open spaces between the veins.
radicans, RAD-e-kanz, creeping and rooting.
virginica, vir-JIN-ik-a, Virginian.

Wulfenia, woolf-E-ne-a; after Franz Xavier von Wulfen (1728–1805), Austrian botanical author, teacher and Jesuit abbot. Herbaceous perennials. *Plantaginaceae*.
amherstiana, see *Wulfeniopsis amherstiana*.
carinthiaca, kar-in-the-A-ka, from Carinthia.

Wulfeniopsis, woolf-en-E-op-sis; from *Wulfenia* (which see); *opsis*, resembles, likeness. Herbaceous perennials. *Plantaginaceae*.
amherstiana, am-HERST-e-a-na, after Sarah, Countess Amherst (1762–1838), an amateur botanist who collected plants on her travels in India.

Xanthoceras, zanth-OS-er-as; from Gr. xanthos, yellow; keras, a horn, the projecting horn-like growths between the petals. Trees. *Sapindaceae*.
sorbifolum, sor-bif-O-le-um, *Sorbus* leaved.

Xeranthemum, zer-AN-the-mum; from Gr. xeros, dry; *anthos*, a flower, alluding to the chief characteristics of this plant. The dried flower heads retain their form and colour for years. Annuals. *Compositae.*

  annuum, AN-nu-um, annual. Everlasting flower.

Xerophyllum, zer-o-FIL-lum; from Gr. *xeros*, dry, *phyllon*, a leaf, the leaves being dry and grassy. Herbaceous perennials. *Melanthiaceae.*

  asphodeloides, ass-fo-del-OY-dees, resembling *Aphodelus* (asphodel).
  setifolium, see *X. asphodeloides*

Yucca, YUK-ka; modification of an aboriginal name applied to another plant. Flowering and foliage shrubs. *Asparagaceae.*

  aloifolia, al-o-if-OL-e-a, foliage resembles *Aloe.*
  anceps, AN-ceps, two-edged, flattened.
  baccata, bak-KA-ta, berried, referring to the edible fruits.
  brevifolia, brev-if-OL-e-a, short-leaved.
  filamentosa, fil-a-men-TO-za, thready, referring to the filaments on the leaf margins.
  glauca, GLAW-ka, sea-green – the foliage.
  gloriosa, glor-i-O-sa, glorious.
  gloriosa var. *tristis*, TRIS-tis, square leaved.
  recurvifolia, see *Y. gloriosa* var. *tristis.*
  whipplei, see *Hesperoyucca whipplei.*

Yushania, u-SHA-ne-a; named after Yushan, *Yu shan*, literally Jade Mountain, the highest mountain in Taiwan where the type species was found. Grasses. *Poaceae.*

  anceps, AN-ceps, two-edged, flattened.

Zaluzianskya, zal-u-ze-AN-ske-a; after Adam Zaluziansky (1558–1613), a physician and botanist, of Prague. Half-hardy annuals. *Scrophulariaceae.*

  capensis, ka-PEN-sis, of the Cape of Good Hope.
  selaginoides, see *Z. villosa.*
  villosa, vil-LO-sa, shaggy, hairy.

Zantedeschia, zan-te-de-SHE-a; after Giovanni Zantedeschi (1773–1846), Italian botanist. Herbaceous perennials. *Araceae.*

  aethiopica, eth-i-O-pik-a, Ethiopian.
  albomaculata, AL-bo-mak-ul-A-ta, white spotted, the leaves.
  elliottiana, el-le-ot-e-A-na, in compliment to Capt. Elliott of Farnboro Park, Hampshire.
  pentlandii, PENT-land-e-i, grown by R.Whyte of Pentland House, Lee.
  rehmannii, ra-MAN-e-i, after Anton Rehmann (1840–1917), Polish botanist.

Zanthoxylum, zanth-OKS-il-lum; from Gr. *xanthos*, yellow; *xylon*, wood, the latter being yellow in some species. Trees or shrubs. *Rutaceae.*

  ailanthoides, a-lanth-OY-dees, resembling *Ailanthus.*
  americanum, a-mer-i-KAY-num, of the Americas. The Toothache Tree.
  bungeanum, bunj-E-A-num, after Alexander von Bunge (1803–1890), a Russian botanist.
  bungei, see *Z. bungeanum.*
  piperitum, see *Z. bungeanum.*

Zauschneria, zawsch-NEER-e-a; after Johann Baptist Zauschner (1737–1799), botanist, professor of medicine Prague. Half-hardy shrubby perennial. *Onagraceae.*

  californica, kal-if-OR-nik-a, of California.

Zea, ZE-a; from the Greek name for another cereal. Ornamental foliage, fodder and corn grasses. *Poaceae.*

  mays, may-z, Mexican vernacular name for maize.

Zebrina, see below.

  pendula, see *Tradescantia zebrina* var. *zebrina.*

Zelkova, zel-KO-va; from the vernacular name in the Caucasus. Shrubs and trees. *Ulmaceae.*

  acuminata, see *Z. serrata.*
  carpinifolia, kar-pine-E-fo-le-a, resembling *Carpinus* (hornbeam).
  crenata, kre-NA-ta, notched – the leaves.
  serrata, ser-RA-ta, saw-toothed edge to the leaves.

Zenobia, zen-O-be-a; after Zenobia, once Empress of Palmyra circa AD266. Flowering shrubs. *Ericaceae.*

  pulverulenta, pul-ver-ul-EN-ta, powdered as with dust, the leaves.
  speciosa, spes-e-O-sa, showy.

Zephyranthes, zef-er-AN-thez; from Gr. *zephyros*, the west wind; *anthos*, a flower. In reference to the origin of the genus in the Western Hemisphere. Bulbs. *Amaryllidaceae.*

  atamasco, at-am-AS-ko, old name. The Atamasco Lily.
  candida, KAN-di-da, white.
  carinata, kar-in-A-ta, keeled.
  rosea, RO-ze-a, rose-coloured.

treatiae, tre-AT-e-e, after Mrs Mary Treat, Green Cove Springs, Florida.
versicolor, ver-SIK-o-lor, variously coloured.

Zigadenus, zig-a-DE-nus; from Gr. *zygon*, yoke; *aden*, gland. The glands are sometimes in pairs at the base of the sepals. Bulbs and rhizomatous perennial herbs. *Melanthiaceae*.
angustifolius, see *Stenanthium densum*.
glaberrimus, gla-ber-RIM-us, completely glabrous, without hairs.
muscitoxicum, see *Amianthium muscitoxicum*.
nuttallii, see *Toxicoscordion nuttallii*.

Zingiber, ZING-ib-er; classical name coming from the Sanskrit. Tropical foliage and flowering plants. *Zingiberaceae*.
officinale, of-fis-in-A-le, of the shops. The roots form the Ginger of commerce.

Zinnia, ZIN-ne-a; named after Johann Gottfried Zinn (1727–1759), professor of botany at Göttingen. Half-hardy annuals. *Compositae*.
elegans, EL-e-ganz, elegant.
haageana, ha-ag-e-A-na, after J.N. Haage (1826–1878), German nurseryman.
pauciflora, paw-sif-LO-ra, few-flowered.
verticillata, ver-tis-il-LA-ta, whorled – the leaves.

Zizania, ziz-A-ne-a; from Gr. *zizanion*, a name for a 'tare' or weed of wheat fields, not this. Waterside grasses. *Poaceae*.
aquatica, a-KWAT-ik-a, growing in or near water. Canadian wild rice.
latifolia, lat-if-O-le-a, broad-leaved.

Ziziphus, ZIZ-if-us; from *Zizouf*, the Arabian name for *Z. lotus*. Shrubs and trees. *Rhamnaceae*.
lotus, LO-tus, lotus. The African or Jujube Lotus.

Zygocactus, misapplied see below.
truncatus, see *Schlumbergera truncata*.

× *Zygocolax*, misapplied see below.
veitchii, see *Zygopetalum × veitchii*.

Zygopetalum, ZY-go-PET-a-lum; from Gr. *zygos*, a yoke; *petalon*, a petal, in reference to the segments of the perianth being jointed at their bases. Orchids. *Orchidaceae*.
crinitum, KRYN-it-um, hairy.
intermedium, see *Z. maculatum*.
mackayi, see *Z. maculatum*.
maculatum, mak-ul-A-tum, spotted.
maxillare, max-il-LA-re, shaped like a jaw.
× *sedenii*, sed-E-ne-i, after John Seden, a noted hybridiser for Veitch Nurseries.
× *veitchii*, VEECH-e-i, after Messrs. Veitch, nurserymen of Chelsea, London.

NOTES